Formal Ontology

edited by

Roberto Poli
Department of Sociology and Social Research,
Trento, Italy

and

Peter Simons
Department of Philosophy,
Leeds, United Kingdom

KLUWER ACADEMIC PUBLISHERS
DORDRECHT / BOSTON / LONDON

A C.I.P. Catalogue record for this book is available from the Library of Congress.

ISBN 0-7923-4104-X

Published by Kluwer Academic Publishers,
P.O. Box 17, 3300 AA Dordrecht, The Netherlands.

Kluwer Academic Publishers incorporates
the publishing programmes of
D. Reidel, Martinus Nijhoff, Dr W. Junk and MTP Press.

Sold and distributed in the U.S.A. and Canada
by Kluwer Academic Publishers,
101 Philip Drive, Norwell, MA 02061, U.S.A.

In all other countries, sold and distributed
by Kluwer Academic Publishers Group,
P.O. Box 322, 3300 AH Dordrecht, The Netherlands.

Printed on acid-free paper

TABLE OF CONTENTS

FOREWORD   vii

ROBERTO POLI / *Res, Ens* and *Aliquid*   1

NINO B. COCCHIARELLA / Conceptual Realism as a Formal Ontology   27

JERZY PERZANOWSKI / The Way of Truth   61

FRED SOMMERS / Existence and Correspondence-to-Fact   131

DAVID M. ARMSTRONG / A World of States of Affairs   159

MIECZYSŁAW OMYŁA / A Formal Ontology of Situations   173

KAREL LAMBERT / Attributives, their First Denotative Correlates,
    Complex Predicates and Free Logics   189

LILIANA ALBERTAZZI / Formal and Material Ontology   199

JEAN PETITOT AND BARRY SMITH / Physics and the Phenomenal
    World   233

PETER M. SIMONS AND CHARLES W. DEMENT / Aspects of the
    Mereology of Artifacts   255

INGVAR JOHANSSON / Physical Addition   277

INDEX OF NAMES   289

FOREWORD

The idea of a formal ontology arose around the turn of the present century in the work of Edmund Husserl. It coincides in many respects with what is nowadays sometimes called 'analytic metaphysics' or with attempts to use formal methods to solve classical philosophical problems relating to the notions of being, object, state of affairs, existence, property, relation, universal, particular, substance, accident, part, boundary, measure, causality, and so on. Formal ontology thus includes several sub-disciplines, of which the most developed is the theory of part and whole, as sketched by Husserl in the third of his *Logical Investigations* and later worked out as a formal theory by Leśniewski. Formal-ontological ideas are present also in much contemporary work on naïve physics and in the formal theories of the common-sense world canvassed by workers in the field of artificial intelligence research.

The idea of a formal ontology is placed in a network of conceptual oppositions: it admits of different senses according to which of its two constituent elements is given priority. If the emphasis is placed on 'ontology' then the principal distinction is between 'formal' and 'material' (that is between 'formal ontology' and 'material ontology'); if instead the emphasis falls on 'formal', the contrast is between 'ontology' and 'logic' ('formal ontology' vs. 'formal logic'). This situation raises some important questions: When one speaks of 'ontology', how can its formal aspects be distinguished from its material ones? When we talk about the 'formal', how can we distinguish between logic and ontology?

The papers collected in this volume present a wide range of proposals about many aspects of formal ontology. The notions of being and object are analyzed by Poli, Cocchiarella, and Perzanowski; the notion of existence is considered by Sommers and Lambert; state of affairs, facts and situations are discussed by Sommers, Armstrong and Omyła; predicates are analyzed by Lambert and Cocchiarella; the difference between formal and material ontology is mainly considered by Albertazzi and by Smith and Petitot; these latter consider also naïve physics; the concept of part is discussed by Simons and Dement; the concept of measure by Johansson. But many other aspects are also considered and discussed. As a collection the papers indicate the scope, liveliness, and applicability of formal ontology.

The first idea for this volume arose out of the *International Summer School in Philosophy and Artificial Intelligence* on 'Formal Ontology', organized in Bolzano (Italy), 1-5 July 1991, by the Central European Institute of Culture. Our thanks go to the President of the Institute, Professor Claudio Nolet, for his constant and valuable support.

The Editors

ROBERTO POLI

RES, ENS AND ALIQUID

1. Introduction*

There are conceptual distinctions that have been repeatedly introduced into philosophical reflection and that have been correspondingly disappeared into nothingness without leaving a visible trace of their presence. The systematic constant disappearance of these distinctions after short periods of presence means perhaps that it is a question of false distinctions. But the fact that they keep on appearing again in different philosophical contexts, theories and systems perhaps sends us back to the presence of a theoretical impasse or of a conceptual knot which is not solved yet.

The distinction which we are talking about in this article deals with the thesis that the realms of being are three and not, as we usually believe, two. That is to say that, according to the thesis we are going to discuss, it is not enough to distinguish between concrete and abstract, complete and incomplete, individual and general, but we must proceed to a tripartitioned consideration of the realms of ontology. The thesis we are presenting was suggested, among others, also by schools or scholars who are as different as the Stoics in ancient philosophy, Thomas Aquinas (1225-1274) and Gregory of Rimini (1300-1358) in the Medieval period, Meinong (1853-1920) in contemporary philosophy. Stoics talk of it as of the distinction among *soma*, *on* and *ti*; Thomas distinguishes the natures of things into singular, abstract and absolute natures; Gregory of Rimini distinguishes *res*, *ens* and *aliquid*; finally, Meinong distinguishes a realm of being in a strict sense, including real and ideal objects, from a realm of *Aussersein*, including pure objects.

* I would like to thank in particular Massimo Libardi for his helpful remarks on earlier versions of this paper. I would also thank Liliana Albertazzi, Nino Cocchiarella, Rudolf Haller, Jerzy Perzanowski and Barry Smith for their comments on an earlier version of this paper.

1

Schematically:

(i) The three types of entity considered by the Stoics are the *soma* or the individual, effectively existing body, the *on* or entity, and the *ti* or something indeterminate. That which actually exists, the genuine object, is only the *soma*. An entity, by contrast, could well be *asomaton* or incorporeal. Thus while the *soma* is subject to the principle of individuation, the *on* admits at most some criterion of identity, and the *ti* admits neither identity nor individuation.[1] For them the *on* can be objective without having to be existent, a *soma*.

ii) For Thomas, singular nature is the primary, individual substance; abstract nature is due to intellect and concerns the conceptual consideration of individual substance; finally, nature that is absolutely considered deals with the essential constituents of individual nature, its definitory characteristics. The latter is considered, Thomas says, "in statu differentiae vel solitudinis",[2] i.e. without considering its exemplifiability or insertibility into a structured theory or context.

(iii) The distinction introduced by Gregory originates from the questions 'What do we know?', 'What is the object of knowledge?'; questions that are posed within a theory that states that (i) the object of knowledge is a complex (= a proposition) because only complexes can be true or false, and that (ii) we gain knowledge of it through analysis (= demonstration). In his early writings Gregory argued that the object of knowledge was neither (1) the conclusion of a demonstration, nor (2) the external thing, but (3) the *meaning* of the conclusion. One may object, however, that the meaning of the conclusion is either an object or it is nothing. If it is nothing, knowledge has no object. If it is an object, it is either a mental or a non-mental object. If it is non-mental, it is a thing external to the mind, and this confutes the thesis (2). If it is mental, it is either a term or a proposition. If it is a term, it cannot be true or false, and it is therefore not an object of knowledge. If it is a proposition, it is the conclusion of a demonstration, and this confutes thesis (1).[3] To save his theory from collapse, Gregory distinguished three kinds of object: the *aliquid*, which denotes every thing, simple or complex, true or false; the *ens*, which denotes only true things; and the *res*, which denotes only the existent.[4] The meaning of a proposition is

---

[1] Laerzio 1925, ch. VII. See Melandri 1989, 69-70.

[2] Thomas, *Quod.* VIII, q.1 a. 1; *De ente et essentia*, ch. 4. Cited by Fausti 1947, 73-4.

[3] Elie 1936, 26.

[4] Gregory refers his theory directly to Aristotle. Cf. Aristotle, *Categories*, 12b 6-15 and *Metaphysics*, 7, 1017 31-34. See Elie 1936, 27-8.

therefore something in the first or the second sense, but not in the third. This is to say that a meaning could be an *ens* or an *aliquid*, but not a *res*.

(iv) Meinong's *Gegenstandstheorie* considers objects from the point of view of their nature. The distinction between complete and incomplete objects is consequent. Complete objects, in their turn, are classified into real, those that of their nature can exist, and ideal, those that of their nature cannot exist. The realm of complete objects is the realm of being, that of the incomplete objects is the realm of *Aussersein*, a realm that cannot be scientifically considered because of its extreme plentitude. And in a passage recalling the preceding quotation from Thomas's, Meinong affirms that it is a question of "*a strange kind of desert* where no mental progress is possible".[5]

There is an interpretation that allows us to sustain that, in spite of the differences which are clearly verifiable among the theories of such different authors, all of them use the same tripartite division. This is the interpretation according to which the above-mentioned distinctions deal with the classification of the furniture of universe into objects that by their nature are objectively describable and can exist (*soma*, singular nature, *res*, real), objects that by their nature are *objectively* describable even if they cannot exist (*on*, abstract nature, *ens*, ideal) and a third remaining category of objects that is so different from those of the first two categories that the community of philosophers has still not succeeded in finding a generally accepted name for them. As for the aforementioned partitions we speak of the class of what was called *ti*, nature in the absolute sense, *aliquid*, pure object. Meinong is probably the author who more than any other tried to characterize what belongs to this class, identifying their distinctive traits in comparison with real and ideal objects.

We should consider that all these authors accept the thesis according to which what exists or can exist is also objectively describable. That is to say that those objects present some form of (ontological) independence from their description. This means also that from the point of view of the study of being, real things are just a subset of objectively describable things that can be identified by having the property of existence (or, in its modal version, they are what can exist).

Setting real and ideal objects against pure ones, Meinong notices that the main distinctive characteristic is that the objects of the first two classes are *complete*, while those of this third class are *incomplete*. This single distinction allows Meinong to maintain that incomplete objects, simply because of their

---

[5] See Findlay 1933, 57.

partiality, are *ausserseiend*.⁶ To this realm belong impossible, literary, fantastic, mythical objects, as well as concepts, ideals, imaginations. In an expression, all objects of imaginations and fantasy, with no limitation, belong to it. Husserl calls it the first level of logic, a level which is so rich that it may collapse precisely because of its richness.⁷ We can characterize it by saying that in its broadest form the realm of aliquid is the realm of the imaginary.

In this paper we deal with two questions. On the one hand we try to describe the main distinctive traits of the operations connecting the different realms of being. In this sense we shall proceed to distinguish abstraction from idealization, where we mean that abstraction is the operation that (i) connects the realm of *res* with that of *ens,* and that (ii) it enters the realm of *ens* itself as a procedure of classification of the individuals composing it. Idealization is instead that kind of procedure connecting both *res* and *ens,* on the one hand, with *aliquid,* on the other. This second procedure, unlike the first one, has an ontological commitment.

Having delineated the connections joining the realms we have distinguished, we shall devote particular attention to *Aussersein,* facing the problem of how we can succeed in speaking of the objects pertaining to it in absolutely neutral terms, without surreptitiously introducing conceptual frameworks or theoretical constraints that belong to our way of speaking of things and do not belong to things in themselves. This problem is particularly dramatic for objects of *Aussersein,* because in their generality those objects are extremely weak and *sensitive to the way in which we speak of them.* We understand the reason for such a state of affairs if we come back to Meinong's description of that realm.

Objects possessing *Sein* are complete objects. That is to say, they are objects able to maintain their individuality and to 'resist' the descriptions concerning them. Concerning such a kind of object, we can see if their description is faithful or false, adequate or inadequate. *Aussersein* objects, on the contrary, just because of their incompleteness, are instead 'fragile' and sensitive to the descriptions involving them. In other words, when we speak of an *Aussersein* object, it is always possible to attribute to it aspects, dimensions or structures that do not pertain to it, without realizing that, *under the description,* the original object becomes a *different* object. That is why we face the problem of the directly depicting language, i.e the problem of the characteristics that a neutral language must possess to be able to speak correctly of *Aussersein.*

⁶ Meinong 1960, 83 ff.
⁷ Husserl 1969.

2. Individual and General Presentations

The distinction between objects having being and *Aussersein* objects has been often brought back to the distinction between individual and general objects. This distinction in its turn turns one to the parallel distinction between individual and general presentations, i.e. between presentations of individual objects and presentations of general objects.

A useful reference for the distinction between individual and general presentations is Twardowski's book on the relationship between the act, content and object of presentation.[8] The main point of his argumentation is the recognition that there are no presentations to which more than one object corresponds. Each presentation has its own unique object. The usually adduced example of complex presentations in which it is affirmed that it is possible to list the different objects composing them contains in fact a subtle mistake. When the objects which should correspond to such presentation are listed, as a matter of fact we refer to the objects of new presentations and these are as many in number as the considered objects. Twardowski's example is clear: if we want to count the pictures hanging in a room, we must singularly represent the single pictures to ourselves.

Neverthless we talk of general presentations, setting them against the individual ones. Twardowski defines the object of general presentations as the object of those presentations dealing with 'what is common as such' to different single presentations. The definition recalls the Aristotelian one of universal. We must anyway keep in mind that we are talking of objects, and neither of contents nor of concepts. Once it is recognized that the object of general presentation is common to different individual presentations, we have also recognized that the objects of the two kinds of presentations we have just considered are different. The object of the individual presentations is different from the object of the general ones. In order to exemplify this, Twardowski reminds us

---

[8] On Twardowski's thought see Ingarden 1939-40. Ingarden notes that the opinion that Twardowski was the first to introduce the distinction between act, content and object of presentations is not only historically inaccurate but neglects the fact that Twardowski 1894 gave the first articulated theory of the object since scholasticism and Carl Wolff's ontology. And this was well before Meinong's and Husserl's work; these being writers, moreover, who paid specific attention to Twardowski. The act, content, object distinction reaches back, in fact, to Zimmermann and Kerry: for the latter, see Kerry 1885-1891. According to Ingarden, Twardowski generalized Kerry's theory and equipped it with better arguments. It should also be pointed out that the difficulties, if not the aporia, present in Twardowski's theory provided a point of reference and a cue for Leśniewski and Kotarbiński's analyses, which, I would argue, are also an attempt to solve Twardowski's difficulties. On the connections between Wolff and Twardowski, see Poli 1992b.

that the general presentation of a triangle is neither the presentation of an equilateral triangle nor the presentation of a triangle with a determined area. If we then affirm that a general triangle (as object of a general presentation of a triangle) is neither equilateral, nor isosceles, nor scalene, then we conclude that general objects are incomplete and that for them the principle of the excluded middle is not valid. Twardowski's general objects thus share one of the main characteristics of Meinong's *Aussersein* objects.[9]

Twardowski adds then a further characterization: general objects are wholes constituted by a group of parts which are common to several individual objects. That is to say, the object of general presentations is constituted by characteristics. And this is the keypoint of the whole dispute: general objects are exhausted by the characteristics explicitly composing them. Anticipating the analysis we will develop in § 10 ff., we therefore understand why an intrinsically elementary language must be extremely weak: it must deal only with what is *explicitly* given. Any inference allowing us to obtain new data inserts the object into a theoretical context that structures and transforms it. If we want to study the framework of *Aussersein*, we must pay close attention to any condition we impose to it. It is clear that some conditions, even if only local, must be introduced, otherwise we cannot do anything at all. It is not accidental that Thomas speaks of 'statu solitudinis' and Meinong of 'mental desert'. What is important is to study carefully the consequences of the different conditions that are introduced, starting from the simplest and weakest.

As distinct from individual presentation, the general one is always indirect and non-intuitive. In fact nobody is able to present a triangle that is neither equilateral, nor isosceles, nor scalene. But there are indirect presentations of such triangles, "as well as there are indirect presentations of a white black horse, of a steel cannon made of wood and of other similar things".[10]

Twardowski adds that the general object constitutes in a certain way a metaphysical constituent of the single objects subordinated to it. And it is particularly interesting to notice that in the languages which have maintained the definite article, the proper noun for a general object is normally the substantive connected to it. That is to say that general objects are denoted by terms which are prefixed by the definite article, such as in '*the* table' or '*the* red'.

---

[9] For a modern formal analysis of the problem, see Fine 1985 and Santambrogio 1987. For a philosophical discussion see Santambrogio 1992, Albertazzi 1992, Poli 1992c, chs. 13, 14, 17 and 19. Consider that, in addition to the objects violating the excluded middle, also contradictory objects, i.e. those violating the principle of non contradiction, belong to the realm of *Aussersein*.

[10] Twardowski 1977, § 15.

3. Parts and Properties

Twardowski talks also of the object of presentation and of content as the mode in which this object is presented.[11]

For Twardowski, the object is a whole which may be formed of material and formal parts. The material parts of the object can be divided into simple parts and complex parts. The former are those parts which cannot be broken down any further, the latter are those that can in turn be divided into parts. Complex material parts are either more immediate parts (1st order material parts) or more remote parts (2nd, 3rd, etc. order material parts). For example, we may say of a book that its pages are its 1st order material parts, while the shape, colour, etc. of the pages are the 2nd order material parts of the book and the 1st order material parts of the page.

Complex parts can be broken down further into what can be called transitive parts and intransitive parts according to whether the whole is completely or incompletely decomposable in such parts. An example of decomposition into transitive parts is the division of the hour into minutes and minutes into seconds. These are transitive parts because the hour is completely decomposable in minutes and the minute is completely decomposable in seconds. As a side effect of the repeated complete decomposability of the whole in its parts it is just as meaningful to say that the hour is composed of minutes as it is to say that the hour is composed of seconds. An example of intransitive parts is the decomposition of a city into the houses of which it is composed, and of these latter into their windows.[12]

A third typology concerns the independence and dependence of the parts with respect to the whole that contains them.

Formal constituents are constituted by the relations among the material constituents and the whole (primary formal constituents) or by the relations among the different constituents of the whole (secondary formal constituents). Primary formal constituents are then further subdivided into constituents in the strict sense, like those that connect the whole to its parts, and constituents in the non-strict sense, like those that enable us to state that the whole is greater than its parts, that it is like its parts in certain respects and unlike them in others, that there is coexistence or succession between whole and parts. Further relations may hold between the various formal constituents of a whole. Because

[11] This position could find support in some Aristotelian passages. See *Metaphysics* Z, 10, 1035 21-22: "the notion has the same relationships with respect to the thing as do its parts with respect to the parts of the thing".

[12] Twardowski 1977, § 9. Traditional philosophy distinguishes here between parts homonymous with the whole and non-homonymous parts.

these have the primary relations as their objects, they are second-degree relations. Proceeding in this manner, we obtain relations of the third, fourth, etc. degree.[13] Twardowski uses the term 'order' for material constituents and 'rank' for formal ones.

Like the object, the content of presentation also has material and formal parts. In general, the content of the presentation of a complex object, which is presented as complex, is made up of three groups of 1st order material constituents: (i) presentations of the object's 1st order material constituents; (ii) presentation of the property relations between object as a whole and its 1st order material constituents; (iii) presentation of the object's secondary formal constituents.

The material constituents of the object determine the material constituents of its content.[14] The reverse does not hold, however, in the sense that *not all* material constituents of the content have the material constituents of the object as their object, given that there are material constituents of the content that correspond to the formal constituents of the object.

Twardowski's analysis leads to the distinction between part and property. One may say, for example, that a soldier is part of an army but that he is not a property of the army, just as a minute is part of an hour but not a property of an hour. We may follow Twardowski in calling the properties of an object its metaphysical parts; that is, the parts that can be *distinguished* in a whole by abstraction but which cannot be materially *separated* from it. Metaphysical parts are therefore extension, colour, weight, identity, etc. In short, metaphysical parts are moments.[15] This definition enables us to articulate the concept of property into at least two distinct cases. In the first, a property is that relation which designates whatever part of the whole relative to the whole itself. In this sense, *having* minutes as parts is a property of the hour, just as *having* a colour is a property of the body. The second distinction regards metaphysical parts and concerns the designation of one only of the terms of the relation, leaving the whole of which they are parts out of consideration. Twardowski adds that "in this sense one speaks of things and their properties".[16] The difference lies in the differing role of the auxiliaries used. One says of the metaphysical parts that they *are* parts of an object, of non-metaphysical parts that an object *has* this or that part.

---

[13] Twardowski 1977, § 10.
[14] Twardowski 1977, § 12.
[15] Twardowski 1977, § 13. See the essays in Smith 1982.
[16] Twardowski 1977, § 10.

4. The object

I shall use the term 'object' synonymously with the traditional 'entity'. 'Entity' is the translation of the Aristotelean term 'on', which corresponds to the medieval Latin 'ens', participle of 'esse'. These terms can be used in a variety of ways, and many philosophical misunderstandings have arisen from the overlapping of their various senses. One possible distinction is between the distributive meaning and the collective meaning of 'object'. Used *distributively*, 'object' means 'thing'. Every man, every thing, every fact is an object or entity in the distributive sense. Used *collectively*, 'object' means 'whole'. The definition itself of metaphysics as the science of being states in effect that metaphysics does not occupy itself with the entities of this or that genus but with the whole, the totality, the entirety.[17]

A different distinction concerns analysis of objects either with respect to their *effective composition*, or with respect to the *concepts of which they are instances*, or with respect to the *form* of these instances. I shall say that the object as a *whole* admits its decomposition into parts, as a *thing* its classification into *genera* and *species*, after separation of form from matter, and that the object as *something* can be categorized.

Terms like 'whole', 'individual', 'thing', 'something' are often taken to be synonymous; a linguistic abundance that borders on wastefulness. There are, in fact, cogent reasons for framing these various terms within a systematic network of relations and dependences. One of the best of these is the series of distinctions we have mentioned at the beginning of the paper. Considering for instance Gregory's distinction between *aliquid*, *ens* and *res*, we can update Gregory's formulation to a more modern context saying that the *aliquid* is indifferent to the being or non-being of what it denotes, that it covers the possible and the non-possible, the actual and the non-actual; the *ens*, instead, is restricted to the realm of abstract being (comprising the abstract consideration of the real beings), while the *res* considers the concrete being, the existent. We may also say that the *res* is the whole, the *ens* is the thing, and the *aliquid* the form of instances. We will see that the *aliquid* as form of instances has an incredibly wide range of possible variations and depends on the way in which we define 'form'.

---

[17] Czezowski 1948, 70.

5. The Whole and the Thing

The distinction between that which exists (as *res*) and the thing (as *ens*) stands in perfect parallel to that between collective and distributive. As early as the 12th century, Abelard drew a clear distinction between the two cases in his theory of the different kinds of whole: integral or collective (*res*) and distributive (*ens*).

For Abelard, the integral or collective whole: (i) is not predicated by its constitutive elements; (ii) is not a universal whole, (iii) is composed of parts even though it is not reducible to its parts; (iv) involves only a singular predication. The distributive whole on the other hand: (j) is predicated by its constitutive elements; (jj) falls within the doctrine of genera and species; (jjj) is a universal whole; (jv) involves a universal predication.[18]

Let us take the example of 'horse'. The collective class of the things that form the horse – head, legs, etc. – do not constitute the horse (cf. (i)). The horse of which we speak is that particular horse, that specific and unrepeatable individual (cf. (ii)) formed of parts but which is not simply the sum of its parts, because it, the horse, is not the simple aggregate of such parts (cf. (iii)). The difference between x-part and part-of-x, to use Henry's terminology,[19] comes into play here. The x-parts are the constituents of the horse insofar as they subsist independently of their conjunction. That is, they are the constituents in their autonomous ontological givenness. The parts-of-x, instead, owe their subsistence to the x itself and exist as parts-of-x only if x exists. The passage from x-part to part-of-x requires the imposition of a definition which transforms what might otherwise be simply a mass into a real and proper whole.[20] This whole, finally, entails a strictly individual predication (cf. (iv)); that is, it cannot be properly considered a universal.

Distributive wholes, on the other hand, can be predicated of their elements. Of every individual belonging to a class one may say that it is of that class; that is, it possesses the defining features of that class. Every single instance of a horse is a horse (cf. (j)), since it can be analysed by genus and by species (cf. (jj)): the individual belonging to the class 'horses' (species) is the same individual that belongs to the class 'animals' (genus). They can be properly considered to be universals (cf. (jjj)) and usual predicate theory applies to them.

---

[18] Abelard 1969, 166, 193.

[19] Henry 1972, 124; Henry 1984, § 4.541, Henry 1991, §§ 1.4, 2.3 and 3.41.

[20] The point is a subtle one and relies on an accurate reading of Aristotle's mereology. On this see Poli, Dappiano and Libardi 1993.

One of the chief consequences arising from the distinction between collective (material) wholes and distributive (objectual) wholes is that the conceptual correlates of distributive wholes – i.e. those that have an abstract individuality – are governed by the principle of extensionality: two classes are identical if they have the same members. Put otherwise, the principle of individuation by classes coincides with their criterion of identity. This, however, does not apply to the conceptual correlates of material wholes.

6. Properties and Forms

Abstraction is the typical procedure by which properties are characterized. Abstraction takes us from the lowest species to the highest genera, like 'material thing', 'living being', etc. The relationship between species and genera, on the one hand, and the individuals that exemplify them on the other, is a relationship of instantiation or exemplification. I may say, therefore, that the table in front of me is an instance of 'table', just as the whiteness of its surface is an instance of 'white'. Quite different from the process of abstraction or generalization is that of formalization or idealization. It is clear that the scheme '$((p \rightarrow q) \wedge p) \rightarrow q$' is not the *genus* of its instances but the *form* of all the instances of this kind. Idealization does not produce species and genera but what Husserl called conceptual essences. The objects obtained by idealizations are not classifiable into genera but are essences which give origin to specific regional ontologies. The concept 'object in general', for example, is not a genus under which the species 'number' and 'material object' are subsumable. The realm of essences is therefore mapped by the categories concerned: some of these are coextensive with the entire sphere of the essences, others are constitutive of particular regions internal to it.

The concept of essence or form is extremely complicated.[21] For instance if we intend it in the sense of logical form, we can say, using a doctrine ascribable to Quine[22] and Kaplan[23], that the logical form is the way in which we evaluate the truth-value of an utterance. In this sense the concept of form is a semantic notion, determined by the norms of evaluation of the language that tell us how to 'build' the semantic value of of an expression starting from the value of its logically simple constituents. But if we adopt a formal structure

[21] For some references see Albertazzi's article in this volume.
[22] Quine 1960.
[23] Kaplan 1970.

that is sensitive not only to the truth-values, but also to other constituents (for example, to the meaning connections between antecedent and consequent), then semantics incorporate other aspects of the propositions in addition to their truth-value and to the forms of composition.[24] But it is also possible to refuse the tradition inaugurated by Frege and Russell and to attest that it is not true that the truth-conditions of an utterance determine its syntax. The objection to this choice is that utterances with the same form can possess different conditions of truth. Consider for example the propositions 'the horse captured by Bellerophon was white' and 'the horse that won the race is grey'. Pre-analytically, both are true, but the second only has an *existential* truth-condition, that is 'the horse that won the race exists'. Traditional logic,[25] and with it modern *free logic*, do not require that utterances with the same logical structure have the same truth-conditions. How ample the possible choices are may be seen if we go on reading the recent reconstructions of Meinongian semantics. On the one hand, for instance, Parsons accepts that there are partial objects, but he does not consider the difference between existence and subsistence; on the other, Zalta distinguishes between abstract and concrete objects, but he considers that all objects are complete; from a still different point of view, Lambert and Routley base their own reconstructions starting from the rejection of the principle of abstraction.[26]

The acceptance of abstract objects or of pure objects (or of both) allows also to distinguish different kinds of predication. If Parsons recurs to the distinction between nuclear and extranuclear predication, Zalta distinguishes instead, more than the traditional form of predication as exemplification (that is clearly valid for real objects), also predication as encoding. In this case we shall not say that the object exemplifies this or that property, but that the object is composed of or (internally) determined by this or that property.[27] The same results are also obtainable by developing the theory of nominalization, according to the perspective inaugurated by some observations of Frege (and of Twardowski, recall the last lines of § 1) and developed by Cocchiarella.[28]

[24] See for instance Epstein 1990.

[25] Sommers 1982, 107-8.

[26] Parsons 1980; Zalta 1983, 1988; Lambert 1983; Routley 1980.

[27] In traditional terms, this is the case that is usually considered as inherence. Both distinctions may be led back to some observations of Ernst Mally, who is probably Meinong's main pupil. See Mally 1904, 1912. See also Poli 1990 and 1993b.

[28] Cocchiarella 1972, 1974, 1978, 1986a, 1986b, 1989a, 1989b, 1991 and the essay in this volume.

7. The *Aliquid*

In terms of my present analysis, the *aliquid* is some form of (the instances of) things. In traditional terms, this is an area of analysis that belongs to metaphysics, in particular to the theory of transcendentals. An important aspect of traditional enquiry is that, since the *aliquid* is considered apart from the thing, it is based on the distributive meaning of object (= *ens*). Hence one may say with Albertus Magnus: *quodlibet ens est unum, verum, bonum.*[29]

The traditional meaning of 'transcendental' is historically and conceptually much more sophisticated than is generally believed, even though it seems that it was never given definitive treatment. Using a terminology derived from Kant and Husserl, we may say that transcendentals are those categories that constitute a sphere of enquiry.

Aristotle foresaw something of the kind when, by constructing his theory of categories, he gave them joint ontological, logical and linguistic value. In effect, every operation that seeks to give foundational priority to one only of these aspects is not only philologically mistaken but has devastating effects on the whole theoretical corpus of the Stagirite. Both the interpretations that from Valla onwards has reduced the categories to linguistic-grammatical categories, as well as those that have otherwise sought to demonstrate the pre-eminence of logical over ontological meaning, erroneously transmute what for Aristotle was an *enumeration* into a *deduction*. From an Aristotelian point of view, in fact, it is impossible to deduce the categories because they are irreducible genera. In other words, apart from their not being reducible one to the other, there is nothing from which they can be deduced.[30]

8. Abstraction and Idealization

'Abstracting' means 'leaving aside', 'omitting'. According to the interpretation adopted in this paper, it does not mean 'extracting' something or 'drawing something forth'. When one abstracts, one does *not* obtain a new ob-

---

[29] Ueberweg 1915, 470. The entity is one in the case of presentation, it is true in judgement, it is good with respect to volitional acts. 'True' in this context means that it is the object of knowledge, and 'good' signifies that it functions as an object of will. See Aquinas, *De veritate* I, qu. 16, art. 1: *Sicut bonum nominat id, in quo tendit appetitus, ita verum nominat it, in quo tendit intellectus.* See also Twardowski 1977, § 7.

[30] Zanatta 1989, 82-3.

ject. Abstraction does not break the object down into its constitutive parts or constituents. If abstraction is taken to its fullest extent, what are we left with? If all aspect of material and content are abstracted from the object, what is ultimately left is its form. This cannot be abstracted because it is not something that the object has and which can be left aside or omitted. Form is instead something which the object exhibits or shows. The form under discussion here, as the nature of this something that is shown, can only be analysed by a science that is not the theory of objects (intended like *res* or like *ens*).

On the other hand, if forms (in the sense given to them here) are to be studied, they must be made into the objects of possible enquiry; a transformation made possible by idealization.

The main difference between abstraction and idealization is that idealization constructs new objects (by nominalization).[31] From what I have said, care must be taken to avoid confusion between idealization and abstraction. Although they are often confused, the conceptual and operative characteristics of abstraction and idealization are very different.

Abstraction is an operation that takes place within a particular universe of discourse. It involves the setting aside of a particular section of the universe with regard to the predicates being considered. Let us consider the universe U of individuals I. Each individual of the universe is defined with regard to the predicates of the theoretical language describing the universe. For the sake of abstraction, we shall select those individuals of the universe that possess one or more particular features in common (or which do not possess such features). In this sense, abstraction is an equivalence relation over the individuals of the universe of discourse. Abstractive theories therefore transform the structure of a theory's universe of discourse without modifying the individuals of the universe. In this sense, abstraction allows us to classify the individuals of an universe. This is an epistemological and not an ontological type of procedure. For abstraction, individuals are given, like the characteristics of which they are composed. In this sense, abstraction may be understood as also connected with the inductive moment of a theory. The procedure of concretization, compared with an abstractive theory, is a procedure of individuation brought about by imposing a relation of order. The path to abstraction requires the introduction of equivalences. The path to individuation requires the introduction of an order, possibly total and strict. Nothing else is necessary because individuals are already given.

---

[31] For Vaihinger, the first philosopher to have made systematic use of the concept of idealization was Wolff (Kant himself was perfectly aware of its value). See Poli 1992b.

The case of idealizational theories is rather different. We have to distinguish two different types of idealization: *a posteriori* (descriptive) idealization and *a priori* (constitutive) idealization. Let us look first at descriptive idealization.

9. Descriptive Idealization

With descriptive idealization we do not have a transformation of the structure of the universe but a modification of the individuals of the universe, and therefore the construction of an ontologically different universe. If abstraction involves the subdivision of the universe into the set of individuals in possession of property P and the set of individuals not possessing property P, idealization eliminates from the theory's language both the affirmation and the negation of a certain property. In other words, that particular property is eliminated. This has two possible consequences with regard to the universe: (i) the individuals of the universe are no longer determined in relation to that property, (ii) the disappearance from the universe of discourse of those individuals which (a) were determined by the eliminated property or (b) whose definition was determined, either individually or collectively, by the eliminated property. In the first case, we have an ontological transformation of the universe through the transformation of its individuals. In the second case, we have a transformation of the universe due to the elimination of a part of the same.

The complexity of idealization obliges us to proceed with care and to examine some exemplary cases in detail. The simplest case is (ii.b). Let us begin therefore with this. Let us suppose that our universe of discourse is the astronomical universe. We wish to study our solar system. To do so we construct a new theoretical universe composed of the sun and the nine planets that revolve round it. In this way, we eliminate from the start all the other stars and planets of the universe. We can thus easily construct a model of the working of the solar system, without taking the entire astronomical universe into consideration. Naturally, this model will not demonstrate exactly how the solar system works in reality because we have eliminated the rest of the astronomical universe, and therefore also a whole series of forces which affect the actual working of the real solar system. Idealization, in this case, is an example of how a reduction in the complexity of the universe may allow us to master a part of it. An operation of concretization in situations of this type consists in introducing a suitable correction factor that balances the elimination of real forces due to the sought after reduction of complexity. The case of the individuals eliminated as a result of the elimination of that essential property by which they are determined is similar to the preceding case and does not offer particular difficulties once it is understood that the essential properties are those that constitute the object by defining it.

The remaining case is by far the most interesting. Idealization, in this case, is not limited to the redefinition of the boundaries of the universe, but *constructs a new universe with new individuals*. The real problem here concerns the relations between the primitive universe and the new universe. In other words, the problem is that of the relations between the individuals of the old universe and the individuals of the new one. Such individuals in fact are still genetically the same individuals. The problem therefore is that of genetic identity against ontological difference. Let us consider the following examples. Let us suppose that we wish to construct a theory of rational action. In this case, the individuals of the universe are the agents of the theory. These are defined independently of the physical or chemical properties of their bodies and by subjecting the expectations and motivations that influence their actions to particular restrictions. In the world, we never encounter agents, but rather persons endowed with bodies with a particular chemical and physical structure and an extremely varied set of motivations and expectations. In our passage from the universe of the theory of persons to the universe of the theory of agents, radical transformations have been imposed on the individuals of the first universe. The reasons are clear: persons are too complex for our scientific tools. Agents, on the other hand, possess a complexity that can be treated mathematically and therefore allow the construction of formal theories, thus enabling us to make previsions. It is obvious that, strictly speaking, only persons exist whilst agents have an existence of a theoretical nature: they are therefore fictional constructions that allow us to regulate and manipulate a certain set of data. They exist, therefore, only in the model. On the other hand, the individuals of the universe of persons must have particular relations to the individuals of the universe of agents. We are really still speaking, in a way, of the 'same' individuals, of the 'same' fragment of the world.

10. Constitutive Idealization

Constitutive idealization occurs when the possible forms of objects are determined. Unlike descriptive idealization, this is an *a priori* discipline. To avoid misunderstandings, I should clarify the sense in which I employ the terms '*a priori*' and '*a posteriori*'. Perhaps the best way to provide them with unequivocal meaning is to say that an *a posteriori* idealizing procedure is one that aims to construct a model of something. Evidently, in order to construct a model of an entity, one must first have an idea of how this entity is made or of how it acts. An *a priori* procedure, on the other hand, is a constitutive procedure, one that creates a particular context and the individuals of that context. It is therefore *a priori* with respect to the individuals that it constitutes. In this sense, all procedures have both an *a priori* and an *a posteriori* aspect. The procedure with which a model is constructed is *a posteriori* relative to the object that it seeks to model and *a priori* relative to the object that it has modelled.

Saying that constitutive idealization is *a priori* and therefore determines the possible forms of objects is to attribute to it the same role as that performed by the Husserlian concept of formal ontology.[32]

In formal terms, at issue here are the quantifiable variables of the theory. The traditional interpretation to the effect that being is univocal amounts to admitting only one single type of category, and therefore only one single type of quantifiable variable. Any other kind of variable present admits at most to a substitutive, that is, purely nominal, interpretation of quantification. The presence of only one type of quantifiable variable does not prevent it from being sub-divided into specific sub-classes, which are quantifiable even when taken separately.[33] From this point of view, being is a genus, and from what I have already said, it is clear that this is not a procedure of idealization but of abstraction.

Under the other traditional interpretation, being is analogous (multivalent). In formal terms, this amounts to saying that there are different categories of quantifiable variables which represent different modes or categories of being. What this position must explain, however, is how the different modes of being can be unified in a coherent whole. And the formal instrument used to clarify the structure of such unification is the theory of predication.[34]

Resorting to a typology of quantifiable variables, however, is not enough to distinguish between being as genus (= one only type of quantifiable variable) and multivalent being (= various types of quantifiable variable). Consider, for example, combinatory logic. This has neither variables nor quantifiers, and its structure seems less akin to a conventional predicative structure than to a philosophical position with its roots in Aristotle and reformulated by Brentano and Kotarbiński. The extreme form of nominalism developed by these thinkers,

[32] On the concept of formal ontology see Cocchiarella 1991, Poli 1992c and 1993c.
[33] Cocchiarella 1991, 641.
[34] Cocchiarella 1991, 641-3.

usually called reism, is based on the 'determination of things through things'.
Here we clearly have an ontology with only one type of entity, but if the logic
corresponding to it were a combinatory logic, there would be no variables and
no quantifiers. This means that nominalist metaphysics can be translated into
logic within at least two different categorial frameworks; frameworks, these,
which even if holistically equivalent are nevertheless categorially distinct.

Other fields of enquiry are opened up by the multivalent consideration of
being. Here the distinction between abstraction and idealization comes into effect; a distinction that has no role to play in nominalist theory because it ac-
knowledges only one kind of variable. If various kinds of variable are present
then we must recognize various corresponding categories. It is also evident that
the various categorizations of metaphysical reflection – that is, reflection on the
category 'object' – may give rise to new insights, in particular as regards the
concept of the possible form of the object.

The possibility that there may be different conceptual frameworks for the
same situation (as exemplified previously) enables us to distinguish between
internal semantics and *external* semantics. Semantics internal to the individual
framework study the forms of reciprocal determination among the entities of a
metaphysics in the case where there is one single type of variable, or they ad-
dress the various forms of unification among the entities corresponding to the
diverse categorial variables when there are several types of variable. External
semantics instead represent the various categorial frameworks within a single
conceptual space, and this allows comparison among, and analysis of, the various accounts that have been made of them.[35] The most powerful instrument so
far developed for this purpose is set theory, which therefore seems to take on
the role of a metatheory of ontological theories. But it is also the case of remembering that what we need to know the world is theories, not metatheories.
It follows that internal semantics, even if much more complicated, tangled and
less inclined to a set-theoretic normalization of any external semantics, is by far
the most important of any instrument, from an ontological point of view, which
is structurely appointed to comparative investigations.

11. Directly Depicting Language

Before concluding, it is now the time to come back to the question of which
instruments can be used to describe the objects of the most mysterious realm,

[35] Cocchiarella 1991.

the *Aussersein*. We have already claimed that the objects of this realm are sensitive to their description. For this reason we need a language that is as neutral as possible.

The notion of a directly depicting language has been introduced by B. Smith in his "Characteristica universalis".[36] His purpose is to construct a language "which will enable us to represent the most general structures of reality". In order to realise his purpose, Smith turns to an old tradition of formal ontology and uses a diagrammatic language instead of a propositional language.[37] In what follows, we shall retain his idea of a directly depicting language, but we will opt for a propositional language. The reason for our choice is straightforward: our purpose is to represent (some fragments of) the realm of *Aussersein* and all the intuitions we have of the objects of such a realm are of a linguistic nature.[38]

12. Frege and Wittgenstein

For Frege there is some kind of connection between the categories of ontology and the categories of signs. The two primary ontological categories, namely object and function,[39] are in fact linked to the two principal categories of signs, namely saturated expressions and unsaturated expressions. All the different types of objects are linked to saturated expressions and all the types of functions are linked to unsaturated expressions. In what follows we will consider the two main kind of saturated expressions: names and propositions. As we all know, they have both sense and reference. The sense of the name is its *Sinn*, the *mode* in which reference is given to us, while reference itself, the *Bedeutung*, is the object denoted by the name. As regards propositions, their sense is the *Gedanke*, while their reference is their logical value. It is immediately apparent, therefore, that both categories of signs are articulated into an object (respectively the *Bedeutung* and the logical value) and into the *mode* whereby this object is presented to us (respectively the *Sinn* and the *Gedanke*).[40] The most debatable aspect of this position concerns propositions.

---

[36] Smith 1992.

[37] To put things in a nutshell, he uses Peirce instead of Frege.

[38] Because the objects of such a realms can be only indirectly intuited. Cf. § 13.

[39] Note that function make up a number of other categories (1st level concepts, 2nd level concepts, ..., 1st level dyadic relations, etc.).

[40] I follow Perzanowski's 1993 exposition here. See also Perzanowski 1984 and 1990.

To understand Frege's account we have to distinguish between 'true' and 'false' as properties (that is as unsaturated expressions) from 'the True' and 'the False' as objects (that is as saturated expressions). When speaking of a logical value as the object referred to by a proposition, we are considering the True and the False as objects and not true and false as properties.

Using a suggestion coming from the last works by Suszko we can distinguish two different kinds of valuation: logical valuation and algebraic valuation. Logical valuations involve what are conventionally called the values of truth and falsity (as unsatured expressions), while those that Suszko termed algebraic valuations assign a referent.[41] By admitting the existence of only two referents, Frege's position collapses logical and algebraic valuations together and thus renders them indistinguishable.[42]

Wittgenstein took up a completely different position, where he rejected – this being the difference whence most of his subsequent distinctions stemmed – what Perzanowski called the *principle of semantic homogeneity*. According to this principle, the problem of the reference of names and the problem of the reference of propositions are both resolved using similar structures. This is Frege's case, therefore. For Wittgenstein, however, the solution to the nominal reference problem is *different* from that of the propositional reference problem. For names, the semiotic triangle (name-sense-reference) is reduced by eliminating sense, so that names refer directly to objects and do not require the intermediation of sense. This gives rise to an extremely simple one-to-one correlation. It also means that both names and objects are simple, the one in language the other in reality. By contrast, the simplicity of the name-object semantic relation generates an extremely complex semantic representation for propositions that involves the concepts of 'proposition', 'propositional sign' (preceivable sign of the proposition), 'sense of the proposition' (situation in the logical space connected to the proposition), 'thought' (logical picture of the fact related to the proposition) and 'fact depicted by the proposition'.[43]

---

[41] See Suszko 1975.

[42] The principle according to which there are only two referents for propositions I shall call, following Suszko, *Frege's axiom*. It is interesting to note that the independence of Frege's axiom was demonstrated by Tarski in his doctoral dissertation (1923), where he explicitly compared it with Euclid's Vth postulate. For a brief treatment see Suszko 1977. If all true propositions denote exactly one and the same entity, this means that the real philosophical position underlying the theory is an absolute monism of facts. Suszko's rejection of Frege's axiom prompted him to elaborate his so-called non-Fregean logic. See Suszko 1975 and the paper by Omyła in this volume.

[43] For details see Perzanowski 1993.

It seems, therefore, that there are at least two main different strategies to adopt: if we accept Frege's position that names and propositions are semantically homogeneous entities, we can represent their structures by using the relative semiotic triangles. In this case the procedure is straightforward, and we encounter no major obstacles as long as we accept the idea that Truth and Falsity are in every respect objects of our ontology. If, instead, we follow Wittgenstein and reject the principle of semantic homogeneity, we are stressing that there is an univocal relationship between name and object. On the basis of this relationship each entity is an atom of its universe (the ontological universe in the case of objects, the universe of signs in the case of names). This absolute simplicity as regards names, however, generates major complexity among propositions.

The problem addressed by Wittgenstein was certainly not a new one. The basic issue was whether it was possible to construct an ontologically neutral language. Before Wittgenstein the problem had exercised several other thinkers: Brentano, for example, particularly during his so-called 'reist' phase.[44] The fundamental theoretical problem was how to use language without being trapped by the symbolic features of language itself.

13. Signs and Symbols

From an ontological point of view, the question condenses into whether a directly depicting language is possible, that is, whether we can construct a language that depicts reality directly without the mediation of symbols.[45]

Such a language plays a particularly relevant role in the case of *Aussersein*'s objects, because – as far as we can see – language is the main tool we have in order to be acquainted with them. We are acquainted with complete objects through presentation, that is, they are intuitively given to us. But there are not presentations of incomplete objects. They are indirectly presented to us only through the presentation of other (complete) objects. This is an observation that, as a psychological law, was already stated by Aristotle: nobody can possess a non-intuitive presentation if it is not accompanied by one (or more) intuitive presentations.

A language depicting objects of this kind has very different features from a natural language or a normal formal language. As far as regards the categore-

---

[44] See Poli 1993a and Albertazzi 1991a, 1991b and 1992.
[45] See Smith 1992.

matic constituents of the language, it has signs only for the 'objects' of the two main ontological categories. That is it has names (signs for things) and propositions (signs for states of affairs). But it has no sign for properties, qualities, relations and so on. Seen in this way, it should be apparent that a directly depicting language is closer to a Wittgensteinian viewpoint than to a Fregean viewpoint.

A directly depicting language in our sense is, for example, intrinsically elementary. The concept of 'intrinsic elementariness' is difficult to pin down. In preliminary terms we may say that an intrinsically elementary language is extremely poor. As far as I can see, it is closed only under conjunction and it contains very unusual conditions of identity, of the type analyzed by Suszko when he was able to distinguish propositional identity from double implication. That is, to distinguish the truth conditions of '$\alpha \wedge \beta \leftrightarrow \beta \wedge \alpha$' from the truth conditions of '$\alpha \wedge \beta = \beta \wedge \alpha$'.[46] To give an other example, it means that, providing that '$\neg$' is part or the furniture of our language, we can also distinguish between '$\alpha \leftrightarrow \neg\neg\alpha$' and '$\alpha = \neg\neg\alpha$'.

Needless to say, from the point of view of an intrinsically elementary language, we should maintain '$\alpha \wedge \beta \neq \beta \wedge \alpha$' and '$\alpha \neq \neg\neg\alpha$'.

Any condition which allows connectives to be interdefined, or new connectives to be derived, transforms an intrinsically elementary language into an intrinsically non-elementary one. An intrinsically elementary language contains 'few' connectives, those definable on the basis of apodeictically 'evident' operations.[47] An example can be found in Husserl's *Philosophie der Arithmetik*, where the primitive connectives are negation and conjunction,[48] and in his *Formale und transzendentale Logik*, where the primitive connectives are disjunction and negation.[49] From a formal point of view, the only unproblematic connective that can pertain to an intrinsically elementary language is conjunction.

---

[46] Suszko 1975. See also Omyła's paper in this volume.

[47] The reference here is to Brentano's distinction between 'apodeictic evidence' and 'assertive evidence'. See Brentano 1966.

[48] From negation (= leaving aside) we obtain the simple something, and from the somethings, in the sense of 'this something *and* that something *and* so on', we obtain the multiplicities.

[49] For an analysis of Husserl's latter proposal see Harvey and Hintikka 1991 and Albertazzi 1993. In would be interesting to know why Husserl changed from negation and conjunction to disjunction and negation. Note that in the first case negation is more fundamental than conjunction, while in the second disjunction is more fundamental than negation.

Coming back to the problem of a directly depicting language, one of the most puzzling aspects of such a language is that it is a so-to-say intermediate language between the propositional and the predicative level. It is stronger than a pure propositional language because it does contain signs for things, but it is also weaker than a predicative language because it does not contain signs for predicates. As we said before, a directly depicting language contains categorematic signs only for things and states of affairs.

The underlying intuition is that it is not possible to construct an intrinsically elementary language of a predicative nature, because some degree of measure of symbolization seems inevitable in the passage to the predicative level. To keep the measure of symbolization (or non-elementariness) of predicative language to a minimum, we could bear the difference between properties and predicates in mind. In this sense we can say that properties, for example, are all positive, that is that negative properties do not exist. Likewise, there are no disjunctive properties, whereas it is obvious that there are disjunctive predicates.[50] We shall use the term 'conditions of closure' for the assumptions that enable us to pass from the theory of properties to that of predicates. A language of this kind may be a significant step forward from a directly depicting language of the first type (intrinsically elementary), but we have still not arrived at a real and proper symbolic language. That is to say that from a formal point of view, the collection of properties is a weaker algebra than a Boolean algebra.

Provided that our description of a directly depicting language is correct, it follows that a language of such a nature will have some very peculiar characteristics. Consider, for instance, the fact that we cannot say which theory of predication is applied, for the very simple reason that there are not predicates. But consider also the transformation that should intervene in the theory of quantification or in the concept of existence. All these are very strange features for the standard or paradigmatic sense of logic. But all these are features that we can find in the now quite old proposal of a new logic advanced by Brentano and some of his pupils.[51] Unfortunately, their proposal arrived in the wrong moment, just as the Fregean paradigm was about to burst on the scene. But now that we know both the great power of the Fregean perspective and its strong limitations, it is perhaps time to go back to such a different proposal, armed with the tools and the results achieved over several decades of research.

---

[50] See, for instance, Armstrong 1978 vol. 2 and Grossmann 1983; for a defense of the opposite view, cf. Meixner 1992. For some connected topics, see Forbes 1992, Hochberg 1992 and Simons 1992.

[51] Poli 1993a.

References

Abelardo 1969: *Scritti di logica*, edited by M. Dal Pra, 2 ed., La Nuova Italia, Firenze.

Albertazzi, L. 1989: *Strati*, Reverdito, Trento.

Albertazzi, L. 1991a: "Nominalismo e critica della lingua in Franz Brentano", *Idee*, vol. 13-15, 217-235.

Albertazzi, L. 1991b: "Brentano and Mauthner's critique of language", *Brentano Studien* 2, 145-157.

Albertazzi, L. 1992: "Is there a transcendental object?", in Paśniczek 1992, 26-44.

Aristotle: *Metaphysica*, tr. by W.D. Ross, Oxford U.P., Oxford, 1908.

Aristotle: *Categoriae and De Interpretatione*, tr. by E.M. Edghill, Oxford U.P., Oxford, 1928.

Armstrong, D.M. 1978: *Universals and scientific realism*, Cambridge U.P., Cambridge (vol. 1: *Nominalism and realism;* vol. 2: *A theory of universals*).

Brentano, F. 1966: *The True and the Evident*, Routledge, London (*Wahrheit und Evidenz*, Meiner, Hamburg 1962).

Burkhardt, H. and Smith, B. (eds.) 1991: *Handbook of Metaphysics and Ontology*, Philosophia, Munich.

Chisholm, R. (ed.) 1960: *Realism and the background of phenomenology*, The Free Press, Glencoe, Ill.

Cocchiarella, N. 1972: "Properties as individuals in formal ontology", *Nous* 6, 165-87.

Cocchiarella, N. 1974: "Formal ontology and the foundations on mathematics", in Nakhnikian 1974, 29-46.

Cocchiarella, N. 1978: "On the logic of nominalized predicates and its philosophical interpretations", *Erkenntnis* 13, 339-69.

Cocchiarella, N. 1986a: "Conceptualism, ramified logic and nominalized predicates", *Topoi* 2, 75-86.

Cocchiarella, N. 1986b: *Logical investigations of predication theory and the problem of universals*, Bibliopolis, Napoli.

Cocchiarella, N. 1989a: "Conceptualism, realism, and intensional logic", *Topoi* 5, 15-34.

Cocchiarella, N. 1989b: "Philosophical perspectives on formal theories of predication", in Gabbay and Guenthner 1992, 254-326.

Cocchiarella, N. 1991: "Ontology II: formal ontology", in Burkhardt and Smith 1991, 640-47.

Czezowski, T. 1948: *O metafizyce, jej kierunkach i zagadnieniach* [Metaphysics, its directions and problems], Ksiegarnia naukowa, Toruń.

Elie, H. 1936: *Le complexe significabile*, Vrin, Paris.

Epstein, R.L. 1990: *The semantic foundations of logic. Volume I: Propositional logics*, Kluwer, Dordrecht.

Fausti, G. 1947: *Teoria dell'astrazione*, Cedam, Padova.

Findlay, J.N. 1963: *Meinong's theory of objects*, Oxford U. P., Oxford (1933).

Fine, K. 1985: *Reasoning with arbitrary objects*, Blackwell, Oxford.

Forbes, G. 1992: "Worlds and states of affairs: how similar can they be", in Mulligan 1992, 118-132.

Gabbay, D. and Guenthner, F. (eds.) 1989: *Handbook of philosophical logic*, vol. IV, Dordrecht, Reidel.

Grossman, R. 1983: *The categorial structure of the world*, Indiana U. P., Bloomington.

Haller, R. and Gombocz, L. (eds) 1984: *Ästhetik / Aesthetics*. *Proceedings of the 8th International Wittgenstein-Symposium*, I, Hölder - Pichler - Tempsky, Wien.

Haller, R. and Brandl, J. (eds.) 1990: *Wittgenstein. Eine Neubewertung. Towards a Re-evaluation. Proceedings of the 14th International Wittgenstein-Symposium*, Hölder - Pichler - Tempsky, Wien.

Harvey C.W. and Hintikka J. 1991: "Modalization and modalities", in Seebohm, Føllesdal and Mohanty 1991, 59-77.

Henry, D. 1972: *Medieval logic and metaphysics*, Hutchinson University Library, London.

Henry, D. 1984: *That most subtle question (Questio subtilissima): The metaphysical bearing of medieval and contemporary linguistic disciplines*, Manchester U. P., Manchester.

Henry, D. 1991: *Medieval mereology*, Grüner, Amsterdam / Philadelphia.

Hochberg, H. 1992: "Truth makers, truth predicates, and truth types", in Mulligan 1992, 86-117.

Husserl, E. 1969: *Formal and transcendental logic*, Nijhoff, The Hague (*Formale und transzendentale Logik*, Husserliana XVII, 1974; 1st ed. 1929).

Ingarden, R. 1939-40: "The scientific activity of Kazimierz Twardowski", *Studia philosophica*, 17-30.

Kaplan, D. 1970: "What is Russell's theory of descriptions?", in Yourgrau 1970.

Kerry, B. 1885-1891: "Über Anschauung und ihre psychische Verarbeitung", *Vierteljahrsschrift für wissenschaftliche Philosophie*, (8 papers: 9 (1885), 433-493; 10 (1886), 419-467; 11 (1887), 53-116; 11 (1887), 249-307; 13 (1889), 71-124; 13 (1889), 392-419; 14 (1890), 317-353; 15 (1891), 127-167).

Laerzio, D. 1925: *Lives of Eminent Philosophers*, 2 voll., London.

Lambert, K. 1983: *Meinong and the principle of independence*, Cambridge U. P., Cambridge.

Mally, E. 1904: "Untersuchungen zur Gegenstandstheorie des Messens", in Meinong 1904, 121-262.

Mally, E. 1912: *Gegenstandstheoretische Grundlagen der Logik und Logistik*, Barth, Leipzig.

Meinong, A. 1904: *Untersuchungen zur Gegenstandstheorie und Psychologie*, Barth, Leipzig.

Meinong, A. 1960: "The theory of objects", in Chisholm 1960, 76-117 ("Über Gegenstandstheorie", in *Untersuchungen zur Gegenstandstheorie und Psychologie*, Barth, Leipzig 1904).

Meinong, A. 1983: *On Assumptions*, University of California Press, Berkeley (*Über Annahmen*, Barth, Leipzig (1902; 2nd amply revised ed. 1910)).

Meixner, U. 1992: "On negative and disjunctive properties", in Mulligan 1992, 28-36.

Melandri, E. 1989: *Contro il simbolico. Dieci lezioni di filosofia*, Ponte alle grazie, Firenze.

Mulligan, K. (ed.) 1992: *Language, Truth and Ontology*, Kluwer, Dordrecht.

Nakhnikian, G. 1974: *Bertrand Russell's Philosophy*, Duckworth, London.

Parikh, R. 1975: *Logic Colloquium*, Springer, Wien.

Parsons, T. 1980: *Nonexistent Objects*, Yale U. P., New Haven.

Paśniczek, J. (ed.) 1992: *Theory of Objects: Meinong and Twardowski*, Lublin, KUL.

Perzanowski, J. 1984: "Some Ontological and Semantical Puzzles of Wittgenstein's Tractatus", in Haller and Gombocz 1984, 224-30.

Perzanowski, J. 1990: "Towards Post-Tractatus Ontology", in Haller and Brandl 1990, vol. 1, 185-99.

Perzanowski, J. 1993: "What is Non-Fregean in the Semantics of Wittgenstein's *Tractatus* and Why?", *Axiomathes* 4, 357-372 ("Ce qu'il y a de non Frégéen dans la sémantique du *Tractatus* de Wittgenstein, et pourquoi", in Sebestik and Soulez 1992, 163-77).

Poli, R. 1988: "Astrazione e idealizzazione", *Verifiche* 17, 189-207.

Poli, R. 1990: "Ernst Mally's theory of properties", *Grazer Philosophische Studien*, vol 38, 115-38.

Poli, R. 1992a: "La scomparsa del logoforo. Alle radici del declino della metafisica", forthcoming in *Idee*.

Poli, R. 1992b: "Twardowski and Wolff", in Paśniczek 1992, 45-56.

Poli, R. 1992c: *Ontologia formale,* Marietti, Genova.

Poli, R. 1993a: "Ontologia e logica in Franz Brentano: giudizi categorici e giudizi tetici", *Epistemologia*, 16, 39-76.

Poli, R. 1993b: "Understanding Mally", forthcoming in the proceedings of the Mally conference, Salzburg 1992.

Poli, R. 1993c: "Husserl's Conception of Formal Ontology", *History and Philosophy of Logic* 14, 1-14.

Poli, R., Dappiano, L. and Libardi, M. 1993: "Aspetti della teoria aristotelica delle parti e dell'intero", *Paradigmi* 11, 593-626.

Quine, W.V.O. 1960: *Word and Object,* Wiley, New York.

Routley, R. 1980: *Exploring Meinong's Jungle,* Philosophy Department, Australian National University, Canberra.

Santambrogio, M. 1987: "Generic and Intensional objects", *Synthese* 73, 637-663.

Santambrogio, M. 1992: "Was Frege right about variable objects?", in Mulligan 1992, 133-156.

Sebestik, J. and Soulez, A. (eds.) 1992: *Wittgenstein et la philosophie aujourd'hui,* Méridien Klincksieck, Paris.

Seebohm T.S., Føllesdal D. and Mohanty J.N. (eds.) 1991: *Phenomenology and the formal sciences,* Kluwer, Dordrecht.

Simons, P. 1992: "Logical atomism and its ontological refinement: a defense", in Mulligan 1992, 157-179.

Smith, B. 1982: *Parts and Moments,* Philosophia, München.

Smith, B. 1992: "Characteristica universalis", in Mulligan 1992, 48-77.

Sommers, F. 1982: *The Logic of Natural Language,* Clarendon, Oxford.

Suszko, R. 1975: "Abolition of the Fregean Axiom", in Parikh 1975, 169-239.

Suszko, R. 1977: "The Fregean Axiom and Polish Mathematical Logic in the 1920s", *Studia Logica* 36,151-55.

Twardowski, K. 1977: *On the Content and Object of Presentations,* Nijhoff, Amsterdam (*Zur Lehre vom Inhalt und Gegenstand der Vorstellungen*, Hölder, Wien 1894; reprint Philosophia, München 1982).

Überweg, F. 1915: *Geschichte der Philosophie*, II, Mittler, Tübingen (12th ed.).

Vaihinger, H. 1911: *Die Philosophie des Als ob*, Meiner, Hamburg.

Yourgrau, W. et. al., *Physics, Logic and History,* Plenum Press, New York.

Zalta, E. 1983: *Abstract Objects,* Reidel, Dordrecht.

Zalta, E. 1988: *Intensional logic and the metaphysics of intentionality,* MIT Press, Cambridge (Mass.).

Zanatta, M. 1989: "La genesi e il significato dottrinale delle categorie", introduction to Aristotele 1989: *Le categorie*, Rizzoli, Milano, 7-298.

NINO B. COCCHIARELLA

CONCEPTUAL REALISM AS A FORMAL ONTOLOGY

1. Introduction

A formal ontology is both a theory of logical form and a metaphysical theory about the ontological structure of the world. What makes it a theory of logical form is that different ontological categories or modes of being are represented in it by different logico-grammatical categories. It is specified in this regard by what might be called an ontological grammar that determines how the expressions of those logico-grammatical categories can be meaningfully combined so as to represent different ontological aspects of the world.

There is more to a formal ontology than ontological grammar, however. In particular, besides determining the ways that the expressions of the different logico-grammatical categories can be meaningful combined, a formal ontology also determines the ways those expressions can be deductively transformed as well – i.e., the ways those expressions determine the valid formulas of that ontology. As a theory of logical form, a formal ontology involves not only an ontological grammar, accordingly, but also ontological laws determining the valid formulas of that grammar.

What is central and fundamental in determining both of these functions of a formal ontology as a theory of logical form is how the metaphysical system it represents interprets the nexus of predication. That is because, whether directly or indirectly, it is the nexus of predication that determines how the expressions of the different logico-grammatical categories of a theory of logical form can be both meaningfully combined and deductively transformed – which is to say that it is in terms of this nexus that the unity of the different categories or modes of being of the formal ontology in question is ultimately to be understood.

27

R. Poli and P. Simons, Formal Ontology, 27–60.

Historically, there are three major types of theories of predication corresponding to the three types of theories of universals that have been propounded. Here, by a universal, we do not mean just any abstract entity at all (such as a set or class, or even a number, as W.V. Quine would have it) but what has traditionally been understood ever since Aristotle – namely, an entity that can be predicated of things (*De Interpretatione*, 17a39). The three types of theories of universals are nominalism, conceptualism, and realism. Nominalism is the most restrictive of the three, because according to nominalism there are no universals that can be predicated of things other than the predicate expressions of language – where what it means to say that a predicate expression can be predicated of things is simply that the expression is *true of* those things (or that those things *satisfy* the expression). Hence, according to nominalism, there is no nexus of predication other than what occurs in language.

In conceptualism and realism there are universals other than the predicate expressions of language, and, at least in conceptualism and *logical realism*, it is these universals that provide the semantic grounds for the correct use of predicate expressions – i.e., it is these universals that determine when a predicate expression is true (or false) of things. In conceptualism such universals are called *concepts*, whereas in realism they are generally called *properties* and *relations*. Concepts are what underlie predication in thought and language, which in conceptualism means that concepts cannot exist independently of the socio-biologically based capacity humans have for thought and language. The universals of realism, on the other hand, are what underlie predication in reality – e.g., the states of affairs that obtain in the world (as in *natural* realism), or the propositions that constitute the objective truths and falsehoods of the world (as in *logical* realism). These universals are assumed to exist independently of the human capacity for thought and language – and in logical realism (as a modern form of Platonism), unlike natural realism (as a modern form of Aristotelianism), they are assumed to exist independently of the causal structure of the world as well, and even independently of whether they are logically realizable or not.

In both nominalism and logical realism, the representation of ontological categories by the logico-grammatical categories of a theory of logical form is direct – although, as we explain below, the representation in logical realism is perhaps even more direct and simple than in nominalism. In conceptualism and natural realism, the situation is not so direct or simple as that. The properties and relations of natural realism, for example, are posited to account for the causal structure of the world; and, in that regard, they are not assumed to be the semantic grounds for the correct or incorrect application of predicate expressions except when those predicate expressions are explicitly assumed to represent such a natural property or relation – an assumption that can be made only *a posteriori*. Natural properties and relations are not the 'meanings', or intensions, or cognitive capacities that underlie our use of predicate expressions; rather, they are what in the causal order may correspond to some, but by no means all, of the concepts we can form and the predicate expressions we can introduce in our use of language. We may use a predicate expression to represent a natural property or relation (and, in terms of that property or relation, a predication in reality, i.e. a state of affairs), but, in order to do so, the semantic grounds for the correct use of that expression must already be determined and explained in terms of some other theory of predication. In this regard, we maintain that in order for us to posit natural properties and relations in our scientific theories – and, therefore, in order for natural realism even to be formulable as a formal ontology – it must be assumed that in principle natural realism is able to provide a natural, causal account of predication in both language and thought. If natural realism is to be a viable formal ontology at all, in other words, then in principle it must be able to provide the causal ground for one or another form of conceptualism – or, to be more precise, of one or another form of conceptual natural realism (see Cocchiarella 1989a, sections 13-14).

Conversely, conceptualism, as a socio-biologically based theory of the human capacity for thought and language, must in turn presuppose a causal ground for that capacity, and the most natural causal ground is an evolutionary theory based upon some applied form of natural realism. In addition, without some associated form of realism, natural or otherwise, conceptualism is at best only a truncated ontology, and it is dubious that it alone can provide an adequate account of the different modes or categories of being, including in particular (1) the states of affairs that obtain in the causal order, (2) the abstract objects that are normally assumed to exist in mathematics, and (3) the intensional objects that we seem to be committed to in our various theories and speculations about the world, whether true or false – which may well be the same as the intensional objects of fiction, or of stories in general, whether true or false.

Conceptual realism, as opposed to conceptualism *simpliciter*, does provide the general framework of a formal ontology that can accommodate both a natural realism and an intensional realism, as in *conceptual natural realism* and *conceptual Platonism* – or, instead of conceptual Platonism, as in *conceptual intensional realism*, where abstract objects are intensional objects that come about as products of cultural evolution. But the representation of the different ontological categories by logico-grammatical categories is not given in the direct and simple way in conceptual realism as it is in logical realism or nominalism. Instead, conceptual realism must represent the different formal modes of being in an indirect way. It is the explanation of this indirect way that is our primary concern in this essay.

2. Substitutional versus Ontological Interpretations of Quantifiers

As a formal ontology, nominalism maintains the metaphysical thesis that being is a genus – which is not at all the same as to say that there cannot be different *kinds* of being. Traditionally, nominalism also maintained that whatever the different kinds of being there are, all are forms of concrete being – though, as recognized today, this does not seem to be necessary to nominalism as a formal ontology (see Goodman 1956). The important point to notice here about nominalism as a formal ontology is that although there are different logico-grammatical categories (such as singular terms and predicates), there is nevertheless just one ontological category – namely the category of individuals or objects. In other words, the fact that predication unites expressions of different logico-grammatical categories does not mean that there must then be different ontological categories. The representation of ontological categories is not always quite as simple as that.

In nominalism, it is only the logico-grammatical category of singular terms that has ontological significance. This means that only objectual quantifiers – i.e. the first-order quantifiers that reach into the positions that singular terms occupy in the formulas (sentence-forms) of predicate logic – are indicative of nominalism's ontological commitments (see Goodman 1956). It is for this reason that most contemporary nominalists restrict themselves to the theory of logical forms described in first-order predicate logic.

A formal ontology for nominalism need not preclude the introduction of predicate quantifiers, however. Rather, the point is that if predicate quantifiers are to be allowed at all in nominalism, then they must be interpreted only substitutionally, which means that the logic of predicate quantifiers must be restricted to what is now called standard 'predicative' second-order logic (see Cocchiarella 1986, chapter one). Such a restriction involves imposing certain constraints on the logico-grammatical category of predicate expressions and how those expressions can be deductively transformed. In particular, in such a framework no formula (with n free variables) in which a predicate quantifier occurs can be taken as a proper/genuine substituend of the bound (n-place) predicate variables (or, in the case of standard ramified second-order logic, no formula in which there occurs a predicate quantifier of a ramified 'level' higher than, or equal to, any given 'level' can be a proper substituend of the bound predicate variables of that 'level').

A substitutional interpretation of quantifiers of any given type will not affect the general understanding that *to be* of a given ontological type (or category) of a formal ontology *is to be the value of a variable bound by a quantifier regarding that type* – i.e. a quantifier that can reach into positions in formulas occupied by expressions of the corresponding logico-grammatical type (or category). For a variable bound by a quantifier interpreted substitutionally will have no values at all but only substituends – i.e. expressions that can be properly substituted for that variable – and, in that regard, the logico-grammatical category represented by that variable (and its substituends) will have no ontological significance. But again, a substitutional interpretation, if it is not to be confused with an ontological interpretation, will bring with it certain important constraints regarding the logico-grammatical behavior of expressions of the category in question. It is in terms of those constraints that a formal ontology will distinguish a substitutional from an ontological interpretation.

Now it is significant that the constraints on the logic of predicate quantifiers in *constructive* conceptualism, as opposed to *holistic* conceptualism, are not unlike the constraints in nominalism. For unlike holistic conceptualism, constructive conceptualism does not allow for the formation of so-called 'impredicative' concepts – i.e. concepts that can be represented only by a formula in which a predicate quantifier (of the same or higher 'level' in the case of a ramified logic) occurs. In this regard, constructive conceptualism is also represented by a 'predicative' second-order logic – but, because predicate quantifiers do have a referential or ontological significance in conceptualism, such a predicative logic is not the same as the predicative logic that represents the nexus of predication in nominalism. The difference between the standard predicative logic of nominalism and the 'nonstandard' predicative logic of constructive conceptualism indicates that the distinction between an ontological and a substitutional interpretation of predicate quantifiers is somewhat more subtle than the different distinction between a 'predicative' and an 'impredicative' logic – because, although an impredicative logic clearly precludes a substitutional interpretation of predicate quantifiers, the same cannot be said for a predicative logic. (For more on the distinctions between constructive and holistic conceptualism on the one hand, and the 'predicative' second-order logics of nominalism and constructive conceptualism on the other, see Cocchiarella 1986.)

3. The Importance of the Notion of Unsaturatedness in Formal Ontology

Predicate quantifiers have ontological significance in conceptualism because they are interpreted there as referring to concepts; but the sense in which they refer to concepts is not the same as (nor is it really even comparable to) the sense in which first-order, objectual quantifiers refer to objects. That is because concepts (as understood here) are not objects of any kind at all, but rather are unsaturated cognitive structures, which in the case of predicable concepts are based on cognitive capacities to identify, characterize and relate objects to one another in various ways. Referential concepts are cognitive capacities that are complementary to predicable concepts, and it is by their means that we are able to refer (or at least purport to refer) to objects in various ways. It is the exercise or realization in thought and speech of concepts as cognitive structures based upon such capacities that is what informs our speech acts, and our mental acts in general, with a predicable and referential nature, respectively. (For convenience, we ignore concepts other than predicable and referential concepts here.) Predicable concepts, for example, are based upon cognitive capacities that underlie our ability to follow the rules of language regarding the correct use of predicate expressions – and, in that regard, they are what determine the truth conditions that we associate with those expressions. Similarly, referential concepts are based upon the cognitive capacities that underlie our use of referential expressions (e.g. proper names, definite and indefinite descriptions, and quantifier phrases in general).

The terminology of unsaturatedness that we are using here is adopted from Frege, who also held that concepts have an unsaturated nature. Only, for Frege concepts are not cognitive capacities or mind-dependent entities at all. Rather, they are independently real functions from objects to truth values (the true and the false), which he also called properties and relations. These properties and relations are properties and relations in the logical sense, i.e., they are logically real properties and relations, because, as functions from objects to truth values, many of them have no instances (i.e. they assign the truth value the false to all objects), and, indeed, some are such that, logically, it is impossible for them to have any instances at all. The formal ontology that is associated with Frege's theory of logical form, accordingly, is a version of logical realism. In addition, because all and only (saturated) objects are values of the individual variables, and all and only (unsaturated) functions are values of function variables, with (onto)logically different types of functions being the values of logico-grammatically different types of function variables, the different ontological categories of Frege's ontology are represented by expressions of different logico-grammatical categories. Here, we have a good example of a formal ontology in which ontological categories are represented in a direct and simple way through logico-grammatical categories, and where all and only the entities of any one ontological category are values of the variables bound by quantifiers respecting the corresponding logico-grammatical category.

The nexus of predication in Frege's formal ontology is explained in terms of what he took to be the unsaturated nature of functions, which means that in his version of logical realism the nexus of predication is really just a form of functionality. Such an interpretation is odd in a way because the only explanation Frege ever gave of the unsaturated nature of a function turned both on the unity of a sentence (which is based on the unsaturated nature of a predicate expression as a linguistic function) and the unity of the proposition (*Gedanke*) expressed by a sentence. Thus, in regard to the unsaturated nature of a predicate as the nexus of predication in a sentence, Frege claimed that "this unsaturatedness ... is necessary, since otherwise the parts [of the sentence] do not hold together" (Frege 1979, 177). Similarly, in regard to the unsaturated nature of the nexus of predication of a proposition (*Gedanke*), Frege argued that "not all parts of a thought [in the sense of an independently real proposition] can be complete; at least one must be 'unsaturated', or predicative; otherwise, they would not hold together" (Frege 1952, 54).

Bertrand Russell, whose original framework was also a version of logical realism (but not the same as Frege's – cf. Cocchiarella 1987, chapter 2), reversed the order of priority and explained functionality in general in terms of predication and the notion of a proposition. That is, a function, according to Russell, is really just a many-one relation, where it is the notion of a relation as the nexus of a predication, i.e. as a relating relation, that 'embodies' the unity of a proposition. What holds the constituents of a proposition together, according to Russell, is a relation relating those constituents in a certain particular way, i.e. a relation as the nexus of a predication in reality.

Unfortunately, unlike Frege, Russell (at least until 1913) also took properties and relations to be objects, i.e. entities that could themselves be related by relations (of a higher-order/type) in the nexus of predication; and, in consequence, he was forced to reject the idea of properties and relations having an unsaturated nature. This led to certain difficulties in his theory of predication, and therefore in his formal ontology. In time, through being prodded by Wittgenstein (in 1913), he came to change his formal ontology from logical realism to logical atomism as a version of natural realism – though, in doing so he was no longer able to justify the ontological logicism that was his motive for originally adopting logical realism (see Cocchiarella [1987], chapter 5, for a detailed explanation of this last claim). It was

Wittgenstein in the *Tractatus Logico-Philosophicus* – and Russell who later followed him in this – who replaced Frege's unsaturated logically real properties and relations (as functions from objects to truth values) with unsaturated natural (or 'material') properties and relations as the modes of configuration or nexuses of predication in atomic facts or states of affairs. It is because of their unsaturated nature as modes of configuration or nexuses of predication, Wittgenstein came to see, that natural properties and relations cannot themselves be objects in such configurations.

It is not our purpose to describe or defend logical atomism here as a formal ontology – and, in fact, we do not think that it can succeed in fulfilling certain conditions of adequacy that any viable system of formal ontology must fulfill. We reject, in particular, the metaphysical notion of an ontologically simple object (which some regard as a bare particular) that is central to this ontology, as well as the thesis that all meaning and all analysis must ultimately be based upon such ontologically simple objects and the atomic states of affairs in which those objects are configured. Aside from requiring that all predicate expressions must be analyzable (and in that sense reducible) in strictly logical terms to the simple predicate expressions that stand for the natural properties and relations that are the modes of configuration of atomic states of affairs, such an analysis would also require (as in Rudolf Carnap's state descriptions) the semantic reduction of all quantifier expressions in favor of the simple proper names, or individual constants, that would occur in the atomic sentences of the formal ontology. All reference, in other words, is to be explained in logical atomism in terms of the singular reference involved in the use of such individual constants, which means that all mental acts of asserting or thinking a proposition must be analyzable in terms of the mental assertion of atomic propositions and the immanent, simple mental objects that are their constituents (and that stand in a projective relation to the objects that they represent).

These consequences of logical atomism are rejected in both conceptualism and conceptual natural realism – where, in the latter framework, there are natural properties and relations but no ontologically simple objects such as are involved in logical atomism, and where it is false that all of the predicate expressions of language are assumed in principle to be logically analyzable in terms of the predicates that stand for natural properties and relations. Indeed, even without the assumption that there are any natural properties and relations at all, it is false in the kind of conceptualism we have in mind here that ultimately all reference must be explained in terms of the singular reference of proper names – or even in terms of the singular reference of proper names together with definite descriptions and other kinds of singular terms.

Conceptualism has an entirely different interpretation of the nexus of predication than is given in either Frege's logical realism or Wittgenstein's logical atomism – even though it too, like each of them, involves the notion of unsaturatedness in that explanation in a fundamental way. One important difference, for example, is that the primary unity of the categories that is achieved in conceptualism through the notion of unsaturatedness is the unity of thought as expressed in a mental act, which includes the unity of a speech act when a mental act is overtly expressed in language in a context of use. In Frege's logical realism, on the other hand, and in Wittgenstein's logical atomism (as a version of natural realism), the primary unity is the unity of a proposition or of an atomic state of affairs, respectively.

4. Referential and Predicable Concepts Versus Immanent Objects of Reference

Predicable concepts, we have said, are unsaturated cognitive capacities, or cognitive structures based upon such capacities, to identify, characterize, and relate objects to one another in various ways. Referential concepts are complementary capacities by which we are able to refer (or purport to refer) to such objects as well. It is the exercise or realization in thought and speech of concepts as cognitive capacities which is what informs our mental acts (which include our speech acts) with a referential and a predicable nature. That is because as capacities to identify, characterize, and relate objects, as well as to refer to such objects, concepts are also the capacities that underlie our ability to follow the rules of language regarding the correct use of predicate and referential expressions. Indeed, unlike propositional knowledge – i.e. knowledge that certain propositions are true – our 'knowledge' of the rules of language regarding the correct use of different kinds of expressions is really a matter of our having concepts in the sense of cognitive capacities, and our following those rules is really a matter of our exercising those concepts as capacities. It follows, accordingly, that concepts in the sense intended here do not exist independently of the more general capacity humans have for language and concept-formation – which does not mean that they are merely subjective entities and do not have a status as objective universals. Indeed, as intersubjectively realizable cognitive capacities, or cognitive structures based upon such capacities, that are common to different people, and that underlie the means by which people think and communicate with another, concepts are objective entities – even if they are not 'objective' in the sense of existing independently of the human capacity for thought and language, as is commonly assumed in logical realism (which, as in the case of Frege and Russell, identifies concepts with properties and relations).

Concepts, accordingly, are neither mental images nor ideas in the sense of particular mental occurrences – nor are they mental *objects* of any other kind as well (and hence they are not *object*-ive entities in that sense as well). Instead, as cognitive capacities that may in fact never be exercised, or that may be exercised at the same time by different people, or by the same people at different times – i.e. as intelligible or cognitive universals – concepts have an unsaturated nature. In addition, predicable concepts have an unsaturated nature that is complementary to the unsaturated nature of referential concepts. Indeed, it is because of the complementarity of predicable and referential concepts as unsaturated cognitive structures that we are able to make, e.g., a categorical judgment or statement, which is just the result of jointly exercising (and mutually saturating) a predicable and referential concept. As a mental act (which is overtly expressed in the case of a speech act), a categorical judgment or statement is an event, which means that it is an object of a special kind. But neither of the concepts that are realized – i.e. that are mutually saturated – in that event are themselves objects of any kind at all.

A general thesis of conceptualism regarding the complementarity of referential and predicable concepts is that every affirmative assertion (speech act) that is syntactically analyzable in terms of a noun phrase and a verb phrase (regardless of the complexity of either) is also semantically analyzable in terms of an overt application of a referential and a predicable concept, and that the assertion itself is the result of their mutual saturation in that joint application. It is in just this sort of joint application that we are to understand how conceptualism interprets the nexus of predication. A speech act in which 'All ravens are black' is asserted, for example, is the result of jointly applying the referential concept that 'all ravens' stands for – which, formally, can be represented by '$(\forall x \text{ Raven})$' – with the predicable concept that 'is black' stands for – which, formally, can be represented by 'Black( )', or, using λ–abstracts (which are needed in any case to formally represent complex predicates), by '$[\lambda x \text{ Black}(x)]$'. (We ignore the difference between singular and plural here, though we now believe that conceptualism is committed to giving some logical account of that difference, i.e. an account in terms of logical forms.) Thus, in conceptualism the logical form of the sentence 'All ravens are black' is given as '$(\forall x \text{ Raven})\text{Black}(x)$', or, equivalently, as '$(\forall x \text{ Raven})[\lambda x \text{ Black}(x)](x)$'. The logical form of 'Some ravens are not black', which, assuming that the negation is internal to the predicate, we also view as an affirmative assertion, is given as '$(\exists x \text{ Raven})[\lambda x \neg \text{Black}(x)](x)$', where the internal negation (represented by '¬') is now clearly part of the predicate expression.

Denials, or negative assertions, although equivalent in intensional content to an affirmative assertion in which the negation is internal to the predicate – as 'No raven is white' is equivalent in intensional content to 'Every raven is such that it is not white' – are not themselves affirmative assertions and should not be represented as such. The negative aspect of a denial such as 'No raven is white' is an external negation, which in this case can be represented as '¬(∃x Raven)White(x)'. In such a negative assertion, the referential concept that the quantifier expression that '(∃x Raven)' stands for has been 'deactivated', by which we mean that no referential act to a raven is involved in such an assertion. Such an act is involved in the equivalent affirmative assertion, but an equivalence of intensional content is not the same as an identity of cognitive structure, which is determined by the referential and predicable concepts (among possibly others as well) whose activation, or deactivation, is involved in the assertion in question.

Singular reference, as in the use of a proper name or a definite description, is not essentially different from a general reference, as in the use of 'some' and 'all' with a common name (and as in the use of such determiners as 'most', 'few', 'several', etc., with a common name as well – which we shall not go into here). Indeed, the category of names in conceptualism can be be taken to consist of common names and proper names as two distinct subcategories, where proper names and most common names are taken to stand for a sortal concept. Here, by a sortal, we understand a concept whose use in thought and communication is associated with certain identity criteria, i.e. criteria by which we are able to identify and count objects of the sort in question. Thus, just as the common name 'raven' stands for a sortal concept by which we are able to identify and refer to one or more ravens, so too a proper name such as 'Socrates' stands for a sortal concept by which we are able to identify and refer to a single individual. In general, the use of a proper name brings with it the identity criteria provided by the most specific common name sortal associated with that proper name.

Because singular reference is not essentially different from quantifier forms of reference, the referential use of a proper name in a conceptualist theory of logical form should also be represented by a quantifier phrase. In addition, because a proper name can be used both with and without an existential presupposition, it is appropriate that we use the same quantifiers ∃ and ∀ with proper names that are already used with common names. Thus, for example, we can use '(∃x Socrates)' to represent a referential use of the proper name 'Socrates' that is with, as opposed to without, an existential presupposition, and, similarly, we can use '($\forall$x Socrates)' to represent a referential use of 'Socrates' that is without such an existential presupposition. That both kinds of uses occur in thought and language is a well-known phenomena, which we shall not review and go into here. The important point here to note is that in both kinds of cases the referential concept is an unsaturated cognitive structure and not, for example, an 'idea' as a mental occurrence, and certainly not a 'bare particular' that is immanent to the mental act. The exercise of such a concept, or saturation of such a structure, together with a predicable concept results in a mental/speech act occurrence, and it is the functional roles of both concepts that informs that mental/speech act with a referential and predicable nature – but in neither case is the concept an object immanent to such a mental act. If by representationalism is meant the view that concepts are immanent objects of reference in our various mental acts (as it is sometimes maintained in historical accounts of conceptualism), then conceptualism is not a form of representationalism. But then, perhaps this way of characterizing representationalism is both misleading and historically wrong – in which case there may no incompatibility at all between conceptualism and representationalism after all.

Definite descriptions are also referential expressions that can be used both with and without existential presuppositions. An assertion of 'The King is wise', for example, as made by someone in a country (and at a time) in which there is a king, can be represented by '($\exists_1$x King)Wise(x)', where $\exists_1$ is a special quantifier representing a use of the determiner 'the' that is with, as opposed to without, an existential presupposition. The truth conditions of such an assertion in the kind of context indicated are essentially those described by Russell in his (1905) theory. That is,

$$(\exists_1 x \text{ King})\text{Wise}(x) \leftrightarrow (\exists x \text{ King})[(\forall y \text{ King})(y = x) \wedge \text{Wise}(x)]$$

is a valid thesis of the conceptualist theory of logical form in question here. But this is not to say that a representation of the truth conditions of a mental/speech act is the same as a representation of the cognitive structure of that act. Among other things, the latter should include, in particular, a representation of the referential and predicable concepts being exercised in that act, and that is not what a Russellian analysis of the truth conditions represents. (For more on this distinction, see Cocchiarella 1989b.)

For a use of the determiner 'the' that is without an existential presupposition, we need another special quantifier, $\forall_1$, that is dual to $\exists_1$. Given such a quantifier, we can take '($\forall_1$x King)Wise(x)' to represent an assertion of 'The King is Wise' in a context in which the definite description 'the King' is not being used with an existential presupposition regarding the existence of a (unique) king. The truth conditions of such an assertion can be similarly indicated by the following equivalence (as a valid thesis of conceptualism's theory of logical form):

$$(\forall_1 x \; King)Wise(x) \leftrightarrow (\forall x \; King)[(\forall y \; King)(y = x) \rightarrow Wise(x)].$$

These kinds of analyses can be applied to the well-known cases that are commonly brought up in the literature – such as Meinong's example of 'The round square is round and square', or, as in Descartes's version of the ontological argument, 'The perfect being is perfect'. (Contrary to what Meinong maintained about definite descriptions in general, both of these sentences, assuming the reference is with existential presuppositions, will be analyzed as false, which is as it should be, regardless of what Meinong thought about the matter.) Here, 'the round square' can be rephrased (with 'round' as part of a relative clause) as 'the square that is round', which can be represented by '$(\exists_1 x \; Square / Round(x))$'. The truth conditions of such a relative clause can be unpacked through having

$$(\exists_1 x \; Square/Round(x))F(x) \leftrightarrow$$
$$(\exists x \; Square)[(\forall y \; Square)(Round(y) \leftrightarrow y = x) \wedge F(x)]$$

as an instance of a general law for such clauses in definite descriptions. (For more details on the use of complex definite descriptions and non-sortal common names, such as 'being' in 'the being that is perfect', see Cocchiarella 1989b.)

There is no general presumption in any of these cases that that the exercise of a referential concept (i.e. the use of a concept by which we purport to refer) is always successful – i.e. that there always are entities that are the referents of our referential acts. This is particularly noteworthy in those cases of singular reference, such as the use of a proper name or a definite description, that are with, as opposed to without, existential presuppositions.

This last sort of observation was also made by Brentano, whose own ontology has striking similarities to conceptual natural realism (as a modern form of Aristotle's conceptual realism). Brentano noted, for example, that although "all mental references refer to things, ... in many cases, the things to which we refer do not exist" (1973, 291). This is not to say that such 'things' have 'being as objects', such as the intentional or 'immanent objects' of Brentano's early work. Rather, according to Brentano, "all it means is that a mentally active subject is referring to them" (ibid.). The intentionality of a mental act consists, in other words, only in the activation or exercise of a referential concept as one of the determinants of that mental act, and not in the 'being' of an object that is either immanent or transcendent to that act.

Brentano did not distinguish, as we have, between a concept as an unsaturated cognitive capacity and the event that is the result of exercising such a capacity in a mental act. His main concern was with what he called the mental content (Inhalt) of such an act, which in conceptualism corresponds to the referential aspect of the act, i.e. that aspect of the act that is 'informed' by the exercise of a referential concept. Nor, we should note, did Brentano allow in what has come to be called his reism, or concretism, any reference to objects other than concreta, i.e. objects that exist in the space-time causal manifold. In conceptual intensional realism (described in section 6 below), on the other hand, there can be reference to objects that do not (and, in fact, cannot) exist (as concreta in the space-time causal manifold). But then, even aside from such abstract objects, there can be reference in conceptualism in general to objects that could exist but which in fact do not exist (at the time of reference) – such as past or future objects, and perhaps also merely causally possible objects, such as the oak tree that a now destroyed acorn could have grown into (as a matter of natural possibility). In other words, regardless of whether there are abstract intensional objects or not, concrete existence, according to conceptualism, is not the same as being, which is a concept that past and future objects fall under even if they do not now exist, and which perhaps even merely causally possible objects fall under as well (depending on our view of causal possibility as an ontological mode of being). (See Cocchiarella 1989a, section 12, for more on the distinction between existence and being in conceptualism.)

The distinction between being and (concrete) existence is not a material but a formal distinction in conceptualism. It corresponds, in particular, at least on the level of objects, to the difference between a use of the quantifier phrase, 'there be (is, are)', and a use of the related, but different, quantifier phrase, 'there exist(s)', which in a conceptualist theory of logical form can be represented by the logico-grammatical difference between $\exists$ and $\exists^e$ as quantifiers (or perhaps $\exists^a$ instead of $\exists^e$ to emphasize that it is existence in the sense of actual/concrete being that is in question). Being and (concrete/actual) existence, in other words, are formal, 'logical' concepts according to conceptualism, and not properties, or attributes, that things might or might not have. Thus, whereas *to be* (an object) is to be a value of an individual variable bound by $\exists$, *to exist* (as an object in the space-time causal manifold) is to be a value of an individual variable bound by $\exists^e$, which, formally, can be defined as follows:

$$E!(x) =_{df} (\exists^e y)(x = y).^1$$

In the framework of conceptualism, accordingly, there is such a concept as (concrete) existence – which is not the same as to say that there is a property, or attribute, of existence in the sense of either logical or natural realism. It is the latter thesis that Brentano was particularly concerned to deny, we maintain, and not the former. (see, e.g., Brentano 1973, 208). Thus, to say that Socrates exists is not to ascribe an attribute, or property, of existence, to Socrates, any more than to say that Pegasus does not exist is to ascribe an attribute, or property, of nonexistence to Pegasus. All we do in both cases, according to Brentano, is either affirm or deny 'the object' in question – by which he means only that we affirm or deny 'the object' as a mental content (or 'immanent objectivity') through which the intentional act of reference is made. In conceptualism, as already noted, this mental content corresponds to that aspect of an assertion that is 'informed' by the application, or activation, of a referential concept, which, as an unsaturated cognitive structure, is not in any sense an object immanent to the act of reference.

This suggests that Brentano's view of what it means to say that Socrates exists, or that Pegasus does not exist, can be reconstructed (or represented) in conceptualism in terms of the logical forms '$(\exists x \text{ Socrates})E!(x)$' and '$\neg(\exists x \text{ Pegasus})E!(x)$', respectively. Here, in the denial of existence in particular, where the referential concept is deactivated, there is no need to speak of 'objects' that do not exist as objects that are immanent to our mental acts. Nor is there any need to speak, as Meinong does, of the being of *Nichtseinsobjektiven*, or states of affairs, having nonexistent objects as components – a position that Brentano rejected very emphatically (op. cit., 292).

---

[1] The absolute quantifier '$(\exists^e y)$' abbreviates '$(\exists^e y \text{ Object})$', where the non-sortal common name 'Object' is taken as the common name that is the ultimate superordinate of all common names. As discussed in Cocchiarella 1989b, we leave open whether such an ultimate superordinate is a new primitive notion or is contextually defined in terms of quantification over sortal concepts as follows:

$(\forall x \text{ Object})\phi =_{df} (\forall S)(\forall x \, S)\phi$,

$(\exists x \text{ Object})\phi =_{df} (\exists S)(\exists x \, S)\phi$,

and similarly for '$(\forall^e x \text{ Object})\phi$' and '$(\exists^e x \text{ Object})\phi$'. Thus, to refer to every object, on this analysis, is to refer to every object of *whatever sort*, and to refer to some object is to refer to some object *of some sort or other*.

5. Conceptual Natural Realism and the Analogy of Being Between Natural and Intelligible Universals

Conceptualism, without any associated form of realism, is at best only a truncated ontology. Yet, as a socio-biologically based theory of the generic capacity humans have for language and thought, it would seem that conceptualism must presuppose some form of natural realism as the causal ground of that capacity. Conversely, natural realism, it would seem, cannot stand on its own, but must, in turn, presuppose some form of conceptualism by which to explain how it is possible for us to form concepts and use language in our various theories and descriptions of the world, including in particular our ability to posit natural properties and relations as part of the causal order. There is a natural affinity between conceptualism and natural realism, we maintain, in that each seems to presuppose the other as part of a more general, supporting framework, which we shall call *conceptual natural realism*.

Concepts, we have said, do not exist independently of the capacity humans have for language and thought, whereas natural properties and relations do. Unlike the properties and relations assumed in logical realism, however, natural properties and relations are not assumed to exist independently of the causal structure of the world, and in particular they are not assumed to exist independently of the causal possibility of their being realized, i.e. of the causal possibility for there to be (concrete) objects having those properties and relations. The important point for us here at the moment, however, is not the difference between the properties and relations of natural realism and those of logical realism, but the difference between concepts and natural properties or relations. This is no less true even in those cases in which a natural property or relation may correspond to a concept, i.e. in which, properly speaking, a concept may be said to represent a natural property or relation.

The historical antecedents of conceptual natural realism seem to have been confused on just this point. Peter Abelard, for example, in his *Glosses on Porphyry*, does not distinguish the predicable concepts we exercise in thought from the universals (in the sense of a moderate realism) that exist as a common likeness in things. That is, a universal, according to Abelard, seems to 'exist' in a double way, first as a common likeness in things (prior to, and independent of, our having any concepts regarding that likeness), and then as a predicable concept in the human intellect through our capacity to abstract the likeness in things from our perception of them. Here, it is clear that the properties and relations in question exist only in the causal or natural order as likenesses in things – and yet, were those things to cease to exist, according to Abelard, they would still somehow exist in the human intellect as a universal concept.

Aristotle also seems to describe the natural kinds and properties of his conceptual natural realism in this double way, i.e. as having a mode of being both in things and, through an inductive abstraction (*epagoge*), in the human mind (*nous*) as well – though it is possible to interpret him otherwise. The point, in any case, is that when conceptualism is combined with natural realism, we must be careful not to confuse concepts with natural properties and relations, but at best to speak only of there being a correspondence between some predicable concepts and some natural properties and relations – a correspondence in which such a concept may be said to represent the corresponding natural property or relation.

One reason why the universals of natural realism were confused with predicable concepts (as universals that exist only in the intellect) is that both can be designated by predicates – or, more precisely, that a predicate that stands for a concept for which it is assumed there is a corresponding natural property or relation can also be taken (in a secondary, or derived, sense) to stand for the corresponding natural property or relation. A predicate can be taken to stand for a natural property or relation, in other words, as well as for a concept – even though the sense in which it stands for the former is derived from, and secondary to, the sense in which it stands for the latter. The sense in which a predicate stands for a concept is primary because it is the concept that determines the functional role of the predicate and the conditions under which it can be correctly used. It is only by assuming that there is a natural property or relation that corresponds to the truth conditions determined by the concept – a natural property or relation that may in fact be the causal basis for our construction of the concept – that we then can say, in a secondary sense, that the predicate also stands for a natural property or relation. Thus, even though the natural property or relation is prior in the order of being, nevertheless, the concept that the predicate stands for is prior in the order of conception.

The distinction between concepts in the order of conception and natural properties and relations in the order of being does not mean that there should also be a distinction in the theory of logical form of conceptual natural realism between predicates that stand for concepts and predicates that stand for a natural property or relation. The same predicate may be taken to stand in a double way both for a concept (in the primary sense) and a natural property or relation (in the secondary sense). Thus, it is not that the same universal can exist in a double way, as Abelard assumed, first in nature and then in the mind, but rather that, semantically, the same predicate can stand in a double way both for a concept and a natural property or relation – though it stands first for a concept, and then derivatively, and only in the sense of an empirical hypothesis, for a natural universal in nature as well.

Similarly, just as a predicate constant can be taken to stand in double way both for a concept and a natural property or relation, so too an (n-place) predicate variable can be taken in a double way to have both (n-ary) concepts and (n-ary) natural properties and relations as its values. The difference between the universals in the one order and the universals in the other is reflected not in a difference between two 'types' of predicate constants and variables – where the one 'type' stands for concepts and the other stands for natural properties and relations – but in the kind of second-order reference that is made by means of predicate quantifiers, i.e. the quantifiers that can be affixed to predicate variables and that determine the conditions under which a predicate constant can be substituted for a predicate variable so bound. In this way, the difference is reflected not in a difference of 'types' of predicate variables to which predicate quantifiers can be affixed, but in a difference between the predicate quantifiers themselves.

What we need to add to the second-order conceptualist theory of logical forms already briefly indicated, accordingly, are special quantifiers, $\forall^n$ and $\exists^n$, that can be applied to predicate variables, and that, when so applied, can be used to refer to natural properties and relations. Thus, for example, the fundamental thesis, (NR), of natural realism that every (j-ary) natural universal is causally realizable can be stated in terms of such a quantifier as follows:

(NR) $(\forall^n F^j)\Diamond^c(\exists^e x_1)...(\exists^e x_j)F(x_1,...,x_j).$

Here, the modal operator $\Diamond^c$ represents only a causal (or natural) possibility, and not a logical or merely conceivable possibility. With the modal operator deleted, the thesis (NR) can be taken to represent a form of Aristotle's moderate realism, in which it is assumed that properties and relations exist only *in re*, i.e. only in the concrete objects that have those properties and relations. With the modal operator for causal possibility (in the sense of what is possible in nature), (NR) represents a *modal moderate realism* according to which natural properties and relations have a mode of being within the causal structure of the world, and in particular a mode of being that does not depend on whether or not there are objects having those properties and relations – and therefore a mode of being that is in that sense *ante rem* – but not a mode of being that is independent even of whether or not there could be (in the sense of a natural possibility) objects having such properties and relations. When the universe was first formed, there were only elementary particles and no atoms of any kind – or at least certainly not atoms or compounds of any complex kind. Many of the natural properties and relations that we assume to now structurally characterize atoms and compounds as complexes did not at that time characterize any objects at all – which does not mean that they did not have any real mode of being within nature's causal matrix. Indeed, there may well yet be some transuranic substances, and natural properties of such, that will, as a matter of contingent fact, never be realized in nature by any objects whatsoever, but which, nevertheless, as a matter of a natural or causal possibility, could be realized. The being of such a natural property or relation does not consist of its being a characteristic of some object at some time or other, i.e. its being *in re*, but rather the causal possibility of its being *in re* – a possibility that can be accounted for only by that property or relation having a mode of being as such within the causal structure of the world. That is why conceptual natural realism rejects Aristotle's moderate realism and replaces it with a modal moderate realism as formulated in (NR).

The fact that only concrete objects can have a natural property or relation is reflected in the following additional law of conceptual natural realism:

$$(\forall^n F^j)[F(x_1,...,x_j) \rightarrow E!(x_1) \wedge ... \wedge E!(x_j)],$$

where, as already indicated, we use E! to stand for the formal concept of (concrete) existence (in the causal space-time manifold).

The assumption that there is a natural property or relation corresponding to the (j-ary) concept that a given (j-place) predicate constant or (open) formula $\phi(x_1,...,x_j)$ stands for – i.e. the assumption that such a predicate expression stands (in the secondary sense) for a (j-ary) natural universal – can be formulated as follows:

$$(\exists^n F^j)\square^c(\forall x_1)...(\forall x_j)[F(x_1,...,x_j) \leftrightarrow \phi(x_1,...,x_j)].$$

A natural property or relation can be completely specified in this way, it should be noted, because, unlike concepts, natural properties and relations are 'identical' when, as matter of causal necessity, they are coextensive. As part of the causal structure of the world, in other words, natural properties and relations retain their 'identity' as such across all causally accessible worlds. Formally, we can express such a cross-world causal 'identity' of universals as follows:

$$F^j =_{\overline{c}} G^j =_{df} \square^c(\forall x_1)...(\forall x_j)[F(x_1,...,x_j) \leftrightarrow G(x_1,...,x_j))].$$

Thus, using λ-abstracts for the specification of complex concepts, the above way of stipulating that there is a natural property or relation corresponding to a given (j-ary) concept $[\lambda x_1,...,x_j\ \phi]$ can be more succinctly stated as follows:

$$(\exists^n F^j)[[\lambda x_1,...,x_j\ \phi] \equiv_{\overline{c}} F].$$

Here, it is important to note that, unlike the comprehension principle of logical realism, such an assumption is at best only a scientific hypothesis, and as such must in principle be subject to confirmation or falsification.

Natural properties and relations are not intensional objects, it should be noted, nor are they objects of any other kind as well. Indeed, natural properties and relations, as universals that might have no concrete instances in the world at all, are not contained within the space-time causal manifold the way that concrete objects are, but rather are *unsaturated* causally determinate structures within that manifold. In this regard, natural properties and relations have a mode of being other than that of concrete objects – a mode of being that, in fact, is analogous to (though not the same as) the unsaturated mode of being of predicable concepts. Thus, although the unsaturated mode of being of natural properties and relations is not the same as that of predicable concepts, nevertheless they are said to 'be' in a sense analogous to the way that concepts are said to be – namely, as values of bound predicate variables (albeit bound by $\forall^n$ and $\exists^n$, instead of $\forall$ and $\exists$). In addition, just as predicable concepts are said not to exist independently of the general capacity humans have for language and concept-formation, so too natural properties and relations are said not to exist independently of nature and its causal matrix. That is why, just as the laws of compositionality for concept-formation can be said to characterize the logical structure of the intellect as the basis of the human capacity for language and thought, so too the laws of nature regarding the causal connections between natural properties and relations (especially as structural aspects of natural kinds) can be said to characterize the causal structure of the world. (See Cocchiarella 1989a for more on this issue.)

6. Conceptual Natural Realism and Aristotelian Essentialism

In addition to the natural properties and relations that may correspond to some, but not all, of our predicable concepts, there are also natural kinds that may correspond to some, but not all, of our sortal concepts. By a natural kind we understand here a type of causal structure, or mechanism in nature, that is the basis of the powers or capacities to act, behave, function, etc., in certain determinate ways that objects belonging to that natural kind have. Indeed, according to Aristotelian essentialism, natural kinds are the causal structures, or mechanisms in nature, that determine the natural laws regarding the different natural kinds of objects that there are, or can be, in the world.

The question of to which of our sortal concepts there corresponds a natural kind is, as in the case of the correspondence of natural properties and relations to certain of our predicable concepts, an empirical matter that is always subject to confirmation or falsification. The assumptions we make regarding such correspondences are hypotheses of scientific theories and are never validated on logical grounds alone, i.e. in terms of a theory of logical form for conceptual natural realism.

It is possible to construe natural kinds (as I have done in Cocchiarella 1989a) as natural properties, albeit subject to special laws that do not apply to natural properties in general. I now think, however, that it is more appropriate to see a difference of ontological type, or category, between natural kinds and natural properties – a difference that should be reflected in the theory of logical form for conceptual natural realism. This ontological difference corresponds in fact to the conceptual difference between sortal (common name) concepts and predicable concepts and the way that referential concepts based on the former may be saturated in thought by the latter. Thus, just as a (one-place) predicate may stand in a double way for both a concept and a natural property, so too a sortal common name may stand in a double way for both a sortal concept and a natural kind. Similarly, just as the quantifiers $\forall^n$ and $\exists^n$ can be applied to predicate variables, whereby we are able to refer to natural properties and relations, so too additional quantifiers, e.g., $\forall^k$ and $\exists^k$, can be introduced and applied to common name (sortal) variables, whereby we are able to refer to natural kinds. Similarly, just as a referential concept based upon a sortal concept can be saturated by a predicable concept in a judgment as a mental act, so too the natural kind corresponding to a sortal concept may be thought of as an unsaturated causal structure, which, when realized by an object belonging to that natural kind, can be saturated by a natural property or relation in a state of affairs having that object as a constituent. In this regard, a natural kind is not a 'conjunction' of natural properties and relations that objects belonging to that natural kind have, but rather is the causal ground or nexus of each of the states of affairs corresponding to such a conjunction. (The rejection of natural kinds as 'conjunctive' properties is typical of the way Aristotelian essentialism has been misrepresented.)

Even though natural kinds are not themselves properties, the thesis of natural realism that every natural property or relation is causally realizable applies to natural kinds as well. This thesis can be formulated as follows:

(K1) $(\forall^k S)\Diamond^c(\exists^e x)(\exists y\ S)(x = y)$.

Here, we should note that the expression '$(\exists y\ S)(x = y)$' says, in effect, that 'x is (identical with) an S', so that the thesis can be read as asserting of every natural kind S that it is causally possible for there to exist an object x that is an S. For convenience, we can symbolize 'x is an S' more simply as '$x\ S$' by adopting the following definition:

$$xS =_{df} (\exists y\ S)(x = y).$$

The quantifier phrase '$(\exists^e x)$' ('there exists') in (K1) can be replaced by the more general phrase '$(\exists x)$' ('there is'), incidentally, because we assume that only (concrete) existents (i.e. values of variables bound by $\exists^e$) belong to natural kinds; that is, because

(K2) $(\forall^k S)(\forall x)[xS \rightarrow E!(x)]$

is assumed to be a valid thesis of this version of Aristotelian essentialism.

The most fundamental law of natural kinds as (natural) 'essences' is that an object can belong to a natural kind only if being of that natural kind is essential to it – i.e. only if it *must* belong to that natural kind whenever it exists:

(K3) $(\forall^k S)(\forall x)[xS \rightarrow \Box^c[E!(x) \rightarrow xS]]$.

If we adopt the following abbreviatory notation for common names,

$$S_1 \leq S_2 =_{df} \Box^c(\forall x)[x\ S_1 \rightarrow x\ S_2],$$

$$S_1 < S_2 =_{df} (S_1 \leq S_2) \wedge \neg(S_2 \leq S_1),$$

then *the partition principle* for natural kinds can be stated as follows:

(K4) $(\forall^k S_1)(\forall^k S_2)[\Diamond^c(\exists x)[xS_1 \wedge xS_2] \rightarrow S_1 \leq S_2 \vee S_2 \leq S_1]$

If two natural kinds are not necessarily disjoint, then, according to (K4), one must be subordinate to the other. Thus, the family of natural kinds to which any object may belong forms a chain of subordination of one natural kind to another – where each natural kind in the chain is, as it were, a template structure that is causally more determinate and finer-grained than the natural kinds to which it is subordinate.

An important consequence of (K3) and (K4) is the thesis that an object can be of two natural kinds only if, as a matter of a natural or causal necessity, it belongs to the one kind when and only when it belongs to the other:

$$(\forall^k S_1)(\forall^k S_2)(\forall x)[\Diamond^c(x S_1) \wedge \Diamond^c(x S_2) \rightarrow \Box^c[x S_1 \leftrightarrow x S_2]].$$

In terms of this view of natural kinds as template causal structures that can fit one within another, it is only natural to assume a *summum genus principle* to the effect that any chain of subordination between natural kinds must have a summum genus as an ultimate, initial template structure within which all of the natural kinds of that chain must fit. It is only in this way that the individuation of natural kinds of objects can even begin to take place in the universe as an ontological process. Formally, the thesis can be stated as follows:

(K5) $\quad (\forall^k S_1)(\forall x)[x S_1 \rightarrow (\exists^k S_2)[x S_2 \wedge (\forall^k S_3)(x S_3 \rightarrow S_3 \leq S_2)]].$

Thus, any object that belongs to a natural kind belongs, according to this thesis, to a natural kind that is a summum genus – that is, a natural kind that has subordinate to it every natural kind to which that object belongs. Given the partition principle, (K4), (K5) is equivalent to the following alternative way of stating the summum genus principle – namely, that every natural kind is subordinate to a natural kind that is properly subordinate to no other natural kind:

$$(\forall^k S_1)(\exists^k S_2)[S_1 \leq S_2 \wedge \neg(\exists^k S_3)(S_2 < S_3)].$$

The dual of a summum genus as the ultimate, initial causal template structure of a natural kind of object is the infima species of that object. This is the finest grained template structure determining the causal nature of that object. The *infima species principle* stipulates, accordingly, that if an object belongs to a natural kind, then it belongs to a natural kind that is subordinate to all of the natural kinds to which that object belongs:

(K6) $(\forall^k S_1)(\forall x)[xS_1 \rightarrow (\exists^k S_2)[xS_2 \wedge (\forall^k S_3)(xS_3 \rightarrow S_2 \leq S_3)]]$.

A consequence of (K6) is the following alternative version of the infima species principle – namely, that every natural kind has subordinate to it a natural kind to which no other natural kind is subordinate:

$$(\forall^k S_1)(\exists^k S_2)[S_2 \leq S_1 \wedge \neg(\exists^k S_3)(S_3 < S_2)].$$

There are other theses of Aristotelian essentialism that we could mention here as well – such as that every genus is the sum of its species, or that all of the natural kinds that are immediate species of a genus are either the 'same' species of that genus or are necessarily disjoint, etc. – but these are matters that we shall not go into here. (See Cocchiarella 1989a, section 14, for a discussion of such additional theses.)

7. Conceptual Intensional Realism versus Conceptual Platonism and the Logic of Nominalized Predicates

We have explained in the last two sections how the theory of predication of a truncated ontology such as conceptualism can be analogically developed into a realistic Aristotelian ontology (which we have called conceptual natural realism) that can account for various ontological categories or modes of being in the natural world of the space-time causal manifold. (An indication of how the categories of time and space are constructed in conceptualism in terms of tense operators of both the local time determined by a continuant and the cosmic time based on the signal relation of a causal network of continuants can be found in Cocchiarella 1984, sections 13-15.) It is no less significant that such a theory of predication can also be developed into a Platonist or intensional ontology of abstract objects, including in particular the abstract objects of number theory and the intensional objects of fiction.

The fundamental insight into the nature of abstract objects, according to conceptualism, is that we are able to intellectually grasp and have knowledge of them only as the correlates of concepts. Historically, this correlation has come about through the development and institutionalization of the rule-based linguistic process of nominalization, which, conceptually, represents a kind of reflexive abstraction in which we attempt to represent what is not an object – e.g., an unsaturated cognitive structure underlying our use of a predicate expression – as if it were an object. In predicate-nominalization, for example, a predicate phrase (such as 'is triangular', 'is wise', 'is just', etc.) becomes transformed into an abstract singular term (such as 'triangularity', 'wisdom', 'justice', etc.), by which we purport to denote an abstract object as the intensional content of the concept that is expressed by that phrase. It was Plato who first recognized the ontological significance of such a transformation and who built his ontology around it.

Formally – i.e. within our conceptualist theory of logical form – we can represent the nominalization of a predicate expression of the form 'F( )' by simply deleting the parentheses (and commas in the case of a relational predicate) that are part of the functional role of that expression as a predicate. As a complex predicate expression, a λ-abstract, '$[\lambda x_1...x_n \; \phi](\;)$', can be similarly nominalized, resulting in '$[\lambda x_1...x_n \; \phi]$' as an abstract singular term. (Frequently, for brevity, we use 'F' and '$[\lambda x_1...x_n \; \phi]$' without parentheses and commas to refer to the predicate expressions themselves as well – but the parentheses and commas are always present when these expressions are actually being used as predicates.) Thus, where 'F' is a one-place predicate, we now have not only 'F(x)' but also 'F(F)' as a well-formed formula.

There are forms of conceptualism that reject the hypostatization of abstract objects as concept-correlates. Abelard, for example, who, for reasons already indicated, might well be interpreted as a conceptual natural realist, acknowledged that the same (conceptual/natural) universal might well be shared by different objects – the way Socrates and Plato shared the universal of being human – but he rejected the idea that such a universal could itself be a 'thing', i.e. an object. In our present context, where predicate variables represent both the category of concepts and the category of natural properties and relations as unsaturated universals, and the individual variables 'x', 'y', etc. represent the category of objects, we can represent the Abelardian thesis as

(Abelard*) $(\forall F^j)\neg(\exists x)(F = x),$

and

(Abelard$_n^*$) $(\forall^n F^j)\neg(\exists x)(F = x),$

where the first applies to concepts, and the second to natural properties and relations, as unsaturated universals. Here, for example, although the initial quantifier of (Abelard*) refers to an arbitrary (j-ary) concept, the nominalized occurrence of the predicate variable in the embedded identity formula purports, as an abstract singular term, to denote an abstract object as the correlate of that concept. What the Abelardian thesis maintains is that any such 'purporting' to denote by a nominalized predicate can never succeed – i.e. that every such abstract singular term must be denotationless. (For more on the Abelardian thesis, see Cocchiarella 1986, chapter 4.)

The Platonist – or, more properly, the conceptual Platonist – takes the opposite position, namely, that every nominalized predicate, ?~ an abstract singular term, denotes an abstract object – and, in particular, th. the object it denotes is the real intensional content of the concept that the predicate otherwise stands for in its role as a predicate. Formally, the Platonist thesis can be stated as follows:

(Plato*) $(\forall F^j)(\exists x)(F = x)$.

Note, however, that because of the unsaturated nature of concepts, any (j-ary) concept that the initial predicate quantifier refers to cannot itself be the object purportedly denoted by the nominalized predicate that occurs in the identity formula that follows. That is why we speak of the object denoted as the correlate of the concept, or simply as a concept-correlate, by which we mean an 'object-ified' reification of the intension of the concept, or, equivalently, a reified 'object-ification' of the truth-conditions determined by the concept. Thus, by starting out from concepts as (unsaturated) cognitive capacities underlying our use of language, we are able to grasp the intensions of our concepts as abstract objects by means of a reflexive abstraction corresponding to the process of nominalization.

Now it is noteworthy that the abstract objects that nominalized predicates are assumed to denote are also usually called properties and relations – a usage that, unfortunately, has led to a conflation of these entities with the unsaturated properties and relations of natural realism. This in turn has led to an inappropriate opposition between conceptual natural realism and conceptual Platonism, which, historically, has been represented by the opposition between Platonism and Aristotelianism. There need be no such opposition in *conceptual realism*, however, by which we now mean not just conceptual natural realism but conceptual natural realism together with a conceptual Platonism – or, preferably, with the alternative conceptual intensional realism described below. For, just as it is only concepts as unsaturated cognitive capaciti: that are the basis of predication in thought, it is only the analogically projected unsaturated natural properties and relations of natural realism that are the basis of predication in the states of affairs that obtain in nature. As abstract objects, properties and relations in the Platonic sense are really not (unsaturated) predicable entities at all – which is not to say that they do not reflect in the intensional order some of the aspects of predication in thought or reality, including in particular their role as constituents of propositions, which in turn are the abstract objects that nominalized sentences denote as abstract singular terms.

The way intensional objects (e.g. properties in the Platonic sense) mimic the role of concepts can be seen in the following analysis of *exemplification*, which clearly indicates the conceptual priority of predication over exemplification:

$$x \; \varepsilon \; y =_{df} (\exists F)[y = F \wedge F(x)].$$

In strictly extensional contexts – i.e. applications of conceptual realism in which an extensionality axiom for nominalized predicates is assumed – this definition can also be taken as an analysis of membership in a class in the logical sense (i.e. as the extension of a concept). That is, in strictly extensional contexts, the intension of a concept can be taken as the extension of that concept, so that just as we are able to apprehend the intension of a concept by starting out from the concept, so too are we able to apprehend the extension of a concept by starting out from the concept. In this way the well-known construction of numbers and other mathematical entities in terms of classes as extensions can also be given in terms of the concept-correlates of conceptual realism. (See Cocchiarella 1992 for more on how certain well-known foundational theories of membership in a class can be contained in conceptual realism.)

Despite the prevalence today of having only a theory of membership as a foundation for mathematics, it is important to emphasize that it is predication and not membership that is primary and fundamental in the analysis of numbers and other mathematical objects. This is not only because any representation of membership (and exemplification) will presuppose a superseding theory of predication, but also because, as a result of Russell's paradox, not all concepts can be 'object-ified', i.e. reified as objects, and therefore not all concepts will have an extension or intension as a concept-correlate. A theory of membership (or exemplification), in other words, can give at best only a limited and imperfect reflection in the intensional order of the role of concepts in the nexus of predication of the order of thought, and in that regard it cannot be taken as a foundation for mathematics that can stand on it own as an alternative to predication. It is only by understanding how predication in thought and language is possible at all that we can begin to explain how membership in a class, and, similarly, how exemplification of a property (in the Platonic sense), are ultimately to be understood and given a foundation of their own. (See Cocchiarella 1989b, section 3, for more on the significance of Russell's paradox in conceptualism.)

Whether viewed as intensions or extensions, all abstract objects, according to conceptual realism, are concept-correlates, which means that they have their being, at least in an epistemological sense, in the concepts whose correlates they are. Thus, even though abstract objects may be assumed, as they are in conceptual Platonism, to 'exist' in a realm that transcends space, time and causality – and therefore 'preexist' the evolution of consciousness and the cognitive capacities we exercise in thought and language – nevertheless, from an epistemological point of view, no abstract object is assumed to 'exist' as an object of reference otherwise than as the correlate of a concept.[2] It is only in this way that we can explain how, by starting out from concepts as cognitive capacities, we can have knowledge of abstract objects, be they Platonic forms (i.e. properties or relation in the Platonic sense), or classes in the logical sense (i.e. classes as extensions of concepts), among either of which we can include the abstract objects of mathematics.

Conceptual Platonism is not the only way in which abstract objects may be assumed to 'exist', however; and, in fact, there is a form of *conceptual intensional realism* in which the Platonist assumption that abstract objects 'exist' outside of space, time, and causality, and therefore 'preexist' the evolution of consciousness, is rejected. The being of all abstract objects, i.e. all concept-correlates, on this view, is to be explained in terms of the evolution of language and culture. It is not only that our knowledge and grasp of abstract objects depends upon their being concept-correlates, but even the nature of their being as abstract objects is understood, on this view, to consist entirely of their being concept-correlates. Abstract objects have a dependent, or relational, mode of being, in other words, because their role as concept-correlates is essential to their being understood as objects of thought at all.

All abstract objects, on this view, are products of language and culture, and, despite the fact that they have a certain degree of autonomy, they do not have any being of their own independently of the role they play in language and culture.[3] On this view, it is not only our grasp and knowledge of intensional

---

[2] We place scare-quotes around 'exists' here so as distinguish the being of abstract objects from that of concrete objects. Both kinds of objects are individuals, and, as such, have *being* as values of the individual variables bound by the objectual quantifier, 'there be', which we have represented by '$(\exists x)$'. Only concrete objects are 'actual' or *exist* in the sense of being values of the individual variables bound by the objectual quantifier, 'there exists', on the other hand, which we have represented by '$(\exists^e x)$'.

[3] See Popper and Eccles 1977, chapter 2, for a description of a related view of abstract objects. Intensional objects, according to Popper and Eccles, belong to what they call World 3,

objects that has come about primarily through the development and use in language of the process of nominalization, i.e., the process whereby predicates and other expressions are transformed into abstract singular terms, but even the very abstract being of those objects as well. It is the evolution of this process of nominalization, which began with the first rudimentary attempts to reflexively abstract the intensional content of our concepts – i.e. to reify, or 'object-ify', the rule-based cognitive capacities that underlie our use of language – that is the ultimate, explanatory ground of the mode of being of abstract objects. It is only through the evolution and institutionalization of this process that humanity has been able to grasp and talk about abstract objects at all, and, because such a process is essential to our knowledge of such objects, it is only in their status as products of cultural evolution, i.e. as concept-correlates, that their being as abstract objects is ultimately to be explained.

Abstract objects are not only products of cultural evolution, but are themselves the means by which the further evolution of culture is possible. For in addition to the abstract objects of mathematics, which are essential to the development of science and technology, there are also propositions as the intensional objects that nominalized sentences denote in their role as abstract singular terms. A standard form of such a nominalized sentence is a *that*-clause, such as occurs in statements expressing a propositional attitude – e.g., a statement of belief, which has the form 'x believes that ϕ', or a statement of desire, which has the form 'x desires that ϕ', etc.

As objects in the intensional order, propositions are not the same as states of affairs, which are part of the causal order of the natural world. Nevertheless, as intensional objects, propositions enable us to construct a 'bracketed world' of intensional content within which we are able to freely speculate and construct various hypotheses and theories about the natural world. Whether true or false, all theories about the natural world consist of a system of propositions, which we are able to contemplate independently of whether or not there are any states of affairs in the natural world corresponding to them. In this way, as intensional

---

as distinct from World 1, which is the universe of physical entities, and World 2, which is the world of mental states, both conscious and unconscious. This terminology of different worlds is adopted from Frege, who, unlike Popper and Eccles, thought of World 3 as independent of the space-time causal manifold of World 1.

It should be perhaps be noted here that although conceptual realism is compatible with, and may even be taken to support, the Popper-Eccles interactionist theory of mind, nevertheless, it does not presuppose that theory. Indeed, conceptual realism is also compatible with the view that World 2 is a part of World 1, and may be further divided into a variant in which (a) World 2 is reducible to the strictly physico-chemical part of World 1, as opposed to a variant (b) in which World 2 is an emergent, irreducible part of World 1.

objects, propositions serve to advance the development of science and technology, and thereby the further evolution of culture.

Propositions also make up the content of our fables and myths, and, in fact, they are the content of stories of all kinds, both true and false. In this way propositions and the abstract objects that are their constituents also serve the literary and aesthetic purposes of culture. In reading a fictional story, for example, we are given to understand that none of the references made in the story are to be taken literally, i.e. that all of the referential expressions occurring in the sentences of the story are understood to be deactivated, by which we mean that we are dealing with the intensional content of those referential expressions and not with any real objects that those expressions might otherwise be used to refer to in direct discourse. The same is true of stories that are put forward as descriptions of reality – except in those cases we indirectly re-activate the referential function of the expressions used in those stories by indicating, even if only implicitly, that the stories are to be taken as true. (Here, we see the significance of the law '(that ϕ is true $\leftrightarrow \phi$)', wherein an assertoric occurrence of a propositional form ϕ is connected with a nominalized occurrence of ϕ.) All stories are to be interpreted in this regard as a form of indirect discourse – such as the contexts that occur within the scope of an 'In-the-story' operator, which often is only implicit when we read, or are being told, a story. For it is only by first understanding the content of a story that we can then raise the question of its veracity, i.e. the question of whether or not there are states of affairs in the space-time causal manifold corresponding to the propositions that make up that story.

All fictional characters, on this account, are intensional objects – namely, the intensional objects that are the correlates of referential concepts. These intensional objects are accounted for in conceptual realism through a double correlation first of referential concepts with predicable concepts, and then of the latter with their concept-correlates. Formally, the predicable concept that corresponds to a referential concept, as represented, e.g., by the quantifier phrase '($\mathcal{Q}$x S)', can be specified as follows:

$$[\mathcal{Q}x\ S] =_{df} [\lambda y\ (\exists F)(y = F \wedge (\mathcal{Q}x\ S)F(x))].$$

By λ-conversion, an intensional object falls under this predicable concept if, and only if, the concept whose correlate it is falls within the referential concept; that is,

$$(\forall F)[(\mathcal{Q}x\ S)F(x) \leftrightarrow [\mathcal{Q}x\ S](F)],$$

which, in conceptual realism, amounts to a version of Frege's double correlation thesis (correlating second-level concepts with first-level concepts and the latter with their extensions). The intensional object that is the correlate of the referential concept expressed by '$(\mathfrak{Q}x\ S)$', accordingly, is the concept-correlate of the predicable concept represented by '$[\mathfrak{Q}x\ S]$'. It is such an intensional object that is the real constituent of a proposition, rather than the object, or objects, that the referential concept whose correlate it is might otherwise be taken to refer to in direct discourse. (See Cocchiarella 1989b for a detailed description of this double correlation, including how it generates the natural numbers as the correlates of our numerical quantifier phrases.)

In a specific story, say, A, both the propositions and the intensional objects involved in the referential expressions of that story may be relativized as follows,

$$[\mathfrak{Q}x\ S]_A =_{df} [\lambda y\ (\exists F)(y = F \wedge In(A, [(\mathfrak{Q}x\ S)F(x)]))],$$

where '$[(\mathfrak{Q}x\ S)F(x)]$' is a nominalization of the formula '$(\mathfrak{Q}x\ S)F(x)$', and 'In(A, [...])' represents the formula-operator 'In (the story) A, ...'. Thus, the referential expression 'Sherlock Holmes' will be taken to have one intensional object as its content in Conan Doyle's novel *The Hound of the Baskervilles* and a different intensional object in Conan Doyle's *The Valley of Fear*. (Because the singular term 'Sherlock Holmes' is used with existential presupposition in the fictional worlds of both novels, it is represented as having the logical form '$(\exists x$ Sherlock Holmes$)$' in the sentences that make up the written text of those novels; and therefore the intensional objects that are the constituents of the propositions making up the content of those novels are represented by, e.g., '$[\exists x$ Sherlock Holmes$]_{Baskervilles}$' and $[\exists x$ Sherlock Holmes$]_{Valley}$', respectively.) Though these intensional objects are not identical, they are counterparts to one another in much the sense of David Lewis's counterpart theory. It is here among the intensional objects of our various stories – and not the among the concrete objects that exist in, and across, different causally possible worlds – that David Lewis's counterpart theory has its proper application.

It is the relativization of intensional objects in this way that explains the so-called 'incompleteness' of fictional objects. There are many predicate expressions of English, for example, that can be meaningfully applied to humans but that are neither affirmed nor denied of the character Sherlock Holmes in any of Conan Doyle's novels. Neither the formula 'In(A, [($\exists x$ Sherlock Holmes$) F(x)]$)' nor 'In(A, [($\exists x$ Sherlock Holmes$) \neg F(x)]$)' will then be true of the concept (as a value of 'F') that such a predicate might stand for, in order words, regardless which of Conan Doyle's novels we consider as a value of 'A'; and therefore, neither '$[\exists x$ Sherlock Holmes$]_A(F)$' nor '$[\exists x$ Sherlock Holmes$]_A([\lambda x \ \neg F(x)])$' will be true as well – which is to say that, in the story A, the character Sherlock Holmes falls under neither the concept F nor its complement, and is, therefore, 'incomplete' in that regard.

Meinong's impossible objects, when construed as fictional characters or objects (or as intensional objects of someone's belief-space), are also 'incomplete' in this way. Thus, whereas 'The round square is round and square' is false as a form of direct discourse – i.e., as analyzed as in section 4 above – nevertheless, it could be true in a given fictional context. Suppose, for example, we construct a story called, *Romeo and Juliet in Flatland*, which takes place in a two-dimensional world (Flatland) at a time when two families, the Montagues and the Capulets, are having a feud. The Capulets, one of whom is Juliet, are all circles, and the Montagues, one of whom is Romeo, are all squares. (Juliet has curves and Romeo has angles.) Unknown to the two families, Romeo and Juliet have an affair and decide to live together in secret. In time, Juliet becomes pregnant and, given the difference in genetic makeup between Romeo and herself, gives birth to a round square. Although Romeo and Juliet both love their baby, the round square, the two families, the Montagues and the Capulets, become enraged when they discover what has happened. They kill Romeo and Juliet, and their baby, the round square. But, not wanting it to be known that a round square – which, given the cruel social mores of Flatland society, would have been considered a monster – was born into either family, the Montagues and Capulets keep the birth, and death, of the round square a secret. They then pass it around that Romeo and Juliet were ill-starred lovers who committed suicide in despair of the open hostility between their respective families. The story ends with Romeo and Juliet being eulogized and buried together – but without their baby, the round square, whose body was cremated and reduced to ashes.

As this story makes clear, we can meaningfully talk about 'impossible' objects as if they were actual objects – although such talk can be true only when relativized to a context of indirect discourse, such as a story, and perhaps the belief-space of someone with inconsistent beliefs. Thus, for example, as part of the story, *Romeo and Juliet in Flatland*, it is true to say that the round square is round and square, which, formally, can be represented as follows:

$$In(R\&J\text{-}in\text{-}Flatland, [(\exists_1 x \ Square/Round(x))[\lambda x \ Round(x) \wedge Square(x)](x)]).$$

Thus, even though both

$$[\exists_1 x \; Square/Round(x)]([\lambda x \; Round(x)]),$$

and

$$[\exists_1 x \; Square/Round(x)]([\lambda x \; Square(x)]),$$

are false regarding the intensional content of 'The round square' simpliciter, nevertheless, both

$$[\exists_1 x \; Square/Round(x)]_{R\&J\text{-}in\text{-}Flatland}([\lambda x \; Round(x)]),$$

and

$$[\exists_1 x \; Square/Round(x)]_{R\&J\text{-}in\text{-}Flatland}([\lambda x \; Square(x)]),$$

are true of the intensional content of 'The round square' relativized to the story, *Romeo and Juliet in Flatland*. Nevertheless, as an objet of a fictional, intensional world – as opposed to the objects of the actual world of nature – such an 'impossible' object will be 'incomplete' with respect to the different kinds of things that are in fact said of it in its fictional world. It is in this way that conceptual realism is able to explain the 'incomplete' and 'impossible' objects of Meinong's theory of objects. (See Cocchiarella 1987, chapter 3, for a more detailed account of how Meinong's theory can be reconstructed in the kind of framework we have in mind here.)

8. Concluding Remarks

As this informal sketch indicates, conceptual realism, by which we mean conceptual natural realism and conceptual intensional realism together, provides the basis of a general conceptual-ontological framework, within which, beginning with thought and language, a comprehensive formal ontology can be developed. Not only does conceptual realism explain how, in naturalistic terms, predication in thought and language is possible, but, in addition, it provides a theory of the nature of predication in reality through an analogical theory of properties and relations. In this way, conceptual realism can be developed into a reconstructed version of Aristotelian realism, including a version of Aristotelian essentialism. In addition, through the process of nominalization, which corresponds to a reflexive abstraction in which we attempt to represent our concepts as if they were objects, conceptualism can be developed into a conceptual intensional realism that can provide an account not only of the abstract reality of numbers and other mathematical objects, but of the intensional objects of fiction and stories of all kinds, both true and false, and including those stories that we systematically develop into theories about the world. In this way, conceptual realism provides a framework not only for the conceptual and natural order, but for the mathematical and intensional order as well. Also, in this way, conceptual realism is able to reconcile and provide a unified account both of Platonism and Aristotelian realism, including Aristotelian essentialism – and it does so by showing how the ontological categories, or modes of being, of each of these ontologies can be explained in terms a conceptualist theory of predication and its analogical extensions.

References

Brentano, F. 1973 (1874/1924): *Psychology from an Empirical Standpoint*, edited by O. Kraus, London, Routledge and Kegan Paul.

Cocchiarella, N.B. 1984: "Philosophical Perspectives on Quantification in Tense and Modal Logic", *Handbook of Philosophical Logic*, vol. II, D. Gabbay and F. Guenthner, eds., Dordrecht, D. Reidel, 309-353.

Cocchiarella, N.B. 1986: *Logical Investigations of Predication Theory and The Problem of Universals*, Naples, Bibliopolis.

Cocchiarella, N.B. 1987: *Logical Studies in Early Analytic Philosophy*, Columbus, Ohio State University Press.

Cocchiarella, N.B. 1989a: "Philosophical Perspectives on Formal Theories of Predication", *Handbook of Philosophical Logic*, D. Gabbay and F. Guenthner, eds., Dordrecht, D. Reidel, 253-326.

Cocchiarella, N.B. 1989b: "Conceptualism, Realism, and Intensional Logic", *Topoi* V, 75-87.

Cocchiarella, N.B. 1992: "Conceptual Realism versus Quine on Classes and Higher-Order Logic", *Synthese* 90, 379-436.

Frege, G. 1952: *Translations from the Philosophical Writings of Gottlob Frege*, P. Geach and M. Black, eds., Oxford: Blackwell.

Frege, G. 1979: *Posthumous Writings*, H. Hermes, F. Kambartel, and F. Kaulbach, Oxford: Blackwell.

Goodman, N. 1956 "A world of Individuals", in *The Problem of Universals*, University of Notre Dame Press, Notre Dame, 15-31.

Popper, K.R. and Eccles, J.C. 1983: *The Self and Its Brain*, London, Routledge and Kegan Paul (First published Berlin, Springer Verlag, 1977.)

JERZY PERZANOWSKI

THE WAY OF TRUTH

1. Introduction
2. Beings, the Being and Being
3. Ontological Connection
4. Towards a Theory of Ontological Connection
       Language
       Logical Axioms
       The Basic Ontological Definitions
       Objectiva
       Collections
       Ideas
5. Some Classical Ontological Questions
6. A Linguistic Intermezzo
       Some Etymology
       Comparative Grammar: Greek, Latin, English, German, Polish
       Instead of a Conclusion
7. An Outline of a Primitive Theory of Being – **PTB**
       The Theory
       Results
       Models
       Comments
       An Alternative Approach
8. Towards an Extended Theory of Being – **ETB**
       Collections and Ideas
       Empty Ideas
       Connections of Abstract Concepts
       Identity
       Qualities of Abstractors
       ETB
       Supports and Forms
       Infinity
       Final Remarks
9. Parmenidean Statements Reconsidered and Classical Questions Answered
10. Summary
Acknowledgements
References

R. Poli and P. Simons, Formal Ontology, 61–130.
© 1996 *Kluwer Academic Publishers. Printed in the Netherlands.*

1. Introduction

1.1 The Parmenidean 'way of truth' concerns what there is and what there is not: *estin te kai os ouk esti me einai.*[1] It concerns the basic ontological items: beings and nonbeings, as well as (the) being and (the) nonbeing.

As we have learned from Parmenides, Zeno and Plato,[2] the way of Parmenides is the way of difficult truth, the way of metaphysical paradox.

1.2 Quite often the principal truth of Parmenides is formulated as the *ontological principle of identity*: *being is and nonbeing is not.* Usually this principle is considered tautologous[3] or even trivial.

I disagree. Triviality presupposes clarity. The principle, however, is neither clear nor evident. Also it is not obvious.

Is it true?

1.3 Both 'being' and 'is' are immediate derivatives of the verb 'be'. The verb itself has several variants.

Can all these derivatives and variants be presented in a uniform way? Is, for example, 'Being is' a more adequate expression of the thought of Parmenides than 'Whatever is, is'?

Next, to which items does the Parmenidean statement refer: to particular beings – like me, you, a ship, this pencil; or to their totality – the being; or to their unity – Being? Should Parmenides' statement be understood as 'the being is and the nonbeing is not', or rather as 'a being is and a nonbeing is not', i.e., 'any being is and no nonbeing is' or 'beings are and nonbeings are not'?

1.4 The problem was pointed out and discussed by Plato in *Sophist* as the crux of his refutation of the sophistic claim that nothing is false.

Parmenides' spokesman, the Eleatic Stranger, is arguing there for Plato's conclusion that "nonbeing has an assured existence and a nature of its own",

---

[1] Cf. Diels 1906, *Parmenides* B2.3. Notice a rather subtle problem connected with the translation of this claim (see Bodnár 1988b). *Inter alia*, the following translations have been offered: Diels 1906: "dass [das Seiende] ist und dass es unmöglich nicht sein kann", Bormann 1971: "dass [das Seiende] ist und das Nicht-Seiende ist nicht", Kirk and Raven 1957: "that it is and that it cannot not-be", Burnet 1957: "It is, and... it is impossible for it not to be", Tarán 1965: "it is and to not be is not", Mannheim in Heidegger 1961: "it is, and... nonbeing is impossible".

[2] For Parmenides and Zeno cf. Kirk and Raven 1957, for Plato cf. *Parmenides* and particularly the *Sophist* in Plato 1961.

[3] Cf. Tatarkiewicz 1958.

recalling at the same time the warning of Parmenides: "For never shall this thought prevail, that non-beings are, but keep your mind from this path of inquiry".[4]

1.5 The answer to Plato's problem clearly depends on an explication of the four notions involved: *being, nonbeing, is* and *is not*.

From a metalogical point of view it is also determined by the related logics: the logic of our reasoning and an appropriate logic of being.

1.6 Hereafter, the ontological notions are explained according to the *qualitative* approach to the notion of being: *a being is a subject of some qualities; the being is the totality of all beings; Being is the unity of all beings.*

These quite ancient but yet obscure formulas are crucial for traditional ontology and they therefore deserve clarification.

Such a clarification requires an appropriate theory of qualities, as well as a suitable theory of ontological connection connecting qualities with subjects. It is the latter, above all, which will be outlined in the present study.

1.7 Clarification comes, *inter alia*, through formalization. Formalization requires logic. In what follows I rely exclusively on classical logic. To be more exact, standard classical logic is used as the logic of reasoning, whereas a suitable applied version of classical logic will serve as our logic of being.

1.8 In what follows a very general theory of ontological connection is provided.

In spite of its generality this theory enables us, as we shall see, to reconsider the classical ontological claims of Parmenides and to refute an anti-ontological claim that the notion of being is syncategorematic.

Also certain ontological theorems will be proved, including: *Being is and Nonbeing is* (sic!). *A being is, whereas a nonbeing is not.* Also: *Whatever is, is* – which is shown to be equivalent to *Whatever is not, is not.*

1.9 The paper is organized as follows: I start with general remarks concerning ontology and different approaches to the notion of being. Next, several classical questions of traditional ontology are discussed. After making our problems clear, I will introduce a formalism enabling us to study them in their full generality. Finally, the results of the paper are discussed in a manner introducing perpectives for a subsequent theory of qualities.

---

[4] Cf. *Sophist*, 258 b-d.

2. Beings, the Being and Being

2.1 Ontology is the discipline of being. It is the theory of what there is, why and how.

As the tradition makes clear, the verb 'to be' used here is ambiguous. It refers either to the domain of existing objects, depending therefore on an appropriate theory of existence, or to what *really* exists (in a metaphysical sense) – to *logos* which is behind existing items and behind the facts. The latter realm emerges when emphasis is placed on the second part of the above definition, i.e., on the questions: *why* and *how*?

The answer we are looking for is of the form: *there is x* because *x is possible* and in addition for *existing* objects *x satisfies certain specific conditions of existence*. Possibility is frequently explained as a matter of consistency or coherence, whereas existence conditions are specified in terms of stability, homeostasis, actualization, etc.

2.2 Ontology is distinguished by its extreme generality and by the richness and fertility of its basic notions.

The most basic ontological notions are notions of *a particular being* and *the being*. Both notions can be approached in at least three ways: possibilistically, connectionally (or qualitatively), and through what we shall call verb-type-ontologies.

2.3 In the verb-type-approach both notions – of a being and the being – are obtained from the verb 'to be' by transformations and nominalizations.

The theory behind the latter is quite complicated, much more than is the grammar of the verb 'to be' itself, and this is complicated enough. In most Indo-European languages we must distinguish at least eleven variants of the verb 'to be', which leads to a rather rich variety of verb-type-ontologies.

A being here is defined as any item which *is* in a sense specified according to an appropriate variant of the verb 'to be'.

The verb 'to be' has its basic form in the context 'S is P', where it denotes a binary relation. The most general verb-type-ontology is therefore the general theory of relations. By specification of variants of the verb 'to be' we obtain variants of the verb-type-ontology, for example the ontology of things and properties and the set-theoretic ontology.

2.4 In the possibilistic approach a being is defined as any possible object, hence the ontological universe is understood as the space of all possibilities. Its ontology is therefore the general theory of possibility.

2.5 The qualitative or connectional approach deals with the most traditional concept of a being, defined as any item having some quality (or as a subject of qualities).

Here at least three topics need further elaboration: the ontological connection itself and the items connected: qualities and subjects. In consequence, there are four variants of this type of ontology: the qualitative one, stressing qualities, the subjective one, putting emphasis on subjects (individuals); the connectional one, stressing the formal side of the ontological connection, and the eclectic one, which tries to develop all three factors in unison.

In the present essay I shall consider several fundamental topics of connectional ontology.

2.6 The above three approaches differ in their ideas of particular beings. They do however use the same devices to define the being as the totality of all beings and Being as the unity or the idea of all beings.

These are quite abstract concepts. To formalize them we need two abstractors; one to collect objects satisfying a suitable condition, and another to unify objects belonging to some family.

3. Ontological Connection

3.1 Consider a typical qualitative statement: *My sweater is red.* Here three components can immediately be differentiated: the subject 'my sweater', the qualitative phrase 'red', and the connector 'is'.

According to the qualitative approach, the *sweater* is indeed a being, for it is the subject of some quality, or it is connected with a quality – in our case with *redness*.

3.2 Hereafter we emphasize the ontological connection. Usually such a connection is made by means of a suitable connector, in most cases by an inflection of the verb 'to be'.

The verb-type and the connectional approaches will coincide at just this point, because the connector 'is' is a derivative of the verb 'to be', which is basic for verb-type-ontologies.

3.3 Now, we may ask: Is an *explicit* connector, like 'is', necessary for a connection to be made?

Certainly not. In English we say 'John is at home' but in Russian we can say this in a much simpler way 'Ivan doma', without any explicit connector.

Therefore, looking for a general view on ontological connection, we should abstract from particular connectors and simply write 'yx' to express the situation that an item x is ontologically connected with an item y, with the further idea in mind that x is a subject of the quality y.

3.4 What is connected in a given ontological connection?

Consider 'yx'. Here the right-hand argument is the connection's subject.

The idea of a subject is rather clear. A subject is any object characterized, determined, formed, framed, modified or described by its connected companion. Simply, a subject is the subject *for* something or *of* something.

What the left-hand argument is, however, is unclear and ambiguous.

Notice the relative and formal character of both connected items. In particular, an item that is subject in one connection can be a feature or someting similar in another.

3.5 To be free of misleading associations we fix our terminology in a more neutral, purely formal way. The right-hand argument, its subject, will be called the *objectum*, whereas the left-hand argument will be called the connection's *objectivum*.

3.6 In different connections the place of the objectivum is taken by qualities, determiners, characters, traits, modifiers, properties, attributes, features, concepts, etc. The place of the objectum can be taken by things, individuals, conscious subjects, situations, facts, events, processes, etc.

As we can see, both families are very broad and heterogenous.

3.7 The ontological connection in general is also not uniform. Two basic intuitions concerning it should at least be distinguished: yx means either that x *has* y, that y *describes* or *characterizes* x; or that y *determines, forms* or *frames* x.

The first intuition has dominated logico-linguistic investigation of connection and prevails in *thought-* and *language-ontologies*, whereas the second plays the keyrole in scientific investigation of the world and prevails in what might be called *being ontologies* in the proper sense.[5]

---

[5] On the differentiation between being, thought and language ontologies cf. Perzanowski 1988 and 1990.

Notice the grammatical difference between typical *objectiva* of the first and second sorts. The former is expressed in an adjective-like form like *red*, the latter in a noun-like form, like *spin* of an electron or *platonicity* of Plato.

3.8 The above remarks are very sketchy. They mark only the distinctions which have to be made clear. In particular, the notion of a quality needs more detailed discussion, for which see Perzanowski 1993a and 1993b.

4. Towards a Theory of Ontological Connection

4.1 I shall outline a theory of ontological connection suitable for studying the controversy between Parmenides and Plato concerning being and nonbeing.

We start by introducing a language appropriate to study both beings and the being defined along the lines of the qualitative approach. To this end we need a language with a binary connective for ontological connection and suitable abstract operators to define the being and Being.

Next, we use classical logic to deduce ontological theorems from these definitions and some further theorems via additional axioms.

4.2 Which version of classical logic should we use?

Ontology is the most general discipline; it deals with any object at all. At the beginning of the ontological investigation objects should not be differentiated without essential reasons. Each of them has to be taken at the same level with every other.

It is important, therefore, not to start with any classification of beings imposed by the language we use, even with an elementary distinction between names and sentences or individual expressions and predicates. Natural classifications should arise as a result of research.

4.3 To express the most basic ontological notions we need quantifiers and abstract operators. We need therefore a suitable version of the classical quantifier logic.

But not a predicate one. The differentiation between names and predicates, individuals and complexes, etc. which is usual for predicate calculi is clearly not ontologically innocent. Predicate languages are *too* connected with language and thought ontologies (in particular with the common ontologies of things and properties) to be accepted as the starting point for *general* ontology.

Thus we need a more neutral version of classical quantifier logic.

4.4 Hence in general ontology and in being-ontology we shall employ languages with only *one* basic category of expression. These ontologies are thus analogous in their linguistic machinery to calculi of names, to propositional logic and to algebraic logic.

Because we need quantifiers and abstraction operators we shall work within a version of classical propositional logic with quantifiers and abstractors, similar to the protothetics of Leśniewski, cf. his 1991b.

LANGUAGE

4.5 *The alphabet.* We use only one sort of designators: *x, y, z,...* denoting objects, because we wish to speak about all objects without prior differentiation.

Eight designators are fixed, for the sake of the definitions to follow: B, -B, N, -N, U, -U, D, -D.

The alphabet includes also the concatenation symbol '*', usually omitted, to express the ontological connection, two abstraction operators {_: _____} and [_: _____] as well as the standard functors of classical logic: *negation* ¬, *conjunction* ∧, *disjunction* ∨, *implication* →, *equivalence* ↔, *universal and particular quantifiers* ∀ *and* ∃, *and identity* =.

4.6 Expressions, like objects, are either simple or complex.

Atomic expressions are built up, at the first stage, by concatenation of designators and, in the next stages, by application of the two operators of abstraction.

More exactly:
(i) *Any designator is an atomic expression.*
(ii) *If A and C are atomic expressions, then (A)(C) is also an atomic expression.*

We accept the convention of cancelling brackets containing designators as well as brackets associating to the left. For example, instead of $(x)(y)$ we write simply xy; $((x)(y))(z)$ is equivalent to xyz and $(x)((y)(z))$ to $x(yz)$.

4.7 Notice that complex connections, like xyz or $x(yz)$, are not available in elementary predicate languages, because the iteration of predicates is there syntactically forbidden.

This is, in fact, the major advantage of propositional (or algebraic) languages in the realm of general ontology where, for essential reasons, we need iterated connections.

4.8 *Expressions* are produced in the usual way, cf. Mendelson 1979, from atomic expressions by means of the classical connectives: ¬, ∧, ∨, →, ↔, ∀, ∃ and =. Also the notion of a *bound* and a *free occurrence* of a designator (variable) and the notion of a substitution of a designator by atomic expressions are standard.

$A(x/C)$ denotes the result of replacing all free occurrences of x in A by an atomic expression C, provided that C is free for x in A, i.e., each variable occurring freely in C remains free after substitution.

4.9 *Concept expressions.* Concepts are objects made by abstraction or ideation in several ways, including comparison, classification, joining together, unification, variation, etc.

To form concepts we use operators, usually one for each way. In our case, it is convenient to work with at least two such operators:

{_: _____} to form *collections*, and

[_: _____] to form *ideas*.

Indeed, in qualitative ontology we are interested in distinguishing extensional and intensional aspects of totalities.

4.10 We extend the formation rules of the language by the following:
(iii) *If A is an expression, then both* {x: A} *and* [x: A] *are atomic expressions.*

Both abstractors bind designators which are their first arguments. Designators therefore can be bound either by means of quantifiers or by means of abstractors.

Finally, to obtain *all expressions of the extended language* we repeat formation rules a suitable number of times.

Notice that the syntax of our language is more Leśniewskian than Hilbertian.

LOGICAL AXIOMS

4.11 We accept the usual axioms of classical quantification logic with identity (cf. again Mendelson 1979) adapted to our propositional language.

This is acceptable because the ontological universe is clearly non-empty. Indeed, you are reading this essay. Hence at least you and I, the essay and the reading are objects in the universe of all objects, i.e., in the ontological universe.

4.12 In what follows, two families of *specific* axioms of our theory will be introduced: firstly the basic ontological definitions and secondly axioms for abstractors.

THE BASIC ONTOLOGICAL DEFINITIONS

4.13 I start with an informal clarification of abstractors.

The inscription $A(x)$ is used to mark the fact that the designator x occurs freely in the formula A. $A(x)$ is connected in a usual way with its *extension*, i.e., the family of all As containing all objects satisfying it.

Now, $[x: A(x)]$ is understood as *the idea of A*, i.e., as the general concept of As. It is therefore a natural objectivum: $[x: A(x)]y$ means that y *falls* under the concept A or, using the terminology of Plato, that y *participates* in the idea of A. Conversely, $y[x: A(x)]$ means that y is an objectivum, i.e., a determiner, a property or an idea of the concept A.

As regards collectors, $\{x: A(x)\}$ is understood as *the collection of all objects satisfying A*. This is also a typical objectivum. $\{x: A(x)\}y$ means that y *belongs* to $\{x: A(x)\}$, which in the set-theoretical notation can be expressed by $y \in \{x: A(x)\}$. The reverse, *objectum* position of collectors will be discussed later.

Both concepts clearly conjugate. Quite often they are identified, as in the standard Zermelo-Fraenkel set-theory **ZF**; sometimes they are implicitly[6] or explicitly differentiated.

The above clues will be used in the future as the starting-point for the axiomatization of our two abstractors.

4.14 Observe that in the present framework we can distinguish *four* aspects of a given object: two 'extensional' and two 'intensional'.

$Q(x):= \{y: yx\}$ The *qualification* of x, in which all qualities (objectiva) of x are collected.

$E(x):= \{y: xy\}$ The *extension* of x, collecting all the objecta of x.

$F(x):= [y: yx]$ The *form* of x, which is the unity, togetherness, of all its qualities (objectiva).

$S(x):= [y: xy]$ The *support* of x, which is the unity of all the objecta of x.

The above concepts are clearly interconnected, in a way which will become clear once we have introduced suitable axioms for abstractors.

---

[6] Cf. Kisielewicz 1989 and his modification of **ZF** into the double extension set-theory.

4.15 Fix now a given connection yx. This is an open formula with both x and y occurring freely in it.

Binding one of these designators and using negation in all possible ways we obtain *eight* elementary formulas expressing basic ontological situations. Four of them are *positive*: $\exists y\ yx$, $\forall y\ yx$, $\exists x\ yx$, and $\forall x\ yx$; four are *negative*: $\neg\,\exists y\ yx$, $\neg\,\forall y\ yx$, $\neg\,\exists x\ yx$ and $\neg\,\forall x\ yx$.

In consequence, we get[7] exactly eight basic ontological qualities, eight connected totalities and eight ideas.

OBJECTIVA

4.16 Notice that the first formula '$\exists y\ yx$' says that the object x is qualified, i.e., that it has a quality or, more formally, an objectivum y. This, according to the qualitative approach, means that x is *a being*. On the other hand, its negation '$\neg\,\exists y\ yx$' says that x is *a nonbeing* or *a naked* object, i.e., an item without qualities.

Formally, let us put:

$Bx\ := \exists y\ yx$

$-Bx := \neg\,\exists y\ yx$

defining thus two really basic ontological notions: x is *a being* and x is *a nonbeing*.

4.17 The remaining six notions are defined as follows:

$Nx\ := \exists y\ xy$	x is *nonempty* iff x is not a *floating* objectivum, i.e., it is possessed by some objectum;
$-Nx := \neg\,\exists y\ xy$	x is *empty* iff x is an *unrealized* objectivum, i.e. without an objectum;
$Ux\ := \forall y\ xy$	x is *universal* iff it is a *tautologous* objectivum, i.e., such that any object is its objectum;
$-Ux := \neg\,\forall y\ xy$	x is *non-universal* iff it is an objectivum which some object does not have;
$Dx\ := \forall y\ yx$	x is *defective* iff any object is its objectivum, i.e., its qualification is *full*
$-Dx := \neg\,\forall y\ yx$	x is *non-defective* iff it is an objectum possessing only some objectiva, if any.

---

[7] In a way resembling, to some extent, the manner of Bolzano in his 1975. Cf. also Bolzano 1914-15. I owe this reference to P. Simons.

We have introduced eight basic ontological categories. Four of them are positive: B, N, U, D. Four are negative: -B, -N, -U, -D. Four are general: -B, -N, U, D; four are particular (existential): B, N, -U and -D.

COLLECTIONS

4.18 Collecting suitable objects together, we obtain eight basic ontological collections:

B	:= {*x*: B*x*}	*The being,* which is the collection of all beings;
-B	:= {*x*: -B*x*}	*The nonbeing,* which is the collection of all nonbeings;
N	:= {*x*: N*x*}	*The nonemptiness,* which is the collection of all nonempty objects;
-N	:= {*x*: -N*x*}	*The emptiness,* which is the collection of all empty objects;
U	:= {*x*: U*x*}	*The universality,* which is the collection of all universal objects;
-U	:= {*x*: -U*x*}	*The nonuniversality,* which is the collection of all nonuniversal objects;
D	:= {*x*: D*x*}	*The defectiveness,* which is the collection of all defective objects;
-D	:= {*x*: -D*x*}	*The nondefectiveness,* which is the collection of all nondefective objects.

IDEAS

4.19 Analogously, unifying suitable objects into one, we obtain the following eight basic ontological ideas:

B	:= [*x*: B*x*]	*Being,* which is the unity of all beings;
-B	:= [*x*: -B*x*]	*Nonbeing,* which is the unity of all nonbeings;
N	:= [*x*: N*x*]	*Nonemptiness,* which is the unity of all nonempty objects;
-N	:= [*x*: -N*x*]	*Emptiness,* which is the unity of all empty objects;
U	:= [*x*: U*x*]	*Universality,* which is the unity of all universal objects;
-U	:= [*x*: -U*x*]	*Nonuniversality,* which is the unity of all nonuniversal objects;
D	:= [*x*: D*x*]	*Defectiveness,* which is the unity of all defective objects;
-D	:= [*x*: -D*x*]	*Nondefectiveness,* which is the unity of all nondefective objects.

4.20 As in the case of qualities, so also ontological collections and ontological ideas can be categorized into positive and negative, and also into general and particular.

A collection or an idea is respectively positive, negative, general or particular, if its definitional quality is such.

4.21 Notice that by definitional replacement the above concepts can be made more explicit:

$B = \{x: \exists y\, yx\}$, $\mathbf{B} = [x: \exists y\, yx]$, $-B = \{x: \neg\, \exists y\, yx\}$, $-\mathbf{B} = [x: \neg\, \exists y\, yx]$, etc.

4.22 Observe the self-referential, quasi-paradoxical character of our collections and ideas.

Being, i.e., the idea of beings, falls under itself, if Being is a being (we will see that it indeed is). Similarly, the being, i.e., the collection of all beings, belongs to itself if the being is a being (which indeed holds: cf.§ 7.12).

Analogous claims can be made concerning our other concepts as well.

All of this is nothing surprising. Similar connections are well-known for the general (Cantorian) notion of set. They, however, are notorious for their power to generate inconsistencies. We must therefore check them very carefully, for we would of course like to produce a consistent ontology.

4.23 Definitions are implicit axioms.

The above 24 definitions are rudimentary axioms of the theory of ontological connection.

Later on, in chapter 8, our list of axioms will be extended by suitable axioms for abstractors. But even the present list enables us to answer several traditional questions of ontology, including some raised by Parmenides, Plato, Aristotle and Kant.

5. Some Classical Ontological Questions

5.1 We start with the famous problem of Parmenides answered by him in the positive:

Q.1   *Is there being?* i.e.: *Is being in being?*

Notice the ambiguity of these questions caused by the ambiguity of the name 'being'. Having distinguished three variants of the corresponding notion, we can either ask:

Q.1a   *Is there a being?*   i. e.: *Is a being in being?* or
Q.1b   *Is there the being?*   i. e.: *Is the being in being?* or finally
Q.1c   *Is there Being?*   i. e.: *Is Being in being?*

5.2 Observe that the claim *There is x*, whose purely ontological meaning is: *x is in being*, is expressed in our formalism by the formula Bx: *x is a being*.

Therefore Q1 in each of its three versions can be paraphrased as:

Q.1'a   *For a being x, does Bx hold?*
Q.1'b   *Does BB hold?*
Q.1'c   *Does $\mathbf{BB}$ hold?*

5.3 Observe first that Q1'a can trivially be answered in the positive.

Indeed, it in turn can be paraphrased into: *Given Bx, does Bx hold?* i.e., *Does $Bx \rightarrow Bx$ hold?*

The last implication is a case of a well-known theorem of classical logic. Therefore, Q1'a has the emphatic answer: YES.

5.4 The question Q1 in its remaining versions (including Q1a) is, however, somewhat more tricky.

Notice, that putting 'B' or '$\mathbf{B}$' instead of 'x' in the formula 'Bx' and applying next the definition of qualification Q we immediately obtain

(1) $BB \leftrightarrow \exists y\, yB \leftrightarrow Q(B) \neq \varnothing$ and $\mathbf{BB} \leftrightarrow \exists y\, y\mathbf{B} \leftrightarrow Q(\mathbf{B}) \neq \varnothing$.

In plain words: BB (or $\mathbf{BB}$), i.e., *the being (Being) is in being iff it is a being iff it has some qualities*, i.e., *its qualification is nonempty, or it has a content.*

The above explication made clear the self-referential character of both concepts involved: B – the being – and $\mathbf{B}$ – Being in itself.

5.5 The story now is clear: both general concepts of being are self-referential iff they are from an essential point of view 'nonempty', i.e., if they have content.

Indeed, by (1), Parmenides' question can be reformulated as follows

Q.2a   *Has the being content?* In other words: *Is the being qualified?*
Q.2b   *Has Being content?* i.e.: *Is Being qualified?*

Both answers occur in philosophy. The answer YES is given by Parmenides and his followers, the answer NO by Aristotle.[8]

5.6 The question of Parmenides is not only of historical importance. Using the above reformulation we see that it is indeed crucial for qualitative ontology.

For if Being (the being) has a content which is not trivial, then ontology itself is not tautologous.

Parmenides' position means, therefore, that the notion of a being as well as the notions of the being and Being are categorematic. Hence ontology, which is the most general of all disciplines, is still essential.

On the other hand, the Aristotelian position in its extreme form means that the notion of the being (Being) is syncategorematic, hence ontology is a purely formal, 'empty' discipline.

What will be shown in this paper seems to lead Aristotelians in qualitative ontology into troubles, provided that they respect classical logic.

5.7 The universality question is as follows: is 'to be a being' universal or not? In other words: *Is any object a being?*

In formal terms:

Q.3a *Does $\forall x\, Bx$ hold?* i.e., *Is B universal*: *UB?*

Observe that
(2) $\forall x\, Bx \leftrightarrow \forall x \exists y\, yx \leftrightarrow \forall x\, Q(x) \neq \varnothing$.

Every object is a being iff every object has some quality iff every object has a content.

5.8 In the future refinement of the present formalism, after clarifying the meaning of the connections Bx and $\mathbf{B}x$, a similar explication will also be made regarding the universality question concerning the being and Being:

Q.3b *Do $\forall x\, Bx$ and $\forall x\, \mathbf{B}x$ hold?* In other words, *Are B and **B** universal*: *UB?*, respectively: *U**B**?*

Both Q3a and the first part of Q3b will be answered in the positive, whereas the second part of Q3b will be answered in the negative.

---

[8] Cf. Owens 1973 and Poli 1992. The Aristotelian position was defended forcefully by Twardowski in 1894.

5.9 We may ask a similar question regarding qualities: Are there universal, or tautologous, qualities? More formally:

Q.4   *Is there an object y such that $\forall x\ yx$?* In other words: *Is the extension of the idea of universality empty?*

5.10 By classical logic and under the proviso that the ontological universe is non-empty, which we took for granted at § 4.11, we have:

(3) *The answer YES for Q3 implies the answer YES for Q4.*

5.11 Finally, let me ask a rather naive question:

Q.5   *Is the being (or Being) an object?*

Observe that

(4) *The answer NO for Q1 but YES for Q3 implies the answer NO for Q5.*

5.12 The conclusion of (4) is somewhat paradoxical. Some philosophers, like Twardowski and Quine, who support the assumption of (4), might interpret it as a refutation of the categorematicity of the notion of being.

However, they usually equate the notion of a being with the most general notion of all, that of an item or object.

Let me stress that in qualitative ontology beings are *qualified* objects, i.e., objects enjoying some qualities.

5.13 In what follows we shall see that a suitable version of classical logic enables us to answer all five questions in the positive.

6. A Linguistic Intermezzo

6.1 Since their origin in ancient Greek philosophy ontological expressions like those studied in the present paper have been notorious because of their difficulty and obscurity.

As was previously mentioned in footnote 1, even the translation of small fragments of Parmenides' poem causes serious problems, like Patin's problem of 'the subject of *estin*' at B2 (cf. Bodnár 1988b).

6.2 I do not wish to go into details as to the complex philological and historico-philosophical discussion concerning this matter. The content of the Parmenidean poem is, in the main, not a problem of philology and history of philosophy, but a problem of ontology. In discussions of it, both philological and historical analyses are auxiliary, not decisive.

The problem needs rather a discussion and development of an appropriate theory (or theories) of being.

6.3 A brief linguistic discussion can still, however, be rewarding.

It is interesting to know, *inter alia*, whether we can easily express in natural languages the meaning of expressions like BB and other formulas used in the previous chapter.

6.4 Indeed, it is an interesting philosophical exercise to collect and compare ways in which the Parmenidean formula BB, with its conjugate forms, can be expressed in several languages.

First of all, a discussion of such matters can illuminate the problem itself. On the other hand, it can throw light on a metaphilosophical question: to what extent is philosophy, which is – like any human activity – produced by human beings born, educated and thinking in particular languages, determined by those languages?

SOME ETYMOLOGY

6.5 To begin, let me report, after Brückner 1971, Heidegger 1961 and *The Shorter Oxford English Dictionary*, what is known about the etymology of the verb 'to be'.

The verb itself and its derivatives – including 'is', 'beings', 'the being', etc. – came from at least three different roots. The first two are common to all Indo-European languages, the third occurs only in some of them.

6.6 The first Indo-European radical is Sanskrit *bhu, bheu, bhawati* – which means 'to grow' or 'to emerge'. It is present in Greek: *phuo, phumai*; in Latin: *fui, fuo, futurus*; in English: *be, been, become*; in German: *bin, bist*; in Polish: *być, bawić, przebyć, przybyć*.

The second stem is the Aryan *es-*, or Sanskrit *as-, asus, asmi, esmi, esi, esti* – which means 'to live', 'to be and stand in itself'. In Greek: *es-, estin, eimi, einai*; in Latin: *es-, ens, est, esum, esse*; in English: *is*; in German: *ist, Seiende, Sein*; in Polish: *jest, mieszkać*.

The third stem is *wes-*. In Sanskrit *was-, wasami* which means 'to remain', 'to dwell', 'to sojourn'. In English: *was*; in German: *was, war, es west, wesen, gewesen*; in Polish: *bytować, bywać, przebywać*.

In English and in several other languages also a fourth stem *ar-* can be distinguished, present in the plural of 'is': *are*. Its origin is unknown.

6.7 The word 'being' is equivalent to Greek 'eon' ('on') or 'einai', to Latin 'ens' or 'esse', to German 'das Seiende' or 'das Sein', to Polish 'byt', to French 'l'être', to Italian 'essere', to Spanish or Portuguese 'ser'.

All of these are obtained by production outlined above.

6.8 The story, however, is more complicated. The notion of being is also related to the conjugate family of synonyms belonging to the above second and third etymological line, including the Latin or Italian verb *'sta'*, *'stare'*, German *'stehen'*, English *'to stay'*, Polish *'stać'*, *'pozostać'*, Spanish or Portuguese *'estar'*.

Observe that the notion of 'a state', meaning conditions or manner of being, is derived from this fifth family in a way similar to the generation of the notion of being from the first.

As a matter of fact, in ontology beings and states are closely related. It seems that, at least from an etymological point of view, they can be treated as parallel bases for ontology.

6.9 Observe, however, a certain remarkable improportionality.

The usual ontological conceptual network is built by means of derivatives of the verb 'to be'. It would be interesting to know a parallel net of concepts derived from the verb 'to stay'.

Parallel to *a being* is, of course, *a state of affairs* or *a situation*. Which item is, however, the collection of all states? Is it the being? Or, is it the ontological space? Is *a complex* the most general notion of the ontology of states?

Next, identify the unity, or the idea, of all states. Is it *the form*, like *essence, logos* or *nous* in the case of beings?

6.10 To conclude, the concept of being is a common abstraction mixing different sources, which results in a remarkable wealth of variants and makes quite a lot of applications possible.

COMPARATIVE GRAMMAR

6.11 I hope now that we are sufficiently awake to concentrate on the question: which variant of the verb 'to be' is used, in different languages, to express the statements of the Parmenidean sort.

I will test five languages in this regard: Greek, Latin, English, German and Polish.

We are particularly interested in ways used to differentiate particular beings, their collection and their idea.

That means that we should like to distinguish in a careful way between six notions involved: *a being, the being, Being, a nonbeing, the nonbeing* and *Nonbeing.*

The chief mark of distinction is that the four general notions have *only* singular form – no plurals for *the being, Being, etc.*; whereas both particular notions have also plurals: *beings* and *nonbeings.*

GREEK

6.12 The standard Greek ontological vocabulary is drawn from the verb *eimi (esti)*, which belongs to the line generated by the second Indo-European stem *es-*.

Three forms of it are particularly important: the infinitive *einai*, the feminine form *ousia* and the neutral form *eon (on)*.

6.13 A particular being, like you, me or an earthquake I am experiencing just now, is *to eon (to on)*. In the plural: *ta eonta*. Notice that *to eon (to on)* can also denote the plurality of all beings, i.e., the being.

The infinitive *einai* is also ambiguous. As a matter of fact, it can be used to denote all three ontological objects under scrutinization: a particular being, all beings, the idea or essence of beings.

Ousia is usually reserved for the third use denoting, for example, in Plato's writings, the being itself or its unity, its nature. In Aristotle's works on the other hand it denotes substance.

6.14 The grandfathers of ontology had at their disposal a quite sophisticated, but ambiguous, vocabulary.

Therefore from the very beginning they tried to delineate both the linguistic and the theoretical distinction between the three notions involved.

To this end, Parmenides was playing with the idea that there is an intimate connection between apprehension and being: *to gar auto noein estin te kai einai – thinking and being is the same* (cf. Diels 1906, Parmenides B5). This leads to the idea that the unity of being, i.e. Being, is Nous, i.e., Reason or the Mind.

On the other hand, Heraclitus seems to be the first to deal with the idea of logos as the intrinsic togetherness, unity, of beings: *tou logou d'eontos sonou* (Kirk and Raven 1957: *"although the Logos is common* [to essents – J.P.]", Mannheim in Heidegger 1961: *"though the logos is this togetherness in the essent"*).

Notice that it was exactly in this way Plotinus was using his notion *hen* (One) to enforce the notion of Being.

6.15 In fact, Greek philosophers sharply distinguished three notions of being. They used *to eon (ta eonta)* for the first, *to eon* or *to einai* for the second, and *to einai, to ousia, nous* or *logos* for the third, most general, notion.

6.16 To produce Parmenidean sentences we need two types of negation: *nominal*, which is used to produce negative notions and *sentential*, which is used to produce negative statements.

The grammar of Greek is standard. Names are negated by means of the negation particle *me*: *to me eon* – a nonbeing, *ta me eonta* – nonbeings, *me einai* – the nonbeing, *to me einai* – Nonbeing. The negation of a simple affirmative sentences is achieved by means of the adverb *ouk*.

Thus the basic Parmenidean statements are as follows:

to eon esti	–	a being is
to me eon esti	–	a nonbeing is
to me eon ouk esti	–	a nonbeing is not
ta eonta eisi	–	beings are
ta me eonti ouk eisi	–	nonbeings are not
esti gar einai	–	the being is
einai ouk esti	–	the being is not
me einai esti	–	the nonbeing is
me einai ouk esti	–	the nonbeing is not
to einai esti	–	Being is
to einai ouk esti	–	Being is not
to me einai esti	–	Nonbeing is
to me einai ouk esti	–	Nonbeing is not

6.17 We return to the problem of the metaphysical subject in Parmenides' poem. In most cases Parmenides is using the ambiguous *einai*. In the crucial point, which was emphasized twice by Plato in *Sophist* (cf. ft. 4), he used, however, the plural form *eonta: ou gar mepote touto damni einai me eonta* (for never shall this thought prevail, that nonbeings are).

Taking into account the distinctive mark of plurality, which was pointed out in § 6.12, we can conclude that Parmenides was considering beings at the beginning of his lesson, approaching next more abstract levels of them.

Therefore claims which can and have to be attributed to him are as follows: *Beings are. Nonbeings are not.* Also, *Being is.*

Whether Parmenides rejected the claim *Nonbeing is* remains unclear.

LATIN

6.18 Philosophical Latin was created over the centuries after the influence of Greek distinctions.[9]

Its basic vocabulary is drawn from the verb *sum (fui, esse)*, in which the first two Indo-European stems are mixed: *es-* is present in *sum* and *esse*, *bhu-* is present in *fui* and *futurus*.

In its developed form the vocabulary contains: *ens* and *entia* denoting respectively *a being* and *beings*. The name *ens* is also used to denote *the being*.

In order to avoid misuse, medieval scholars sometimes used the Greek determinate article *to* to mark a more general use of the word: *to ens* equals *the being*.

For the most general notion, i.e., for *Being* the word *Esse* or *Essentia* is usually reserved.

6.19 Latin syntax, too, is regular.

First, notice that both the nominal and the sentential negation is the same: *non*. Hence *non ens* means either a nonbeing or the nonbeing, *non esse* means Nonbeing, etc.

The basic Parmenidean statements are as follows:

A being is   –   *Ens est*, or *Ens existet*
Beings are   –   *Entia sunt*, or *Entia existent*
The being is   –   *(to) Ens est*, or *(to) Ens existet*

---

[9] For a very illuminating discussion of the development of ontological terminology in Greek and Latin cf. Kahn 1973.

Being is   –   *Esse est*
A nonbeing is   –   *Non ens est*, or *Non ens existet*
Nonbeing is not–   *Non esse non est*, or *Non esse non existent.*

6.20 The above duplication of forms: *est - existet* is remarkable. It seems that the first predicate 'est', coming from the same stem as *ens - esse*, is the natural one.

The second predicate 'existet' is, however, more technical. It comes from *existere*, which is drawn not from the verb *sum*, but from its ontological counterpart (cf. § 6.8) *sto - stare*: *existere = ex + sistere = ex + stare*, which means, literally: extract or essence of staying or standing in itself.

This invention of Latin philosophers was spread among most European philosophical languages. In this way two ontological lines converged, connecting beings with states. In particular, the question of being comes close to the problem of existence (esse = existentia, etc.), in a way which sometimes seems however rather to obscure than to clarify the problems in hand.

ENGLISH

6.21 Not only Being is self-referential. Also a text can be such. Now writing in English, hence using its fundamental be-constructions I would like to discuss them.

As a matter of fact, the previous text makes quite clear what I am going to summarize here.

6.22 The English vocabulary of being contains two families of terms.

One is used throughout this paper. It comes from the verb 'to be' and contains the name 'being' obtained from the verb via gerund-nominalization.

In this essay, having in mind the importance of singular-plural symmetry, and using both articles available, I shall exploit the following sequence of terms listed in the order of increasing generality: a being, beings, the being, Being.

The second family is adopted from Latin: an entity / an essent, entities / essents, the entity / the essent, Essence.

6.23 The level of mixing different stems in the forms of the verb 'to be' is also worth observing. Each of the four stems is, in fact, present: *bheu* in *to be*, *es* in *is*, *was* in the past form *was*, and *ar* in the plural *are*.

The last one is really interesting, because it suggests a lost verb used to speak about the plurality of beings.

6.24 English syntax, like that of Latin, is quite regular.

There are three basic negations: *not*, which is both nominal and sentential, *no*, which is sentential, and *non*, which is nominal.

Negative concepts follow immediately: *a nonbeing* or *a not-being*, etc.

6.25 As regards Parmenidean sentences, I will, for the sake of further discussion carefully list sentences from the first group, concerning beings, both in the positive and in the negative form:

1.	There is a being	There is not a being
2.	A being is	A being is not
3.	A being exists	A being does not exist
4.	A being is in being	A being is not in being
5.	A being is in existence	A being is not in existence
6.	Beings are	Beings are not
7.	There are beings	There is no being.

Sentences concerning the being and Being are constructed in a similar manner.

6.26 Positive Statements. The first positive statement, using an abstract predicate-phrase 'there is', is the most neutral.

The next two are standard: 2 is still neutral, whereas 3, imitating a technical Latin phrase, expresses existential presupposition.

Notice that 1 and 2 preserve the connection of the state of being with being itself, for both 'being' and 'is' are derivatives of the verb 'to be', coming, however, from two different stems. Taking this into account and recalling § 6.6 we can risk the suggestion that the original meaning of both sentences is 'what emerges and stands in itself'.

Sentences 4 and 5 are more technical, they develop the second statement. Their form, however, is quite complicated, introducing problems with additional use of 'is' and 'in', as well as – in 5 – delicate questions of existence.

In conclusion, the two first forms seems be the best way to express in English the first Parmenidean statement.

GERMAN

6.27 The general structure of the relevant German phrases is quite similar to the Latin and English ones.

The basic ontological vocabulary comes from the verb 'sein'. It includes: *ein Seiendes* for a being, *Seiende* for beings, *das Seiende* or *alles Seiende* for the being, and *das Sein* for Being itself.

To build negative forms we operate with the negation *nicht*, both nominal and sentential.

The corresponding negative concepts are thus: *ein Nicht-Seiendes, Nicht-Seiende, das Nicht-Seiende* and *das Nicht-Sein.*

All relevant forms, with exception of *existieren* accommodated from Latin come from the stem *es-*.

6.28 The paradigmatic sentences are as follows:

1.a	*Es gibt ein Seiendes*	There is a being
1.b	*Ein Seiendes ist*	A being is
1.c	*Ein Seiendes existiert*	A being exists
2.a	*Es gibt Seiende*	There are beings
2.b	*Seiende sind*	Beings are
2.c	*Seiende existieren*	Beings exist
3.a	*Es gibt das Seiende (alles Seiende)*	There is the being
3.b	*Das Seiende ist*	The being is
3.c	*Das Seiende existiert*	The being exists
4.a	*Es gibt das Sein*	There is Being
4.b	*Das Sein ist*	Being is
4.c	*Das Sein existiert*	Being exists.

Similarly for the remaining forms, including negations. For example: *Ein Nicht-Seiendes ist nicht – A nonbeing is not*, etc.

6.29 Four comments follow:

First, German has a quite distinctive structure of ontological notions, differentiating what indeed should be differentiated.

Second, 'es gibt' is the most neutral affirmator, like 'there is' or 'there are' in English.

Third, the verb 'existieren' in German presupposes at least existence in time.

Fourth, the regularity and symmetry of German phrases is amazing. For each case there are at least three expressions increasing in ontological commitment.

POLISH

6.30 Finally, let me pass to my mother tongue.

In the main this is similar to the four languages which were studied previously. However, it shows also some interesting dissimilarities.

6.31 The basic Polish ontological vocabulary is drawn from the verb 'być' which, in its different form, refers to all three of the relevant Indo-European stems: *być* to *bheu*, *jest* to *es*, *bywa* – *bytowanie* both to *bheu* and *was*.

6.32 The standard line of the basic ontological notions is as follows: *byt* both for a being and the being, *byty* for beings, *Byt* or *Istota* for Being.

It is interesting to observe that in traditional Polish we can find a different line: *jestestwo* – *jestestwa* – *Jestestwo*. Moreover, in old Polish Being was named by means of *Bytność*, made from *Byt* by means of the abstractor -*ość* (i.e. -ness).

To sum up, I propose: *poszczególny byt* for a being, *byty* for beings, *byt* for the being, and *Byt* or *Istota* for Being.

6.33 Negative terms are built up by means of the negation *nie* which in general is both nominal and sentential. Hence we have: *niebyt* for nonbeing, etc.

6.34 The most peculiar is, perhaps, the form of the negative Parmenidean statements.

Let me illustrate this by analysing statements concerning Being:

1.	*Byt bytuje*		
2.	*Byt jest*	–	Being is
	Bytu nie ma	–	Being is not
3.	*Byt istnieje*	–	Being exists
	Byt nie istnieje	–	Being does not exist

Positive statements occur in three different forms (1-3). The last: *Byt istnieje* in Polish is as specific as in German; *istnienie* in its natural meaning presupposes reality of some kind.

The second sentence *Byt jest* is neutral, like *Being is*; whereas the first *Byt bytuje* is purely ontological.

Bytowanie is the Gerund form of *bytować*, like *bycie* is the Gerund of *być*. Therefore, the meaning of the Polish equivalent of BB: *Byt bytuje* is: *Being is in its characteristic state of being*.

The negative statement *Bytu nie ma* is, as was said before, rather peculiar: *ma* comes from *mieć* (to have) taken in the following meaning: it is possible to find (among the things which are at one's disposal). Therefore, *nie ma* has a purely logical meaning: it is impossible to find.

6.35 Both pecularities of ontological Polish lend it a comparative flexibility and allow it to speak, at least in the realm of ontology, in a neutral and abstract way.

INSTEAD OF A CONCLUSION

6.36 I think that the above comparison says nothing for or against the philo-sophical flexibility of particular natural languages.

It is rather an argument for not limiting ourselves to this or that language when doing philosophy. It also suggests the superiority of suitable formal lan-guages in discussion of formal philosophical questions. Usually such languages are more neutral and more adaptable to the problems under discussion than natural languages are.

Sometimes natural languages are not so flexible as we need.

7. An Outline of a Primitive Theory of Being – **PTB**

7.1 What we need is to *prove* ontological *theorems* concerning both being and nonbeing. To this end we must rely on some formalism.

Is the formalism introduced in chapter 5 relevant? And is it sufficiently flexible and useful?

To find out we should use it, try to answer our questions, judging the theory by judging its fruits.

THE THEORY

7.2 The theory **PTB**, which I am going to develop in the present chapter, is primitive in this sense, that its theorems are deduced from the first eight definitions (given in the sections 4.16 and 4.17) alone, without referring to further definitions concerning abstractors, or to additional, specific axioms.

Therefore, its primitives are these nonlogical symbols which occur in the definitions of § 4.16 and 4.17, i.e., the binary connective * and the eight constants: B, -B, N, -N, U, -N, D and -D. The remaining 16 ontological constants, which denote the abstract concepts, are distinguished not in the present framework, but in its subsequent extension **ETB**.

7.3 The following list of axioms of **PTB** is provided to avoid any misunderstanding:

LOGICAL AXIOMS

(A0) The standard axioms and rules of classical elementary logic, including the rule of extensionality

SPECIFIC AXIOMS

(A1) $Bx \leftrightarrow \exists y\, yx$

(A2) $-Bx \leftrightarrow \neg\exists y\, yx$

(A3) $Nx \leftrightarrow \exists y\, xy$

(A4) $-Nx \leftrightarrow \neg\exists y\, xy$

(A5) $Ux \leftrightarrow \forall y\, xy$

(A6) $-Ux \leftrightarrow \neg\forall y\, xy$

(A7) $Dx \leftrightarrow \forall y\, yx$

(A8) $-Dx \leftrightarrow \neg\forall y\, yx$

ONTOLOGICAL METAPRINCIPLES

(M1) Everything we can speak about is, *prima facie*, an object. An ontological universe contains, without any differentiation, all objects which can be treated consistently.

(M2) The objectiva B, -B, N, -N, U, -U, D and -D are ontological objects.
(M3) Variables range over objects in the ontological universe.

7.4 The *ontological universe* of **PTB** is any ontological universe satisfying
the above axioms. I.e., it is an ontological universe with a natural network of
basic ontological notions, characterized by (A1)-(A8).

Does such a universe exist at all? In other words, can the basic network of
ontological concepts be used both in accordance with classical logic and in a
consistent way?

We are going to prove that this indeed can be done; not in all universes,
however, but only in some.

7.5 Metaprinciples are introduced to clarify presuppositions of the **PTB**-
proofs.

(M1) expresses the extreme generality of ontology which, by definition,
concerns everything, i.e., each and every object. In ontology, in particular, we
are trying to differentiate consistent (possible) objects from inconsistent (impossible) ones. In the main, ontology deals with consistent objects. Inconsistent
objects are also treated, under the proviso, however, that they can be elaborated
in a consistent way.

(M2) expresses our presumption that the basic ontological notions can indeed be investigated, whereas (M3) guarantees unrestricted use of the classical
calculus of quantifiers.

7.6 Specific axioms (A1)-(A8) were commented upon already in §§ 4.16
and 4.17. It would be useful, I think, to comment upon them once again, before
use.

We should distinguish two ways of understanding the specific axioms:
purely formal and ontological.

From an applicative, ontological point of view axioms are formulas of qualitative ontology. I.e., the connection *yx* expresses an *ontological connection*
between the objectivum (quality) *y* and the objectum (subject) *x*. Hence, for
example, the formula *yx* says: *x is qualified by y*, or *x is the subject of the quality y*.

On the other hand, from a purely formal, relational point of view the connection *yx* says only *that y is related to x*. Now, the formula *yx* says that something is related to *x*, i.e., that *x* is complex with respect to a given relational
network.

7.7 For the sake of further discussion let me introduce the standard relational terminology.

Consider a relational frame ordered by the relation R. We say that:

x is *simple*	iff	nothing is related to it: $\neg\exists y\, yx$
x is *complex*	iff	it is not simple, i.e., something is related to it: $\exists y\, yx$
x is *co-simple*	iff	it is related to nothing, i.e., $\neg\exists y\, xy$
x is *co-complex*	iff	it is not co-simple, i.e., it is related to something: $\exists y\, xy$
x is *a root*	iff	it is related to everything: $\forall y\, xy$
x is *a co-root*	iff	everything is related to it: $\forall y\, yx$.

If x is the only root (or the only co-root), it is called *the smallest* (or *the biggest*) one.

7.8 Now, it is easy to grasp the meaning of axioms under scrutiny.

(A1) says, ontologically, that B is a quality characteristic for items possessing qualities, i.e., a quality characteristic for beings. On the other hand, from a relational point of view, (A1) says that B indicates complexes, i.e., is related to complexes only.

Therefore, from a purely formal point of view, beings are qualitative complexes.

Interpreted in ontological terms, (A2) says that -B is the characteristic quality of nonbeings, i.e., items without qualities; whereas, in relational terms, -B indicates (is related to) simples. From a purely formal point of view, nonbeings therefore are qualitative simples.

Notice the paradoxical character of a quality characteristic for nonbeings, or a relational indicator of simples. Cf. Theorem 7 below.

(A3) and (A4) characterize respectively N and -N as the qualities of nonemptiness or emptiness. In formal terms, N and -N serve respectively as an indicator of objects which are not co-simple or as an indicator of co-simples.

In (A5) and (A6), U and -U are presented as characteristic respectively for universal (non-universal) qualities. In relational terms, they are, respectively, indicators of roots (not-roots).

Finally, (A7) and (A8) say something similar for objecta. D and -D are, respectively, characteristic for defective and non-defective objecta, i.e., items possessing all (not all) qualities. In relational terms, D indicates co-roots, whereas -D does the same for objects which are not co-roots.

7.9 The special axioms of **PTB**, on first reading, are interesting from the point of view of qualitative ontology; a second reading is interesting from the point of the verb-type, or relational ontology however. They are among the bridge-formulas and concepts which connect two of the three basic types of ontology: qualitative and relational ones.

RESULTS

7.10 By classical logic we have the following interconnections between our eight notions:

(5). i $Dx \to Bx$:   *Anything defective is a being,*

       $-Bx \to -Dx$:   *Nonbeings, if there are any, are not defective,*

(5).ii $Ux \to Nx$:   *Universals are nonempty,*

       $-Nx \to -Ux$:   *Empty qualities are not universal.*

On the other hand:

(6) Bx, Dx, Ux and Nx *are in contradiction with respectively*: $-Bx$, $-Dx$, $-Ux$ *and* $-Nx$.

Therefore, in general, the above eight formulas form two logical squares:

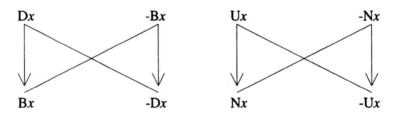

Here arrows indicate implication, whereas diagonals indicate logical contradiction.

In **PTB** however, the first square can be remarkably reduced.

7.11 Observe first that:

(7) *Anything is a being*: $\forall x\, Bx$

Proof. Take an arbitrary object x. By (M2), both Bx and -Bx are meaningful and legitimate. By the law of the excluded middle, either x is a being or it is not: B$x \lor \neg$Bx. By (A1) and (A2), $\neg$B$x \leftrightarrow$ -Bx. Hence, either x is a being or it is a nonbeing: B$x \lor$ -Bx.

To finish the proof it suffices, by the disjunctive syllogism law, to refute -Bx. To this end suppose that -Bx holds. Applying again (A2) we obtain: $\neg \exists y\ yx$. On the other hand, by the existential generalization law, which due to (M2) and (M3) can be used here, -Bx implies $\exists y\ yx$, which contradicts the previous claim.

Therefore $\neg$(-Bx), hence Bx. In conclusion, $\forall x$ Bx, for x was taken arbitrarily.

7.12 A number of corollaries follow:

(8) *The quality of being is universal*: UB, *hence nonempty*: NB. *On the other hand, the quality of nonbeing is empty*: -N-B, *hence not-universal*: -U-B.

Proof. Apply (A5) to (7), next use (6).

(9) *The extension of being is universal*: E(B) = OB, *where* OB *is the family of all ontological objects*.

(10) *Everything is complex*: $\forall x \exists y\ yx$.

Proof. By (7) and (A1).

(11) i) *Everything has a content*: $\forall x\ Q(x) \neq \varnothing$.
      ii) *The intersection of all contents is non empty*.

Proof. Ad (i): By (7) and definition of Q.
        Ad (ii): Indeed, B is a common objectivum of everything.

(12) i) *Both the quality of being B and the quality of nonbeing -B are beings*: BB, B-B.
      ii) *Moreover, the remaining six ontological qualities are also beings*: BN, B-N, BU, B-U, BD, B-D.
      iii) *If appropriate ontological concepts*: B *(the being)*, **B** *(Being)*, -B *(the nonbeing)*, **-B** *(Nonbeing) etc. satisfy* (M1), *then they are beings*: B**B**, **B**B, B-*B*, B-B, *etc*.

Proof. Ad (i) and (ii): Apply (7), (M2) and (M3). Ad (iii): Similarly, because (M1) is the general formal proviso for (M2) and (M3).

Notice that 12(i) is particularly striking in the case of the quality of being B. Indeed, the formula BB makes clear the self-referential character of the notion of being.

Observe also that for the conclusion of 12(iii) we need an appropriate investigation of the concepts involved. This will be done in the extended theory **ETB**.

Finally, notice the negative reformulation of (7) and (10):

(13) *There are no nonbeings, i.e., nonbeings are not*: $\neg\exists x\text{-}Bx$.
(14) *There are no simples*: $\neg\exists x\forall y \neg yx$.

7.13 The above proofs clearly depend on use of some characteristic laws of classical logic. This I will comment on later. I would now like to analyse the role of the axiom (A2).

First of all, it expresses, in a straightforward way, the idea of nonbeings in qualitative ontology, as items without qualities. As it was noted previously and made clear in the proof of (7), this idea is paradoxical.

This is even more transparent when we are using the relational explication: it indicates *simples*, i.e., items to which *nothing is related*, hence in any given *relational* network they cannot be indicated. Characteristic for simples, if there are any, is that they cannot be indicated.

This does not mean, however, that simples cannot be collected, but only that no collection of simples is based on or generated by an indicative quality of them.

An important lesson follows: *collection does not imply or presuppose the existence of any characteristic quality for the collected items.*

7.14 By the way, with the above remarks in mind, it is easy to see the level of logical consequence in traditional philosophy and theology which, indeed, is remarkable.

Recall traditional discussions of simples and God. Quite often, God was claimed to be simple either with respect to analyses of the world, or with respect to essential or qualitative analyses, or with respect to both (being in this case *absolutely* simple).

The first option was taken, among others, by Leibniz; the second and the third by several gnostic or mystical thinkers, including Meister Eckhart.

To be consistent anyone should either consider God (and any *natural simple being* as well) to be complex from the point of view of qualitative analysis, or to claim that God (and any qualitative or absolute simple) cannot be qualified and indicated, that It is (they are) out of any essential characterization.

It is nice to recognize that these moves were indeed taken, the former *inter alia* by Leibniz, the latter among others in negative theology.

7.15 Return to deduction. The second objectivum which, in fact, cannot be instantiated is the indicator of defectiveness D. Indeed

(15) *For any x, x is defective iff x is contradictory.*

Proof. For the right-hand implication assume that x is defective: Dx. By (A7), $\forall y$ yx. By (M2) and (M3), D and -D are ontological objects, both in the range of y. Therefore, by general particularization, Dx and -Dx hold. Applying (A7) and (A8), we obtain -D$x \leftrightarrow \neg$Dx. Thus D$x \wedge \neg$Dx, hence x is contradictory.

For the reverse implication assume that x is the subject of contradictory characterization: $A(x) \wedge \neg A(x)$. By Duns Scotus' Law, $A(x) \wedge \neg A(x) \rightarrow \forall z$ zx. Hence $\forall z$ zx, i.e. Dx, as required.

Observe now

(16) *Every object is not defective*: $\forall x$ -Dx.

Proof. Assume, for the sake of contradiction, that x is defective: Dx. Hence x is contradictory. For example, D$x \wedge \neg$ Dx. This, however, contradicts the well-known classical principle of non-contradiction: $\neg$(D$x \wedge \neg$Dx).

Hence, for any x, -Dx, as claimed.

7.16 Again, a number of corollaries follow.

The first square of § 7.10 collapses, for

(17) $\forall x$ B$x \leftrightarrow \forall x$ -Dx *and* $\forall x$ -B$x \leftrightarrow \forall x$ Dx.

Proof. By (7) and (16), the formulas from the first equivalence are true, whereas these from the second equivalence are false.

(18) *The quality of nondefectiveness is universal*: U-D, *hence nonempty*: N-D. *On the other hand, the quality of defectiveness is empty* -ND, *hence non universal*: -UD.

(19) *There is no qualitative co-root*: $\neg\exists x\forall y\ yx$.

Proof. By (16) and (A8).

(20) *Nothing has the full content*: $\forall x\ Q(x) \neq OB$.

Confronting this with (11) we obtain

(21) *Everything has an intermediate content*: $\forall x\ \varnothing \neq Q(x) \neq OB$.

(22) *Each of the eight ontological objects under investigation is nondefective*:
-DB, -D-B, -DN, -D-N, -DU, -D-U, -DD, -D-D.

7.17 Iterations of the eight ontological objects under investigation were previously shown several times to be important. Now I shall study them systematically.

There are 64, i.e. 8×8, such iterations, which are divided into two basic families.

The first one, with 32 formulas, concerns the size of whatever is the relevant content. This is so because

(23) *For any x*:

Bx	iff	$Q(x) \neq \varnothing$,	-Bx	iff	$Q(x) = \varnothing$
-Dx	iff	$Q(x) \neq OB$,	Dx	iff	$Q(x) = OB$

Previously, in (7) and (16), the formulas occurring on the left side of the equivalences from the first column were proved. In consequence, in (12) and (22), the following sixteen iterations were included among the theorems of **PTB**: BB, B-B, BN, B-N, BU, B-U, BD, B-D; -DB, -D-B, -DN, -D-N, -DU, -D-U, -DD, -D-D.

The remaining sixteen iterations, which start with -B or D, are not provable in **PTB**, because they contradict **PTB**-theorems and in the next subchapter **PTB** will be shown to be consistent.

7.18 To characterize the remaining 32 iterations take one, say -N-U, and, using axioms calculate:

-N-U	$\leftrightarrow$	$\neg\exists x$ -Ux	by (A4)
	$\leftrightarrow$	$\neg\exists x\neg\forall y\ xy$	by (A0) and (A5)
	$\leftrightarrow$	$\forall x\forall y\ xy$	by (A0).

Hence N-U is equivalent to the standard quantifier formula saying that everything is connected with everything.

7.19 Taking into account that for a given two-variable connection '*xy*' there are exactly 12 combinations of negation with both general and existential quantifiers binding variables *x* and *y*, and repeating the above calculation for the remaining 31 formulas we obtain

(24) i) *Each of the conditions -N-U, UU, UD, -N-D is equivalent to $\forall x \forall y\, xy$, i.e. to the thesis that everything is ontologically connected to everything else, or: Any object is both objectum and objectivum to each and every other object.*

  ii) *Each of the conditions N-U, -UU, -UD, N-D is equivalent to $\neg\forall x \forall y\, xy$: Some objects are not ontologically connected.*

  iii) *Each of the conditions NN, -U-N, -U-B, NB is equivalent to $\exists x \exists y\, xy$: Some objects are ontologically connected.*

  iv) *Each of the conditions -NN, U-N, U-B, -NB is equivalent to $\neg\exists x \exists y\, xy$: Nothing is ontologically connected.*

  v) *Each of the conditions NU, -U-U is equivalent to $\exists x \forall y\, xy$: Something is an objectivum (a quality) of everything.*

  vi) *Each of the conditions -NU, U-U is equivalent to $\neg\exists x \forall y\, xy$: Nothing is an objectivum of everything.*

  vii) *Each of the conditions UN, -N-N is equivalent to $\forall x \exists y\, xy$: Any object is an objectivum (quality) for something.*

  viii) *Each of the conditions -UN, N-N is equivalent to $\neg\forall x \exists y\, xy$: Some object cannot be an objectivum.*

  ix) *Each of the conditions UB, -N-B is equivalent to $\forall y \exists x\, xy$: Any object is an objectum for something, or: Everything in the qualitative universe is complex.*

  x) *Each of the conditions -UB, N-B is equivalent to $\neg\forall y \exists x\, xy$: Something cannot be an objectum.*

  xi) *Each of the conditions ND, -U-D is equivalent to $\exists y \forall x\, xy$: Some object is the universal objectum.*

  xii) *Each of the conditions -ND, U-D is equivalent to $\neg\exists y \forall x\, xy$: Nothing is the objectum for everything.*

The above twelve quantifier formulas describe all *general* situations occurring in graphs of binary relations: everything is connected, something is not connected, something is connected, nothing is connected, etc. The second group of ontological iterations contain therefore expressions having a quite clear relational meaning.

Which of them hold in **PTB**?

7.20 As a matter of fact, **PTB** with respect to these general possibilities is complete: exactly half of suitable formulas are its theorems.

They are listed, with the previous numbering, below.

(25) *The following formulas are theorems of* PTB:

(ii)   N-U, -UU, -UD, N-D *and* $\neg\forall x\forall y\, xy$

(iii)   NN, -U-N, -U-B, NB *and* $\exists x\exists y\, xy$

(v)   NU, -U-U *and* $\exists x\forall y\, xy$

(viii) -UN, N-N *and* $\neg\forall x\exists y\, xy$

(ix)   UB, -N-B *and* $\forall y\exists x\, xy$

(xii)   -ND, U-D *and* $\neg\exists y\forall x\, xy$.

Proof. Notice that, by (25), the formulas collected in the successive rows of the above theorem are known to be equivalent. Therefore, to check that they indeed are theorems of **PTB**, it suffices to check that at least one of them is such.

Ad (ii). By (18), N-D is a theorem of **PTB**.

Ad (iii). By (8), NB is a theorem of **PTB**.

Ad (v). Again by (8), UB is a theorem of **PTB**, *a fortiori* NU is such.

Ad (viii). By (13), -N-B, hence by (A0), (M2) and (M3), $\exists x$ -Nx. Applying (A4) we obtain that N-N is a theorem of **PTB**.

Ad (ix). By (8), UB is a theorem of **PTB**.

Ad (xii). By (18), U-D is a theorem of **PTB**.

7.21 In conclusion: Exactly half of all sixty-four possible iterations happen to be theorems of **PTB**. The remaining thirty-two are their negations. Hence they cannot be theorems of **PTB**, provided that the theory is consistent.

And this, indeed, is the case.

MODELS

7.22 To prove consistency we need models. A model of a given theory is any interpretation of its language, which respects logical entailment and satisfies the axioms of the theory.

The language of **PTB** is that part of a language introduced in chapter 4 which suffices to express the axioms of the theory. Because abstractors are not used, they can be here left out of account.

The syntax of the language of **PTB** is therefore standard.

7.23 Which models model **PTB**?

PTB is a theory of the ontological connection and the eight notions involved: B, -B, N, -N, U, -U, D and -D.

Its natural models are therefore *relational frames* with eight distinguished elements, endowed with corresponding interpretations: $F = <O, R; b, \underline{b}, n, \underline{n}, u, \underline{u}, d, \underline{d}>$.

Here b, $\underline{b}$, n, $\underline{n}$, u, $\underline{u}$, d, $\underline{d}$ belong to the universe O; whereas R is a binary relation on it.

Let *FOR* denote the family of all formulas in the language of **PTB**.

An *interpretation* is any mapping f: $FOR \rightarrow O$ such that

(i) $f(B) = b$, $f(-B) = \underline{b}$, $f(N) = n$, $f(-N) = \underline{n}$, $f(U) = u$, $f(-U) = \underline{u}$, $f(D) = d$ and $f(-D) = \underline{d}$;

(ii) $f(AC) = f(A)Rf(C)$;

(iii) f respects classical connectives and quantifiers.

We say that a model $<F, f>$ is a **PTB** *model* if all axioms of **PTB** are valid in it.

7.24 It is easy to see that quite a lot of relational models are not **PTB** models.

By (24), **PTB** models must:

i) Interpret all specific symbols of **PTB**, hence they must include indicator of simples $\underline{b}$;

ii) They therefore must contain only complexes;

iii) Also, they must have roots and co-simples, but not co-roots;

iv) They cannot be discrete (for something must be connected);

v) They cannot be full (for something should not be connected).

The crucial point is to verify (A2). There are no simples, hence $\underline{b}$ should indicate them in vain. Therefore $\underline{b}$ must be co-simple.

7.25 It is easy to see that the six-element model given below is a **PTB** model.

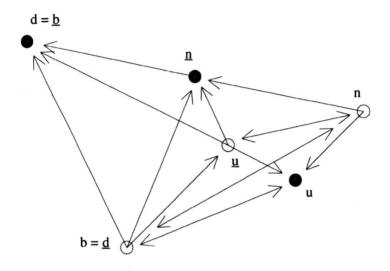

Convention: in the diagram reflexive (irreflexive) points are depicted by empty (nonempty) dots: ○ (●).

The model verifies, in fact, a stronger theory than **PTB**, for, in addition, it verifies

(A9) $\forall x(Bx \leftrightarrow -Dx)$, i.e., B and -D as well as -B and D are equivalent.

7.26 In conclusion

(26) **PTB** *is consistent.*

Therefore, by remarks in § 7.21, **PTB** really answers all *primitive* questions which can be expressed in its language.

COMMENTS

7.27 Some comments are in order. Are the above results convincing? Are they made in an ontologically innocent way? What are their presuppositions?

7.28 Two main questions can be raised. The first concerns the language of **PTB**, the second draws attention to the logic of the above proofs.

7.29 It is well-known that standard, i.e. classical-like logics enjoy a certain freedom in considering all syntactically correct formulas as meaningful despite ease of introduction of self-contradictory formulas.

The proofs under investigation depend on the correctness of all formulas involved, *inter alia*: Bx, $-Bx$, BB, NB, etc. They are, for sure, made in a correct way and have a rather clear meaning. However, they presuppose that B can be both objectivum and objectum, that both B and -B can be objectiva of any object, etc.

These linguistic presuppositions are, however, implicit in the metaprinciples (M1)-(M3).

7.30 On the other hand, our language might be thought to be too poor.

We are using only *one* primitive ontological connective (and eight parameters). Someone might prefer to use more connectives: one to define 'to be being' and 'to be nonbeing', another one for connection between an object and its qualities or ideas, etc.

In such a case, more freedom is available, for the conceptual framework is broader. As a matter of fact, this option was developed by F.J. Pelletier in his recent 1990. For its outline see the next subchapter.

7.31 In particular, someone can prefer to use in 'Being is' distinct symbols for 'Being', say B, and for 'is', say E, i.e., to write 'EB' instead of 'BB'.

This, however, suggests the basic, primitive distinction between 'being' and 'is', despite the results of our previous linguistic discussion. Remember that both 'is' and 'being' are derivatives of the verb 'to be'. And I like to preserve this connection.

The proper proportion of formal distinctions is perhaps the most subtle factor of any formalization. We can of course make as many verbal or notational distinctions as we wish. However, each distinction needs further elaboration. The more notions we have, the more work is needed for their elaboration.

I prefer a reasonably economic framework. Taking into account the extreme generality of the pure ontological investigation and the status of the present investigation, which is the starting point for further development, I chose the most economical ontological framework of all: with *only one* primitive connection, plus parameters and, of course, logical functors. The rest is derived.

7.32 Turn now to the logical side of the arguments under scrutiny, i.e., reconsider the proofs of (7) and (16).

Both proofs depend heavily on use of a few characteristic classical laws: the law of the excluded middle, which in use seems to have a rather strong ontological meaning, the law of existential generalization, the double negation law, Duns Scotus' Law, the law of disjunctive syllogism.

Notice that the *formal proviso* to existential generalization: nonemptiness of the ontological universe, is indeed acceptable (cf. § 4.11). But what about an *ontological proviso*, if any?

Observe that a suitable assumption is implicit in our meta-axioms (M2) and (M3).

7.33 The law of the excluded middle has a deep ontological tenor in itself. Indeed, read $A(x) \vee \neg A(x)$: *For each (property) A and each (individual) x, either A(x) is the case or it is not.*

In our case, its tenor is even stronger. $Bx \vee -Bx$: *For each x, either x is a being or it is a nonbeing.* Can such a formula be ontologically innocent?

It seems that it cannot. Recall the well-known arguments of Łukasiewicz 1910 against an ontological justification of the law of the excluded middle and the law of noncontradiction as well as Scholz's 1941 arguments for the claim that they are, in fact, ontological statements.

7.34 Therefore, the laws of classical logic on which my proofs depend in the present ontological context should be treated not as purely formal, neutral logical principles, but rather as specific, ontological axioms of the theory.

7.35 Someone can argue that this is sufficient reason to limit the use of classical logic in ontology. But which logic should be used instead?

I am not going so far in my self-criticism. Any revision is revision of something. Before revising onto-logic, i.e. logic of being, we must therefore develop it in a standard, classical way. And this is my present task.

7.36 Finally, a metaphilosophical remark. Some pecularities of the present formalism are, in a sense, illuminating.

It is half-predicative, half-algebraic. Our formulas, like BB, resemble rather the formulas of combinatory logic than those of the standard, predicate calculus.

This option has been chosen for essential reasons, discussed in chaper 4. In practice it indeed shows some usefulness.

It seems therefore that the algebraic framework is more appropriate for general ontological investigation; whereas the standard, predicate formalism is more adequate to deal with language ontologies and perhaps also with the metaphysics of the common-sense world.

AN ALTERNATIVE APPROACH

7.37 Let us compare the framework of the present essay with that outlined by Pelletier at the end of his impressive analysis of Plato's 'Sophist', cf. Pelletier 1990.

Pelletier adopts as primitives two binary predicates $DK(\_,\_)$ and $X(\_,\_)$ introduced to formalize two types of *participation*. He also uses two parameters 'b' and 'n' for suitable forms of Being and not-Being.

Pelletier's principles are as follows:

(P1) $\forall y[\exists x DK(x,y) \leftrightarrow X(y,b)]$
(P2) $\forall y[\neg \exists x DK(x,y) \leftrightarrow X(y,n)]$

7.38 It is easy to find equivalents of Pelletier's formulas among ours:

B$y := X(y,b)$; -B$y := X(y,n)$, and $xy := DK(x,y)$.

Thus (P1) and (P2) correspond respectively to our definitions of a being and a nonbeing.

The axiom behind this reduction is the following one:

(PP) $DK(x,y) \leftrightarrow X(y,x)$

7.39 Substituting 'b' and 'n' for 'y' respectively in (P1) and (P2) we obtain the following four formulas:

(P3) $\exists x DK(x,b) \quad \leftrightarrow X(b,b)$
        $\exists x DK(x,n) \quad \leftrightarrow X(n,b)$

$$\neg \exists x DK(x,b) \leftrightarrow X(b,n)$$
$$\neg \exists x DK(x,n) \leftrightarrow X(n,n)$$

We immediately have

(27) $X(b,b) \leftrightarrow \neg X(b,n)$
        $X(n,b) \leftrightarrow \neg X(n,n)$

7.40 By (27), the following three pairs of formulae constitute all maximally consistent subcollections of X-formulas, which are involved in (P3):

I   := $\{X(b,b), X(n,b)\}$
II := $\{X(b,b), X(n,n)\}$
III := $\{X(n,b), X(b,n)\}$

In my notation, **I** = {BB, B-B}, **II** = {BB, -B-B} and **III** = {B-B, -BB}.

I corresponds to the family *asserted* in **PTB**, **II** constitutes Pelletier's *axiomatic choice* of Parmenidean statements, whereas a rather counterintuitive family **III** constitutes a logical challenge to Parmenideans in the framework of Pelletier.

7.41 Let me stress, that the family **I** occurs, *mutatis mutandis*, both in **PTB** and in the more liberal approach of Pelletier; whereas **II** and **III** are lost in **PTB**.

Restrictiveness is reasonable not only for economic reasons. Sometimes in a restrictive framework we can prove something which is lost in more liberal one.

In Pelletier's approach, **I** is one of the three options which can be chosen axiomatically; in the more restrictive **PTB**, formulas belonging to it are *provable*.

8. Towards an Extended Theory of Being – **ETB**

8.1 In the Extended Theory of Being, in short **ETB**, which is an extension of **PTB**, we deal in addition with two abstract concepts of being: the being B, which is the collection of all beings and Being **B**, which is the unity or idea of all beings.

Both notions are abstract concepts arrived at by means of suitable abstractors: $B := \{x: Bx\}$ and $\mathbf{B} := [x: Bx]$.

ETB therefore relies on an appropriate theory of both abstractors, which is rather a delicate topic.

COLLECTIONS AND IDEAS

8.2 Hereafter, the full language introduced in chapter 4 will be used, with all its pecularities commented upon there.

Recall that the inscription $A(x)$ is used to mark that the variable x occurs freely in the formula A. $A(x/C)$ denotes the result of *correct* substitution of a variable x by the formula C in the formula A.

$A(x)$ is connected in the usual way with its extension, i.e., the family of all objects, say As, realizing it. Clearly, the exact definition of realization must presuppose either a given theory (in which A is provable), or a class of models satisfying it.

8.3 The collector $\{\_:\_\}$ is understood as an operator collecting families of differentiated and determined objects. In particular, $\{x: A(x)\}$ is the collection of all objects realizing A.

It is a typical objectivum, studied in set theory. $\{x: A(x)\}y$ means that y belongs to $\{x: A(x)\}$ (what, in set-theoretical notation, is expressed by:
$y \in \{x: A(x)\}$).

8.4 Ideas or unities are built from multiplicities by their unification, if possible. Unvoid unification clearly presupposes compatibility, i.e., that items realizing a given condition *can be taken into one*.

Formally, ideas are formed by means of unifiers $[\_:\_]$. Thus, $[x: A(x)]$ denotes the idea of As or the unity of all As. It is also a typical objectivum: $[x: A(x)]y$ means, in Plato's terms, that y *participates* in the idea of As.

8.5 Both abstractors need a careful axiomatic elaboration. This can be done in at least two ways.

In the standard option our attention is directed to two appropriate relations: the well-known relation of membership $\in$, characteristic for collectors; and the not so elaborated relation of participation characteristic for unifiers. Here both abstractors are implicit.

I prefer a more economic option: to work with *one* connection plus *two* abstractors. They can occur either as objectivum, on the left side of connection, or as objectum, on the right side, or even on both.

8.6 As a matter of fact, we need to characterize four situations:

$\{x: A(x)\}y$ – y belongs to the collection of *A*s;

$y\{x: A(x)\}$ – y qualifies or characterizes or contains the collection of *A*s;

$[x: A(x)]y$ – y participates in the idea of *A*s;

$y[x: A(x)]$ – y qualifies or determines or forms the idea of *A*s.

8.7 Usually people are dealing only with the objectivum position, working with:

Comprehension Principle: $y \in \{x: A(x)\} \leftrightarrow A(x/y)$, or

Abstraction Axiom: $[x: A(x)]y \leftrightarrow A(x/y)$.

The Comprehension Principle was common in intuitive set theory and is still used in some of its refinements, whereas the Abstraction Axiom is one of the basic principles in formal theories of properties. Both of them are notorious for their capacity to produce paradoxes.

In what follows I am trying to approach the problem from its roots.

8.8 Consider first the case of abstractors as qualities.

Two fundamental, partly opposed intuitions concerning the interrelations between realization, collection and unification are leading.

8.8.1 According to the first, unification presupposes collection and, in turn, collection presupposes realization. Suitable implications are accordingly here *accepted* as axioms:

From unities to collections:

(UC) $[x: A(x)]y \rightarrow \{x: A(x)\}y$ *If y participates in the idea of As then y belongs to the collection of As (is one of the As)* .

From collections to realized cases:

(CR) $\{x: A(x)\}y \rightarrow A(y)$ *If y is among the As, then y realizes A.*

The question arises: Do the reverse implications hold as well?

8.8.2 In the second option exactly the reverse implications:

(RC) $A(y) \rightarrow \{x: A(x)\}y$
(CU) $\{x: A(x)\}y \rightarrow [x: A(x)]y$

are chosen as basic axioms.

I.e., it is claimed that if y realizes A, then y belongs to the collection of all As and, in turn, if y belongs to this collection, then y falls under the general concept of As, i.e., it participates in the idea of As.

Here it seems to be taken for granted that everything can be collected and that each collection can be unified. The first assumption seems to be reasonable, provided that collecting is considered to be a purely mental, *a priori* activity. The second assumption, however, is much more doubtful, because unification requires objective compatibility and that there is a corresponding form.

8.9 Combinations of both options are, of course, possible and are indeed often practised.

Notice that the Comprehension Principle is equivalent to the conjunction of (CR) and (RC), whereas the Abstraction Axiom easily follows from the conjunction of all four axioms.

8.10 If we choose, as I do, the first option, but not everything from the second, then the question of restrictions for appropriate equivalences arises naturally.

By our previous discussion they should be suitable compatibility conditions. Looking for such conditions we see that in the present framework there are, in fact, only two *natural* candidates for such a condition. And both will be used.

8.10.1 For a given formula A, its *downward compatibility*, DC(A), means that some object z is the common objectivum of (or, is related to) all objects realizing A:

$$DC(A) := \exists z \forall y (A(y) \rightarrow zy)$$

Thus, for a down-compatible formula A, examples of As enjoy a common quality, which is the reason for their compatibility.

8.10.2 Similarly for *upward-compatibility*:

$UC(A) := \exists z \forall y (A(y) \rightarrow yz)$.

Items realizing an up-compatible condition A are instantiated by (or, are related to) the same object, which is another sort of guarantee of As compatibility.

8.11 Using the above conditions, it is easy to distinguish different kinds of tranformation unifying *many into one*.
They are expressed in the following three axioms, *accepted* for further use:

(C) $\{x: A(x)\}y \leftrightarrow A(y)$ Comprehension Axiom

Everything described by a linguistically correct condition can be comprehended, i.e., collected mentally.

Comprehension, however, does not presuppose compatibility. Hence not all mentally achieved collections are coherent. Coherence appears in stages:

(PC) $[x: A(x)\}y \leftrightarrow \{x: A(x)\}y \wedge DC(A)$ Proper Collection Axiom

Proper collections are multiplicities produced by down-compatible conditions.

(U) $[x: A(x)]y \leftrightarrow [x: A(x)\}y \wedge UC(A)$ Unification Axiom

Unities are proper collections achieved by up-compatible conditions.

8.12 Immediately from these definitions we obtain

(27) i) $[x: A(x)\}y \leftrightarrow A(y) \wedge DC(A)$
      ii) $[x: A(x)]y \leftrightarrow A(y) \wedge DC(A) \wedge UC(A)$

Hence, y participates in the idea of As iff it realizes A, which can be unified, i.e., is both down- and up-compatible.

Observe that by the axiom (U), unities of incompatible collections are not excluded. Such ideas, however, must be empty.

(28) *If the collection of As is incompatible, i.e.* $\neg DC(A)$ *or* $\neg UC(A)$, *or if A is not realizable, then no y participates in the idea of As:* $\neg \exists y \ [x: A(x)]y$.

Similarly for incompatible proper collections, which also must be empty.

Now *consistent collections* are defined as *proper* collections with *nonempty*, i.e. instantiated, ideas.

8.13 Observe that (U) entails the Abstraction Axiom for *compatible* formulas:

(29) $DC(A) \wedge UC(A) \rightarrow ([x: A(x)]y \leftrightarrow A(y))$.

8.14 It is instructive to see the meaning of the above axioms in the set-theoretical realm (cf. Fraenkel, Bar-Hillel and Levy 1973 and Mendelson 1979).

Down-compatibility on A is like Zermelo's restriction, introduced by him for reasons similar to ours. To see this, recall Zermelo's Separation Axiom:

For every formula A and every set a there exists a set whose elements are exactly those of a realizing the formula A:

$\exists x \forall y [y \in x \leftrightarrow A(y) \wedge y \in a]$ (*x is not allowed to occur in A*).

Observe that in set-theoretical terms $DC(A)$ is equivalent to:

$\exists x \forall y (A(y) \rightarrow y \in x)$, which, to some extent, resembles Zermelo's condition.

On the other hand, up-compatibility means that the family of all *A*s is *centred*, which is an important condition in the theory of filters:

$UC(A) \leftrightarrow \exists x \forall y (A(y) \rightarrow x \in y) \leftrightarrow \bigcap \{y: A(y)\} \neq \emptyset$.

Both conditions of compatibility have therefore a well-known and recognized meaning in the realm of sets. Proper collections are sets in a modified sense of Zermelo:

$y \in [x: A(x)\}$ *iff* $A(y) \wedge \exists x \forall y (A(y) \rightarrow y \in x)$;

whereas unities, or consistent collections are proper collections which generates proper filters:

$y \in [x: A(x)]$ *iff* $A(y) \wedge (\exists x \forall y (A(y) \rightarrow y \in x) \wedge (\bigcap \{y: A(y)\} \neq \emptyset))$.

EMPTY IDEAS

8.15 It is reasonable to accept the thesis that there are unities for *all* collections, i.e., for all conditions. But in some cases they are *nonempty*, i.e. something really participates in them; whereas in some cases they are *empty*, because nothing participates in them.

As a matter of fact, there are quite a lot of cases leading to empty ideas. I am going to characterize some of them. First of all

(30) *Inconsistent conditions lead to empty collections and, in turn, empty collections end with empty ideas.*

8.16 On the other hand conditions tolerating inconsistencies also lead to empty ideas.

To be more exact, a formula A is said to *tolerate inconsistencies* iff there are x and $\underline{x}$, both realizing A, such that $\underline{x}$ is a quality opposite to x: $\exists x \exists \underline{x}(A(x) \wedge A(\underline{x}) \wedge \forall z(\underline{x}z \leftrightarrow \neg xz))$.

Now, applying the principle of noncontradiction it is easy to see that

(31) *If A tolerates inconsistencies, then the idea of As is empty:* $\neg \exists y \, [x: A(x)]y$.

Proof. Take some A tolerating inconsistencies. Assume UC(A), i.e., $\exists z \forall y \, (A(y) \rightarrow yz)$.

By assumption, for some opposite x and $\underline{x}$: $A(x)$ and $A(\underline{x})$. Hence, by UC(A), xz and $\underline{x}z$, i.e., xz and $\neg xz$, which contradicts the principle of noncontradiction. Thus $\neg$UC(A), therefore, by (U), the idea of As must be empty.

In conclusion

(32) *Very general conditions lead to empty ideas.*

Indeed, what is truly general is common for everything, hence also for inconsistencies. Hence a truly general condition tolerates inconsistencies, therefore, by (31), its idea is empty.

8.17 Further, notice that:

(33) *If A tolerates simples or co-simples, then it produces an empty idea.*

Proof. By definition, *A tolerates simples (co-simples)* iff it is realized by some simple (co-simple) object: $\exists y\,(A(y) \wedge \neg\exists x\,xy)$ or $\exists y(A(y) \wedge \neg\exists x\,yx)$.
In the first case, $\neg DC(A)$; whereas in the second, $\neg UC(A)$. Therefore, by (U), no y participates in $[x: A(x)]$.

8.18 Finally, let me pass to qualitative particulars and universals.
Particulars are qualified, but not qualifying objects, i.e., x is *a particular* iff it is qualified but not qualifying: $Q(x) \neq \varnothing$, or $\exists z\,zx$, but x itself is not a quality: $\neg\exists z\,xz$.

Universals are qualifying objects, i.e., x is *a universal* iff for some z, x is its quality: xz.

Void objects, i.e., objects both simple and co-simple, are neither particulars nor universals.

Particulars are unvoid co-simples. The rest are universals.

Observe that

(34) *Only universals can be unified in a fruitful way.*

This is because, by (33),

(35) *If A tolerates (i.e. is realized by) void objects or particulars then its idea is empty.*

CONNECTIONS OF ABSTRACT CONCEPTS

8.19 Abstract concepts are given in order of increasing abstraction.
We start with particular cases of A: $A(y)$, which are then mentally collected into $\{x: A(x)\}$. This collection sometimes can be turned into the proper collection $[x: A(x)\}$ which, in turn, sometimes can be fruitfully unified into the idea $[x: A(x)]$.

It is rather reasonable to expect that each of the above concepts falls under its more general companions. I.e., that not only the cases of As, but also their collections and ideas participate in the idea of As.

8.20 To be more exact, let a denote one of the A-abstractions: $\{x: A(x)\}$, $[x: A(x)\}$, $[x: A(x)]$. Ask: when does a participate in $[x: A(x)]$, i.e., $[x: A(x)]a$?

By the axiom (U), $[x: A(x)]a$ is equivalent to the conjunction of the three conditions:

(i) $A(a)$. In particular:
      (*) $A(\{x: A(x)\})$, or $A([x: A(x)\})$, or $A([x: A(x)])$, which are typical
            fixed-point conditions;
(ii) $DC(A)$,
(iii) $UC(A)$.

By $UC(A)$, for some z:
      (**) *If $A(y)$ then yz.*
By (*) from (i), the following holds: $\{x: A(x)\}z$, or $[x: A(x)\}z$, or $[x: A(x)]z$.
Applying suitable axioms and (**) we finally obtain that zz. Hence we proved

(36) *If at least one of A-abstractions participates in the idea of A then*
     (i) The condition A enjoys a suitable fixed-point property,
     (ii) The ontological universe $<OB, *>$ is not irreflexive: $\exists z\ zz$.

8.21 Therefore

(37) *In a standard set-theoretical universe no abstractor participates in its conjugate idea.*

This is so, because the standard set-theoretical realm is *regular*, hence: $\neg \exists z\ z \in z$. In the set-theoretical universe the connection zz means $z \in z$, hence regularity contradicts (36.ii).

8.22 In which way should our axiomatics be completed?
Quite a lot of candidates can, in fact, be considered. Most of them, however, are either artificial or produce paradoxes.

In the present essay, I am limiting myself to rather safe conditions, introduced in order to guarantee logical extensionality: *the same effect for equivalent formulas.*

IDENTITY

8.23 First consider the problem of identity, which is usually characterized by coextensiveness.

Let A and C be any conditions expressible in the language of qualitative ontology. They are either formulas with *one* free variable or they are abstractors.

In the case of abstractors we accept the convention that they are realized by objects instantiating them, i.e., for a given abstractor a, $a(x) := ax$.

Conditions can be compared. In particular, *two conditions are said to be coextensive, $A \equiv C$ iff they are logically equivalent, i.e., they are realized by the same objects*:

$$A \equiv C := \forall x(A(x) \leftrightarrow C(x)).$$

Observe that by the convention and by the axiom (C) coextensivity concerning collections is reduced to coextensivity of appropriate formulas. For example:
$$\{x: A(x)\} \equiv C(x) \quad \leftrightarrow \quad \forall y(\{x:A(x)\}(y) \leftrightarrow C(y)) \leftrightarrow \forall y(\{x:A(x)\}y \leftrightarrow C(y));$$
$$\leftrightarrow \quad \forall y \, (A(y) \leftrightarrow C(y)) \leftrightarrow A \equiv C.$$

Similarly, but with additional requirements involved, in the case of the remaining two abstractors.

8.24 Following Leibniz's clue we accept the principle of the identity of indiscernibles, with unavoidable relativization to language:

(L) $x = y$ *iff* $\forall A \, (A(x) \leftrightarrow A(y))$.

Two objects are identical if they cannot be distinguished (by conditions expressible in the language.

8.25 We can try to weaken this principle further. Are *all* conditions necessary for identity? Can we limit ourselves to some basic conditions?

In the framework of qualitative ontology we can try limitation only to conditions delineating objects' qualities and subjects. This leads to the idea of *coequity*:
$$x \approx y \; iff \; \forall z \, (zx \leftrightarrow zy) \wedge \forall z \, (xz \leftrightarrow yz)$$

Two objects are *coequal* iff they have the same qualities and they qualify the same objects. That is

(38) $x \approx y$ *iff* $Q(x) = Q(y) \wedge E(x) = E(y)$.

Clearly, in our language equity implies coequity:

(39) $x = y \rightarrow x \approx y$.

8.26 What are the reasonable conditions for reversing this implication? As a matter of fact, in the *real* ontological universe even a weaker condition should suffice, because the original principle of Leibniz says:

(LP) $x = y$ *iff* $Q(x) = Q(y)$.

Objects with the same qualities are identical, which is the principle accepted in qualitative ontology.

8.27 Observe that all requirements outlined above exclude quite a lot of relational frames from the realm of qualitative ontologies. For example:

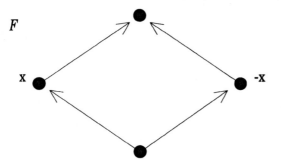

is not ontological, because x and $-x$ are different but indistinguishable in the F-network.

This, in fact, is an ontological reason for troubles with *ontic* negation. To solve it, we must refer to structures big and complex enough to differentiate items which must be distinguished.

8.28 We accept the usual *axiom of extensionality for collections*

(EC) $\{x: A(x)\} = \{x: C(x)\}$ *iff* $A \equiv C$.

8.29 What about ideas? First of all, observe that

(40) *Ideas generated by coextensive conditions have the same extension:*
      $A \equiv C \rightarrow E([x: A(x)]) = E([x: C(x)]).$

Indeed, it is easy to see that the conditions of participation in ideas defined by equivalent formulas are equivalent.

However, the above implication is not reversible (cf. the next subchapter). Hence the coextensivity of two conditions is logically stronger than the coextensivity of the corresponding ideas.

Therefore, coextensivity might be used to characterize identity of ideas, as in the following *axiom of extensionality for ideas*:

(EI) $[x: A(x)] = [x: C(x)]$ *iff* $A \equiv C.$

Immediately

(41) $[x: A(x)] = [x: C(x)]$ *iff* $\{x: A(x)\} = \{x: C(x)\}.$

Identity of ideas is equivalent to identity of collections.

8.29 However, some doubts concerning (EI) remain.

Surely, coextensionality regulates the problem of equality of extensions. Is it sufficient for equality of ideas, which seems to depend on some essential or intensional factors?

Observe that coextensive ideas can be different. For example, Being **B** and Nonbeing -**B** are coextensive (cf. (49) below) but, by (EI), they are different, for conditions defining them are not equivalent.

QUALITIES OF ABSTRACTORS

8.30 Consider now the problem of characterization of the determiners or qualities of collections or ideas.

A minimal requirement seems to be preservation of provable equivalences, expressed in the following *axiom of preservation*:

(CP) $C\{x: A(x)\} \rightarrow \forall E((E \equiv A) \rightarrow CE)$

This axiom immediately entails

(42) *If* $C\{x: A(x)\}$, *then CA*
(43) *If* $E \equiv A$, *then* $Q(\{x: E(x)\}) = Q\{x: A(x)\}$

Therefore (CP) entails the weak form of extensionality:

(44) *If* $E \equiv A$, *then* $\{x: E(x)\} \approx \{x: A(x)\}$

8.31 In the next subchapter, it will be pointed out that, in general, the qualities of conjugate collections and ideas are different.

(45) *Neither* $C\{x: A(x)\}$ *implies* $C[x: A(x)]$ *nor, conversely, does* $C[x: A(x)]$ *imply* $C\{x: A(x)\}$.

Therefore the analogous axiom of preservation for ideas is not acceptable.

An important and difficult question as to what are the acceptable axioms characterizing qualities of ideas is left open for further study.

ETB

8.32 The Extended Theory of Being, in short **ETB**, is an extension of **PTB** obtained by: i) use of the full language, as defined in chapter 4, and ii) application of the list of definitions from chapter 4 plus the above axioms concerning abstractors.
Thus in **ETB** axioms (C), (PC), (U), (LP), (EC), (EI) and, with some reserve, (CP) are applied to ontological concepts determined by the eight ontological qualities: B, -B, N, -N, U, -U, D and -D.

8.33 First of all, observe that by (7) each condition is down-compatible, hence in each linguistically detactable case collections and proper collections are coextensive, hence, by (EC), equal.

(46) *For any formula A,* $DC(A)$. *Therefore* $\forall y([x: A(x)]y \leftrightarrow A(y) \leftrightarrow \{x: A(x)\}y)$, *i.e.* $[x: A(x)] \equiv \{x: A(x)\}$, *hence* $[x: A(x)] = \{x: A(x)\}$.

Indeed, by (7), $\forall y(A(y) \to By)$. Therefore $\exists x \forall y(A(y) \to xy)$, i.e. DC($A$). Next, use axioms (C) and (CP) and logic.

8.34 In consequence, all appropriate ontological collections defined in § 4.18: B, $-B$, etc. are proper and co-extensive with suitable qualities:

(47) *For any y*: $By \leftrightarrow By$, $-By \leftrightarrow -By$, $Ny \leftrightarrow Ny$, $-Ny \leftrightarrow -Ny$, $Uy \leftrightarrow Uy$, $-Uy \leftrightarrow -Uy$, $Dy \leftrightarrow Dy$ *and* $-Dy \leftrightarrow -Dy$.

Therefore, by suitable theorems proved in **PTB**

(48) *i)* *B and -D are universal collections*: $B = OB = -D$,

  ii) *-B and D are empty*: $-B = \varnothing = D$; *whereas*

  iii) *N, -N, U, -U are intermediate, i.e., neither universal nor empty*: $\varnothing \neq N \neq OB$, *etc.*

Proof. Cases i) and ii) immediately follow from (7) and (16); whereas for iii) it suffices to remind oneself that NB, -N-B, UB and -U-B.

8.35 Return to the paradoxical quality -B. By the axioms of **PTB** it produces a legitimate collection $-B := \{x: -Bx\}$, which is empty and equal to $\{x: \neg\exists y\, yx\}$.

As was pointed out in §§ 7.8 and 7.13 simples cannot occur in **PTB** models. This means that in universes with qualitative simples the axiom (A2) must be cancelled.

In such cases delineation of simples, for example by the collection $\{x: \neg\exists y\, yx\}$, cannot be treated as *objective*, i.e. determined by quality which really *is* in the universe, but at best as purely subjective, *a priori*, delineation.

8.36 As regards ideas:

(49) *Four of them*: **B**, **-B**, **D** *and* **-D** *are, for general reasons, empty*.

Proof. By (7) and (16), qualities B and -D are universal, hence tolerate inconsistencies. Therefore, by (31), they must be empty.

On the other hand, qualities -B and D are empty. Hence, by (30), their conjugate ideas are also empty.

(50) *The idea of nonuniversality is empty as well*: $E(-U) = \varnothing$.

Proof. Notice first that its conjugate quality -U is known to be non-empty. For example: -U-B. Therefore, by (46), we should check only whether -U is up-compatible: UC(-U)?

It is not. Assume UC(-U), i.e., $\exists z \forall y$ (-Uy → yz). Fix this z. Therefore, *inter alia*, -U-B → -Bz. By the example mentioned previously and by detachment, -Bz. This, however, is in contradiction with the known **PTB** description of -B, which must be co-simple.

On the other hand

(51) *The idea of universality is not empty*: $E(U) \neq \varnothing$. *In particular, qualities of being and nondefectiveness participate in it*: **UB, U-D**.

Proof. For the first claim, it suffices to check up-compatibility of the quality U. By (A5), $\forall y$ (Uy → yx). Therefore, $\exists x \forall y$ (Uy → yx), i.e. UC(U), as required: As to the second claim, it suffices to remind ourselves that, by (7) and (16), both UB and U-D. Applying now (29) we obtain that UB and U-D.

Finally

(52) *Both the idea of nonemptiness and the idea of emptiness are empty*: $E(N) = \varnothing = E(-N)$.

Proof. As usual, it suffices to disprove an alleged up-compatibility of scrutinized ideas.
Assume first UC(N), i.e., $\exists x \forall y$ (Ny → yx). Fix this x. We know that both UB and -U-B, hence NU and N-U. Therefore Ux and -Ux, i.e., x is contradictory. This, however, itself contradicts the principle of noncontradiction.
Assume now UC(-N), i.e., $\exists x \forall y$ (-Ny → yx). Fix x. We know that nonbeing is empty: -N-B. Therefore -Bx, which, by (7), is impossible.

8.37 To resume: From the eight basic ontological ideas, only one idea is nonempty and instantiated. It is the idea of universality: **U**.

It clearly delineates the subrealm of general or universal beings, as items participating in it.

8.38 Now, it is easy to see reasons against that *ontological extensionalism* in which the investigation of abstract notions is reduced to investigation only of their extensions.

Indeed, the ideas of being and nonbeing, i.e., Being and Nonbeing or **B** and -**B**, by (49), are co-extensional. But they are transparently different, and differentiated even by (EI), because they are *not* coextensive. I.e., E(**B**) = E(-**B**), but ¬(B ≡ -B).

Extensionalism is simply too strong, and therefore must produce paradoxes, like the paradox to the effect that Being and Nonbeing are the same.

8.39 We now also see reasons for the reservations expressed in §§ 8.28 and 8.32.

In fact, (40) is not reversible, because as was pointed out just above, E(**B**) = E(-**B**), but ¬(B ≡ -B).

On the other hand, (45) is indeed correct. As we know, N*B* but -N*B*. Hence, *C**B** does not imply *C***B**, and also *C***B** does not imply *C**B**.

SUPPORTS AND FORMS

8.40 Finally, turn to the four general notions introduced in § 4.14, i.e., for arbitrary *x* the form, qualification, support and extension:

$$F(x) := [y{:}yx]$$
$$Q(x) := \{y{:}yx\}$$
$$S(x) := [y{:}xy]$$
$$E(x) := \{y{:}xy\}$$

First observe that by the two axioms of extensionality, (EC) and (EI), we have the following particular case of (41):

(53) F(x) = F(y) *iff* Q(x) = Q(y), *and* S(x) = S(y) *iff* E(x) = E(y):
Identity of forms is equivalent to identity of qualifications and identity of supports is equivalent to identity of extensions.

Whereas the first equivalence is rather difficult to apply because of lack at the present time of satisfactory knowledge of qualities characteristic to ideas and other objects studied here, the second one generates some interesting results.

8.41 To see this, notice that the supports of our eight ontological qualities are their corresponding ideas: $S(B) = B$, $S(-B) = -B$, $S(N) = N$, $S(-N) = -N$, $S(U) = U$, $S(-U) = -U$, $S(D) = D$ and $S(-D) = -D$.

Thus the logical relations, including identity and difference, between those ideas are, by (53), reduced to relations between appropriate extensions. But they, at least in part, are known:

(54) i) $E(B) = OB = E(-D)$

   ii) $E(-B) = \varnothing = E(D)$

   iii) *The remaining four extensions*: $E(N)$, $E(-N)$, $E(U)$ *and* $E(-U)$ *are neither empty nor full, and each of them is different from the remaining seven.*

Proof. Cases i) and ii) immediately follow by (7) and (16).

Ad iii): Consider first $E(N)$. It differs:

from $E(B) = E(-D)$, because $-B \in E(B) - E(N)$; from $E(-B) = E(D)$, because $B \in E(N) - E(-B)$; from $E(-N)$, for $B \in E(N) - E(-N)$; from $E(U)$, because $U \in E(N) - E(U)$; and from $E(-U)$, because $-D \in E(N) - E(-U)$.

Next, take $E(-N)$. It is neither empty, as $-B \in E(-N)$, nor full, for $-D \notin E(-N)$, hence it differs from four extensions considered in i) and ii). $E(-N) \neq E(N)$, by the example provided previously. $E(-N) \neq E(U)$, because $-N \in E(-N) - E(U)$; and $E(-N) \neq E(-U)$, because $N \in E(-U) - E(-N)$.

Finally, consider $E(U)$. It suffices to note that $E(U)$ differs from $E(-U)$, indeed they are in fact disjoint.

8.42 Applying now (53) we obtain

(55) i) $B = -D$ *and* $-B = D$,

   ii) $B, -B, N, -N, U, -U$ *differ one with another.*

Observe that the above situation is in full accordance with the model of § 7.25.

8.43 Taking into account the results of § 8.36, we obtain

(56) *The following seven ideas are coextensive*: $B \equiv -B \equiv N \equiv -N \equiv -U \equiv D \equiv -D$, *whereas the idea of universality* U *differs in extension from each of them.*

8.44 By the two previous claims we have that

(57) *In* **ETB** *coextensivity of ideas does not imply their identity.*

Indeed, by (EI), identity of ideas is equivalent not to their coextensivity, but to coextensivity of conjugate collections.

8.45 Consider, for example, Being and Nonbeing.

By (53) and (54), they are different: **B** ≠ -**B**, because the extension of their conjugate qualities differ one with another: $E(B) \neq E(-B)$.

But, by (49), both ideas are co-extensive, i.e. they have common extension: $E(\mathbf{B}) = E(-\mathbf{B})$.

In conclusion: **ETB** *is not an extensional theory.* Some objects, like **B** and -**B** are provably different in it, with, however, common extension.

8.46 Observe that Being and Nonbeing have the same support: $S(\mathbf{B}) = S(-\mathbf{B})$, provided the standard set-theoretical axiom of extensionality.

Indeed, by (53), $S(\mathbf{B}) = S(-\mathbf{B})$ iff $E(\mathbf{B}) = E(-\mathbf{B})$. But, under the above proviso, $E(\mathbf{B}) = \varnothing = E(-\mathbf{B})$, which entails the conclusion.

Query: Characterize the common support of Being and Nonbeing.

8.47 Last, but not least, consider forms.

The form of x, $F(x)$, is the unity of all its qualities or, in other terms, traits or determiners: $[y: yx]$. Is it a real, or coherent, unity? What is the participation in a form?

As a matter of fact, in general we know very little about forms. In **ETB**, however, we can answer both questions in the positive.

(58) *For each* x: i) *Its form,* $F(x)$, *is coherent; and*
ii) *Participation in the idea of* x *is equivalent to qualification or determination of* x: $F(x)y \leftrightarrow yx$.

Proof. For a form $F(x)$ its corresponding condition is $F_x(y):= yx$. By (7), it is, like any condition, down-compatible: $DC(F_x)$.

It is also up-compatible. This is so because $UC(F_x) := \exists u \forall y (F_x(y) \rightarrow yu)$, which is equivalent to $\exists u \forall y (yx \rightarrow yu)$. But this formula is a theorem of classical logic. Hence $UC(F_x)$.

In consequence, $F(x)$ is coherent, hence nonempty.

Applying now (29) we obtain: $F(x)y \leftrightarrow [z: zx]y \leftrightarrow yx$.

8.48 Notice that each universal quality is formal (in the ontological sense). That is

(59) *Universal qualities participate in all forms*: $\forall y \forall x (Uy \rightarrow F(x)y)$

INFINITY

8.49 As a matter of fact, there are quite a lot of forms, *a fortiori* quite a lot of ideas. Namely, infinitely many.

To see this first recall (53): $F(x) = F(y)$ *iff* $Q(x) = Q(y)$, which combined with Leibniz's Principle (LP) gives:

(60) $F(x) = F(y)$ *iff* $x = y$.

That is, *the mapping* $F: x \mapsto F(x)$ *is one-to-one.*

On the other hand, by (58), *each form is a coherent, i.e. nonempty, idea.*

Consider now the family of all objects OB, i.e. the full ontological universe, and its subcollection FM containing all forms. Clearly

(61) FM *is a proper subcollection of* OB: $FM \subset OB$.

Proof. Take, for example, the idea **B**. By (49), **B** is empty. Therefore it is an object which does not belong to FM.

In conclusion, there is *one-to-one* mapping F of the ontological universe OB *onto* its *proper* subcollection FM; $F: OB \mapsto FM$.
Therefore

(62) *The ontological universe* OB *is infinite in the Bolzano-Dedekind sense.*

But FM itself is equinumerous with OB. Hence also

(63) *The family of all forms* FM *is infinite.*

8.50 The above infinity results are rather unexpected in purely ontological research (cf. Russell 1919). Therefore its proof deserves scrutinization.

First of all, the results are not immediate. In a sense, the main body of **ETB** is used in the proof.

Indeed, in the proof that the mapping F is one-to-one all three axioms of extensionality: (EC), (E) and (LP) were used. On the other hand, to prove that FM is a proper subcollection of OB we used (58), which depends on (7) as well as on (49), which in turn depends on classical logic and the axiom (U).

Therefore the axiomatic background of the proof is as follows: classical logic, **PTB** axioms (A1) and (A2), the unification axiom (U), Leibniz's Principle (LP) and both axioms of extensionality: (EC) and (EI).

8.51 Notice that by (62) models of the theory outlined above, *a fortiori* models of **ETB**, are infinite.

8.52 Axioms of extensionality, which play such an essential role in our proof, are usually considered as reducing the size of their domain.

Therefore, the ontological universe seems to be infinite also without extensionality axioms, provided that forms are still present in it.

Query: Prove or disprove this hypothesis.

FINAL REMARKS

8.53 The being, i.e. the universe of beings is very broad indeed. Hence its idea is also very general. Too general to be nonempty.

But some ideas are nonempty. Moreover, ideas are interrelated by means of logical relations between appropriate conditions. Hence in the realm of *non empty* ideas some ideas are more general than others.

Therefore we can and should search after regions of the being which are *metaphysically coherent*, i.e., such that their objects participate in common (or compatible) ideas.

8.54 From a metaphysical point of view, a *possible world* is any region of the being which is maximal with respect to participation in ideas.

8.55 I would like to finish the present study of being by asking certain simple questions which are, for sure, easier to ask than to answer:

What is the idea or ideas delineating the real world?

Is it the idea of reality, or the idea of existence, or both?

Are these two ideas different?

Which is their relation to the only nonempty idea among the basic ontological ideas: the idea of universality?

9. Parmenidean Statements Reconsidered and Classical Questions Answered

9.1 Parmenidean statements concern the status of being and nonbeing: *being is, being is not, etc.*

Previously *three* variants of being were distinguished. A particular being, say *a being x*: B*x*, *the being*: *B* and *Being*: **B**. Similarly for nonbeing: *a nonbeing x* (-B*x*), *the nonbeing -B*, and *Nonbeing* **-B**.

My plan is to use the above distinctions to express in our formal language different versions of the Parmenidean statements and next to discuss them.

9.2 Variables denote objects. Beings are qualified objects, whereas nonbeings are objects without qualities. I.e., the variable *x* varies over the *full* ontological universe OB. Its restriction to the (improper) subuniverse of *beings* is made by means of the objectivum B, whereas the restriction to the (empty) subuniverse of nonbeings is made by means of the objectivum -B.

The remaining relevant concepts: *B, -B,* **B** and **-B** are four objects distinguished within the realm OB.

9.3 B is, above all, an objectivum. It is made from the verb 'to be' by the gerundial construction: *being = be + ing*.

According to the analysis provided in chapters 4, 5 and 6 it has several readings. B*x*, in its primary use, means: *x is*, which through paraphrasing becomes: *x is be-ing* or, as I prefer to say, *x is in being*. This, in qualitative ontology, is clarified by: *x is a being*.

9.4 The basic principle of qualitative ontology is therefore:

(QB) *x is iff x is in being iff x is a being*

9.5 Analogously, *Bx* means: *x is the being,* whereas the standard reading of **B***x* is: *x is Being*.

9.6 Similarly for negative phrases.

-B*x* means, primarily, that *x is not*. Via paraphrases analogous to those made in the case of B, it is also read: *x is in nonbeing* or *x is a nonbeing*.

-Bx means: *x is the nonbeing*, whereas **-B***x*: *x is Nonbeing*.

9.7 With this key it is easy to find formulas expressing Parmenidean statements.

'Being is' is, depending which kind of being is taken into account, either BB or B*B* or **BB**.

'Being is not' is either -BB or -B*B* or -**BB**.

'Nonbeing is' is either B-B or B-*B* or B-**B**.

'Nonbeing is not' is either -B-B or -B-*B* or -**B**-**B**.

9.8 By the above paraphrases we have the following unfolding of the basic Parmenidean statements:

A being is	*iff*	*A being is in being*
	iff	*A being is a being*
A being is not	*iff*	*A being is in nonbeing*
	iff	*A being is a nonbeing*
A nonbeing is	*iff*	*A nonbeing is in being*
	iff	*A nonbeing is a being*
A nonbeing is not	*iff*	*A nonbeing is in nonbeing*
	iff	*A nonbeing is a nonbeing*
The being is	*iff*	*The being is in being*
	iff	*The being is a being*
The being is not	*iff*	*The being is in nonbeing*
	iff	*The being is a nonbeing*
The nonbeing is	*iff*	*The nonbeing is in being*
	iff	*The nonbeing is a being*
The nonbeing is not	*iff*	*The nonbeing is in nonbeing*
	iff	*The nonbeing is a nonbeing*
Being is	*iff*	*Being is in being*
	iff	*Being is a being*
Being is not	*iff*	*Being is in nonbeing*
	iff	*Being is a nonbeing*
Nonbeing is	*iff*	*Nonbeing is in being*
	iff	*Nonbeing is a being*
Nonbeing is not	*iff*	*Nonbeing is in nonbeing*
	iff	*Nonbeing is a nonbeing*

9.9 Observe the metaphysical tenor of the equivalences made above and, in turn, some virtues of our formalism.

The formalism of **PTB** and **ETB** indeed enables us to answer which of the statements under scrutiny is true. On the other hand, it also makes for fluency in dealing with these rather obscure metaphysical formulas.

9.10 To see this, let us scrutinize the positive Parmenidean statement 'Being is'. As we know, this has at least three variants, one for each of the three sorts of being. In addition, two versions of it should be distinguished: *ontological* and *logical*.

9.11 In the ontological version the predicate 'is' has a purely ontological meaning: *to be* means *to be in being*, which is expressed by means of the objectivum B.

But, by (7), we know that *everything is*: $\forall x Bx$.

Therefore, by (QP), *everything is in being* or *everything is a being*.

A fortiori, being of each sort is a being. Among others, BB: *being itself is* or *being is in being* or *being is a being*.

Furthermore, B*B*: *The being is*, or *the being is a being*. Also, B**B**: *Being is*, for *it*, like everything, *is in being* or *is a being*.

And, in the case of nonbeing, B-B: *nonbeing is*, B-*B*: *the nonbeing is*, and B-**B**: *Nonbeing is* (sic!)

9.12 The logical, or quantifier version says: *Whatever is, is*. Or: *Whatever is, is in being*. Or: *Whatever is, is a being*.

This is a bit ambiguous. It either says 'Whatever is a being, is (a being)': $\forall x(Bx \rightarrow Bx)$.

Or it could be understood as 'Whatever is an object, is (a being)': $\forall x Bx$.

Both versions, in fact, are true: the first by classical logic, whereas the second is true by **PTB**.

9.13 Consider now forms using *B* and **B** instead of B.

9.13.1 As we know, *Bx* means: *x is the being*.

It is also ambiguous. Its ontological reading, developed in **PTB** says: *x is in the being*, which, by axiom (C), is equivalent to B*x*, i.e., *x is a being*.

Hence, again by (7), *everything is in the being*: $\forall x Bx$. *A fortiori*, B*B*: *being is in the being*, B*B*: *the being is in the being*, and B**B**: *Being is in the being*.

Similarly for the three sorts of nonbeing.

On the other hand, the logical version of Bx stresses the identity-reading. I.e., x *is the being* means x *is identical with the being*: Bx iff $x = B$.

This is so because B is a distinguished object of the universe.

It is easy to see that in the logical version the claim that *everything is the being* as well as the claim that *each being is the being*, etc. implies a weak monistic thesis: *there is at most one object.*

Indeed, the first claim is simply $\forall x(x = B)$; whereas the second one is $\forall x(Bx \rightarrow x = B)$, which, by (7) is also equivalent to $\forall x(x = B)$.

In conclusion, the logical version of the statement 'x is the being' can easily be used to entail a monistic thesis.

9.13.2 As regards Bx, which means: x is Being, notice first that its ontological explication says that x *participates in Being*.

In **ETB**, by (49), we have that nothing participates in Being, hence all suitable *positive* Parmenidean statements are false.

The logical reading of Bx says: x *is the same as Being*. Therefore, claims like 'Everything is Being' or 'Each being is Being', interpreted logically, imply monism; wheras under the ontological reading they imply contradiction.

9.14 Passing to the negative statements:

9.14.1 In **PTB**, *nothing is not*: $\neg \exists x\text{-}Bx$, because, by (7), *everything is*: $\forall x Bx$.

A fortiori, all negative Parmenidean statements under the ontological interpretation are false.

9.14.2 The logical version of 'Nonbeing is not' is: *Whatever is not, is not.*

This is a quantifier statement which, in virtue its inherent ambiguity, can be formalized in one of the following three ways:

(i) *Whatever is not an object, is not*: $\forall x(x \text{ is not an object} \rightarrow \neg Bx)$.

The notion of an object is, however, the most general of all, i.e., everything is an object. Therefore, the antecedent of (i) is false, hence, by classical logic, the implication (i) is valid.

(ii) *Any object which is not, is not*: $\forall x(\neg Bx \rightarrow \neg Bx)$.

It, like the first formalization of the appropriate positive formula (cf.§ 9.12), is a classical tautology.

And, finally, a purely logical reading:

(iii) *For no x, x is not*: $\neg \exists x \neg Bx$, which is equivalent to $\forall x Bx$, i.e., UB.

This formalization, like the second one in § 9.12, is a theorem of **PTB**.

9.15 The positive and the negative Parmenidean statements in their *logical* versions are formalizable in *two equivalent* ways. They are either classically true or equivalent to the theorem of **PTB**: UB.

This equivalence was recognized, among others, by Leibniz, but not by Kant. Recall that Leibniz was using[10] only the positive version of the logical Parmenidean principle, indicating it as one of the few basic principles of human knowledge. About eighty years later Kant used[11] both versions introducing them as *two* different axioms of his precritical metaphysics.

However, by classical logic, Kant's distinction is only verbal, because both versions are equivalent.

9.16 Finally, I am going to answer the classical ontological questions of chapter 5.

Ad Q1. Yes: *Being is*, in each version and variant considered in the present paper. In particular: *Beings are.*
Also: *The nonbeing is.* And, *Nonbeing is,* But, *nonbeings are not.*

Ad Q2. Yes: *Each variant of being has content*, for *everything has a content*:
$\forall x \, B \in Q(x)$.
N.B., nonbeings have empty content by definition, but there is no nonbeing.

Ad Q3. Yes: *The quality* B 'to be in being' *is universal.*

Ad Q4. Yes: *Some objects are universal.* For example, B is universal: UB.

Ad Q5. Emphatically yes. Being is well-defined and, as the theory shows, a nontrivial object.

9.17 As regards the argument against categoremacity of being, pointed out in § 5.12, observe that:
The most general notion in the given ontological framework, in our case the notion of *an object*, must be syncategorematic. Indeed, it is used like a general variable. Hence it can be defined only contextually, by use. An essential definition is not available, because any such definition must refer to at least one more general, or at least one foreign, term. This, however, is impossible in the

---

[10] Cf. Leibniz 1969.
[11] Cf. Kant 1986.

ontological framework, due to its extreme generality and, in consequence, to the most general status of its basic notion.

Someone can try to apply the same argument to other universal notions, among others to the notion of being. It indeed, by (7), is universal.

In vain, however. Universality is not generality. The notion of a being is in virtue of its definition not the most general notion. It was defined by means of the notion of ontological connection, which in the framework of **PTB** is more primitive, hence a *more general*, notion.

The notion of a being is universal, i.e., it qualifies any object. It was found to be such by means of a calculation, relying on classical logic and referring to the primitive notion of **PTB**, i.e., the notion of ontological connection.

Therefore, the notion of a being as well as the two subsequent notions of being are categorematic, though universal.

10. Summary

10.1 In the main, the present essay is an exercise in qualitative ontology.
To solve questions arising in traditional ontology two formal theories of being were introduced: **PTB** devoted to the quality 'to be a being' considered as an object; and its extension **ETB**, introducing formalism necessary to deal with abstract concepts of being.

10.2 The chief result of **PTB** is that everything is a being, hence nothing is a nonbeing.

As regards **ETB**, its remarkable contribution is, I think, the characterization of ideas and participation, with the main observation that nothing participates in ideas which are too general, that their extensions are empty. In particular, nothing participates in the idea of being, in spite the fact that everything is a being.

As by-product we obtain that forms are coherent, hence nonempty, ideas and, in consequence, that the ontological universe is infinite.

10.3 As regards Parmenidean statements it was shown *inter alia*:
That beings are in being.
That the being, as well as the nonbeing, is a being; hence both of them are in being.
That Being, as well as Nonbeing, is a being; hence both of them are in being.

10.4 Hence, in the light of logic, the way of truth is:

Being is and Nonbeing is;
beings are, but nonbeings are not.

Acknowledgments

The paper covers the first two of the five topics of my lectures 'A Theory of Qualities' read at the International Summer School in Philosophy, 'Formal Ontology', Bolzano, Italy, July 1-5, 1991. Its first version was presented at the University of Trento in May 1990.

The first draft of the paper was prepared during my stay at Universidade Federal da Paraiba, João Pessoa, PB, Brasil. The support of the CNPq grant no. 30.0095/90 is thankfully acknowledged. Its final version was written during my stay at the Internationale Akademie für Philosophie im Fürstentum Liechtenstein, prepared as a part of a project sponsored by the Swiss National Foundation for Scientific Research on the topic 'Formal Ontological Foundations of Artificial Intelligence Research'. Thanks go both to the SNF and the IAP for their support and hospitality.

I would like particularly to thank Prof. Matias F. Dias and Prof. Barry Smith for their kind invitations and providing me in both places with excellent conditions to work.

I also owe thanks to a number of scholars, in particular C. Gorzka, A. Pietruszczak, R. Poli, P. Simons and B. Smith for inspiring remarks, as well as I. Bodnàr, R. Lüthe, B. Mezei and R. Olvera-Mijares for discussions concerning linguistic mysteries of the verb 'to be'.

Last, but not least, I like to thank Cz. Porębski for his friendly help.

References

Bodnàr, I.M. et al. (eds) 1988a: *Intensional Logic, History of Philosophy and Methodology* , Budapest.

Bodnàr, I.M. 1988b: "Parmenides B2.3 and 5: The Implications of a Degenerate Case", in Bodnàr 1988a, 121-125.

Bolzano, B. 1975: *Gesamtausgabe, Bd.7: Einleitung zur Grossenlehre und erste Begriffe der allgemeinen Grossenlehre*, Friedrich Fromann Verlag, Stuttgart.

Bolzano, B. 1914-5: *Wissenschaftslehre*, 2 Bde, Felix Meiner Verlag, Leipzig.

Bormann, K. 1971: *Parmenides: Untersuchungen zu den Fragmenten*, Felix Meiner Verlag, Hamburg.

Brückner, A. 1970: *Słownik etymologiczny języka polskiego*, Wiedza Powszechna, Warszawa.

Burkhardt, H. and Smith, B. (eds.) 1991: *Handbook of Metaphysics and Ontology*, Philosophia Verlag, München.

Burnet, J. 1957: *Early Greek Philosophy*, Meridan Books, New York.

Diels, H. 1906: *Die Fragmente der Vorsokratiker*, Weidmannsche Buchhandlung, Berlin.

Fraenkel, A.A., Bar-Hillel, Y., Levy, A. and Dalen, D. van 1973: *Foundations of Set Theory*, Amsterdam.

Heidegger, M. 1961: *An Introduction to Metaphysics*, trans. by R.Manheim, Anchor Books, Doubley & Co. Inc., New York.

Kahn, Ch. H. 1973: *The Verb ' Be' in Ancient Greek*, Reidel Publ. Co., Dordrecht.

Kant, I. 1986: *Kant's Latin Writings,* Translations, Commentaries and Notes by Lewis White Beck. In collaboration with Mary J.Gregor et al., Peter Lang, New York.

Kisielewicz, A. 1989: "Double Extension Set Theory", *Reports on Mathematical Logic* 23, 81-89.

Kirk, G.S. and Raven, J.E. 1957: *The Presocratic Philosophers*, Cambridge University Press, Cambridge.

Leibniz, G.W. 1969: *Philosophical Papers and Letters*, A Selection Translated and Edited, with an Introduction by Leroy E. Loemker, D. Reidel Publ. Co., Dordrecht.

Leśniewski, S. 1991a: *Collected Works*, Kluwer, Dordrecht / Boston / London, 2 vol.

Leśniewski, S. 1991b: "On the Foundations of Mathematics", in Leśniewski 1991a, 174-382.

Łukasiewicz, J. 1910: *O zasadzie sprzeczności u Arystotelesa*, Wyd. Akademii Umiejętności w Krakowie, Kraków.

Mendelson, E. 1979: *Introduction to Mathematical Logic*, 2nd ed., D. van Nostrand Co., New York.

Munitz, M.K. (ed.) 1973: *Logic and Ontology*, New York University Press, New York.

SOED: *The Shorter Oxford English Dictionary*, 3rd ed., Clarendon Press, Oxford.

Owens, J. 1973: "The Content of Existence", in Munitz 1973, 21-35.

Paśniczek, J. (ed.) 1992: *Theories of Objects: Meinong and Twardowski*, KUL, Lublin.

Pelletier, F.J. 1990: *Parmenides, Plato, and the Semantics of Not-Being*, The University of Chicago Press, Chicago.

Perzanowski, J. 1988: "Byt", *Studia Filozoficzne* 6/7 (271/72), 63-85.

Perzanowski, J. 1989: *Logiki modalne a filozofia*, The Jagiellonian University Press, Kraków.

Perzanowski, J. 1990: "Ontologies and Ontologics", in Zarnecka-Biały 1990, 23-42.

Perzanowski, J. 1991: "Ontological Arguments II - Cartesian and Leibnizian", in Burkhardt and Smith 1991, 625-633.

Perzanowski, J. 1993a: "A Theory of Qualities and Substance I: The Ontological Theorem" (in preparation).

Perzanowski, J. 1993b: "A Theory of Qualities and Substance II: Elements of Elementologic" (in preparation).

Perzanowski, J. 1993c: "Ideas" (in preparation).

Perzanowski, J. 1993d: *Badania Onto-Logiczne* (in preparation).

Plato 1961: *Collected Dialogues*, ed. by E. Hamilton and H. Cairns, Princeton University Press.

Poli, R. 1992: "Twardowski and Wolff', in Paśniczek 1992, 45-56.

Quine, W.V.O. 1953a: *From a Logical Point of View, Logico-Philosophical Essays*, Harvard University Press, Cambridge Mass.

Quine, W.V.O. 1953b: "On What There Is", in Quine 1953a, 1-19.

Rijk, L.M. de 1986: *Plato's Sophist. A Philosophical Commentary*, North-Holland Publ. Co., Amsterdam.

Rosen, S. 1983: *Plato's Sophist*, Yale University Press.

Russell, B. 1919: *Introduction to Mathematical Philosophy*, Allen and Unwin, London.

Scholz, H. 1941: *Metaphysik als strenge Wissenschaft,* Staufen Verlag, Cologne.

Taràn, L. 1965: *Parmenides*: *A Text with Translation, Commentary and Critical Essays,* Princeton Univ.Press.

Tatarkiewicz, W. 1958: *Historia Filozofii,* PWN, Warszawa.

Twardowski, K. 1894: *Zur Lehre vom Inhalt und Gegenstand der Vorstellungen. Eine psychologische Untersuchung,* Hölder, Wien.

Zarnecka-Biały, E. (ed.) 1990: *Logic Counts,* Kluwer Academic Publishers, Dordrecht-Boston-London.

FRED SOMMERS

EXISTENCE AND CORRESPONDENCE-TO-FACT*

I

In the early portions of this paper I review the central teaching of modern analytic philosophy on existence, whose negative doctrine derives from Kant and whose positive doctrine derives from Frege. I show how Frege's view, that existence is a property of concepts, is inhospitable to the classically realist conception of truth as correspondence to reality. I proceed to examine the principal argument for judging the idea of correspondence-to-fact to be 'an idea without content', pointing out that this judgment is an illegitimate extension of Kant's thesis that predications of existence are otiose and without content. I present a theory of fact based on a classical (non Fregean) conception of existence as a property of reality and argue that facts, so construed, serve for the ontological relatum of traditional correspondence theories of truth. Later sections compare the theory presented with several theories popular in Anglo-American philosophy on such topics as demonstratives, belief and the role of context in determining propositional content.

FREGE'S LEGACY

1.1. In refuting the ontological argument, Kant argued successfully that the existence of an omnipotent being was not an attribute on a par with its omnipotence. More generally, if x is a Q-thing then its Q-ness is a nontrivial property of x, but its existence is not. Kant's arguments are by now familiar: thinking of a sleeping snow leopard as existing is not different from thinking of a snow

---

* I am grateful to George Englebretsen, Eddy Zemach, Palle Yourgrau, Ted Denise, David Kelley and Glenn Branch for comments that led to improvements on earlier drafts.

R. Poli and P. Simons, Formal Ontology, 131–158.
© 1996 *Kluwer Academic Publishers. Printed in the Netherlands.*

leopard that is sleeping. Other ways of showing that 'existence is not a predicate' approach the topic from the negative side. We may truly say that 'Chinese snow leopards do not eat turnips'. But 'Mexican snow leopards do not exist' poses the problem known as Plato's Beard (an allusion to the need for trimming it with Occam's Razor). For we cannot coherently be ascribing a failure to exist to Mexican snow leopards.

In any case it is now accepted that just as the nonexistence of Mexican snow leopards is not a property of Mexican snow leopards, so the existence of Chinese snow leopards is not a property of Chinese snow leopards. Modern logic enforces this Kantian insight by rewriting 'snow leopards (do not) exist' in a way that removes existence from predicate position, giving it merely 'syncategorematic' status, in such paraphrases as 'there are no snow leopards' or 'there is an (no) x such that x is a snow leopard'.

1.2. Having paid syntactic tribute to the thesis that existence is not a property of the things denoted by the grammatical subject of ordinary sentences, analytic philosophy still faced the question of saying what existence *is*. For whatever one understands by *the existence of horses and the nonexistence of centaurs,* they are responsible for the truth of such synthetic statements as 'there are horses' and 'there are no centaurs'. So they must in some sense be 'nontrivial'. We need to characterize a nontrivial sense of existence and nonexistence responsible for truth and falsity. Another way of putting the question that Kant has left over is: 'if existence is not a property of the snow leopard, of what *is* it a property?

Frege has dealt with an analogous problem in his efforts to understand predications of number. For it was clear to him early on that predicating number of things that are (grammatically) numbered wouldn't do. For example, we speak of nine solar planets but being nine unlike being solar is not a property of the planets. Indeed Frege realized that the prohibition against attributing number to things that are numbered and the prohibition against attributing existence to the things that exist are one and the same. We do grammatically say that solar planets exist and that they are nine in number but in neither case do we have a property of the things that surface grammar is leading us to think is the subject of our predications. All the same, number, like existence, is nontrivially predicated and if not of the things that are numbered, then of what? Frege's answer is that both existence and number are predicated of concepts.

[E]xistence is analogous to number. Affirmation of existence is in fact nothing but the denial of the number nought. Because existence is a property of concepts the ontological argument for the existence of God breaks down.[1]

Note that Frege offers his positive doctrine of what existence is, while alluding to Kant's negative thesis on what existence is not. Frege learned much of his philosophy by attending to the logical form of sentences he rescued from the surface obfuscation of natural language. And Kant's negative thesis reinforces the doctrine that a general statement like 'an inhabited planet exists' is very unlike a singular statement such as 'The Earth is a planet'. In the singular statement, the subject 'Earth' denotes the Earth, and the predicate 'is a planet' denotes the concept PLANET; the statement is a claim that what the subject denotes falls under the concept denoted by the predicate. By contrast, the general statement, 'An inhabited planet exists', properly construed as 'there exists an inhabited planet', is about the concept denoted by 'is an inhabited planet'. The claim is that this concept is nonempty. (In logical syntax 'exists' is treated as a 'second level predicate', predicated of a concept denoted by a first level predicate.)

Frege's analysis of general statements had several attractive features that recommended it to perhaps the majority of analytic philosophers. (1) It accommodates Kant's skeptical view that existence is not a property of things that exist and does so in the canonical logical language. (2) It responds to our intuitions that existence must, in some sense, be a nontrivial property even though (as Kant had rightly insisted, not of the things that are said to exist). (3) It does this while trimming Plato's beard. For in saying that centaurs do not exist I am not talking about 'what is not' but about something that exists, attributing to the concept CENTAUR the property of having nothing fall under it (characterizing it as an empty concept).

Russell too recognized the need to explain existence in a positive way and his proposal was similarly constrained by the new logical notation that removed existence from predicate position. According to Russell "existence is essentially a property of a propositional functions" which, as he explained, "means that propositional function is true in at least one instance".[2] For example, 'horses exist' asserts that 'x is a horse' is true in at least one instance or that it is 'sometimes true'. Russell's proposal was entirely in the spirit of Frege but with the difference Russell had no theory of concepts and so seems to be

---

[1] Frege 1952, 53. For an excellent discussion of the doctrine that existence is an attribute of concepts see Williams 1981, ch. 2.

[2] Russell 1966b, 232 ff.

reduced to taking the propositional function itself as the subject for a predication of existence.

1.3. Note that neither Russell nor Frege can be taken literally when they say that they have found subjects for non-trivial predications of 'exists'. Frege, who takes concepts to be the subject, construes 'exists' as 'is nonempty'. In Russell, 'exists' becomes 'is sometimes true'. Thus both proposals are 'definitions in use' that offer paraphrases of existence in ways that may well strike one as not sufficiently attentive to the original definiendum.

Russell's approach proved unpopular for at least two reasons. First, it uses an undefined notion of truth in explaining existence. That seems wrong-headed since we normally think that what is true is so in virtue of what exists or does not exist. Second, treating propositional functions as the subject of predications of existence seems wrong. The truth of 'there are black holes in our galaxy' seems to be a matter of how the world is characterized, not how some propositional function is characterized.

Frege's concepts are real, eternal and independent of language. So his account is not vulnerable to the point made against Russell that existence must be language independent. Nevertheless that advantage is not unmixed; to accept Frege's positive conception of existence requires us to accept his platonist doctrine of mind-independent, language-independent eternal thoughts and concepts. Moreover, even if we do accept it, construing the existence of black holes as a property of a concept may appear unsatisfactory. Intuitively we think that it is the universe or 'reality' (and not some concept, however eternal) that is characterized by the existence of black holes.

The idea that the existence of horses characterizes reality is associated with the classical conception of truth according to which a statement is true if it 'agrees with' or 'corresponds' to reality. Russell was open-minded about correspondence conceptions of truth, but Frege rejected all such theories and with them the notion of ontological facts to which true statements correspond and which make them true. For Frege a 'fact' was just a true proposition, a true 'thought'. Let FACT be used for 'true proposition' or 'true thought'. Then the relation between my statement and a FACT is not one of correspondence and truth making, but of expression: my statement, if true, expresses a FACT. Frege's familiar 'compositional' account of how the statement satisfies the conditions for being true makes no appeal to truth-making facts. As for FACTS, it is far more correct to say that a statement's being true makes the thought it expresses a FACT, than to say that a thought's being a FACT renders the statement expressing it true. Frege is the father of modern philosophy of language and his influence prevailed. In the sections that follow, we shall see how some of the most influential philosophers of language came mistakenly to believe that correspondence theories are not merely false but unintelligible and 'without content' and to regard the very idea of an ontological facts to which true statements correspond logically absurd.

II

2.1. A classically realist account of truth holds that a true proposition corresponds to an objective, non linguistic relatum – a fact or state of affairs that makes it true. Correspondence theories have been discredited in part because Frege frowned on them but mainly because of the persistent failure on the part of correspondence theorists to coherently identify ontological facts and to specify their nature. In this part I present the principal argument for the thesis that correspondence theories must inevitably fail to come up with a coherent notion of the objective relatum of correspondence and I refute this in blunt Johnsonian fashion by offering an account in which facts are construed as existential properties of reality.

2.2. What makes a true statement true? Correspondence theories are in general disarray because this question has not been properly answered. Crucial to a correspondence theory of truth is an adequate account of the objective, nonlinguistic correlates (the facts or 'states of affairs') to which true propositions correspond. But the search for something in the world that could serve as the objective relata of correspondence has produced no plausible candidates. Philosophers from C.I. Lewis to Peter Strawson and Donald Davidson became convinced that such a search could not possibly succeed.

The failure to identify ontological facts was underscored in a famous debate some thirty-five years ago between Peter Strawson and John Austin in which Strawson criticized Austin's version of correspondence theory, persuasively showing that none of Austin's suggestions for the ontological relatum made any sense. Strawson argued that statements are not like names or descriptive expressions; those parts of the statement directs us to things in the world, but the statement as a whole does not:

That (person, thing, etc.) to which the referring part of the statement refers, and which the describing part of the statement fits or fails to fit, is that which the statement is *about*. It is evident that there is nothing else in the world for the statement itself to be related to... The only plausible candidate for (what in the world) makes statements true is the fact it states; but the fact it states is not something in the world... Roughly, the thing referred to is the material correlate of the statement... the fact to which the statement 'corresponds' is the pseudo material correlate of the statement as whole.[3]

If Strawson is right, truth realism cannot come up with the ontological facts it needs for correspondence. For the truth realist holds that the statement as a whole corresponds to a fact, an objective relatum that makes it true. Strawson concludes that "the demand that there should be such a relatum... is logically absurd".[4]

In *The Structure and Content of Truth* (given as The Dewey Lectures in 1989) Donald Davidson cites Strawson with approval and says that correspondence theories "cannot be made intelligible" and that we must "give up facts as entities that make sentences true". The real objection is that such theories fail to provide entities to which truth vehicles (whether we take these to be statements, sentences, or utterances) can be said to correspond. If this is right, and I am convinced it is, we ought to question the popular assumption that sentences or their speech tokens, or sentence like entities or configurations in our brains, can properly be called 'representations' since there is nothing for them to re-present.[5]

From the alleged incoherence of correspondence Davidson draws two conclusions. The first is the vacuity of metaphysical realism:

It is futile either to reject or to accept the slogan that the real and the true are 'independent of our beliefs'. The only evident positive sense we can make of this phrase, the only use that consorts with the intentions of those who prize it, derives from the idea of correspondence and this is an idea without content.[6]

The second is that theories of mental representations are otiose.

If we give up facts as entities that make sentences true, we ought to give up representations at the same time, for the legitimacy of each depends on the legitimacy of the other.[7]

These skeptical doctrines are taken to be consequences of Davidson's twofold conviction that truth-making nonlinguistic facts cannot possibly be found in the world and that only such facts will do for realism and correspondence. Davidson applauds C.I. Lewis for having "challenged the correspondence

---

[3] Strawson 1971b, 194-5.
[4] Strawson 1971b, 194.
[5] Davidson 1990, 304.
[6] Davidson 1990, 305.
[7] Davidson 1990, 304.

theorist to *locate* the fact, or part of reality, or of the world, to which a true statement corresponds". To deny that true judgments are made true by a mind-independent reality to which they correspond is to regard man, not reality as the measure of all truth. The judgment that correspondence-to-fact theories are essentially incoherent, has been especially effective in bringing influential philosophers of language into the camp of what Rorty calls the 'anti-repre-sentationalists', a term he applies to philosophers who do "not view knowledge as a matter of getting reality right, but rather as matter of acquiring habits of action for coping with reality".[8]

2.3. Davidson's and Rorty's harsh verdict leads one to wonder whether the original challenge to 'locate the facts' was not misplaced; one must suspect a challenge to produce X followed by the communiqué that X is not the sort of thing that could possibly be produced. Suspicion grows when one considers that any fact is either a fact of existence or a fact of nonexistence. The Lewis/ Strawson/Davidson requirement to locate something in the world that makes a true statement true is not sufficiently attentive to this feature of facts. For it is plain that the existence of gray whales is the fact that makes 'some whales are gray' true and that the nonexistence of orange whales is the fact that makes 'no whale is orange' true. So the truly challenging question concerning facts is the question left over from Kant's skepticism: What *do* such phrases as 'the existence of gray whales' and 'the nonexistence of orange whales' refer to? We shall find that the most straightforward answer puts one in a good position to see that those who announce the demise of correspondence are overly hasty. More to the point, a clear answer makes it plain that existence and nonexistence (of gray whales, of orange whales, etc.) are real properties, admirably suited for the truth-making role played by the objective, nonlinguistic correlates of a classical correspondence theory of truth.

3.1. Existence and nonexistence are nontrivial properties but, as Kant had advised, not of the things that are said to exist or not to exist. Just as the nonex-istence of elves is not a property of elves, so the existence of elks is not a prop-erty of elks. Of what else then? Since elk-existence and elf-nonexistence are facts this is tantamount to asking: What are facts? To 'both' questions the real-ists' answer is simple and direct: (the fact of) elk-existence and (the fact of) elf-nonexistence are properties of the world.

[8] Rorty 1991, 1.

THE WORLD'S EXISTENTIAL ATTRIBUTES

A world or domain is a totality of things existentially characterized by the presence in it or absence from it of certain constituents. For example, the contemporary world is characterized by the existence of birds and the nonexistence of dinosaurs. The domain of natural numbers is characterized by the existence of an even prime number and by the nonexistence of a greatest prime number. Tolkien's world is characterized by the presence of elves and the absence of elks. Anything in a domain under consideration is a thing, a mere 'existent', in the uninformative sense that Kant derided. In the *informative* sense, to exist or to fail to exist is to characterize the world by *specified* presence or absence. The existence of elks and the nonexistence of elves are properties of a world distinguished by the presence of elks and the absence of elves. Existence is then always Q-presence, non-existence, Q-absence. Quine's dictum, 'to be is to be the value of a variable', meets the condition of specified existence but falls short of recognizing that Q-existence is an attribute of the world. For example, Quine's existence is an attribute of the world: a world characterized by the nonexistence of Quine would be significantly different.

Call a domain that has (one or more) K (things) in it, '{K}ish'. Call a domain that has no J (things) in it, 'un{J}ish'. {K}ishness and un{J}ishness are attributes of that world. The real world is {Quine}ish but not {Loch Ness Monster}ish, {elk}ish but not {elf}ish. {Elk}ishness – the existence of elks – and un{elf}ishness – the nonexistence of elves – are mondial properties or 'states of affairs', which is to say, they are objective existential properties of the world.

Getting clear about existence and nonexistence as properties of totalities or domains is the decisive step to demystifying correspondence. For we then understand what it means to say that the existence of Quine and the nonexistence of Santa Claus are the facts that make true the statements 'Quine exists' and 'Santa Claus does not exist'. Holding fast to the doctrine that facts are mondial properties delivers us from temptation: we have got free of the thought that facts are something we might find in the world. The search for such 'facts' is indeed futile. To think of a thing's presence as present in the world is a 'category mistake'. Quine's presence is a fact but while Quine himself is present in the world, Quine's *presence* is not, no more so than Santa's absence. Quine's properties (e.g., his acumen, his pertinacity, his repute, etc.) may be thought of as being in the world but to look for the fact of his presence is to take a bite from Anselm's apple by thinking of Quine's existence as just another property of Quine.

Strawson rightly identified what is wrong with any In-World Correspondence Theory when he pointed out that to say a fact or state of affairs 'obtains' is not the same as saying it exists. The existence of mangy cats 'obtains'; for the traditional correspondence theorist, it is the fact signified by 'some cats are mangy'. The states that obtain – the presence and absence of things of various kinds – make true statements true. The existence of mangy cats in Maine is 'a state of affairs' that makes 'there are mangy cats in Maine' true. But *such* states of affairs are not situated anywhere; *they are states of the world, not states in the world.*

The positive and negative existential states of the world (its {elk}ishness, its {Quine}ishness, its un{elf}ishness, etc.) are the most suitable candidates for the facts of a traditional correspondence theory of truth. The world's existential states are the facts, the 'objective nonlinguistic correlates' of correspondence that 'make true statements true'. Elementary facts are positive or negative. The existence of elks makes 'there are elks' true, the nonexistence of an animal that eats no food is the elementary negative fact that makes 'every animal eats some food' true. The existence of elks and the nonexistence of animals that eat no food is the compound fact that makes the compound statement 'there are elks and every animal eats some food' true.

STATEMENTS, PROPOSITIONS, DOMAINS

3.2 A statement is an asserted sentence, which is to say, it is a sentence uttered as a claim about a given domain. A true statement signifies a fact, the world *characteristic* that makes it true. A false statement is vacuous with respect to signification: it fails to signify a fact. But any statement expresses a proposition that purports to characterize the domain under consideration. The proposition expressed is a mondial *characterization* that may or may not be true of the world (may or may not correspond to a mondial *characteristic*). Expressions denoting characteristics will be written in lower case letters. Expressions that denote characterizations will be written in upper case letters. For example, 'there are elks' expresses the proposition THAT THERE ARE ELKS (THE EXISTENCE OF ELKS, THERE BEING ELKS, {ELK}ISHNESS). This proposition, is a *characterization* that correctly characterizes ('is true of') the world. By contrast, the existence of elks (that there are elks, {elk}ishness), is a *characteristic*, a property that the world possesses. In the case of 'there are elks', the characterization expressed ({ELK}ISHNESS) corresponds to a (world) characteristic ({elk}ishness). In the case of 'there are elves', the false proposition, THERE BEING ELVES, does not correspond to any existential characteristic of the world.

THE DOMAIN UNDER CONSIDERATION

3.3 Any given statement or asserted utterance is a claim made with respect to some domain or 'universe of discourse'. We refer to the domain under consideration as the 'DC of the statement'. Where several statements are involved, for example as conjuncts in a conjunction or as premises of an argument, the DC is jointly determined; it is the universe common to the statements in that conjunction or argument. Broadly speaking, the context of utterance determines the DC. A DC may be fictional. In the context of a discussion on the fauna of Greek mythology I might say 'there are flying horses' and then add 'but there are no flying kangaroos' and my statements will have expressed propositions that correctly characterize the domain in question. The domain of 'some prime number is even' is the set of natural numbers; the claim is that this domain is {even prime}ish or, equivalently, that the EXISTENCE OF AN EVEN PRIME NUMBER obtains. Here, 'to obtain' is to be a FACT, i.e., to correctly characterize the domain. Equivalently, the existence of an even prime number obtains. Here 'to obtain' is to be a fact, a positive or negative existential characteristic of the domain.

Most commonly, the domain under consideration is the real world or some spatio-temporal part thereof. Saying that there are no longer any saber-toothed tigers I make an existential claim; my statement is true if the nonexistence of saber-toothed tigers is a characteristic of the real (contemporaneous) world. If (looking into a drawer) I say 'there's no screwdriver (here now)', the domain of the claim consists of the objects currently in the drawer and the claim is that the domain in question is characterized by the nonexistence of screwdrivers, that it is an un{screwdriver}ish domain.

4.1 We can now see why the Lewis-Strawson-Davidson challenge to correspondence was an improper challenge that could not possibly have been met by the truth realists. Strawson's arguments were well directed against Austin's misguided attempt to identify facts with 'historic situations' in the world. In-World correspondence theories are indeed untenable. Unfortunately, Strawson and Davidson believed that in putting paid to In-World theories they had put paid to all theories that postulate 'objective nonlinguistic' truth making facts, leaving us, as Davidson says, with "nothing interesting or instructive to which true statements might correspond".

Note that Strawson's and Davidson's verdict that the idea of an objective fact in the world was without content is very much like Kant's judgment on the idea of existence as a property of things on a par with other properties of things in the world. And, indeed, Davidson and Strawson have unwittingly *rediscovered* that ontological facts – the existence and nonexistence of things – cannot logically be thought of as being in the world. Unfortunately, they remained unaware that their negative judgment about facts was that rediscovery and so they failed to see that Kant's healthy skepticism concerning existence as a property of things in the world still left for analytic philosophy the challenge of specifying a *nontrivial* sense for the existence and nonexistence of things that serve as truth making facts. Lacking, as they thought, any 'plausible candidates' for the ontological side of correspondence, Strawson and Davidson prematurely concluded that correspondence was a mystifying, futile doctrine that needed to be abandoned. The idea that the facts of existence and nonexistence are truth making, nontrivial properties (not of things in the world but) of the world seems to have escaped them altogether.

A WORD ABOUT 'REPRESENTATIONS'

4.2 Davidson rightly understood that nothing in the world will serve as a truth making fact but he then went on to recommend that we give up facts as entities that make sentences true, and give up representations at the same time, "for the legitimacy of each depends on the legitimacy of the other".

The correspondence theorist will point out that nothing has been given up since the whole idea of correspondence as a 'mirror' to the facts is a mistake of those who have not got free of the idea that objective facts, if such there be, must be in the world. Both Davidson and Rorty connect the fate of 'representations' to the fate of truth making facts. Both therefore announce a double victory over the truth realist. Not only does he lose facts, he also loses 'representations' of them. But a classical correspondence theory tied to existence and nonexistence as nontrivial mondial attributes is unaffected on both counts. What we picture, represent or mirror must be something in the world. Elks are in the world but their presence is not. We can represent elks; we cannot represent their presence. Nor, *a fortiori*, can we represent the absence of elves. Elk-presence and elf-absence are objective nonrepresentable truth makers. The philosopher with a clear notion of fact as presence and absence is the last one to be tempted to think of propositional content as 'representing' the ontological correlate to which it 'corresponds'. Rorty's and Davidson's objections to a 'mirror' semantics thus miss their primary target.

5.1 THERE BEING ELKS is a *proposition*, an existential characterization applicable to the world. By contrast, BEING AN ELK is an ordinary characterization applicable to things in the world. The correspondence between propositions (mondial characterizations) and facts (mondial characteristics) is better understood by attending to the more familiar correspondence that holds between the characterizations of things in the world (e.g. BEING WISE, BEING AN ELK) and the characteristics of those things (wisdom, elkhood).

The true statement

(1) Being wise characterizes Socrates

may be construed as being about a characteristic that Socrates possesses or about a characterization that may or may not be true of Socrates. In these two construals 'being wise' and 'characterizes' are given different readings.

(1a) BEING WISE is a (correct) characterization of Socrates.
(1b) *Being wise* (wisdom) is a characteristic of Socrates.

Versions of (1b) include 'wisdom characterizes Socrates', '*being wise* is an attribute (property) of Socrates' and Aristotle's '*[being] wise* belongs to Socrates'. Versions of (1a) include 'BEING WISE is true of Socrates' and 'Socrates falls under the concept (BEING) WISE'.[9]

The two construals correspond to distinct ways in which a *term* of a statement is said to be a characterizing expression. In 'Socrates is wise' the term 'wise' will be said to *express* BEING WISE and to *signify* wisdom. We also say that 'wise' *denotes* what 'wise' characterizes (in either sense).

More generally, we may distinguish three modes of meaning of a term. We say that 'Q' *expresses* BEING Q, reading the upper case 'BEING Q' as a phrase

---

[9] Cf. Frege 1977b. In Frege's semantics, a predicate expresses a sense and denotes a concept. The present paper does not recognize a 'real distinction' between concepts and senses. Considered linguistically what a term (sentence) expresses is a 'sense' ('proposition'). Considered epistemically the sense is a 'concept' ('thought'). (The concept must again be virtually distinguished from its mental representation.) A concept or thought is the content I grasp or understand when I grasp or understand a term or sentence. Frege half agrees: though he distinguishes sense and concept for predicates, he agrees that the sense of a sentence is a Thought. The asymmetry is odd.

that refers to a characterization and calling BEING Q the *sense* or *expressive meaning* of 'Q'. We say that 'Q' *signifies* Q-ness or being Q, reading the lower case expression, 'Q-ness' or 'being Q', as a phrase that refers to a characteristic, property or state (the property of Q-ness, the state of being Q) and calling this property the *signification* of 'Q'. And we say that 'Q' *denotes* something that has Q-ness and is correctly characterized as being Q.

Signifying is like denoting; if no one is wise, there is no wisdom and 'wise' is doubly vacuous: it neither signifies a property nor denotes a thing. By contrast, expressing is not subject to vacuity; any meaningful term *expresses* a characterizing sense. Thus 'wise' cannot fail to express BEING WISE. 'Elf' expresses BEING AN ELF although it fails to signify the characteristic of elfhood or being an elf.

The following equivalence states the relation between the expressive and signifying modes of characterization embodied in (1a) and (1b):

BEING Q characterizes *x* iff being Q is a characteristic of *x*.

5.2 We are adopting the view that 'nothing is perfect' entails 'there is no such thing as perfection'. Platonizing philosophers may disagree but others will be content to recognize that denying that the characteristic of perfection exists does not threaten the existence of PERFECTION or BEING PERFECT as a characterization. We assume, then, that such things as being winged or being an elk exist but that 'unhad' properties like being a winged horse or being an elf do not exist.[10]

Suppose nothing in the domain of the claim has the characteristic of Q-ness. Then 'Q' expresses BEING Q, a characterization that characterizes nothing. It is like a representational painting that 'portrays' a subject that is not a portrait of anything or anyone. (By contrast, a photograph is not 'vacuous'; it is a photograph of something or someone 'denoting' its subject and 'signifying' some of its visual properties.) The 'meaning' of a representational picture has a kind of objectivity. So too does the characterization expressed by a meaningful term. The sense or expressive meaning of a term is public. It is cognitively available. As such it exists.

Nevertheless the sense that conventionally attaches to a term is not objectively on a par with the property, if any, that it signifies. What a term like 'gold' denotes and signifies is not the product of human convention: gold and its properties are independently objective. What a term expresses could not

---

[10] According to A.J. Freddoso this view is Ockhamist: "[Ockham's] theory of predication presupposes only the existence of individual substances and [their] qualities". Ockham 1980, 1.

exist independently of linguistic convention but for that very reason, the expression of a sense is not subject to being vacuous. In saying that 'unicorn' expresses BEING a UNICORN, 'expresses' is an internal accusative: 'unicorn' can no more fail to express the characterization that is its sense than a unicorn picture can conventionally fail to portray a unicorn. The sense or expressive meaning of 'unicorn' is in this way analogous to the 'meaning' of a unicorn-picture. Both meanings are characterizations, the one visual and depictive, the other linguistic and descriptive. Both could be used to discriminate, designate or denote a thing or kind of thing that satisfies the characterization. As it happens, there is no such thing.

To summarize: If 'Q' is a term in a statement, let '[Q]' stand for the characterization it expresses and let '<Q>' stand for the characteristic, if any, that 'Q' signifies. 'Q', is meaningful in three ways:

1. It expresses a characterization, [Q], that may or may not be true of something in the world.
2. It may signify a characteristic, <Q>. [Q] is then true of what has <Q>. Also, [Q] may then be said to correspond to <Q>.
3. It may denote a Q thing (in which case it signifies the characteristic, <Q>, that the Q-thing possesses).

[A term is also said to have an extension, defined as the set of things that possess the property signified by the term. In many contexts of its use, a given term will not denote everything in its extension. For example, in the syllogism 'every don is literate, some dons are fools; so some fools are literate' the middle term 'don' denotes some dons in the minor premise and all dons in the major (where it is said to be 'distributed'). It signifies being a don in both premises. We are concerned with terms in use. Unlike denoting or signifying, 'extending' is not something a term in a statement does; it is not, in that sense, a 'mode of meaning'.]

THE MEANING OF STATEMENTS

6.1 What has been said about the meaning of terms applies as well to statements. Consider 'something is a Q'. Corresponding to the distinction between the characterization, BEING Q, and the characteristic, *being Q* or Q-ness, we have the distinction between THE EXISTENCE OF Q, a propositional characterization or content that may or may not characterize or be true of the world, and *the existence of Q* (or {Q}-ishness), a fact or state of affairs that is a characteristic of the world.

The statement 'something is a Q' does *two* things:

1. It expresses the proposition *that something is a Q* (the existential, mondial characterization: SOMETHING BEING A Q, the EXISTENCE OF A Q, THERE BEING A Q THING, {Q}ISHNESS).
2. It claims that SOMETHING BEING A Q characterizes the domain under consideration. As in the case of terms, the relation between the expressive and signifying meaning of a statement holds:

The proposition, SOMETHING BEING A Q ({Q}ISHNESS), characterizes the world (is true, is a FACT) iff the existence of a Q ({Q}ishness) is a characteristic of the world (is a fact). ([s] is a FACT iff <s> is a fact.)

[Any statement (asserted sentence) is a truth claim but truth is primarily a property of the proposition expressed by the statement: to say that 's' is true is to say that [s] is true of the DC of 's'. The DC, which is fixed by the context of assertion, is merely the venue of the truth claim; it plays no part in the proposition expressed for which truth is claimed. For example, 'there's a screwdriver' expresses THERE BEING A SCREWDRIVER. Neither the place nor the time of assertion figures in the propositional content.[11]]

WHAT TRUE STATEMENTS DENOTE

6.2 FACTS correspond to facts. This gives us two ways of stating the truth conditions for a statement:

's' is true if and only if 's' expresses a FACT.
's' is true if and only if 's' signifies a fact.

Any statement makes a claim about a domain. Just as some nonvacuous term, K, signifes a characteristic (being K) and denotes a thing that has the characteristic in question (a K thing), so a true statement, which expresses a true characterization and signifies a fact or world characteristic, denotes the world so characterized. This gives us a *third* way of stating the truth conditions of a statement:

's' is true if and only if 's' denotes its domain.

[11] A statement is an utterance that 'says something'. In the strict sense 'what is said' is simply the existential characterization; it is the proposition expressed by the utterance. In another sense, the domain figures in specifying 'what is said' as a truth claim on the domain under consideration. Let [p] be what is expressed by 'p' and let D be the domain (as fixed by the context in which 'p' is asserted). Then to say that K said that p is to say that K claims that [p] characterizes D. Here 'what is said' is a complex in which the context of assertion that fixes the domain has played a specifying role.

True statements denote the world. False statements are vacuous; they fail to denote the world.

Different true statements, like different nonvacuous terms, signify different characteristics. In 'An Athenian philosopher who influenced Plato was snub-nosed', the nonvacuous terms 'Athenian philosopher' and '(someone) who in-fluenced Plato' signify different characteristics but both denote Socrates. So too, the true statements 'some Eskimos are Danish citizens' and 'no Albanian is an astronaut' signify different (existential world) characteristics, different facts, but both statements denote one and the same world.[12]

6.3 The key elements in the above account of statement meaning and truth conditions are:

'*s*' (a statement or asserted sentence),
[*s*] (the proposition THAT S; the proposition expressed by '*s*'),
<*s*> (the fact, if any, that *s*),
W (the World).

In the favorable case these elements are related as follows:
[*s*] characterizes W (is true of W, 'obtains', is a FACT or true proposition),
<*s*> is a characteristic of W (is a fact),
[*s*] corresponds to <*s*> ,
'*s*' signifies <*s*>,
'*s*' denotes W,
'*s*' is true.

In the unfavorable case,
[*s*] does not characterize W (is not a FACT, is false),
there is no such thing as <*s*>,
[*s*] does not correspond to any fact,
'*s*' does not denote W (fails to denote),
'*s*' is false.

---

[12] In a system of propositional logic, all true statements uniquely denote a common do-main; any compound statement can therefore be construed as a categorical claim about the world. For example, '$p \land q$' can be understood as the claim 'some p (world) is a q (world)'. Since only one world is in question 'some p (world) is a q (world)' entails 'every p (world) is a q (world)' – the categorical transform of 'if p then q'. An argument such as 'if p then q, r and not q; therefore r and not p' is syllogistic: every p world is a q world, some r world is not a q world; therefore some r world is not a p world. For a discussion of categorical propositional logic see my 1993.

The key elements in the account of terms are:

'Q' (a term),
[Q] (the characterization, BEING Q, expressed by 'Q'),
<Q> (the property of being Q, Q-ness),
Q-thing.

In the favorable case 'Q' is nonvacuous and

[Q] corresponds to <Q>,
'Q' signifies <Q>,
[Q] characterizes ('is true of') a Q-thing,
'Q' denotes a Q-thing,
<Q> is a characteristic of a Q-thing.

In the unfavorable case, 'Q' expresses [Q] but is vacuous in not signifying <Q> (there being no such property) and vacuous in not denoting any Q thing (there being no such thing).

III

SOME COMPARISONS

7.1 We compare the views set forth with some current views. (i) In Fregean semantics the Thought, being the sense of the sentence, is akin to what we are calling its expressive meaning or propositional content. Frege thinks of a sentence as expressing a Thought in the way one hits a target already there to be hit. By contrast, we think of the proposition as the *product* of an utterance, produced or expressed when a statement is made (a question asked, a prayer offered etc.). Having been expressed, the proposition exists. Saying something for the first time is like whistling a tune never before heard or thought of. The tune does not exist prior to the act of whistling it. Thereafter it exists and may be whistled again. Similarly, the proposition expressed does not exist except as the product of an initial illocutionary act such as asserting a declarative sentence. But thereafter, like the tune, the expressed proposition is part of the world's (intensional) furniture.

[Though Fregean 'thoughts' are eternal, they are analogous to expressed propositions; on the other hand, we noted the absence in Frege of any analogue to signified facts. By rejecting or overlooking a signifying mode of meaning for statements, Frege ruled out correspondence between what is true (the thought or proposition) and a fact that *makes* it true. According to Frege, a 'fact' just is a true thought analogous to what we are calling a FACT. The (hypostatized) objectivity of a Fregean thought FACT (however 'eternal' and mind independent) is a far cry from the kind of objectivity of truth-making state of affairs such as the existence of elks and the nonexistence of elves that are characteristics of the world. For Fregean FACTS are not truth-makers; we must still ask 'what *makes* a FACT or true thought true?' Frege's answer sends us to the reference of the sentence which in turn depends compositionally on the reference of its categorematic parts.]

7.2 The present account diverges from other familiar doctrines. Due to considerations of space I shall do no more than (baldly) state divergences but in two cases I go into some detail.

(ii) Compare the view that existence is a world attribute with the view that existence is an attribute of concepts.

(iii) Compare the view that statements express 'characterizations' applicable to the world with the view that they express 'Russellian propositions' that may contain real objects as their constituents. The false statement 'Ernest is alive' expresses the proposition ERNEST BEING ALIVE which no more contains the late Ernest Nagel then the characterization BEING ERNEST contains Nagel.

(iv) Compare saying that any true statement denotes the World, characterizing it in different ways, with some popular alternatives, e.g., that it does not denote at all (Ramsey, Strawson) or that it is satisfied by all the world's objects (Tarski) or that it denotes the True (Frege).

(v) Compare the thesis that different true statements may signify different facts with the thesis that all true statements signify one fact (the Great Fact as Donald Davidson has called it).

7.2.1 (vi) Compare the correspondence theorist's facts as states of the world to the situations of 'situation semantics'. Situations are in the world and we have seen reason to agree with those who deny that the state that makes a true statement true is locatable. Moreover, contemporary semanticists who offer technically interesting accounts of situations for an In-World Correspondence Theory are embarrassed by their inability to identify situations that correspond to negative existential statements. Consider 'no raven is yellow'. For the traditional correspondence theorist, the dearth of yellow ravens is the negative state of (not in) the world that makes this a true statement. But what In-the-World could we identify as a situation that makes it true?[13]

CONTENT AND CONTEXT

7.3.1 (vii) Compare, finally, a variety of current doctrines from Frege to David Kaplan to Gareth Evans – holding that the context of assertion contributes to propositional content – to the doctrine here outlined: that the proposition expressed is austerely existential, the role of context being merely to fix the domain being characterized. Looking into a drawer I say 'there is a (no)screwdriver' thereby expressing THERE (NOT) BEING A SCREWDRIVER, a characterization that may or may not be true of the domain under consideration. *Pace* the Fregeans, the here/now context of asserted utterance plays no part in the contents expressed.[14] Instead, by specifying and delimiting the domain, the context determines the venue of the truth claim. The Fregeans hold that the thought expressed is not true or false of anything; it is just true or false. Thus *it must be complete,* including contextual information like time and place in the propositional contents. The austere theory holds that a proposition expressed by a statement is either true or false *of the 'world'*. In asserting

[13] Barwise and Perry, whose theory of situations is an In-World Correspondence theory, have not yet given their answer to this question which so much troubled Russell. But one suspects that any answer they may have will distance us even further from the commonsense meaning of 'situation' that initially attracts one to the idea that true statements correspond to situations. The problem extends to situations that allegedly correspond to conditionals like 'if p then q'. The related problem of correlating valid inferences to an algebra of situations is a formidable one for any In-World theory. Thus Benson Mates pointedly asks how the 'historic situation' to which 'q' corresponds is related to the historic situations to which 'if p then q' and 'p' correspond. Cf. Mates 1974, 395. See Barwise and Perry 1983, 288. On the present account true statements do not signify situations but states of the world and all denote the world whose states they signify. Correlating valid inferences is not problematic. Call the world a p-world when 'p' denotes it. Call it a q-world when 'q' denotes it. Semantically, all arguments are about the world. For example, 'If p then q, p; therefore q' is construed thus: 'If W is a p-world , then it is a q-world, W is a p-world; so it is a q-world'. There being only one world, *modus ponens* may also be reckoned syllogistically: every p-world is a q-world, the world is a p-world ; so it is a q-world. See note 12 above.

[14] Speaking of tensed utterances Frege says: "The time of utterance is part of the expression of the thought". And more generally: "the knowledge of certain conditions accompanying the utterance is needed for us to grasp the thought correctly". Frege 1977a, 10 (cf. also 27-28).

(A) There is a screwdriver,

I claim that THE PRESENCE OF A SCREWDRIVER characterizes the DC, in this case, the contemporaneous set of objects immediately before me – the 'universe of discourse' of the old logic texts. The specification of the domain to be characterized is no part of the characterization. Even when venue-fixing indices are explicitly incorporated in the statement sentence, they still do not figure in the content of the proposition expressed. For example,

(B) There is a screwdriver here now,

again expresses no more than THE PRESENCE OF A SCREWDRIVER, a characterization of the little domain fixed by 'here' and 'now' in the context of assertion. Nor does tense qualify propositional content. In saying that there had been a screwdriver here last week, the propositional content is *again the same* – THE EXISTENCE OF A SCREWDRIVER – only now the claim is that a past totality of objects in the drawer is so characterized.

Kaplan and his school think of 'pure indexicals' like 'here' and 'now' as directly referring expressions whose reference is determined by context. "Clearly" says Palle Yourgrau, "'now' said at noon, refers to noon, said at midnight to midnight". But on the 'austere' view, 'here' and 'now' do not normally refer at all, either directly or otherwise.[15]

[Consider the difference between 'there's no screwdriver (here)' and 'here is a good place to look'. In the former, 'here' is a non-referential syncategorematic index that fixes the DC. In the latter, which *is* about places, 'here' is a demonstrative that refers to *this* place in a DC that includes (alternative) locations as well as objects.]

DEMONSTRATIVES AND PROPER NAMES

7.3.2 Indices like 'here' and 'now' are venue-fixing. So too are demonstratives. Pointing to an object one might say 'that one is a screwdriver'. The speaker then makes a claim about a domain constituted in part by the salient

---

[15] Yourgrau 1991, 1. See the first four essays (two by David Kaplan, one by John Perry and one by Gareth Evans. Kaplan carefully keeps context out of the final sense but he has no place else to put what context *contributes*. Given the character of the sentence, the context determines ('completes' and 'presents') the content. On our account, the content is not 'completed'; the context merely fixes the venue for the evaluation of the content.

constituent demonstratively designated and by some 'background' objects in its neighborhood. A truly 'pure' indexical like 'here' in (B) is 'syncategorematic'; it does not denote any constituent of the domain it helps to specify for the truth claim. By contrast, a demonstrative subject such as 'that' plays a *dual* role. It too partly fixes the domain of the claim as one containing the demonstratum as a salient constituent. In this domain-specifying role, it is like a pure indexical. But then, having stipulated the presence of the demonstratum within 'the domain under consideration', the demonstrative also plays a categorematic role as a term that contributes to the content of the proposition by denoting something in the domain.[16] In using a proper name with whose bearer I am acquainted, I commonly stipulate that the DC of the statement is one that contains the bearer. Anyone visiting Mexico City who asserts 'Mexico City is crowded' makes a claim about a real domain that stipulatively includes Mexico City as a constituent. So used, the proper name has the dual role that a demonstrative has. However a proper name may have a bearer with whom one is not acquainted. If my friend Jen, who is mildly persuaded that the Loch Ness Monster exists, says 'Nessy has been seen by many people', the DC of her statement is the real world, which she believes to contain a monstrous creature lurking in a lake in Scotland. The DC of Jen's statement is not stipulatively fixed as one that has Nessy as a constituent. For she is open to the suggestion that she could well be wrong in which case there is no such creature as Nessy in the DC. Again, since there is no Atlantis, no one can fix and make claims about a real domain that contains Atlantis as a constituent. So the statement 'Atlantis is a beautiful city' (made by someone who believes the ancient myths) is a (false) claim that the existence of a beautiful city, Atlantis, is a fact or, equivalently, that ATLANTIS BEING A BEAUTIFUL CITY is a correct characterization of the world.

7.3.3 Current accounts of propositional content are Fregean in thinking of the proposition as 'complete'.[17] For example, given the meaning (or 'character') of 'I was insulted yesterday', the particular context (say, its assertion by David Kaplan in Los Angeles on April 24, 1973) would determine the pro-

---

[16] Kaplan maintains that the demonstratum itself is a constituent in the propositional contents. According to this, when, pointing to Saturn, I say 'that one has rings' I express a proposition in which Saturn itself is 'trapped'. But on this one must agree with Frege who denied that objects in the world can be constituents of the thoughts we express. The demonstratum is a constituent in the DC and is so by stipulation. That accounts for its immediacy. But the demonstratum itself is not a constituent in 'That one has rings'. The propositional constituent expressed by the demonstrative is rather like the image in the telescope focused on Saturn ('trapped' in the telescope's mirror, if you will).

[17] See note 14 above.

position expressed to be the same proposition as that expressed by the 'eternal sentence', 'David Kaplan is insulted in Los Angeles on April 23, 1973', uttered several weeks later. According to the standard theory both utterances express the proposition or thought that David Kaplan is insulted on April 23, 1973. But on the Austere View, the propositional contents are not 'complete'; even the eternal sentence, when asserted, expresses no more than KAPLAN BEING INSULTED, the same proposition as is expressed by his having said 'I was insulted yesterday'. The proposition is the same but so is the domain. So the truth values are the same. Though both statements say the same thing, they differ in how the DC is specified for the speaker/hearer: contextually and implicitly for 'I was insulted yesterday', verbally and explicitly for 'David Kaplan is insulted in Los Angeles on April 23, 1973'. The domain fixing expressions are a portable feature of the eternal sentence specifying the same domain on any occasion and context of its utterance as a statement.

The Austere View has the virtues of specifying a common existential nature for all propositional contents and of clearly isolating the contribution of context and index (whether explicit or implicit) as that of determining the domain of the characterizing claim. On any such view the propositional content can only be *part* of the information needed by one who fully understands a statement. In addition to knowing the contents expressed by an asserted utterance of S, one must know the domain being characterized. 'There is a screwdriver there' is only partly understood by one who understands the proposition it expresses but doesn't know the context of assertion that would direct him to the domain of the truth claim.

INCORRIGIBLE STATEMENTS

7.3.4 Because its domain is initially fixed by such words as 'here', 'I' and 'now', a statement whose truth is contingent may be incorrigible. For example, anyone, NN, who says 'I'm here now' is claiming that a domain of things in the spatio-temporal region of the utterance made by NN, and which includes NN as a salient constituent, is characterized by THE PRESENCE OF NN. Since the domain of the claim has itself been specified as one that contains NN as a salient constituent, THE PRESENCE OF NN is incorrigibly true of it. The most famous example of such contingent incorrigibility is 'I exist'.[18]

---

[18] Compare Kaplan 1991, 35ff.

Moral: The various ways in which context and index fix the venues of truth claims need a careful (and separate) treatment.

IV

EPISTEMIC NOTES

8.1 A relevant domain often consists of the objects in a visual field. Call this the (immediate) environment. I look out on the pond and see a water lily. Seeing the water lily and correctly taking it to be a water lily I may also be said to see that there is a water lily. Here we distinguish between perceiving a thing in the domain in a certain way and 'apperceiving' the *domain* in a certain way (as $\{Q\}$ish or as un$\{Y\}$ish).

Apperception is mondial experience. Neglect of apperception as a special but fundamental kind of objective experience leaves us without an empirically grounded conception of the facts that make true statements true. The net effect on modern philosophy has been to discredit correspondence, thereby undermining realism and giving preference to pragmatist and coherence conceptions of truth. It is a mistake to think of apperception as secondary or derivatively dependent on object perception. Anyone who has looked for someone knows that the apperception of existence and nonexistence (Q-presence, Q-absence; $\{Q\}$ishness, un$\{Q\}$ishness) is epistemically as fundamental as the perception of objects. The experience of *absence* shows up the independence. Sartre tells of someone entering a restaurant expecting to find Pierre. Not finding him there he keenly experiences his absence; he 'apperceives' the domain as un$\{$Pierre$\}$ish. To apperceive the domain as un$\{$Pierre$\}$ish is to believe that Pierre is not there.

Suppose there are no water lilies on the lake and that I mistook what I saw for a water lily. I then wrongly believe there is a water lily. What does my belief consist in? What has happened is clear: (a) I have taken something to be a water lily (a *de re* belief); (b) I have taken the perceptual domain to be $\{$water-lily$\}$ish. This 'apperceptive' taking is badly named '*de dicto*' belief since '*de dicto* belief' connotes an attitude to a proposition rather than to the world. In believing that there are water lilies out there, I am (wrongly) taking the perceptual environment to be $\{$waterlily$\}$ish. Thus *de dicto* belief is very much like *de re* belief except that, in apperception, the '*re*' is the world itself. And generally, to believe that p is to 'take' the world as a p-world.

Believing that *p* is belief *de mondo*; it is how I take the world to be. Explaining belief in terms of 'taking' and 'mistaking' here treats 'taking' as epistemically primitive. Taking something to be so and so is the sort of thing any sentient creature does to objects in its environment and to the environment itself. Taking *x* to be K(ish) is (ap)perceiving *x* as K(ish). It is what the gosling does when it takes Konrad Lorenz for its mother. It is what Pierre's anguished dog does when, left alone in the house, it apperceives its suddenly desolate domain as un{Pierre}ish.

THE DOXASTIC OBJECT: *DE DICTO* OR *DE MONDO*?

8.2 The theist takes the world to be {God}ish. But the belief that God exists is commonly construed as an attitude to the proposition that 'God exists' expresses, taking it to be true. In the first way of describing the theist's belief, the doxastic attitude is to the world and belief is 'wide'. In the second way of thinking about belief the doxastic attitude is to a *characterization* of the world and belief is 'narrow'. If I believe that my son David is hungry, it seems natural to say that the belief holds dyadically between me, the believer, and the thought or proposition that he is hungry. But this assumes that the thought is informationally complete, the contribution of context having been wholly incorporated in the contents of the proposition or thought, DAVID SOMMERS BEING HUNGRY ON THE MORNING OF JANUARY 20, 1992, that is the object of belief. If we do not think of propositions as complete thoughts, we might view the doxastic attitude as relating the person who believes that *p* to a *truth claim* consisting of the proposition [*p*] and the domain fixed by the context in which [*p*] is entertained. Then to say that I believe the proposition that David is hungry is to say that I am taking the DAVID BEING HUNGRY to be true of the relevant time indexed domain. This alternative, which gives the domain an essential role in my belief (and hence treats belief as wide), may be an acceptable way of construing belief as a 'propositional attitude'.

It may be that a correct theory of mental representation will determine that taking the world to be {Q}ish is no different from taking THE PRESENCE OF A Q THING to be true of the world. It will then be evident that all belief involves propositions and there is no real difference between *de dicto* and *de mondo* accounts of belief. On the other hand, the *prima facie* difference may be real, in which case we are, even now, in a position to say that the *de mondo* account appears to have significant advantages.

In the first place, a propositionless theory of belief avoids problems of substitutivity. Given terms A and B that apply to exactly the same thing or things, the principle of substitutivity says we may substitute A for B in any proposition [...B...] *salva veritate.* Thus Tully (a farmer) is Cicero (the renowned senator) but Flavius, who knows Tully the farmer but does not realize he is Cicero, says and believes that Cicero is a senator but does not believe that Tully is a senator. Let the Roman Senate constitute the DC of Flavius's assertion 'Cicero is a senator'. By the principle of substitutivity which applies to terms within propositions, Flavius's believing [Cicero is a senator] to be true of the Senate seems tantamount to believing [Tully is senator] true of the Senate. There are of course familiar parries, arguing for a difference in cognitive significance. By contrast, substitutivity has no purchase at all in the propositionless account of Flavius's beliefs, according to which Flavius (mistakenly) apperceives the Roman Senate as un{Tully}ish while rightly taking it to be {Cicero}ish.

Second there is plausibility in the conjecture that an animal's belief does not involve propositions except by way of *our* description of what it believes. A dog barks and we say it believes that there is an intruder but the dog's belief may be propositionless; it may consist simply in its taking the domain to be {intruder}ish.

Third, even a proposition [p] that I entertain may not figure in what I believe although we may say of me that I believe that *p*. As a child I once saw my friend's dog being struck by a car and thought it was mine. I believed that my dog, Lucky, had been killed and did not believe that Joey's dog (whose name I have forgotten) had been killed. In the context it may not matter how I had referred to the dog in question: the propositions expressed by 'the dog has been killed by a car' and 'my dog has been killed by a car' may not differ in content. Assuming that the propositional content is simply THAT DOG HAVING BEING KILLED BY A CAR, it would appear the proposition is not central to how we should explain the difference in belief. Propositions aside, there is the world as I apperceived it. My distressing belief may simply consist of a distinct apperception: I apperceived the world *thus* – as a {dead Lucky}ish world.[19]

---

[19] See above section 8.1. Neglect of apperception has diverted philosophers from understanding belief as a *de mondo* experience. Taking the world to be {Q}ish might seem to be equivalent to taking the existence of a Q-thing to obtain. And this would give us states of affairs ({Q}ishness, un{Q}ishness) as a third candidate for the doxastic object. But the equivalence should be rejected. Even a false belief must have an object. It is open to us to deny that such a thing as {elf}ishness is available as an object of false belief to be (mis)taken for something that obtains. (We should still have {ELF}ISHNESS). The third candidate is however an alternative for anyone who holds that all terms and statements signify objective characte-

Consider Kaplan's very similar example:

If I see, reflected in a window, the image of a man whose pants appear to be on fire, my behavior is sensitive to whether I think 'His pants are on fire' or 'My pants are on fire', though the object of thought may be the same.[20]

Kaplan attributes this to the difference in the 'cognitive significance' of the common propositional content when sentences expressing it have different characters. The character determines how the common content is presented (those pants as 'mine', those pants as 'his'). The particular way the proposition is presented to me prompts me to react in a characteristic manner.

Kaplan's solution ingeniously saves propositional belief. Nevertheless, it is simpler bite the bullet by dropping the familiar assumption that believing is an attitude to a proposition (presented in a certain way) and to think of it instead as a particular apperception of the world. So understood, the different reactions are correlated to how the world presents itself to me. Is it a world in which my pants are on fire or his?

Kripke has devised a case where seemingly contradictory beliefs need to be reconciled. Pierre who lived in Paris, said and believed that London ('Londres') is a beautiful city. Later in London (but without realizing he is referring to the same city) he says and believes that London is not a beautiful city. This gives rise to 'a puzzle about belief', for in the circumstances, it is reasonable for Pierre to hold both beliefs simultaneously.[21]

Even if we say that Pierre entertains contradictory propositions we should deny that his beliefs are contradictory. Pierre who is now living abroad and acquainted with London finds his world – a world stipulated to contain London – {ugly London}ish. But, by hypothesis, he also takes it to be characterized by the existence of a city distinct from London whose French name is 'Londres'. Thus Pierre can, without inconsistency, apperceive the world to be {ugly London}ish while also taking it to be {jolie Londres}ish. Of course he's got it wrong since the city whose French name is 'Londres' is none other than London.

Kripke's Londres/London example is an instance of taking a domain to be {J}ish and {K}ish without taking it to be {J&K}ish. For example, though the mayor be a spy, I may take the domain to be {mayor}ish and {spy}ish without taking it to be {spy & mayor}ish.

---

ristics (unhad properties, states of affairs that do not obtain). States that don't obtain are sometimes thought of as states of nonactual worlds ('where' they do obtain).

[20] Kaplan 1991, 42.

[21] Kripke 1979.

EXISTENCE AND REALITY

9. We explain elk existence and elf nonexistence as properties of our world. What of the world itself? Should we speak of it as existing? If we do, we would be understood to say that a domain of (possible) worlds (some of which are {elf}ish) is characterized by the existence of our 'actual' world with *its* peculiar properties ({elk}ishness, un{elf}ishness etc.). As David Lewis recognized, one must then democratically allow for the existence of these other, 'nonactual', worlds all of which exist as members of the domain of worlds. Postulating a domain of worlds is a drastic step to take and it is well to refrain from taking it. What exists is in the world. We need not think of the world itself as existing.

We do nevertheless speak of the real or actual world, opposing it to fictional, mock or nonactual domains. Mock domains (e.g., Tolkien's world, the fauna of Greek mythology) are expressive systems that exist as intensional human products *within* the world, in much the way propositions do. For the actualist, all nonactual worlds exist in that way in the real world.[22]

As for facts, we have seen that it is a profound mistake to think of *them* as constituents of the world. (Facts are 'of' the world, not 'in' it.) Nevertheless, as attributes of the real world facts constitute a real domain in their own right. It is with respect to the world that we say 'there is no such thing (in it) as an elf'. It is with respect to the domain of facts that we say things like 'there is no such thing, no such fact as the existence of elves'.

---

[22] The philosopher who gets by without recourse to possible worlds is an 'actualist'. Abjuring possible worlds, the modern actualist explicates modal propositions by arguing for and attending to the necessary (negative) existential properties of the world. Actualism is classical doctrine. According to Norman Kretzmann and Eleonore Stump, Aristotle's modal logic is "best understood as an attempt to characterize relations between accidental and necessary properties of things in the actual world". The existence of certain things is precluded by "the nature of things"; for example, because the real world is proof against the existence of immortal mammals, it is necessarily true that mammals are mortal. To say that necessarily water (in standard conditions) boils at 100 C is to say the world is proof against the existence of water that fails to boil when heated to that temperature. On the other hand, although there are no trillionaires, the world is not proof against the existence of trillionaires: their existence is possible. *Pace* Anselm, the necessary existential properties of the real world are all *negative* or 'preclusive' so that whatever does exist in it need not have. We may take existential contingency to be a necessary condition for being 'real'. If we do, numbers will constitute a nonreal domain since the domain of natural numbers is characterized by the *necessary* existence of all its constituents. It would seem that not all nonreal domains are fictive. See Kretzmann and Stump 1988, 312 ff.

References

Barwise, J. and Perry, J. 1983: *Situations and Attitudes*, MIT Press/Bradford Books.

Davidson, D. 1990: "The Structure and Content of Truth", *The Journal of Philosophy* 87, nr. 6.

Frege, G. 1952: *Die Grundlagen der Arithmetik,* published with Eng. trans. by J. L. Austin *en face* as *The Foundations of Arithmetic,* Basil Blackwell, Oxford.

Frege, G. 1977a: *Logical Investigations*, tr. P.T. Geach and R. Stoothoff, Oxford.

Frege, G. 1977b: "The Thought" in Frege 1977a.

Kaplan, D. 1991: "Thoughts on Demonstratives", in Yourgrau 1991.

Kretzmann, N. and Stump, E. (eds.) 1988: *The Cambridge Translations of Medieval Philosophical Texts*, Volume One, Cambridge University Press.

Kripke, S. 1979: "A Puzzle About Belief" in Margalit 1979, 239-83.

Margalit. A. (ed.) 1979: *Meaning and Use,* Reidel, Dordrecht.

Mates, B. 1974: "Austin, Strawson, Tarski and Truth", *Proceedings of the Tarski Symposium*; American Mathematical Society, 1974, 385-396.

Ockham 1980: *Ockham's Theory of Propositions,* tr. by A.J. Freddoso and H. Schuurman, Notre Dame.

Rorty, R. 1991: *Objectivity Relativism and Truth,* Cambridge University Press, Cambridge.

Russell, B. 1966a: *Logic and Knowledge,* ed. R.C. Marsh.

Russell, B. 1966b: "Lectures on the Philosophy of Logical Atomism", in Russell 1966a.

Sommers, F. 1993: "The world, the facts, and primary logic", *Notre Dame Journal of Formal Logic* 34, 169-182.

Strawson, P.F. 1971a: *Logico-Linguistic Papers,* Methuen, London.

Strawson, P.F. 1971b: "Truth", in Strawson 1971a.

Yourgrau, P. (ed.) 1991: *Demonstratives*, Oxford Readings in Philosophy, Oxford.

Williams, C.J.F. 1981: *What is Existence?,* Clarendon Press, Oxford.

DAVID M. ARMSTRONG

A WORLD OF STATES OF AFFAIRS

1. States of Affairs Defended

This is a position paper or trailer for a larger work in progress and having the same title. My hypothesis is that the world is a world of states of affairs. I think that I am saying the same thing as those who have held that the world is a world of facts not things. So it may be in order to begin by saying why I use the phrase 'state of affairs' rather than the word 'fact'. This is all the more in order because it is customary among those who patronize facts to use 'state of affairs' to mean no more than *possible* fact. My states of affairs, however, are all existents.

In my view, the word 'fact' is much too closely tied to the notions of statement and proposition. It is natural to think of facts as the tautological accusatives of true statements and propositions. Given this, to each true statement or proposition there corresponds its own peculiar fact. This is quite unsatisfactory for my purposes. I have therefore taken over the phrase 'state of affairs'. It sounds less colloquial and more like a term of art, which is desirable. Those who are lost to all shame and use acronyms in their philosophical publications can abbreviate it to 'SOA'.

The general structure of a state of affairs I take to be this. A state of affairs exists if and only if a particular has a property, or a relations holds between two or more particulars. The relations are all *external* relations, that is, in no case are they dictated by the nature of their terms. In the jargon of possible worlds, it is not the case that in each world in which the terms exist, that is, in which the related particulars exist, the relation also holds.

It is generally conceded by philosophers that what particulars exist is to be determined *a posteriori* as a result of empirical investigation. It is not so generally conceded that what properties and relations exist is to be determined

159

R. Poli and P. Simons, Formal Ontology, 159–171.
© 1996 *Kluwer Academic Publishers. Printed in the Netherlands.*

empirically, but it seems equally important that this concession should also be made. Contemporary philosophy tends to use the terms 'property' and 'relation' in such a way that properties and relations are tautological accusatives of monadic and polyadic predicates respectively. And for certain purposes this is undoubtedly convenient. I will take the liberty of talking in this way way myself where there is need. In that looser way of talking, properties and relations are determined in discourse, not determined empirically. But I make bold to say that the properties and relations that enter into *states of affairs* are the true or real properties and relations. Or, if you recoil from such pre-Moorean language, they are the fundamental properties and relations.

States of affairs have as constituents particulars, properties and relations. I hold that the properties and relations should be taken to be *universals*, thus making it possible for different particulars to instantiate the very same property or different pairs of particulars to instantiate the very same (dyadic) relation. But for those who think that universals, even these non-semantic universals of mine, are creatures of darkness, there is an interesting alternative here. One can take the properties and relations of particulars to be particulars themselves. Using the transitive and symmetrical relation of exact resemblance one can then construct equivalence-classes of these property and relation particulars. It turns out that these equivalence-classes are able to reflect many of the properties of universals (though not all) thus perhaps 'saving the phenomena' without the need to admit universals. (See my 1989, chap. 6, secs. V & VI.) The identification of these equivalence-classes can still be an *a posteriori* affair. For most versions of this *trope* theory, states of affairs will still be required to unite (ordinary) particulars with properties and relations, although the 'rules of composition' will not be exactly the same. Even if one reduces ordinary particulars to 'bundles' of tropes, the various bundlings would still appear to be states of affairs within the meaning of the act.

The necessity for states of affairs be challenged. Why is anything more needed than particulars, properties and relations? The answer to this comes from one of the fundamental assumptions that drive this ontology. It is the need for truths to have a truthmaker (a phrase introduced by C.B. Martin) or an ontological ground (the phrase used by Gustav Bergmann). Let it be the case that the particular a exists, and the property-universal F exists. It is clear that these two entities could exist and yet it fail to be the case that a is F. If the latter is to be true, then some truthmaker is required. The state of affairs of a's being F is suggested as that truthmaker, as the ontological ground.

A spectacular case is provided by non-symmetrical relations. It is unlikely that *loves* is a relation in the true ontological sense. The relation is surely not identical in all cases where an x loves a y, which is required for a universal. But let us here overlook this point. Let *a* love *b*, and *b* love *a*. The two states of affairs are presumably independent. Either could have occurred without the other. Yet the two different states of affairs involve exactly the same constituents. How are they to be differentiated? *Only* by this, it would seem: they are two different states of affairs. Hence we require states of affairs in our ontology.

Alas, one person's modus ponens is another person's *modus tollens*. The case just considered moves David Lewis to deny that there are any states of affairs, conceived as things composed from particulars and properties and relations. For, he reasons, it is impossible that two different things could be made out of *exactly* the same constituents. This leads him to assert that the only way that wholes can be composed out of parts is by that austere form of composition envisaged by the mereological calculus. For in this calculus there is one whole and one alone that a given set of parts compose. So for Lewis there can be no states of affairs. The world must be a world of things. A Quinean ontology, an ontology of the subject alone, with the predicate giving us not ontology but mere 'ideology', seems inevitable (Lewis, 1983). He might allow universals, but they will just be unusual things.

Here is a reason for thinking that mereological composition cannot be 'the cement of the universe'. Mereological wholes *supervene* upon their parts. This, indeed, follows from the fact that, given certain parts, there is only one possible whole which they compose. Different metaphysicians differ in their permissiveness with respect to what things can go together to make a whole. Some censorious persons will not let the Sydney Opera House get together with the square root of minus one. ('What next?', they say.) Lewis is completely permissive in this respect and I go along with him there. For us, Lewis and Armstrong, given that the putative parts are logically compatible, then the whole supervenes. (As indeed the parts supervene on the whole.) What supervenes, however, appears to be *ontologically* nothing more than what it supervenes upon. So, I reason, if mereology really is the only form of composition that there is, then ontologically there is no real composition in the world. This I take to be an absurd conclusion.

So I believe that we should accept the truthmaker argument from predications, non-relational and relational, to states of affairs. It is interesting, and even somewhat surprising, that these entities can differ although their constituents are exactly the same, but I recommend that we simply follow the wind of the argument. Only if someone could come forward with a non-supervenient form of composition that nevertheless allowed only one possible whole to be constructed out of exactly the same parts, would I be inclined to look critically at states of affairs.

States of affairs prove their worth at many points in ontological analysis. They illuminale the topic of causation, in particular singular causation, as will be noted in a later section. Somewhat surprisingly they seem to cast light on the nature of classes (Armstrong 1991). Here it may be of worth to look briefly at the topic of *structural universals* which Lewis, in particular, finds a vexed one (Lewis 1986). Consider a carbon atom, a, which is bonded in the familiar cross-shaped pattern separately to four hydrogen atoms, b, c, d, e. The particular which is the mereological sum $a + b + c + d + e$ is a methane molecule. It is straightforward, *given states of affairs*, to describe the structure of this methane molecule. With C = carbon, H = hydrogen, and B = bonding, we have Ca, Hb, Hc, Hd, He, Bab, Bac, Bad, Bae. To get a description of the (putative) structural universal *being a methane molecule* we should first substitute existential quantifiers for the particulars (together, of course, with non-identity clauses for these quantifiers). This gives us an assertion that the structural universal is instantiated. Abstracting from the assertion of instantiation we have a description of the universal: an individual that is a carbon atom, four further individuals that are hydrogen atoms, and where ... etc., etc. The structural universal is a certain *type* of conjunction of states of affairs. It would, of course, be open to someone to think of this as a structure of universals instead of a structural universal. But although it may not be of the first importance to resolve that dispute, one reason for going the latter way and calling it a universal is to provide for the (epistemic) possibility of 'stuctures all the way down'.

States of affairs are thought to labour under a certain further difficulty, though. It is a difficulty most usually articulated for the particular case of an ontology of particulars and universals, but seems to be a general one. It is the difficulty of predication, the difficulty of the nexus of instantiation (as they say in Iowa), the difficulty of the non-relational tie (W.E. Johnson and P.F. Strawson), the difficulty of the formal distinction (as Scotus put it), the difficulty of participation (as Plato had it). Is not bringing the constituents of a state of affairs, the particulars, the properties and the relations, together into states of affairs, a further relation in which all the constituents stand? But then the new relation is just a further element which requires to be integrated along with the other constituents. Most contemporary opponents of universals take comfort from this argoment. Often it seems to be the only argument they have to set against the multifarious difficulties facing their particular variety of Nominalism!

Well, those of us who accept states of affairs do have to accept what one might think of as an operator that takes constituents of states of affairs to states of affairs (and, in thought, to merely possible states of affairs). But I think that we are under no compulsion to take this 'formation' of states of affairs as a further constituent, something on the same level as the original constituents. One reason for this, I suggest, is that once the putative states of affairs are reached, all further 'relations' in the regress that our Nominalist friends say that we must accept supervene upon the states of affairs. That a state of affairs having certain constituents exists, is, I take it, a contingent matter. But all the alleged further relations in the regress flow necessarily from the structure of the state of affairs. So I suggest this supervenience is a sign that these 'extra' relations do not have to be taken seriously ontologically.

2. States of Affairs Rule

Having said something in defence of states of affairs, let us advance to the proposition that states of affairs are all that there is. It is not denied on this view that there are things – particulars – nor it is denied that there are properties and relations. But it is denied that there is anything that exists outside states of affairs. It is denied that there is anything that is not a constituent of one or more state of affairs. (A point of usage. I generally reserve the word 'part' for mereological parts, speaking instead of constituents of states of affairs. Constituents are parts, too. But they do not obey the axioms of the mereological calculus, so it has seemed advisable to employ another word instead of part.)

If states of affairs are all there is, then there are no 'bare particulars' meaning by this phrase particulars conceived to exist in independence of any state of affairs. (I am here hijacking a term used by Gustav Bergmann and his followers. In their usage bare particulars can be found within states of affairs. But it seems to me that the phrase calls out to be used as I use it.) Equally, there are no uninstantiated universals. Every property is a property of some particular. Every relation holds between two or more particulars. I do not know that there is any very strong pressure to postulate bare particulars. Uninstantiated properties and relations are a different matter. There are semantic arguments for their existence. The idea is that they are required to be the meanings of predicates that, while meaningful, nevertheless fail to apply truly to anything. I think that these arguments can be treated with a certain indifference. But there is a strong *prima facie case* for uninstantiated laws of nature and some of these seem to demand uninstantiated universals. Again, some philosophers have proposed to give an account of possibilities and possible worlds by appealing to uninstantiated universals (Forrest 1986, Bigelow and Pargetter 1990, 4.5). In a complete treatment the arguments from uninstantiated laws and from possibilities would have to be carefully considered. I have tried to deal with the argument from laws elsewhere (1983, Ch. 8). Not everybody thinks I have been successful, but here I will assume this important step in my argument.

I do not suppose that those who accept that there are universals with find it too difficult an idea that properties and relations are literally, if unmereologically, parts of states of affairs. But that particulars should be in the same situation – tables and thunderstorms – may seem a strange, not to say a ratbag, view. I think that the sense of paradox is eased if we draw a distinction between the 'thin' and the 'thick' particular.

The thin particular is the particular considered in abstraction from all its properties. Although not bare, it is very thin indeed. (But you can be thin without being bare.) For me, all thin particulars although numerically different, are, as it were, indistinguishably different. Particulars may be said to have or rather to be haecceities, but they have no mysterious inner and particularized essence that marks off one from another and accounts for their numerical difference. The secret of numerical difference is simply numerical difference. Different particulars may be parts of other particulars, parts which include, I hold, temporal parts, or overlap other particulars. This is the mereological sense of the word 'part' and, with Lewis 1993, I take this identity of parts to be best understood as partial identity. But that is about all that can be said about the thin particular. Notice, however, that it is not hidden, as Locke had it hidden. Even in our most basic. most elementary, perceptions we are aware of particulars, though of course particulars as having certain properties and relations, that is: particulars in states of affairs.

So much for the thin particular. The thick particular is the thin particular considered along with all of its intrinsic, that is, non-relational properties. It is a much more familiar creature. But, on the scheme proposed, what can it be except a state of affairs or conjunction of states of affairs? The existence of conjunctive oniversals is a somewhat controversial but not too important an affair. I allow them, provided that the conjunct universals are all instantatied by the same particular, but some philosophers do not. Suppose we allow them. Then we can roll up all the non-relational properties of a particular into a single, but far from simple, conjunctive universal. We can call it that particular's *nature*. Now consider the state of affairs of that particular's having that nature: *a's having N*. This state of affairs is the thick particular.

I will just note a pleasant anticipation of the thin/thick distinction by Herbert Hochberg. He spoke of 'Socrates' and 'big Socrates' (Hochberg n.d.). In true Iowan style, however, the object he was talking about was not a philosopher but a white square patch.

To gain a somewhat more concrete grip on the doctrine that the world is nothing but a world of states of affairs let us consider another doctrine which I uphold and which I call the doctrine of Naturalism. This is the proposition that the world consists of, and is exhausted by, the single, public, spatio-temporal system. (Naturalism is not to be confused with Physicalism, the doctrine that this space-time world involves nothing more than the entities and laws recognized by a – completed – physics. A Naturalist need not be a Physicalist, although I myself accept both theses.) In the order of knowledge the doctrine of Naturalism must be accorded a higher epistemic credit-rating than the states of affairs doctrine, although I uphold both. After all, the thesis that the world is a world of states of affairs is no more than a *philosopher's* thesis! But in the order of being, if I am right, the space-time world is nothing but a huge conjunction of states of affairs. To *exhibit* this would be a huge undertaking, and, *prima facie*, there are all sorts of ways that we could work out the identification, depending upon the answer to all sorts of scientific and philosophical questions concerning the nature of space and time. For instance, the world might turn out to consist of genuinely atomic particulars which are space-time points; perhaps having field properties, and the concatenation of these points might constitute space-time. This is just one scheme, and not one that I have any particular affection for, although have no particular dislike of it either. But it illustrates a little more concretely, if still unexcitingly, what a world of states of affairs might be like.

It is to be noted that the *unity* of the space-time world is not constituted by the mere conjunction of the state of affairs. A conjunctive state of affairs, as we may call such a conjunction, has a merely mereological unity, which is to say no real unit at all. The real unity is given by the fact that all the particulars are direcly or recursively linked to each other by real, that is external, relations. These relations appear to be exhausted by causal and spatiotemporal relations.

The states of affairs, which includes their constituents, constitute the ultimate truthmakers for all truths. This gives occasion to say something about truth. Two theories of truth, in particular, fight in the breast of any right-minded, not to say clean-living, philosopher. I, at any rate, have oscillated between the two for many years. The first is the Correspondence theory. To say that *p* is true is to say that this proposition corresponds to reality. The other is the Redundancy theory. To say that *p* is true is, fundamentally, to say no more than to say *p*. My suggestion is that both theories have got hold of part of the truth about truth. The Redundancy theory is satisfactory at the more superficial level of usage, formal semantics, and, I think, truth conditions. But our statements and propositions do correspond or fail to correspond to reality. Their correspondent is the *truthmaker*, the ontological ground, for that statement or proposition. But it is vital to realize that the correspondence is not a one-one affair. To think so is to fall into the gravitational field of the Redundancy theory and as a result to postulate a fact peculiar to each true proposition. It is this error, I believe, that has led to dissatisfaction with the supremely natural view that truth is or involves correspondence to reality. The correspondence of truth with truthmaker is actually many-many. It is a totally disorderly affair. I now think that there must be a truthmaker for every truth, even necessary truths, although the later do not require a great deal in the way of truthmaker. It is a, perhaps the, major metaphysical enterprise to determine the general nature of the truthmakers to the various sorts of true discourse. That the basic truthmakers are states of affairs (and of course their constituents) is, I have been arguing, the beginning of ontological wisdom.

3. Higher-Order States of Affairs

One of the attractions of the metaphysics of the *Tractatus* is that the facts that constitute the world are all of the same order. There are no facts about facts. This doctrine is again upheld by Brian Skyrms in his "Tractarian Nominalism" (1981). Unlike Wittgenstein, Skyrms explicitly makes the constituents of his facts particulars and universals, the latter dividing into properties and relations. He might have been privy to my thoughts, He uses the word 'Nominalism', unwisely in my view, not to deny universals but to betoken that he denies the existence of any facts of higher order.

It seems. however, that there is no excape from such facts (states of affairs). The knock-down case, I believe, is the one pointed out to Russell, what he called 'general facts' (1918, 93). I will speak of facts of totality or, in my own terminology, states of affairs of totality. Consider all the electrons, past, present and future. Particular a will have properties sufficient to make it an electron. So will particular b, and so on. Does the conjunction of these states of affairs serve as a truthmaker for the truth that these are *all* the electrons? I don't think it can. For, it is *contingent* that these are all the electrons. These states of affairs could all exist and yet not exhaust the totality of electrons.

This last point might be conceded, it may be objected, why not accept here a truthmaker that would fail to be a truthmaker for the same truth 'in another possible world'? My answer to this is that the truthmaking relation, although many-many, in an *internal* relation, one that supervenes upon, is necessitated by, the nature of the terms. (A view also supported by Kit Fine, 1982.) One point here is that correspondence relation is not a spatio-temporal or a causal relation, and Hume long ago pointed out that these are the only plausible candidates for 'relations of matter of fact' i.e. external relations (see the *Treatise*, Bk. 1, Pt. 1, Sec. V, & Pt. 3, Sec. 1). But the matter can be approached more directly. That it is true that a certain collection of electrons is *all* the electrons is surely only true because there are no more of them. If there are more, then it is not true. That there are no more of them is then part of the truthmaker. But this is a higher-order state of affairs or fact.

It seems, then, that there is allness or totality in the world. Here is one logical constant that does signify. I don't think that the notion can be *analyzed*, but I think we can categorize it a bit further. Allness appears to be a relational property of sorts, in the same sort of way that being a father is a relational property (as opposed to the relation of fathering, on which being a father supervenes). Consider the class of the aggregate (mereological whole) which happens to be the class or the aggregate of the electrons. What makes it *all* the electrons? Is it not that it stands in the totalling relation – the alling relation – to a certain property, the property of *being an electron*? The class or aggregate which happens to be the class of all the protons stands in the very same relation to the property of *being a proton*. It alls being a proton, we might say. We have a relation which is a universal here, it seems, and on it supervenes the allness of certain classes and aggregate with respect to certain properties.

If we admit such 'general facts', then that will have a considerable bearing on the vexed question whether or not to admit *negative* states of affairs. For, as is well known, given all positive states of affairs, and given the further fact of totality that these *are* all the positive states of affairs, then all negative states of affairs supervene. If so, then it would seem that we do not need to postulate negative facts alongside positive ones. It is true that there are some arguments for negative states of affairs to be considered. There appear to be negative perceptions: perceiving that there is nobody in the room. There also appear to be cases of negative causation: lack of water causing death. Ontologically speaking, however, I think it can be made plausible that these are mere surface phenomena. It may be noted that negative properties are as suspect as negative states of affairs.

The account just sketched of totality or allness leads on to a certain view of the nature of number. Consider the salient relation that holds between *being an electron* and *being an aggregate of nineteen electrons* and also between *being a proton* and *being an aggregate of nineteen protons*. Peter Forrest and I have argued that there is a good case for identifying this relation with the natural number nineteen (Forrest and Armstrong 1987). The account appears to generalize smoothly to the rational numbers and to the reals, thus permitting a universal account of these sorts of number. In each case, a unit-universal stands in a certain ratio or proportion to an aggregate universal. With *being one kilogram mass* as unit-property, it stands in the 3.2 ratio to *being 3.2 kilograms mass*. That unit-property also stands in the π relation to *being π kilograms mass*. Perhaps the account can even be generalized to cover the infinitesimals of non-standard analysis.

Allness and the numbers turn out, on this scheme, to have at least a family resemblance to each other, reminding us of the thesis of Grossmann 1983 (Secs. 137-42) that numbers fall into the category of quantifiers. But there is an important difference between allness and the numbers. The 'alling' relation is external. The numerical relations, however, are internal, flowing necessarily from the nature of their terms. That being so, the truthmakers for the holding of the relations are nothing more than the related terms. The relations are of the sort that can hold between windowless monads or the denizens of different possible worlds.

As I see it then, the integration of mathematics into the world of states of affairs should draw its inspiration from the *Tractatus* rather than from the hard-line empiricism of Mill, John Anderson, Quine and others. The states of affairs are contingent, mathematical truths are necessary, and the secret of necessity lies in the reduction of its ontological content.

The consideration of number has taken us away from the topic of higher-order states of affairs, because, unlike allness, the internal relations involved do not call for higher-order states of affairs. This may be the place, nevertheless, to say a word about such mathematical entities as the higher infinite cardinal numbers. The worry here is that there may be no aggregate or class of things which can stand in the right internal relation to some unit-property. But without such a relation, on this theory of number, there would appear to be no such number. To this difficulty I reply by saying that mathematical existence is something less than full-blooded existence. For an infinite number to exist is no more than for the required aggregate or class to be a *possible* one, although this must be absolute not just epistemic possibility. This view (put forward e.g. by Putnam 1967) is a trifle deflationary. But it does help with a difficult epistemological problem. How it is that in mathematics we can arrive at the result that a certain entity exists *a priori*, a result that we do not regard as open to falsification, barring the unusual case of doubt being raised about the original premisses? If all we have really achieved is the weaker conclusion that something is possible, then it becomes easier to accept that such knowledge is possible *a priori*.

Getting back to higher-order states of affairs, it is plausible that causation, singular causation, this causing that, is a relation between states of affairs. It is particulars that act. But they act in virtue of their properties and the effect of their action is determined by the properties of the thing that they act upon. This strongly suggests states of affairs. Putting it in a no doubt oversimplified way, that a is F brings it about that b is G.

Causation naturally leads one on to the topic of laws. Singular causation exhibits a fair amount of regularity, and it is a natural hypothesis that each token of a causal sequence instantiates some law. It is true that there appears to be no *a priori* argument that takes one from singular causation to law, a point emphasized by Anscombe 1971. But, as suggested by Adrian Heathcote, there appear to be good *a posteriori* grounds for identifying singular causal sequences with instantiations of laws (Heathcote and Armstrong 1991).

In the Humean tradition laws are identified with cosmic regularities of a certain sort: 'cosmic coincidences' as that most honest of all Humeans, Jack Smart, calls them. If this traditional Empiricist position can be maintained, then there is no call here to postulate higher-order facts in explaining causes and laws. But, building on the work of many others, I have tried to show how implausible this position is in my 1983. Suppose, instead, as I think plausible, that laws should be seem as relationships holding between universals. We then have higher-order states of affairs, and ones that differ in type from facts of totality and the links between token states of affairs *apparently* present in singular causation.

If we think of a property as a *type* of state of affairs, the property F as the *something is F* type of state of affairs, then one can think of a nomic/causal connection of properties as a state of affairs where one type of state of affairs brings about a further type of state of affairs. But this formulation is not to be understood as a universally quantified truth about tokens of the types in question. It is a 'direct' connection between the state of affairs types, i.e. the universals in question, a connection postulated for its explanatory value. It entails the corresponding universally quantified state of affairs, without being entailed by it. It is not supervenient upon mere first-order states of affairs. As such, it is a higher-order state of affairs.

It is interesting to note here the position of those who accept laws as relations between universals, but who hold that the relation is a necessary one. Since their laws hold in any possible world in which the 'antecedent' universal in the law is instantiated, for them laws supervene upon universals. Such a position seems incompatible with the view, which I defend, that the supervenient is ontologically nothing over and above whatever it supervenes upon. For surely what nomic connections hold between given properties is a substantial matter of fact? (Lewis has pointed out to me that those who hold that laws are necessary might well concede this point but go on to argue that the substantial matter of fact is that these law-bearing universals rather than others are instantiated. I think I can still make my point, but it would certainly take longer.) Laws, then, though relations of universals, involve higher-order states of affairs that are contingent. (By 'laws' are here to be understood the nomic connections themselves, not the true statements that such a connection holds.)

In Dretske, Tooley and Armstrong the sort of laws discussed are usually those linking two properties, generally called F and G in order to make the example as specific and concrete as possible. I think this is excusable. The issues are complex enough without having to concentrate from the beginning on some more lifelike but more tangled case. It remains true, though, that your average law of nature that has some claim to be fundamental will be a functional law that connects two or more quantities. This in turn means that a scientific or *a posteriori* realism about universals will have to concentrate particularly on universals of *quantity*. There are quite pressing problems.

Consider a quantity such as *mass* (or *rest mass*). There is a whole class of *determinate* universals, such as *one kilogram in mass* or *one ounce in mass*. What is the determinable *mass*? Is it also a universal? If it is, then is it a universal whose determinates are its instances, a universal which appears in functional mass-laws? If so, then it seems that we must postulate higher-order properties – properties of properties. A difficulty here, at least for me, is that this supposed higher-order property seems to be supervenient on its first-order property. Determinables entail determinates. Hence I would have to say that we do not get a genuinely higher-order property. Yet we cannot treat a functional law as a mere class of laws – the class of the highly specific laws that govern the individual determinates. That would be a retreat to a Humean theory of functional laws, unacceptable to anybody who is upholding a theory of 'strong' laws.

This has been a survey, inevitably hurrying over many matters that demand a very much fuller treatment. Indeed, much that might have claimed a place has been omitted altogether. But I hope it has shown something of the attraction and, you may think, the problems, that face the metaphysical programme that seeks to exhibit the world as made up of a single sort of constituent: states of affairs having in turn as their sole constituents particulars, property-universals and relation-universals.

References

Anscombe, G.E.M. 1971: "Causality and determination", Cambridge, Cambridge University Press. Reprinted in Sosa 1975.

Armstrong. D.M. 1983: *What is a law of nature?*, Cambridge, Cambridge University Press.

Armstrong. D.M. 1989: *A combinatorial theory of possibility*, Cambridge, Cambridge University Press.

Armstrong. D.M. 1991: "Classes are states of affairs", *Mind* 100, 189-200.

Bigelow, J. and Pargetter R. 1990: *Science and necessity*, Cambridge, Cambridge University Press.

Campbell, K., Bacon J. and Reinhardt, L. (eds.) 1993: *Ontology, causality and mind: essays on the philosophy of D.M. Armstrong*, Cambridge, Cambridge University Press.

Capitan, W.H. and Merrill, D.D. (eds.): *Metaphysics and explanation*, Pittsburgh, University of Pittsburgh Press.

Fine, K. 1982: "First -order modal theories – facts", *Synthese* 53, 43-122.

Forrest. P. 1986: "Ways worlds could be", *Australasian Journal of Philosophy* 64, 15-24..

Forrest P. and Armstrong. D.M. 1987: "The nature of number", *Philosophical Papers* 16, 165-86.

Grossmann, R. 1983: *The categorial structure of the world*, Bloomington, Indiana University Press.

Heathcote, A. and Armstrong, D.M. 1991: "Causes and laws", *Nous* 25, 63-73.

Hochberg, H. n.d.: "Things and qualities", in Capitan and Merrill, 82-97.

Lewis, D. K. 1983: "New work for a theory of universals", *Australasian Journal of Philosophy* 61, 343-77.

Lewis, D. K. 1986: "Against structural universals", *Australasian Journal of Philosophy* 64, 25-46.

Lewis, D. K. (1993): "Many, but almost one", in Campbell, Bacon and Reinhardt 1993.

Putnam, H. 1967: "The thesis that mathematics is logic", in Shoenman 1976. Reprinted in Putnam, H.: *Philosophical papers*, vol. 1, Cambridge, Cambridge University Press.

Shoenman, R. (ed.) 1967: *Bertrand Russell, philosopher of the century*, London, Allen & Unwin.

Skyrms, B. 1981: "Tractarian nominalism", *Philosophical Studies* 40, 199-206. Reprinted as "Appendix" in Armstrong 1989.

Sosa, E. 1975: *Causation and Conditionals*, Oxford, Oxford University Press.

MIECZYSŁAW OMYŁA

A FORMAL ONTOLOGY OF SITUATIONS

The theoretical foundation for this paper is the system of a non-Fregean logic created by Roman Suszko under the influence of Wittgenstein's *Tractatus Logico-Philosophicus*. In fact, we use just a fragment of it called here a non-Fregean sentential logic.

Our basic term is that of a 'situation'. We do not answer the question what situations are. We simply assume that sentences present situations, and we provide a criterion determining when two sentences of some fixed language present the same situation.

The lay-out of this paper is the following. First we set out certain philosophical consequences of the assumption adopted in classical logic that the only connectives of the language in question are the truth-functional ones. Then we sketch out briefly the axiomatics of non-Fregean sentential logic, and of a formal semantics of the algebraic type for it.

Next, for an arbitrary model for a non-Fregean sentential logic, we pick out from the formulae true in that model a theory to be called the 'ontology of situations determined by the model in question' – in contradistinction to all sentences holding contingently in that model, i.e. not determined by its algebra. In the ontology of situations determined by a model we point out those propositions which pertain to possible worlds.

Finally we give a comprehensive bibliography of works concerned with non-Fregean logic.

1. The Fregean Axiom

Contemporary scientific semantics is mostly a theory of interpretation for some fragments of ordinary language and of the languages of particular sci-

R. Poli and P. Simons, Formal Ontology, 173–187.

ences. In semantics these languages are treated usually as predicate languages of the first order subject to classical logic. The standard interpretation of those languages has two essential properties:

1. The reality referred to by the language in question is being considered as a universe of objects (i.e. that universe is ranged over by nominal variables, and its designates objects are denoted by the names of that language) having certain properties and connected by certain relations.

2. The only semantic values of sentences are the truth-values: truth and falsehood.

That interpretation is consistent with the semantics and ontology adopted by Frege. To see this consider an arbitrary language L in which the only extra-logical symbols are the predicates P_1, P_2, ..., P_n. The interpretations for that language are the structures of the following type:

$$M = (A; R_1, R_2, ..., R_n)$$

where A is a fixed set called the universe of the model M, and R_1, R_2, ..., R_n are sets and relations corresponding to the predicates P_1, P_2, ..., P_n, respectively. The model M correlates to the sentences of L their truth-values, their only semantic reference. These, however, do not appear in the model M explicitly. To make the Fregean character of the standard interpretations of the language L explicit observe that the model M may be treated equivalently as the structure:

$$M_F = ((B_2, \{1\}), A, \bar{R}_1, \bar{R}_2, ..., \bar{R}_n)$$

defined as follows:

B_2 is a two-elements Boolean algebra on the set of truth-values $\{0, 1\}$;
$\bar{R}_1$, $\bar{R}_2$, ..., $\bar{R}_n$ are the characteristic functions of the relations R_1, R_2, ..., R_n.

The structure M_F will be called a *Fregean model* for the language L. The structures M and M_F are equivalent models for L in that in both models each sentence of the language in question has the same truth-value.

The gist of interpreting the language L by models of type M_F is that the nominal variables range over a fixed set, and the sentences of L refer to truth-values, with all the other symbols of L being either auxiliary signs or symbols of appropriate functions. This is in accord with Frege's ontology under which everything is either an object or a function, with the objects including a peculiar variety of them called logical objects. Hence Suszko called the model theory for the classic language of the predicate calculus a *Fregean model theory*.

The couple $(B_2, \{1\})$ occurring in the Fregean model for the language of the predicate calculus is the matrix of the classic propositional calculus. In view of the isomorphism of all two-elements Boolean algebras, any two Fregean models determined by the same standard model M differ at most in the elements representing the truth-values.

For any predicate language of the first order interpreted in an arbitrary standard model or in a Fregean model M_F there holds a principle called by Suszko the *semantic variant of the Fregean axiom*. This runs as follows:

(AF) all true sentences of the language in question have one and the same semantic reference, and similarly all the false ones.

Frege adopted the principle (AF) for he viewed it as a consequence of the principles of logical bivalence, of extensionality and of correlation (stating that in a correct symbolism each sign has a unique reference). Following Łukasiewicz, we identify in an arbitrary Fregean model the common semantic reference of all true sentences with Being, denoting it by 1 for short; and similarly the common reference of all the false ones with non-Being, denoting it by 0.

As in any Fregean model the universe of the sentential references contains just two elements, there is no need to introduce sentential variables into the language of the first order predicate calculus, i.e. variables which take sentential formulae for substitution, and whose values come from the set of the sentential references.

Sentential variables differ basically from other kinds of variable in that they are sentential formulae themselves entailing other such formulae (e.g., p entails $p \lor q$). That double role of the sentential variables – i.e. their being both variables and formulae – accounts for the fact that different authors adopt different interpretations of them. Most often we meet with the two following ones: substitutional and objectivist. Under the substitutional interpretation – its main exponent being Quine – sentential variables are not really variables but schematic letters representing sentences of some other language. The best known objectivist interpretations are those

(1) of Frege taking sentential variables to range over the two-elements set of truth-values;
(2) of Łukasiewicz and Post taking them to range over a set of at least two truth-values ordered linearly;
(3) of Wittgenstein and Suszko taking them to range over the universe of situations;
(4) of Kripke and Kit Fine taking them to range over sets of possible worlds.

2. Non-Fregean Logic

In contradistinction to Frege, Wittgenstein regarded sentences not as the names of any logical objects but as the logical pictures of situations. In the *Tractatus* he says:

4.03 ... The proposition communicates to us a state of affairs, therefore it must be *essentially* connected with the state of affairs.
And the connection is, in fact, that it is its logical picture.
4.06 Propositions can be true or false only by being pictures of reality.

According to the *Tractatus* a sentence refers directly to some situation, and only by means of that is it true or false. If the sentence presents an actual situation, i.e. a fact, then it is true, otherwise false. We do not mean to discuss here problems like 'what are situations?', 'how are they represented formally?', or 'what is the import of the concept of a situation to a theory of meaning?'. We just assume that in an arbitrary interpreted language sentences present situations, and that the actual obtaining or not-obtaining of those situations in reality is what makes the relevant sentences true or false. For an arbitrary language L we adopt, moreover, the following criterion of identity for situations: Two sentences of L present the same situation if and only if one may be substituted for the other in all sentential contexts of L without changing the truth-value of such a context.

This criterion may be put down in form of the following schema:

$$\mathbf{h}(\alpha) = \mathbf{h}(\beta) \Leftrightarrow \forall \gamma (\mathbf{v}(\gamma(\alpha)) = \mathbf{v}(\gamma[\alpha/\beta]))$$

where α, β, γ are arbitrary sentences of L, $\mathbf{v}$ is a function mapping sentences into truth-values, and $\mathbf{h}$ is a function mapping sentences into the situations they present.

Roman Suszko (1919-1979), under the influence of various but converging logico-philosophical ideas (we mean the works of authors like Ajdukiewicz 1967a and 1967b, Łoś 1948, Wittgenstein 1922 and Wolniewicz 1968), conceived the project of bringing into one perspective a whole class of logical calculi – like the classic sentential calculus, the classic predicate calculus, some modal logics, and finitely valued logics of Łukasiewicz. According to Suszko those calculi are particular cases of a more general kind of logic which he called the *non-Fregean* one. Their particularity consists in the adoption of certain ontological assumptions with regard of the universe of references for the sentences of the languages in which the logic in question holds. It follows, e.g.,

from the theorems of classic sentential calculus that the universe for its sentential variables must be a two-elements Boolean algebra. From the theorems of
the finitely valued logics of Łukasiewicz it follows that the universe for the
sentential variables is a finitely valued and linearly ordered Post algebra. From
those of intuitionistic logic it follows that the universe in question is a pseudo-
Boolean algebra, and from those of some modal logics that it is a topological
Boolean algebra. However, in all those algebras one element is designated as
the reference of true sentences.

The strongest assumption is adopted in classical logic according to which
the truth-value of any sentence is fully determined by the truth-values of its
clauses. This is so because in a language governed by classical logic the truth-
value of a compound sentence does not depend on the situation presented by it
but merely on the truth-values of its clauses. And this in turn, is so because the
only connectives classical logic takes account of are the truth-connectives.

According to Suszko, to formulate in a given language a fully formalized
theory of the reference of its sentences the vocabulary of that language must
contain, among others, the following symbols:

(1) sentential variables p_1, p_2, ...;
(2) truth-connectives $\neg$ negation, $\wedge$ conjunction, $\vee$ disjunction, $\rightarrow$ implication,
    $\leftrightarrow$ equivalence;
(3) an identity connective $\equiv$;
(4) quantifiers binding sentential variables (i.e. the universal one $\forall$, and the
    existential one $\exists$), and the auxiliary signs (and).

Truth-connectives are necessary to formalize any reasoning, and the identity
connective makes it possible to state that two sentences present the same situation. The quantifiers are needed to formulate general statements about the
universe of situations.

If the language in question does not contain sentential variables then according to Suszko it is not fit for a full formalization of a theory of situations, but at
best for that of a theory of events considered as reified equivalents of situations. (He deals with that question in Suszko 1971b (1993) and 1975).

Now let S be the set of all formulae constructed in the standard way out of
the signs mentioned under (1)-(4). Assume that we have a non-Fregean consequence operator Cn defined on S by selecting some formulae out of S as logical
axioms, and by adopting two proof rules answering to the schemas:

(RO) $a, a \rightarrow b \vdash b$
(RG) $\alpha(p) \vdash \forall p \alpha(p)$

The set Ax.Log of logical axioms splits into three groups:

(A1) The classic axioms for truth-connectives;
(A2) Axioms for quantifiers binding sentential variables which are all the formulae from S represented by the following schemas:

(1) $\forall p\alpha \to \alpha[p/\beta]$, where $\alpha[p/\beta]$ is the result of correctly substituting in the formula α the formula β for the variable p;

(2) $\alpha \to \forall p\alpha$, if p is not free in α;

(3) $\forall p(\alpha \to \beta) \to (\forall p\alpha \to \forall p\beta)$;

(4) $\exists p\alpha \leftrightarrow \neg\forall p\neg\alpha$

(A3) Axioms for the identity connective:

(5) $\alpha_1 \equiv \alpha_2$, where α_1, α_2, differ at most in bound variables;

(6) $\alpha \equiv \beta \to (\alpha \leftrightarrow \beta)$;

(7) $\alpha \equiv \beta \to (\neg\alpha \equiv \neg\beta)$;

(8) $(\alpha \equiv \beta) \wedge (\gamma \equiv \delta) \to (\alpha \,\S\, \gamma) \equiv (\beta \,\S\, \delta)$, where $\S = \wedge, \vee, \to, \leftrightarrow, \equiv$;

(9) $\forall p(\alpha \equiv \beta) \to Qp\alpha \equiv Qp\beta$, where $Q = \forall, \exists$.

The couple (S, Cn) is called a non-Fregean sentential logic. In the literature it is also known as 'SCI with quantifiers' (SCI for 'Sentential Calculus with Identity'). Thus (S, Cn) is that part of non-Fregean logic which is limited to formulae without expressions in the category of names. (A detailed presentation of non-Fregean logic is to be found in Suszko 1968a, 1968b and 1975.)

A formal semantics for non-Fregean logic has been developed by S. L. Bloom and R. Suszko in their 1971 and 1972. Under that semantics we mean by a model for the language of non-Fregean logic the structure defining:

Definition 1. A structure M is called a model for a non-Fregean sentential logic if and only if $M = (\mathcal{U}, F)$ satisfies the following three conditions:

(w_1) $\mathcal{U} = (U; \dashv, \cap, \cup, \to, \leftrightarrow, \circ, \bigcap, \bigcup)$ is a generalized algebra such that $\dashv$, $\cap, \cup, \to, \leftrightarrow, \circ$ are 1, 2, 2, 2, 2, 2-argument operations in the set U, respectively, and $\bigcap, \bigcup$ are operators of the type $U^U \to U$, where U^U is the set of all functions of one argument mapping U into U;

(w_2) $\varnothing \neq F \not\subseteq U$;

(w_3) for any $a, b \in U$ we have:

(i)	$\dashv a \in F$	$\Leftrightarrow$	$a \notin F$
(ii)	$a \cap b \in F$	$\Leftrightarrow$	$a \in F$ and $b \in F$
(iii)	$a \cup b \in F$	$\Leftrightarrow$	$a \in F$ or $b \in F$
(iv)	$a \to b \in F$	$\Leftrightarrow$	$a \notin F$ or $b \in F$
(v)	$a \leftrightarrow b \in F$	$\Leftrightarrow$	$a \in F$ and $b \in F$ or $a \notin F$ and $b \notin F$
(vi)	$a \circ b \in F$	$\Leftrightarrow$	$a = b$

and for any function $g \in U^U$ we have:

(vii) $\bigcap g \in F$ $\Leftrightarrow$ $g(a) \in F$, for every $a \in U$;

(viii) $\bigcup g \in F$ $\Leftrightarrow$ $g(a) \in F$, for some $a \in U$.

Any algebraic structure sastifying condition (w_1) we call a *generalized SCI-algebra*. If, moreover, the universe of a generalized SCI-algebra contains a subset F satisfying conditions (w_2) and (w_3), the structure $\mathcal{U}$ is called a *semi-model* for the language of a non-Fregean sentential logic. For a given generalized SCI-algebra $\mathcal{U}$ the collection of all subsets F such that conditions (w_2) and (w_3) are satisfied by them is denoted by $F_{\mathcal{U}}$.

Let us introduce now more semantic concepts pertaining to the interpretation of non-Fregean logics in their models.

Definition 2. By a *valuation* of the variables of L in the set U we mean an arbitrary function f: Var $\rightarrow$ U, where Var = $\{p_1, p_2, ...\}$ is the set of all the sentential variables of L.

For a given valuation f we define the function:

$$f_k^a(p_i) = \begin{cases} f(p_i), \text{ if } i \neq k \\ a, \text{ if } i = k \end{cases}$$

That function is a valuation of the variables in the set U too, differing from f at most at the variable p_k. For a given valuation f the value function of formulae $\|p_i ; f\|$: S $\rightarrow$ U is defined as follows:

$$
\begin{aligned}
\|p_i ; f\| &= f(p_i) \\
\|\neg\alpha_j; f\| &= \neg\|\alpha_j; f\| \\
\|\alpha \wedge \beta_j; f\| &= \|\alpha_j; f\| \cap \|\beta_j; f\| \\
\|\alpha \vee \beta_j; f\| &= \|\alpha_j; f\| \cup \|\beta_j; f\| \\
\|\alpha \rightarrow \beta_j; f\| &= \|\alpha_j; f\| \rightarrow \|\beta_j; f\| \\
\|\alpha \leftrightarrow \beta_j; f\| &= \|\alpha_j; f\| \leftrightarrow \|\beta_j; f\| \\
\|\alpha \equiv \beta_j; f\| &= \|\alpha_j; f\| \circ \|\beta_j; f\|
\end{aligned}
$$

Definition 3. A formula α is *satisfied in the model* M = $(\mathcal{U}, F)$ by a valuation of variables f if and only if $\|\alpha; f\| \in F$. (Symbolically: $\alpha \in Sat_f(M) \Leftrightarrow \|\alpha; f\| \in F$.)

Definition 4. A formula α is called *true in the model M* if and only if it is satisfied by every valuation of the variables. I.e., putting it down in symbols: $\alpha \in TR(M)$ iff $\alpha \, Sat_f(M)$ for any valuation f.

Definition 5. A formula α is called a *tautology* of a non-Fregean sentential logic if and only if α is true in all models of a language with that logic.

The concepts of valuation, satisfaction, truth, and tautologousness are strictly analogous to the usual ones in the semantics of logical calculi. Specific to a non-Fregean sentential logic is the concept of 'truth in a semi-model'. I.e.:

Definition 6. A formula α is called *true in the semi-model* $\mathcal{U}$ if and only if α is true in all models defined on the algebra $\mathcal{U}$. (Symbolically: $\alpha \in$ Val($\mathcal{U}$) iff $\alpha \in$ TR($\mathcal{U}$, F_i)), for any $F_i \in F_{\mathcal{U}}$.

Next we introduce the concept of a sentence *true in a given class of semi-models:* α is true in a given class of semi-models $\{\mathcal{U}_i: i \in I\}$ if and only if $\alpha \in$ Val($\mathcal{U}_i$), for any $i \in I$. Denote by $\mathcal{X}$ the class of all semi-models for a language L, and by $\mathcal{M}$ the class of models for that language. By the completeness theorem for non-Fregean logic it follows that we have:

$$Cn(\varnothing) = \bigcap\{(TR(M): M \in \mathcal{M})\} = \bigcap\{Val(\mathcal{U}): \mathcal{U} \in \mathcal{X}\}$$

3. Philosophical Interpretations of non-Fregean Sentential Logic

According to the principles of non-Fregean semantics as presented in Omyła 1975, all sentences of an interpreted language have their references. However, not in every such language are we in a position to put forward universal and existential theorems with regard to the structure of the universe of those references. To be in such position the language in question must contain as its sublanguage the language of non-Fregean sentential logic, or at least a significant part of it. As we are not interested here in the universe of any particular language, but only in that of a quite arbitrary one, let us consider now some philosophical aspects of arbitrary models of that kind. Let M = $(\mathcal{U}, F)$ be such a model. The elements of the universe of $\mathcal{U}$ do not generally answer to the intuitions we have about the reference of sentences, and about situations in particular. However, the algebraic structure imposed on $\mathcal{U}$ by the theory TR(M) is the same as that of a possible universe of situations, with regard to the operations corresponding to logical constants. Moreover, the set F has the formal properties of a possible (or 'admissible') set of situations obtaining in that universe. This is so because sentential variables are at the same time sentential formulae, and because the logical constants get in the model M their intended interpretation. Thus for any model M = ($\mathcal{U}$, F) its algebra $\mathcal{U}$ is a formal representation of some universe of situations, and the set F is a formal representation of some admissible set of facts obtaining in some universe of situations. Not all the generalized SCI-algebras represent some algebra of situations; for not all of them contain a set F representing the facts, i.e. such that the couple ($\mathcal{U}$, F) is a model. This depends on how the operations in the algebra $\mathcal{U}$ are defined. For the sake of simplicity the algebra of any model M = ($\mathcal{U}$, F) for the language of a non-Fregean sentential logic will be called the *algebra of situations* occurring in the model M, and the designated set F will be called the set of *facts* obtaining in M. Such a terminology is appropriate here for we are interested only in the formal properties of those universe of situations which in view of our semantic principles find expression in the logical syntax of the language in question, and in consequence operation holding in it. By the completeness theorem for non-Fregean logic it follows that for any consistent theory T in L there is a model M such that T ∈ TR(M). Hence any theory in the language of non-Fregean sentential logic will be called a *theory of situations.*

The term 'ontology of situations' we take over from the title of Wolniewicz 1985, but we understand it a bit differently. By an *ontology of situations* we mean a theory describing the necessary facts of universe of situations fixed beforehand. I.e. an ontology of situations is a set of formulae holding in some fixed universe of situations, independently of which situations there are facts. To be more accurate, by an ontology of situations we mean a set of formulae with the following three properties:

(1) An ontology of situations is a theory having in its vocabulary just one kind of variable – i. e. the sentential one. Under the intended interpretation they range over a universe of situations. (Like in modern set theory there are variables of just one kind, i.e. those ranging over sets.)

(2) An ontology of situations is formulated in a language containing logical symbols only, i. e. logical constants and variables. To justify that postulate let us note that such a basic theory should not presuppose any other terminology except the logical one. At most it might adopt some specific ontological terms as primitive, characterizing them axiomatically. However, we shall deal here only with such ontologies of situations which are expressed exclusively in logical terms.

(3) An ontology of situations describes only the necessary facts in a universe of situations fixed beforehand. I.e., it is a theory dealing with the whole universe of situations, and its propositions apply to such situations as are necessary in the universe given. Let N = {M_i: i ∈ I} = {($\mathcal{U}$, F_i): i ∈ I} be the class of all models for non-Fregean logic defined on the same algebra of

situations $\mathcal{U}$. Thus the models in N are determined by the same set of situations U. Moreover, they are verbalized in L in the same way – which manifests itself only by all the models having a common algebra, and differing merely by the sets of facts obtaining in them.

The set $\bigcap\{F_i: i \in I\}$ is the set of necessary facts in the algebra of situations $\mathcal{U}$; i. e., of those situations which are facts independently of what subset of situations obtains. For open SCI-languages the set mentioned was called by Suszko the core of the algebra $\mathcal{U}$. We use here this terminology too, and we write: $Core(\mathcal{U}) = \bigcap\{F_i: i \in I\}$. In view of the preceding we adopt the following definition of an ontology of situations:

Definition. A set of sentential formulae T of the language of non-Fregean logic is called an *ontology of situations* if and only if T is a theory in L and there is an algebra of situations $\mathcal{U}$ such that $T \subset Val(\mathcal{U})$.

In symbols we put down that definition as follows: $T \in OS_L$ iff $T \in TH(L)$ and $T \subset Val(\mathcal{U})$, where OS_L denotes the set of all ontologies of situations in the language of a non-Fregean sentential logic. (TH(L) is the set of all theories in L.)

Thus defined the notion of an ontology of situations reflects the intuition that an ontology consists of necessary propositions only; i. e., those depending only on the structure of the universe of situations, and not depending on the facts which hold only in some models ('possible worlds') defined on the algebra $\mathcal{U}$.

Having thus defined the notion of an ontology of situations we get immediately three corollaries:

Corollary 1. The set of all logical theorems of a non-Fregean sentential logic is the least ontology of situations in the language L. This is to say that $Cn(\varnothing)$ is an ontology of situations and every such ontology contains it.

The formulae of the form $\alpha \equiv \beta$, where $\alpha, \beta \in S$, we call equalities.

Corollary 2. If T is a theory axiomatizable by equalities and is consistent, then T is an ontology of situations.

By the condition (w_3, vi) in the definition of a model we can see that the truth of the equalities of an algebra depends solely on the structure of that algebra, not on the set of facts designated in it.

Corollary 3. In the language of the classic sentential logic there is just one ontology of situations, i.e. the set of all formulae true in a two-element Boolean algebra.

This follows from the circumstance that in the language of classical logic the identity connective is simply that of equivalence.

In the literature dealing with non-Fregean logic one takes into consideration various theories of situations which at the same time are their ontologies. The least such theory is the set of the propositions of logic. To ascribe its properties we adopt the following definition:

Definition. A situation $a \in U$ is called an *improper fact* in the model $M = (\mathcal{U}, F)$ if and only if a is the reference of some proposition of logic.

By the completeness theorem for non-Fregean logic it follows that $Cn(\emptyset)$ is the set comprising all and only those formulae of L which refer to facts improper in every algebra of situations. The set of all propositions of logic under a non-Fregean sentential logic put no structural or quantitative restrictions on the universe the sentential variables range over – except that there must be at least two distinct elements in that universe. This restriction is expressed by the following proposition of logic: $\exists p \exists q \neg (p \equiv q)$.

To express in the language of logic certain extra-logical presuppositions of ontology pertaining to the structure of the universe of situations, let us adopt the following designations. For any set of formulae A we mean by $Eqv(A)$ the set of all equalities $\alpha \equiv \beta$ such that $(\alpha \leftrightarrow \beta) \in A$; and we mean by D the set of the following seven equational definitions:

$1 \equiv \exists p.p$;
$0 \equiv \forall p.p$;
$\forall p \forall q((p \leq q) \equiv ((q \leq p) \equiv 1))$;
$SFp \equiv (\forall q(q \rightarrow (q \leq p)) \wedge \forall r(\forall q(q \rightarrow (q \leq r)) \rightarrow (p \leq r)))$;
$Inf\ Fp \equiv (\forall q(q \rightarrow (p \leq q)) \wedge \forall r(\forall q(q \rightarrow (r \leq q)) \rightarrow (r \leq p)))$;
$PWp \equiv (\neg(p \equiv 0) \wedge \forall q(q \leq p \vee \neg q \leq p))$;
$RWp \equiv (p \wedge \forall q(q \rightarrow (q \leq p)))$.

Using these designations we are in a position to determine the following theories of situations known in the literature:

$$WBQ =_{def} Cn(Eqv(Cn_0(\emptyset) \cup D);$$
$$WTQ =_{def} Cn(Eqv(\emptyset) \cup D);$$
$$WHQ =_{def} Cn(WBQ \cup H).$$

where Cn_0 is a subconsequence of Cn generated by the sets of axioms (A1), (A2), and by the rules (MP) and (Gen).

H is the set consisting of the two formulae:

$$\forall p \forall q((p \equiv q) \equiv ((p \equiv q) \equiv 1));$$
$$\forall p \forall q(\neg(p \equiv q) \equiv ((p \equiv q) \equiv 0)).$$

The theories WBQ, WTQ, and WHQ – being axiomatizable by equations – are ontologies of situations, and we have: WBQ $\Rightarrow$ WTQ $\Rightarrow$ WHQ.

The theory WBQ contains all the valid Boolean equations written out by means of sentential variables, connectives and quantifiers only.

The terms defined on D have the following intuitive import: 1 is a sentential constant, i. e. it is the abbreviation of some sentence (a formula with no free variables). This sentence says that there is at least one fact. The sentence $\exists p.p$ is a proposition of logic under a non-Fregean sentential logic; thus it presents an improper fact. Consequently, 1 is an improper fact to the effect that in any model the set of facts is not empty. Similarly 0 is the designated impossible situation to the effect that all situations are facts.

The formula 'p $\leq$ q', under any theory containing the set WBQ, is read: 'the situation p is contained in the situation q', or 'the situation p obtains in the situation q', or 'situation p occurs in situation q'. This is justified by the circumstance that in any WBQ-model the counterpart of the connective $\leq$ is an ordering relation on the universe of situations. SFp is to say that the situation p is – under the ordering – the least upper bound of the set of all facts; i. e. it is the sum of all facts. Similarly, Inf Fp says that p is its greatest lower bound.

RWp is to say that p is a fact containing all other facts.

Finally for any model $M = (\mathcal{U}, F)$ of L such that WBQ $\subset$ TR(M), the situation a satisfies the formula PWp if a is co-atom of a generalized SCI-algebra $\mathcal{U}$, the latter being a Boolean algebra with regard to the interpretation of the truth-connectives. To be able to read the formula PWp as 'the situation p is a possible world', we assume that 0 is the only impossible situation in the universe U. This holds for those models in which WHQ $\subset$ TR(M).

Any theory T expressed in the language of a non-Fregean sentential logic such that WBQ $\subset$ T is called a *WBQ-theory*, and its model a *WBQ-model*. (With W for Wittgenstein, B for Boolean algebra, and Q for quantifiers.) Similarly. any theory T such that WTQ $\subset$ T is called a *WTQ-theory*, and its models *WTQ-models*.

Furthermore, any theory T such that WHQ $\subset$ T is called a *WHQ-theory*, and its model a *WHQ-model*.

With T for the topological properties of WTQ-models, and H meaning that the universe of a WHQ-model is a Henle algebra, we get the following:

Metatheorem 1. In any WBQ-theory these formulae are theorems:
(i) $\exists pSFp$;
(ii) $\exists pInfFp$;
(iii) $\nabla p(InfFp,q) \equiv 1$; where ∇ is the description operator definable equationally by logical constants.

By the completeness theorem for non-Fregean logic meta-theorem 1 says that in every WBQ-model there exists the sum of all facts, and also their infimum which is the Boolean unit 1.

Metatheorem 2. In any WHQ-theory these formulae are theorems:
(i) $\exists p(p \wedge PWp) \equiv \exists pRWp$;
(ii) $SFp \rightarrow (p \leftrightarrow PWp)$;
(iii) $SFp \rightarrow (p \equiv 0 \vee PWp)$.

Condition (i) says that the existence of a situation which is both a fact and a possible world is the same as the existence of the real world. Condition (ii) says that if a situation is the sum of all facts then it is a fact if and only if it is a possible world. Condition (iii) says that the situation which is the sum of all facts is either the impossible one or a possible world.

Metatheorem 3. For any WHQ-model $M = (\mathcal{U}; F)$ we have:
(i) with regard to the ordering of situations, the least upper bound of a set of possible worlds is $\|\nabla p(PWp \rightarrow p)\|$;
(ii) the greatest lower bound of such a set is $\|\exists p(p \wedge PWp)\|$.

The values of the formulae occurring in (i) and (ii) – in a fixed model M – do not depend on the valuation of the variables as they do not contain any free variables. Simple proofs of the metatheorems mentioned may be found in Omyła 1986.

From metatheorem 3, and in view of the connection between truth in an algebra of situations and truth in the model defined on that algebra, we get the following:

Corollary 1. In any WHQ-model $M = (\mathcal{U}; F)$ these equivalences hold:
(i) No situation is a possible world in the algebra of situations $\mathcal{U}$ iff $(\exists p(p \wedge PWp) \equiv 0) \in Val (\mathcal{U})$.
(ii) In the algebra of situations $\mathcal{U}$ there are situations which are possible worlds iff $(\neg\exists p(p \wedge PWp) \equiv 0) \in Val (\mathcal{U})$.

(iii) In M there is a situation which is the real world iff $\exists p(p \land PWp)$ is true in M.

(iv) In U each possible situation is contained in some possible world iff $(\exists p(p \land PWp) \equiv 0) \in Val\ (\mathcal{U})$.

(v) Either each possible situation is contained in some possible world, or none is contained in any, iff $(\exists p(p \land PWp) \equiv 0 \lor \exists p(p \land PWp) \equiv 1) \in Val\ (\mathcal{U})$.

Corollary 2. For any model $M = \langle \mathcal{U};\ F \rangle$ of the language of a non-Fregean sentential logic one may try to determine the following sets of propositions: $Cn(\varnothing) \not\subseteq TPW(M) \not\subseteq Val(\mathcal{U}) \not\subseteq TR(M)$, where $TPW(\mathcal{U})$ is a theory of possible worlds in the algebra of situations $\mathcal{U}$, and $Val(\mathcal{U})$ is the greatest ontology of situations true in the model M. The set $TR(M) - Val(\mathcal{U})$ is the set of propositions describing the facts holding contingently in the model M, but which may not hold in other models defined on $\mathcal{U}$.

References

Ajdukiewicz, K. 1967a: "Intensional expressions", *Studia Logica* 20, 63-86.

Ajdukiewicz, K. 1967b: "Proposition as the connotation of sentence", *Studia Logica* 20, 87-98.

Bloom, S. L. 1971: "A completeness theorem for 'theories of kind W'", *Studia Logica* 27, 43-55.

Bloom, S.L. 1974: "On 'generalized logics'", *Studia Logica* 33, 65-68.

Bloom, S.L. and Suszko, R. 1971: "Semantics for the sentential calculus with identity", *Studia Logica* 28, 77-81.

Bloom, S.L. and Suszko, R. 1972: "Investigations into the sentential calculus with identity", *Notre Dame Journal of Formal Logic* 13, 289-308.

Łoś, J. 1948: "Logiki wielowartościowe a formalizacja funkcji intensjonalnych" [Many-valued logics and the formalization of intensional functions], *Kwartalnik filozoficzny* 17, 59-78.

Łoś, J. 1949: "O matrycach logicznych" [About logical matrices], *Travaux de la Societé des Sciences et des Letters de Wrocław*, ser., 19, B.

Michaels, A. and Suszko, R. 1976: "Sentential calculus of identity and negation", *Reports on Mathematical Logic* 7, 87-106.

Omyła, M. 1976: "Translatability in non-Fregean theories", *Studia Logica* 36, 127-138.

Omyła, M. 1978: "Boolean theories with quantifiers", *Bulletin of the Section of Logic* 7, 76-83.

Omyła, M. 1982: "The logic of situations", *Language and ontology,* Wien, 195-198.

Omyła, M. 1986: *Zarys logiki niefregewskiej* [Outline of non-Fregean logic], Warszawa.

Omyła, M. 1990: "Principles of non-Fregean semantics for sentences" (Abstract), *Journal of Symbolic Logic* 60, 422-423.

Omyła, M. and Suszko, R. 1972a: "Descriptions in theories of kind W", *Bulletin of the Section of Logic* 1, 8-13.

Omyła, M. and Suszko, R. 1972b: "Definitions in theories of kind W", *Bulletin of the Section of Logic* 1, 14-19.

Omyła, M. and Zygmunt, J. 1984: "Roman Suszko (1919 - 1979): A bibliography of the published work with an outline of his logical investigations", *Studia Logica* 43, 421-441.

Suszko, R. 1968: "Ontology in the *Tractatus* of L. Wittgenstein", *Notre Dame Journal of Formal Logic* 9, 7-33.

Suszko, R. 1968a: "Non-Fregean logic and theories", *Analele Universitatii Bucuresti, Acta logica* 11, 105-25.

Suszko, R. 1971a: "Quasi completeness in non-Fregean logic", *Studia Logica* 29, 7-14.

Suszko, R. 1971b: "Reifikacja sytuacji" [The reification of situations], *Studia Filozoficzne* 2, 65-82.

Suszko, R. 1975: "Abolition of the Fregean axiom", *Lecture Notes in Mathematics* 453, 169-39.

Suszko, R. 1977: "The Fregean axiom and Polish mathematical logic in the 1920", *Studia Logica* 35, 377-380.

Suszko, R. 1993: "The reification of situations" [English version of Suszko 1971 to appear in *Philosophical logic in Poland,* Synthese Library].

Wittgenstein, L. 1922: *Tractatus Logico-Philosophicus,* London.

Wolniewicz, B. 1968: *Rzeczy i fakty. Wstęp do pierwszej filozofii Wittgensteina* [Things and facts. An introduction to Wittgenstein's first philosophy], Warszawa.

Wolniewicz, B. 1985: *Ontologia sytuacji* [Ontology of situations], Warszawa.

KAREL LAMBERT

ATTRIBUTIVES, THEIR FIRST DENOTATIVE CORRELATES, COMPLEX PREDICATES AND FREE LOGICS

1

English words and phrases of adjectival, verbal, or prepositional form fall in the class of expressions traditionally called *attributive* terms; this is the class of expressions "purport(ing)... to *apply* to things".[1] Examples are 'courageous', 'studies', and 'next to'. English nouns and noun phrases fall in the class of expressions traditionally called denotative terms; this is the class of expressions "purport(ing) to *refer* to things".[2] Examples are 'Russell', 'the author of "On Denoting"', 'courageous things' and 'philosopher'. Of particular interest here are pairs of expressions such as the attributive term 'courageous' and the denotative term 'courageous things'. The second member of this pair is the *first denotative correlate* of the attributive term 'courageous'. (Attributives also have *second denotative correlates*. These are abstract terms that purport to name the property in virtue of which a certain thing is such and such. 'courage', for example is the second denotative correlate of the attributive 'courageous'.) For every attributive term there is a first denotative correlate which can be regimented as an expression of the form 'object x such that x is...' , where '...' is replaced by that attributive term.

It is a dogma in the current logic of terms that a statement of the form

(1) *a* is *P*

is logically equivalent to a statement of the form

---

[1] See Leonard 1967, 196.
[2] Leonard 1967, 196.

R. Poli and P. Simons, Formal Ontology, 189–198.

(2) *a* is an object *x* such that *x* is *P*,

where *P* is an attributive term in both (1) and (2). For instance,

(3) Jules is courageous

is logically equivalent to

(4) Jules is an object *x* such that *x* is courageous.

Henry Leonard has observed that there "is an inclination... to think" of a statement of the form in (1) as "characterizing" its purported subject, and there is also a "temptation to think of" a statement of the form in (2) as "classifying" its purported subject.[3] But whereas many, including Leonard, believe that classifying statements imply the existence of their purported subjects, they do not believe that characterizing statements do.

This collection of dogmas, inclinations, temptations, and implications yields the following inconsistent set of principles: where '*a*' is a singular term and '*P*' is an attributive,

(5) '*a* is *P*' is logically equivalent to '*a* is an object *x* such that *x* is *P*'.
(6) '*a* is *P*' does not logically imply '*a* exists'.
(7) '*a* is an object *x* such that *x* is *P*' logically implies '*a* exists'.

Various ways out of this conundrum are afforded by the different approaches to free logic. For example, a *negative* free logician would accept (5) and (7), but reject (6), given his Russell-like conviction that any simple statement containing the singular term '*a*' implies the statement '*a* exists'. This amounts to a rejection of any proclivity to treat (simple) classifying statements as implying existence, but (simple) characterizing statements as not implying existence. Again, some *positive* free logicians would accept (5) and (6) while rejecting (7), given their Meinong-like conviction that, except perhaps for statements of the form '*a* exists', or their equivalents, *no* simple statement containing the singular term '*a*' implies the statement '*a* exists'. This option also implies a rejection of the basic intuition about the difference between characterizing and classifying noted by Leonard. However, for those free logicians of a positive bent, but whose ontological proclivities are more Russellian than Meinongian, in the sense that the objects are regarded as

---

[3] Leonard, 1964, 33.

coextensive with the existents (a proclivity shared by the author), there is another way out of the above conundrum, a way out which, incidentally, is neutral on the acceptability of the basic intuition mentioned by Leonard.[4] This is the option to be explored in what follows.

2

The major thesis of this essay is that it is the dogma of the traditional logic of terms which is at fault, the doctrine reflected in (5), but that (6) and (7) are true. Consider, first, the first denotative correlates of attributive terms. They have the form:

(8) object x such that x is P.

In contrast to instances of 'P', instances of (8) are always complex predicates. Some notation will be helpful in the following discussion.

Prefixing Δx_1, ..., Δx_n to an open sentence A containing the variables x_1, ..., x_n, yields a complex predicate, and is to be read 'object x_1, ..., object x_n such that $A(x_1, ..., x_n)$. For instance, given the open sentences, respectively, 'x is courageous' and 'x is identical with y', then '$\Delta x(x$ is courageous)' is the complex predicate 'object x such that x is courageous' and '$\Delta x \Delta y(x$ is identical with $y)$' is the complex predicate 'object x, object y such that x is identical with y'. (Hereafter discussion will be limited to complex predicates in one variable, that is, to one place first denotative correlates.)

With this notation, and the convention that concatenation expresses the copula, (1) and (2) can be represented, respectively, as

(9) Pa

and

[4] A negative free logic is one which counts any simple statement containing at least one irreferential singular term false; a positive free logic is one which counts some such statements true. There are also *neuter* free logics; these are free logics which count at least some of the statements in question as neither true nor false, but none as true. Most developments of free logic via supervaluations are positive, rather than neuter. Brian Skyrms' treatment in his 1968 is an example to the contrary.

(10) $\Delta x(Px)a$.

(Since the complex predicate in (10) is the formal counterpart of the first denotative correlate of the attributive in (9), the suppressed copula in (10) must be expressed as 'is an' because attributives are just expressions which go in the place of '...' in 'a is ...', and denotatives are just those which fill the place of '...' in 'a is a (an) ...'.) Remembering Russell's famous recommendation about how to paraphrase of 'I met a man', namely, as 'There exists something which is masculine and I met him', in general, statements of the form in (10) should be treated as logically equivalent to

(11) $\exists x(x = a \land Px)$.

In other words, the denotative term expressed by the complex predicate in (10) conveys existential import to statements of that form. This is because the indefinite article 'a (an)' in the suppressed copula 'is a (an)' of the informal counterpart of (10), following Russell, has existential force, and thus (10) must be logically equivalent to a statement whose scope is governed by an existential quantifier. Indeed, this is quite consistent with standard paraphraseology as practiced in contemporary logic courses.

To borrow one of Leonard's examples, consider now the true statement,

(12) Sherlock Holmes is fictitious,

containing the attributive 'fictitious'.[5] This statement does not imply the existence of Sherlock Holmes, and hence it would be incorrect (for the species of positive free logician now under consideration, the species with the Russellian ontological bent) to treat the formal counterpart of (12) as logically equivalent to the formal counterpart of

(13) There exists something the same as Sherlock Holmes who is fictitious,

because (13) does imply the existence of Sherlock Holmes. (Other attributives which can be used to make the same point and which are favored by the brand of positive free logician under consideration are attributives such as 'identical with' and 'rotates' as in, respectively, 'Sherlock Holmes is identical with Sherlock Holmes' and 'Vulcan rotates'.) In general, then, the traditional dogma that simple statements containing attributives terms are logically equivalent to their

---

[5] Leonard 1964, 34.

simple counterparts in which the attributive is replaced by its first denotative correlate is false, and hence (9) is not logically equivalent to (10). Of course, this is exactly the resolution required of the conundrum above given acceptance of both (6) and (7). It should be noted that the argument for rejecting (5) does not in any way depend on the intuition that classifying statements imply the existence of what is being classified, but characterizing statements do not imply the existence of what is being characterized; in Meinongian terms, the current reason for abandoning (5) skirts the question whether what an object is does (or does not) imply that that object exists.[6]

One of the major benefits of the resolution being proposed is that enables a development of free logic which harmonizes positive and negative free logic, and which, incidentally, provides an analysis of (singular) existence without recourse to an identity predicate, an analysis which accords with ideas laid out perhaps most clearly by Arthur Prior. Let me turn to these matters now.

3

The proof theory of the version of free logic to be sketched is not new. It is essentially that in a paper by Ermanno Bencivenga and me entitled "A Free Logic with Simple and Complex Predicates", and was based on supervaluational semantics.[7] Indeed, the remarks in the first two sections of the current essay can be taken as a different motivation for developing the theory of complex predicates outlined in our paper. However, the resolution of the conundrum manifested in (5)-(7) entertained in Section 2 of this essay is not essentially tied to supervaluations. To establish the point, the version of free logic to be sketched will be based instead on inner-outer domain semantics.

An inner-outer domain semantics construes models (of the formal language) as ordered triples consisting of a set of entities – the inner domain (intuitively, the existent objects), another set disjoint from the first set – the outer domain,

---

[6] Leonard himself, on page 33 of his 1964, notes that the 'temptations' to regard simple statements with attributives in predicate position as not implying existence, but simple statements with denotatives in predicate position as implying existence are 'unreliable'. He writes: "the system of simple cognates is so incomplete in English and the inclination to brevity so strong among users that these temptations become unreliable, or the forms ambiguous. The intention of a speaker using an attributive predicate may well be to classify and that of a speaker using a substantive predicate might well be to characterize rather than to classify".

[7] See our 1986.

and an interpretation function which when applied to singular terms takes as values entities in the union of the inner and outer domains. Perhaps the natural way to think of the outer domain is as the set of nonexistent objects, but that is not the only way. For example, one can think of the outer domain as a set of singular terms *à la* Meyer and Lambert, as the set of *virtual* objects *à la* Scott, or as positions in logical space *à la* van Fraassen.[8] Indeed, if one wishes to cleave to the Russellian equation of the existents with the objects, contra Meinong, the outer domains must be construed in some such way as exemplified in the previous sentence. It will be most convenient here to think of the outer domain as consisting of virtual objects, 'entities' clawing their way toward objecthood.[9]

Assume, then, a standard first order language with identity, the existence symbol 'E!', and singular terms, and suppose that the interpretation function is defined on the attributives (simple predicates) in the conventional way; where P is an attributive, the interpretation function I assigns to P a set of members from the union of the inner domain D and the outer domain D^+ as its extension. For denotatives (complex predicates), I is defined as follows; where P is an attributive, I assigns to $\Delta x(Px)$ the subset of the set assigned to P whose members are members of D as its extension. Intuitively, the extension of the first denotative correlate of the attributive term P is that subset of the set assigned to P consisting just of the existent entities. The existence symbol 'E!' is, as usual, assigned D as its extension.

Except for statements with quantifiers, the characterization of truth is absolutely conventional. For instance, where PR is a predicate, either simple or complex, PRa is true in M just in case a is a member of the extension of PR.

Nevertheless, if 'a' is not assigned a member of D (the set of existents), then 'Pa' could be true when '$\Delta x(Px)a$' is false; for instance 'Pegasus flies' could be true though 'Pegasus is a flying object' is false. However, the quantificational contexts

(14) $\exists x A$

and

---

[8] See Meyer and Lambert 1968; Scott 1967; and van Fraassen 1967.

[9] Virtual objects come in various sorts ranging from Scott's virtual sets to the virtual particles of modern physics. But whereas the latter are genuine physical objects – they exist, after all – the former are not. Virtual objects here are virtual in the sense of Scott, and even earlier, Quine. In other words, as entertained in this essay, they are no more objects than blunderbusses are conveyances filled with mistake prone people ... to paraphrase Nuel Belnap.

15) $\forall xA$

are true in the model M if and only if, respectively, $A(a/x)$ is true in the model M for *some* singular term a having a referent in D (intuitively, the set of existents), and $A(a/x)$ is true in the model M for *all* singular terms a having referents in D. These last conditions on the quantifiers, characteristic of any free logic, guarantee that the quantifiers have existential force in the sense that they are restricted to the existents (or the domain of the objects for the current species of positive free logician).

Given the above conditions on models and truth in a model, it is easy to show that the inference from

(16) Pa

to

(17) $E!a$

is invalid, but the inference from

(18) $\Delta x(Px)a$

to

(19) $E!a$

is valid. Of course, the more general inference pattern '$A(a/x) \supset \exists xA$' fails to be valid (as one would expect) in any free logic. It is also a straightforward matter to show that

(20) $\Delta x(Px)a \equiv (Pa \wedge E!A)$

and

(21) $E!a \supset (Pa \equiv \Delta x(Px)a)$

are logically true. Thus are the intuitions of both negative and positive free logicians accommodated.

One interesting consequence of the preceding development is this: existence can be defined in terms of scope distinction collapse for negation, a view apparently once favored by Arthur Prior.[10] For it is easy to show, in view of (20) and (21), that

(22) $E!a \equiv (\neg\Delta x(Px)a \equiv \Delta x(\neg Px)a)$

is logically true in the current development of free logic. Another pleasant consequence is the following; if a does not exist, then it is not the case that a is an *object* which is P nor is it the case that a is an *object* which is non-P, no matter what P describes. This follows immediately from (22) and the reading of the complex predicate forming operator 'Δ ...' as '*object* ... such that', and comports euphoniously with the view that virtual objects are *not* objects.

4

Consider the natural language statement

(23) Bush is a wimp.

The expression 'wimp' in (23) is a denotative general term. The question arises; how should (23) be paraphrased into the formal language outlined above? The answer is

(24) Bush is an object lacking courage

because, first, there are no simple denotatives in the formal language – and hence (23) must be regarded as containing a suppressed complex predicate such as, for example, 'object lacking courage', and, second, that denotatives in the current formal language include only attributives such as, for example, 'lacks courage'. The model here is, of course, Russell's famous treatment of 'I met a man' as 'I met x and x is human' in *The Introduction to Mathematical Philosophy* in which the attributive 'human' occurs. In the current development, Russell's sentence would be paraphrased more directly as 'I met an object which is human'. This construal of apparently simple denotatives as really complex predicates may not be appealing to everyone. Moreover, there is the

[10] See Williams 1981.

assumption in the preceding that all attributives are simple – despite examples such as 'pastel yellow', an apparently complex attributive – which may also give some cause for pause. Finally, it is misleading to refer to certain words as attributive or denotative; 'human', for instance, can occur in contexts such as 'Bush is human', hence attributively, and also can occur in contexts such as 'Bush is a human', hence denotatively. To accommodate these concerns the barest sketch of another approach within the constraints of free logic follows below.

Return to the basic contexts

(24) '... is ___'

and

(25) '... is a ___'.

The expression replacing '___' in (24) must be attributive, and in (25) must be denotative. So the predicates of the language are now to be treated just as general terms, and not merely as attributive general terms. Additionally, let us add to the formal language two copulas '$\subset$' and '$\subseteq$' corresponding, respectively, to the expressions 'is' in (24) and 'is a' in (25), and the complex predicate forming operators 'Δ' and '∇' (the latter to form complex attributives). In general, then,

(26) $a \subset P$

will be true just in case

(27) Pa

is true, where P is either simple or complex. On the other hand,

(28) $a \subseteq P$

will be true just in case

(29) $E!a \wedge Pa$,

where P is either simple or complex. This bare outline of an alternative approach formulable in free logic adequate to resolving the conundrum described in the first section of this paper does not detail any of the (sometimes obvious) logical relations between '... is ___' contexts and '... is a (an) ___' contexts nor of the intricacies in the structures of the two kinds of complex predicate. The formulation of such a logic is left as an open problem to the interested reader.

References

Bencivenga, E. and Lambert, K. 1986: "A Free Logic with Simple and Complex Predicates", *Notre Dame Journal of Formal Logic* 27, 247-256.

Fraassen, B. van 1967: "Meaning Relations Among Predicates", *Nous* 1, 161-179.

Leonard, H. 1964: "Essences, Attributes and Predicates", *Proceedings and Addresses of the American Philosophical Association*, University of Delaware Press, Newark, Delaware.

Leonard, H. 1967: *Principles of Reasoning*, Dover, New York.

Meyer, R.K. and Lambert, K. 1968: "Universally Free Logic and Standard Quantification Theory", *The Journal of Symbolic Logic* 33, 8-26.

Schoenman, R. 1967: *Bertrand Russell: Philosopher of the Century*, Little, Brown and Co., Boston.

Scott, D. 1967: "Existence and Description in Formal Logic", in Schoenman 1967, 181-200.

Skyrms, B. 1968: "Supervaluations: Identity, Existence and Individual Concepts ", *The Journal of Philosophy* 64, 477-483.

Williams, C.J.F. 1981: *What Is Existence?*, Clarendon Press, Oxford.

LILIANA ALBERTAZZI

FORMAL AND MATERIAL ONTOLOGY

1. Introduction

1. We owe the concept of *formal ontology* to Husserl, who called it the 'formal theory' of objects. However, the concept of *formal* as used by Husserl in his definition should not be understood in the conventional sense, since in his thought 'formal' is equivalent to 'categorial'; it is closely connected with the structures of the intentional acts and, as we shall see, has morphodynamic implications.

In contemporary philosophy, formal ontology has been developed in two principal ways. The first approach has been to study formal ontology as a part of ontology, and to analyse it using the tools and approach of formal logic: from this point of view formal ontology examines the logical features of predication and of the various theories of universals.[1] The use of the specific paradigm of set theory applied to predication, moreover, conditions its interpretation.

The second line of development returns to its Husserlian origins and analyses the fundamental categories of *object, state of affairs, part, whole*, and so forth, as well as the relations between parts and the whole and their laws of dependence – once all material concepts have been replaced by their correlative formal concepts relative to the pure 'something'.[2] This kind of analysis does not deal with the problem of the relationship between formal ontology and material ontology.

[1] Cocchiarella 1972, 1974, 1986 and 1991.
[2] Smith 1978, 1983, 1984a and 1984b; Smith and Mulligan 1982 and 1983; Simons 1986 and 1987; Poli 1992, Ch. 2, and 1993.

R. Poli and P. Simons, Formal Ontology, 199–232.
© 1996 *Kluwer Academic Publishers. Printed in the Netherlands.*

1.1 In a general classification of ontologies, Husserl's ontology belongs to the category of ontologies of layers,[3] that is, those that describe the world using categories of 'dependence' and 'emergence' to explain its various internal configurations.[4]

Hence, the general concept of *ontology* in Husserl should not be understood in the standard sense either, because it is based on two categories which derive from Brentano's ontology: those of *intentional presentation* and of *intentional modification*.[5]

In short, Husserl's concept of formal ontology rests on a categorially prior concept: namely, a *material* ontology which explains its morphological genesis on the basis of the structures of perception.[6]

1.2 More precisely, there are *two different material* ontologies present in Husserl.[7] His *dynamic* material ontology addresses the sphere of the material formation of the objects of presentation, and therefore the realm of perception and its foundations: in short, the realm of the antepredicative structures. The chief categories of this dynamic material ontology, as we shall see, are *intentional inherence*,[8] *temporal extension, place, position, border, surfaces*. Some of these categories – for example, temporal extension, place or position – are absent from his formal ontology, although they maintain their foundational character, that is, they are ontologically prime.[9]

Husserl's *static* material ontology, on the other hand, concerns the higher material genera, the material categories in which the individual ontologies are rooted: in short, it addresses the dependence laws that circumscribe the ontological regions.[10] These regional ontologies of his static material ontology are the higher genera, which include every individual of a given and extremely

---

[3] Husserl 1913, 370 and Husserl 1973, Beilage II, 341. The ontology of 'layers' should be understood as possessing different levels of reality linked by a foundation relationship. It should not, therefore, be taken in the sense of the 'complexity' of organisms. On this see Albertazzi 1989. Another example of an 'ontology of layers' is Hartmann's ontology. See Hartmann 1948, 1949a, 1949b.

[4] For a classification of ontologies see Perzanowski 1990; Poli 1989 and 1992.

[5] Brentano 1874. On the topic of modification in Brentano see Kraus 1930, 1-22; Chisholm 1981, 3-16; Albertazzi 1994-5.

[6] Husserl 1913, II; Husserl 1929, § 38; Husserl 1973.

[7] Husserl 1900-1, Prolegomena and Husserl 1954, § 6, section 1.

[8] Husserl 1900-1, Third Logical Investigation, §§ 8 and 12. On this see Piana 1977, 7-71.

[9] Johansson 1992, 190.

[10] Husserl 1913, 1, § 75. On static (descriptive) and dynamic (genetic) concepts in descriptive psychology see Hedwig 1988 and Albertazzi 1990-1.

general species as a member of its extension. Examples of regional ontologies are those given by the concepts 'animate organism', 'material thing', 'psyche'.

Husserl gives specific treatment and a formal definition only to his static material ontology. At least three series of his lectures, however, those dealing in various ways with the structure of presentation, contain material with which to delineate what I have called his dynamic material ontology.[11]

1.3 From a dynamic point of view, the material ontology precedes the formal ontology because it constitutes its foundational level: it deals, in fact, with the precategorial genesis of the formal notion of 'object'.

From a static viewpoint, however, it is the formal ontology that precedes the material ontology, because it constitutes its highest formal genus.[12] Once the object has been defined in a formal sense, in fact, one can proceed with a descriptive classification of the various kinds of ontological object couched in material terms.

Here I shall describe only the foundational relationship between formal ontology and dynamic material ontology. In particular, I shall provide a description of the categorial structures that underpin the dynamic material ontology and which precede the *pure* formal categories of the formal ontology. Except for some brief references, therefore, my analysis will not concern itself with the static material ontology.

2. Theory of Objects

As Husserl points out, 'object' is a term that stands for many interconnected formations – for example, 'thing', 'property', 'relation', 'relationship of things', 'set', 'order', and so on.[13] These various meanings of 'object' do not lie at the same level but relate to a type of 'primary objectivity' or substratum of which all others are derivates: the 'something in general'.

Husserl uses the term 'object' as well as the term 'part of an object' in the most general manner possible. Because of this extreme generality, in his Third Investigation there is a constant shifting between the concepts of object and

[11] The Husserlian texts dealing with material ontology are various collections of his lectures (Husserl 1966a; Husserl 1966b; Husserl 1973) and two works which, in different ways, describe the 'genealogy of logic' (Husserl 1939 and Husserl 1974).

[12] Albertazzi 1989, Ch. 9, 294 and Poli 1992, Ch. 1.

[13] Husserl 1913, I, § 10.

content, and between the correlated concepts of parts of objects and parts of contents.

2.1 The Third Investigation, moreover, contains a relation which performs an important function. It is twofold in nature and appears in both the material ontology and the formal ontology with substantially similar features. To avoid misunderstandings, I shall use the term *dependence relation* to refer to the relation between real objects, like bodies, and *foundation relation* to refer to the relation between contents, although Husserl tends to collapse the two relations together.[14]

Objects stand in a relationship of dependence or independence, like wholes which are in themselves segmented or segmentable. Within them, their parts are not only discrete in content, but they are also relatively independent of each other.

The laws of dependence and of non-independence, Husserl asserts, are material laws relative to the synthetic a priori: for example, a colour cannot exist without extension. 'Colour' is not a 'relative presentation', the meaning of which includes the presentation of a relationship with something else – in the way in which, for example, 'wife' and 'father' include the presentations 'husband' and 'son'. The existence of a coloured object, in fact, is not grounded 'analytically' in the concept of colour.

2.2 The *part* of an object is that which is *distinguishable* within it or which is *present* (*vorhanden*) within it. There are independent parts (or pieces) and non-independent parts (or moments). Pieces (or fractions) are parts in the strict sense and they are independent of the whole to which they belong. Moments, instead, are abstract and non-independent parts. There are pieces which do not have parts in common and which are therefore discrete. If, although discrete, they are also contiguous – for example, points aligned in a continuum – they may have an abstract part or moment in common – which is their *limit*.

In principle, every part of an object may become an autonomous object as a 'presented content': in fact, we can present a leg to ourselves independently of a body, or a door independently of a house.

As regards contents, their parts are independent if they can be presented separately; or they are non-independent if they cannot be presented separately.

[14] On the part-whole theory see Simons 1987 and Libardi 1990.

Separately presentable, according to Husserl, is "every phenomenal thing and every piece of it, for example the head of a horse or the spatial form filled with sensible qualities".[15]

Non separately presentable is a non-independent content, as in the case of visual quality and extension, or the connection between visual quality, extension and the figure that delimits it.

Although they cannot be presented separately, non-independent contents can *vary* in independent manner. For example, the colour of a particular surface can vary, or the shape of the surface can change while its colour remains the same. In this case, what varies independently is not the content but the species of the moments within the genus.[16] The non-independence of contents is a *functional dependence* by virtue of which, taken independently, they are only partial contents of a whole content.[17] Non-independent contents therefore exist only as parts of more comprehensive wholes of a certain corresponding species: a colour, for example, is by its nature inevitably a part, because it can exist in general only as a moment of an independent content.

2.3 The relations of non-independence among *contents* are expressed by the foundation relation. The foundation can be *unilateral* and *bilateral*, *immediate* and *mediated*.[18]

By *bilateral* foundation is meant the connection between, for example, colour and extension, because both are part of a unitary intuition. A *unilateral* foundation is the connection between the presentations and the judgement which is based upon them, since the presentations need not necessarily function as the basis for the judgement.

As regards independence or relative non-independence, bilateral foundation is undoubtedly a case of relative non-independence, while in the connection between piece and figure, the figure is non-independent with respect to the piece, but is in turn founded on an independent something.

Moreover, as said, the foundation can be mediated or immediate according to the connection among the parts, which can be 'closer' or 'further'. By this Husserl means that, for example, the genus colour is immediately connected to

---

15 Husserl 1901, Third Investigation, § 3.

16 A particular case of this variation is 'phenomenal salience': when we are perceptively affected by a particular colour or by a particular spatial pattern. In this case the phenomenal salience of a colour becomes the basis on which we note another content inherent to it.

17 Husserl 1901, Third Investigation, § 4.

18 It would be more approriate to speak of founded contents rather than non-independent ones. Similarly, the specification of contents in the foundation relation also applies to objects in the laws of dependence.

its specific species of green, yellow, blue, etc. In turn, green, yellow and blue are immediately connected to an extension; colour and extension are consequently connected only mediately. The laws of mediated connection are called analytic laws based on the laws of immediate connection.

2.4 Not all the relations pertaining to the objects of the phenomenological realm exist among the objects of a formal theory: for example, on the phenomenological level there are the two different and specific relations of *distinction* and *fusion*.

Some objects present themselves to intuition as distinct, others instead present themselves fused with the contents connected with them. An example of contents fused with other, simultaneously given contents is provided by the parts of a uniformly white surface. The distinction between fused contents and distinct contents does not regard the ontological level, and hence it does not concern in the strict sense the difference between independent and non-independent contents: in fact, if contents are perceived as distinct they may be equally independent or non-independent.[19]

In general, one may state that a certain content A is 'relatively non-independent' of a content B (that is, of a system of contents determined by B and by its parts) if there exists a rule to the effect that a content of the genus A may exist a priori alone or in connection with other contents belonging to the overall system of content genera determined by B. If such a law does not exist, A is defined as being 'relatively independent' of B.[20]

Let us take the specific case of a momentary intuition in the visual field. The filled visual field is independent of the whole of the visual intuition. Also independent are the pieces of the intuition and every filled section of the visual field. By contrast, the colour of this piece is non-independent, and so is every quality or form of the visual field.

2.5 The parts of a whole are such by *co-penetration* or by *connection*. An example of parts which co-penetrate is provided by the parts of a homogeneous surface of uniform colour, in which the parts are not immediately distinguish-

---

[19] Husserl 1901, Third Investigation, § 9.

[20] Objects and contents may coexist as momentary entities or they may coexist in a duration. If we consider the case of a temporal whole, its determinations, as relations of before and after, segments of the continuum, etc., are part of the system of contents determined by the whole itself. A particular content x with temporal determination t_0 postulates another content with temporal determination $t_1 = t_0 + 1$, and is therefore a non-independent content. This non-independence rule holds for the contents of consciousness which constantly interweave with each other.

able. An example of connected parts is given by the parts of a table, since this is perceived as a unit but the parts of it remain distinct. In this case the pieces of the whole (or independent contents) are the basis of further contents, which are the *forms* that connect them to the interior of the whole.

It is not necessary for all the constituents of the whole to concur in the configuration of its form: this is evidenced extremely clearly by perceptive vision, which involves the wholes presented to it and which is governed by the laws of Gestalt. In the configuration of the wholes that we recognize as a glass, chair or bed, for example, there are parts that are entirely irrelevant or which do not perform any role. This fact applies to the perceptive field, but from a certain point of view it holds for the ontological field as well. The question concerns the ontological identity of wholes: for example, whether, from an ontological point of view, I become something else if I lose a hair, or if a glass is still the same thing should it lose an atom.

In the case of certain wholes it is necessary to presuppose a priori the existence of moments of unity. The sensible forms of unity connect 'relatively' independent parts: for example, the sounds in the unity of a melody, the various colours in chromatic unity, the partial figures in the unity of the complex figure, and so forth. These forms of unity are called *content-forms* by Husserl.

However, as regards the relationship between non-independent parts like extension and colour, there are no forms of connection of unity like the content-forms.

What truly gives unity to *any* type of whole are the foundation relationships, even if the unity which is thus formed, Husserl states, must be understood as a predicate which is applied not to objects but to contents; that is, it is a categorial predicate. In other words, on the basis of the distinction drawn above, the foundation relation is broader than that of the dependence relation.

2.6 All these distinctions, however, as Husserl himself declares, *presuppose* the concept of whole.[21] One may make *general* use of the concept of whole, taking it as the mere subsisting together of contents (parts) to arrive at the concept of whole by means of the foundation relation: every content, in fact, stands in a foundation relationship, directly or indirectly, with another content.

In conclusion, throughout Husserl's Third Investigation – which is devoted to the theory of objects from a mereological point of view – there is a duality in the concept of whole, which is used in the twofold sense of concrete-intuitive whole and formal-abstract whole, and between object and content. Secondly, this duality also exists between the dependence relations and the foundation

---

[21] Husserl 1901, Third Investigation, § 22.

relation. And this same duality is also apparent in the relationship between the dynamic material ontology and formal ontology, that is, between the pre-categorial genesis of the concept of object and the concept of *object in general* or formal object.

3. Formal Ontology

Formal ontology in Husserl concerns the simple 'something': that is to say, it undertakes formal study of the formal region of the 'object in general'.

Formal ontology and formal logic are closely linked. According to Husserl, they constitute a single discipline – to the extent that "every logical-formal law can be transformed into an ontological-formal law".[22] Their 'equivalence' depends on the fact that all forms belong to the 'something in general', the subject-matter of formal ontology.

Formal ontology and formal logic combine to define (i) the *pure objectual categories* (ii) the *pure categories of meaning* and their combinations according to certain laws.

The term 'pure categories', therefore, essentially refers to three things: 1. the forms of the 'something' or of the 'object in general'; 2. the forms of the unification of the lower-order elements of meaning into a proposition;[23] 3. the forms of interconnection among propositions.[24]

Examples of pure objectual categories are 'object', 'state of affairs', 'unity', 'plurality', 'number', 'relation', 'connection'.[25] The Third Investigation also gives 'quality', 'cardinal number', 'order', 'ordinal number', 'whole', 'part', 'magnitude'.[26]

As I said, the relations between pure objectual categories (the subject-matter of formal ontology) and the pure categories of meaning (the subject-matter of formal logic) are governed by rules. The realm of objects is always endowed with meaning because it is constituted by laws belonging to the realm of

[22] Husserl 1913, § 148.

[23] The pure categories of meaning are subject and predicate, disjunction and conjunction, the plural form, and so forth: Husserl 1900-1, Prolegomena, § 68. On this topic see Albertazzi 1989 and Poli 1992.

[24] By *category* Husserl means both a concept in the sense of a meaning and the formal essence expressed by this meaning. Other synonyms for the term 'category' are 'signifying objectivity' and 'objectivity', 'categorial concepts' and 'categorial essences'.

[25] Husserl 1900-1, Prolegomena, § 67.

[26] Husserl 1900-1, Third Investigation, Introduction, § 11.

meaning. Analysis of the categories of the 'something', in fact, is only possible if we use the tools of meaning.[27] However, Husserl argues, although meaning is necessary for explication of the object from the initial level of presentation onwards, this is not to imply that the sphere of meaning is identical with the sphere of objectuality. There are two reasons why object cannot be reduced to meaning: the general doctrine of meaning (with its distinction between *Sinn* and *Bedeutung*)[28] and the distinction between transcendent object and immanent object which, as we shall see in section 5.5, Husserl drew in his dynamic material ontology.

3.1 Husserl divides ontological-formal categories into *syntactic categories* and *substratum* (material) *categories*. *Syntactic categories* are, for example, 'relationship of things', 'relation', 'quality', 'unity', 'multiplicity', 'number', 'order'. They are therefore identical with the *pure objectual categories*.[29] Every logically determinable object assumes different syntactic forms and generates categorial objectualities which can be expressed in meanings. These formations in turn act as the substratum for the formation of other syntactic objectualities. All syntactic objectualities, however, derive from ultimate substrata, from first-degree or lower-degree objects which, as we shall see, no longer contain anything of these ontological forms and bear no trace of syntactic formation.[30]

The *substratum categories* or material categories are syntactic categories deprived of any syntactic form. These objects are no longer syntactic-categorial formations, but mere correlates to the mental functions of attributing, denying, connecting, numbering, and so forth.[31]

In sum, the ontological-formal categories come about, *at their origin*, in relation to the various functions of thought, and they always concern *objects of presentation*. That is, as Husserl puts it, "they may have their concrete basis in the possible *acts* of thought as such or in the *correlates* that can be grasped

---

[27] Husserl 1900-1, Third Investigation, § 11. On the relationship between formal logic and formal ontology see Husserl 1900-1, Fifth Investigation, §§ 34-6; Sixth Investigation, § 49; Husserl 1929, § 5 and § 54 b; Husserl 1913, § 119. On this see Albertazzi 1989 and Poli 1992.

[28] Husserl 1900-1, Fifth Investigation. See Smith 1988, § 5. The distinction is similar to that between signifying intention and fulfilling intention. Since Husserl's theory of meaning is well known, I shall not describe it here. For an interpretation of these categories in terms of material ontology see Albertazzi 1989b.

[29] Husserl 1913, I, § 11.

[30] Ibid.

[31] Ibid.

within them".[32] In this sense, Husserl's formal ontology is deeply rooted in the Brentanian ontology of the act.

3.2 From a *descriptive* standpoint, however, Husserl's formal ontology deals with the various possible forms of meaning of the 'object in general', regardless of the dependence of objects and meanings on the structure of acts. Husserl's analysis of this ontological layer is purely formal and descriptive, even though the supporting structures of the previous ontological layer still remain: namely, the foundation relationship, the theory of parts and the whole, and the laws of dependence.

From a logico-formal point of view it is possible to identify a general morphology of objects which articulates into pure logical grammar and pure logical syntax. Here, as we shall see, the terms 'grammar' and 'syntax' should not be taken in the linguistic sense.

I shall first examine the concept of *pure logical syntax*, which concerns formal propositions and material moments, that is, syntactic forms and syntactic substances (matters), in the proposition.

Although the *syntactic forms* (subject and predicate) may change, their material content, namely their reference to the thing, remains identical. Beneath the syntactic forms, in fact, there lie *syntactic matters* (noun and adjective) which remain the same even though the grammatical form changes.

For example, let us take the term 'table' as the *subject* of the proposition 'the table is white' and then consider it as grammatically modified (that is, declined) as the *object* of the proposition 'I have built the white table'. From the point of view of meaning, independently of its form, the term manifests an identical something which constitutes its objectual reference.[33]

At this purely structural level, analysis does not concern itself with the differing existential statuses of terms like 'table', 'chair', 'centaur' or 'possible world': from a formal-ontological point of view these are only abstract 'indeterminate objects' governed by the same rules.

Syntactic forms and syntactic matters, in fact, are pure forms because the former lack any objectual reference, and the latter, although they constitute the objectual reference, are abstract nuclei of content (*Kerngehalte*). Syntactic form and syntactic matter constitute a concrete unit, the propositional *syntagm* which is formed from identical moments (subject and predicate) and from moments susceptible to change (noun and adjective). The fundamental judgmental form of Husserl's formal ontology is the categorical proposition, which comprises all

---

[32] Husserl 1900-1, Prolegomena, § 67, emphasis mine; Husserl 1891, Ch. 1, § 27.
[33] Husserl 1929, Appendix 1, § 3.

the other forms – existential, copulative, disjunctive, hypothetical, and so forth – as modalizations of the basic ontological-formal structure.[34]

3.3 The *pure logical grammar* addresses other patterns of meaning, that is, the 'nucleus formations' (*Kerngebilde*). Husserl's formal analytic does not consider nucleus formations, in fact, since its purpose is simply to describe the laws of formal consequence.

Syntactic forms (subject and predicate) and syntactic matters (nouns and objects) derive from another type of formation which stands prior to them. This third type of formation is constituted by 'substantiveness and adjectiveness', which Husserl calls the *pure grammatical categories*. These forms are of a completely different kind, since they are no longer syntactic forms, although they are present in syntax, and specifically in the 'syntactic substances' of noun and adjective.

Let us take, for example, the nucleus formations 'beauty', 'beautiful' or 'blueness' and 'blue'. Common to each pair is an essential moment which concerns the syntactic substance but is given in a categorially different manner. Considered from this point of view, the syntactic matters are 'formed' in different ways within the category of substantiveness or within the category of adjectiveness.

As regards the proposition, the subject stands in the nucleus form of objectivity and the determination stands in the nucleus form of adjectiveness.[35] The nucleus forms, however, play a very important role in Husserl's ontology, because they constitute the link between his dynamic material ontology and his formal ontology.

4. Formal Ontology and Material Ontology

Husserl never gave a complete account of the foundation relationship between what I have called his dynamic material ontology and his formal ontology even though, as I said, a series of his lectures did lay the basis for such a theory.[36] Analysis can proceed in either of two directions: from the formal ontology to the dynamic material ontology, or from the dynamic material ontolo-

---

[34] Husserl does not adhere to Brentano's doctrine on the primacy of existential judgements over categorical judgements; Husserl 1974, Appendix I, § 6 c, no. 2.

[35] Husserl 1939, § 50 b.

[36] Husserl 1966a and 1966b.

gy to the formal ontology. I shall begin by following the former route, adopting a procedure of clarification. Then, in the next section, I shall follow a foundational procedure.

At the 'syntactic' level, the syntactic matter (noun and adjective) remains the same, while the syntactic forms (subject and predicate) change because they represent the syntactic *function*. At the 'grammatical' level, substantiveness and adjectiveness ideally express the same structure but, as we have seen, are categorially different formations. In these formations, in fact, substance is identical whereas form varies in its substantival, adjectival, qualitative and relational modifications. 'Redness' and 'red', for example, maintain the same syntactic matter but display a different nuclear formation, which is at times substantival, at times adjectival.

In order to understand the nature of the pure grammatical categories of 'substantiveness' and 'adjectiveness', one must keep the linguistic level quite distinct from the ontological level and examine the connections between them.

There exists, in fact, a multiplicity of modes of intentional presentation, to which corresponds a multiplicity of expressive forms at the linguistic level (active and passive moods, optatives, conditionals, subjunctives, imperatives, future forms).

The multiplicity of the expressive modes corresponds to what Husserl calls the various 'modalizations of belief' intrinsic in the act of actual presentation.[37]

In order to transform the multiplicity of expressive forms back into the original form of the presentation of objects and situation of things, all expressive forms must be reduced to their simplest enunciative form – that is, the categorical statement that 'S is p'. In this primary and original layer of the ontology, S corresponds to the ontological substratum and p to its determination or property. From this point of view, Husserl declares, the categories of substantiveness and adjectiveness constitute the deep structure of the original predication, because they refer to what is recognized in perception – that is, also to the way in which things are originally presented.

The predicative connection at the linguistic level therefore represents the ontological relationship between substratum and determination, that is, between the whole and its parts. The two levels, however, are not connected univocally and necessarily. For example, on the basis of the 'ontological' statement 'there are beautiful things', I can perform a substantivization (nominalization) of the adjective 'beautiful' (which is here a determination of the substratum and a dependent part of the whole) and state that 'beauty is a

---

[37] Husserl 1939, § 21.

virtue'. In this second sentence it is 'beautiful' that functions as the substratum, because there is a different nucleous formation.

In the Indo-European languages examples of adjectivization are rare. This, however, is a separate issue (as Humboldt and Whorf have demonstrated) which does not affect the Husserlian theory. What matters from the theoretical point of view in Husserl's analysis is that it brings out the nexus between the theory of meaning and of linguistic expression and the ontological theory of objects.

This therefore clarifies the above statement by Husserl that substantiveness and adjectiveness constitute the deep structure of (ontological) predication in general: whereas in the proposition the subject performs the role of term, the substantive nucleus form indicates its substantiveness – that is, the fact that it stands for itself and does not depend on anything else. The reverse is true of its predicative determinations. Substantiveness and adjectiveness designate not linguistic forms but, once again, laws of dependence among objects (and contents). The difference among objects (contents) arises from the different forms of linkage that connects their various parts: as we have seen, the presentation of an object, regardless of its ontological givenness (that is, whether it is a thing or a quality) may originally occur, in presentation, either in substantival or adjectival form.[38]

5. Lived Forms

The connection between Husserl's formal ontology and his dynamic material ontology, considered from a foundational perspective, is therefore the problem of how an ontological-formal category is founded on the basis of the modes of presentation. Herein lies the second direction of analysis: from the dynamic material ontology to the formal ontology.

Husserl constantly emphasised the relationship between logic, ontology and aesthetics (in the sense of a categorial theory of perception).[39] More specifically, this is the point where Husserl's formal ontology meets his theory of phenomenological perception based on original and objective *evidence* furnished by the modalities of everyday experience.[40]

[38] Husserl 1939, § 31.

[39] Husserl 1929; 1939; 1966b. See also the Bernauer MS (1917-18) and the Märgener MS (1920-21), respectively on temporal and spatial constitution.

[40] Husserl 1974, § 12 and Husserl 1939, § 8.

Husserl asserts that there are two key features to the 'perception/perceived object' correlation. First – in visual perception, for instance – we are unable to perceive, in the present, all the sides and all the parts of the object. Second, this object is a 'corporeal' one; that is, it is bound up with the physiology of the body, with kinaesthesis and with movement.

A direct 'external' perception is unthinkable from this point of view; and equally unthinkable is an object of perception which can, in the strict sense, be given in its completeness, and from every side with its internal and concealed parts.[41]

In fact, in perception certain sides of objects are presented, and they are presented successively. We therefore have only *perspective aspects* of spatial objects, as *moments* of a substantial nucleus which remains unchanged.[42]

5.1 The laws regulating perception in this first stratum of passivity and receptivity (which corresponds to the duration of the psychic present) are categorial laws of Gestalt character. In operation here, in fact, is a series of syntheses among the various aspects of the object; syntheses which come about by virtue of *similarity* (or affinity), *homogeneity* and *equality*, and by means of *contrast, fusion* and *accretion*.[43] I examine some of these syntheses below.

Synthesis by similarity involves recognition of perceptive features which are 'similar' and therefore pertinent to a certain 'type' of object, although this is still recognized only indistinctly. This process occurs, for example, when two equal triangles, equilateral and of the same colour, appear in our field of vision.

Corresponding to the synthesis by similarity is the *temporal form* (*Zeitgestalt*) which confers unity on the 'multiplicity' which is given simultaneously in the psychic present.[44] Moreover, the synthesis of similarity comes about by means of the *fusion of perceptive contents*.[45]

Fusion is a perceptive component by means of which a multiplicity is realized, even though attention does not necessarily have to be addressed to it. Fusion, moreover, is not a process but a static relation between sensations which is based on the sensations themselves. It is also through fusion that sense data

[41] Husserl 1977, § 1, 25-30.

[42] The background to Husserl's theory, especially as regards his concept of the 'sensation of movement', is provided by the work of Stumpf and Bain. See Stumpf 1873 and Bain 1855.

[43] Husserl 1966b, Ch. 3, § 27-30.

[44] Husserl explicitly states that his analysis is similar to that of the figural synthesis in the first edition of Kant's *Critique of Pure Reason* (1781), Husserl 1966b, § 27, 125.

[45] The notion of fusion was developed by Stumpf, who introduced it in the second volume of his *Tonpsychologie* when discussing the perception of musical chords. See Stumpf 1883-90, II, 101 ff. and 1906, 19.

appear as parts of a whole, not as elements of a sum, according to the laws of Gestalt psychology.

In the above-mentioned case of the presentation of two equilateral triangles of the same colour, the synthesis by similarity is also a synthesis of equality.

The synthesis, by contrast, comes about by opposition (also partial opposition) of perceptive contents: for example, when two triangles, one red and one blue, appear in our visual field. Note that similarity and contrast are not mutually exclusive. For example, in the case of the presentation of a red triangle and a blue triangle, the synthesis is still a synthesis of similarity but not a synthesis of equality.

Similarity, contrast, fusion, but also order and increment, are phenomena of the original level of receptivity in perception, in which the structure of consciousness is closely involved as well.[46]

5.2 Husserl considers oculomotor *kinaesthesis* to be a real and proper field system, with a centre, a periphery and directions of orientation (left, right, upwards, downwards).[47] The form of surfaces is constituted in this field and is grasped as something in motion. The system is organized by *places* and *markers (Wege)*, by means of which it is possible to achieve the optimal appearance of a surface.[48]

As regards the first point, that is, the system of places, the perceptive field is spatially constituted by limiting forms. We identify the limiting form by dividing the perceptive whole into parts: when individual perceptive features overlap each other (*Überschiebung*) – for example, when in some part of the visual field one image is replaced by another with vivid contrast, so that a surface changes colour although its shape remains the same, or when we see a surface of the same colour divided into two different parts. In both these cases, a *boundary* or a dividing line is perceptively drawn between the parts.

The boundary or outline of the perceptive object (and of its parts) gives form to a figure which – insofar as it is delimited or circumscribed with respect to its background – displays certain characteristic properties of things, like *shape, cohesion, individuality*.[49]

5.3 According to Husserl, however, in order to define the nature of the perceptive field, one must be able to formulate *formal* concepts and axioms of a

---

[46] Piana 1988, Ch. 4.

[47] Husserl 1973, 190.

[48] Claesges 1964, § 15. For a treatment of the problem from a linguistic point of view see Bühler 1930, Ch. 1, § 4 and Ch. 3, § 10.

[49] Gurwitch 1964, Part II, Ch. 1b, 110-13.

geographical or topological kind: concepts such as *point, line, surface, distance, direction, series, magnitude*, and so forth.[50]

The visual field can be described as a two-dimensional multiplicity apprehended as a twofold continuous series. According to Husserl, spatial perception at this 'pre-empirical' level does not admit depth and therefore does not admit three-dimensionality.[51]

Here Husserl is in disagreement with Stumpf. In a marginal annotation to his copy of Stumpf's book on the origin of spatio-temporal presentation – where Stumpf argues that also depth is given in the visual presentation – Husserl makes the following criticism: a distinction must be drawn between surface as two-dimensional multiplicity (*Manningfaltigkeit*) and surface as a two-dimensional formation (*Gebilde*) in space.[52] As we have seen, the sensations of movement play a major role in the conversion of the former into latter.

Husserl asserts that this conversion takes place through the connection of multiplicity relative to distance (which is one-dimensional and linear) with multiplicity relative to a change of perspective (*Wendung*) (which is two-dimensional and cyclical).[53]

Time, however, is represented as a straightforward, homogeneous, one-dimensional and continuous series: in short, a straight line. By way of example: once two points of light ('a pair' of points) fused together in the visual field have been subjected to formalization, they become two abstract points. Formalization allows one to take measurements and to approach the concrete limiting form, but this is only possible by means of an abstractive procedure.

5.4 The second feature of the perceptive field is its *markers*, or indicators of objects. These are always present in a contextual field and are connected with practical activities. Markers, whatever form they take, are always closely linked with the objects they refer to: road signs, phonemes, geographical maps, for example, are all markers.

---

[50] Husserl 1966b, Ch. 3, § 31.

[51] Husserl 1973, 165-6.

[52] Claesges notes that the concepts of 'orthoid (linear) multiplicity' and 'cyclical multiplicity' play a major role in Husserl's analysis of the constitution of spatial forms, in particular as regards the problem of how the two-dimensional oculomotor field is converted into the three-dimensional field. The question closely concerns the definition of fixed magnitudes, a problem which had occupied Husserl since 1891, and the difference between real numbers (orthoid multiplicities) and imaginary numbers (cyclical multiplicities); Claesges 1973, xxvi, no. 1.

[53] Husserl 1973, 255.

The system of markers is based on habit. Generally speaking, at the perceptive level markers employ oppositions such as *light-dark, centre-periphery, figure-background*, and so forth.

Corresponding in consciousness to the kinaesthetic system is duration: that is, the unity of a multiplicity of impressions given in the psychic present. The outcome of this bilateral synthesis is the flower that we see in the field, or the series of musical tones we hear in the next room. Every constitution of sense and every parallel constitution of objectuality entails an act of consciousness. In principle, every fundamental type of object is matched by a different intentional structure which operates on the basis of diverse primitive concepts (essences).

5.5 For the purposes of a phenomenological theory of perception, therefore, the difference between *transcendent object* and *immanent object* is the following: from the standpoint of consciousness *esse est percipi*, and this applies above all to the individual *moments-now* of perception. The immanent object, in fact, can only be given in the psychic present and only in some particular aspects. The transcendent object, on the other hand, may be given in an infinity of modes and can only constitute itself in a duration as the substratum (*Unterlage*) of an immanent content (*Gehalt*) which corresponds to the aspect of the object that appears in perception.[54]

The concept of substratum is fundamental here: the substrata comprise individuals in whose individuation consciousness plays a part but to which correspond, moment by moment, what Husserl calls an *original impression* of the transcendent object, that is, something that really exists.

The absolute substrata in the strict sense are, firstly, *bodies* (and these, for Husserl, constitute the *primacy of external perception*);[55] secondly, the objects of external perception, taken also as a plurality; thirdly, the syntactic objectualities founded on the objects of external perception; fourthly, the 'object in general' of Husserl's formal ontology.[56] Thus the point of departure for the dynamic morphogenesis of his formal ontology is the environment or forms of life.

5.6 Finally, we see objects delimited by a corporeal *surface* and qualified by sense which constitute a *base framework* for the object of perception.[57] This

---

[54] Husserl 1966, § 4.
[55] Husserl 1929, § 14.
[56] Husserl 1929, sect. 2; Husserl 1913, I, 28; Husserl 1924, 181.
[57] Husserl 1966b, 23.

form of closed surface is built on the structures of consciousness as a multiplicity of the synthesis of coincidence among the various sides of the object,
which are grasped by intentionality and given, from one moment to another, as
the immanent contents of perception.[58] These latter Husserl calls *experienced*
spatial forms, in the sense that they are not abstract but intuited, and linked to
the environment which surrounds us and which we are accustomed to viewing
as *typical* of it.

In fact, beside their spatial character, the objects of perception are also
physiognomic, a feature which renders them immediately recognizable.[59] We
always see colours as inseparable from both the surfaces and the type of structure that they belong to, and we see them whether the surface is smooth, porous
or whatever;[60] or we see that the corners, as perceptive data, have a certain
directionality, with a vector that orients them towards a certain locus; or, again,
we see that three unaligned points in the perceptive field organize themselves
in a certain way; and so forth.[61]

These perceptive contents, as colour and texture, also furnish us with information about the composition of the substance currently being observed by
us.[62]

6. The Material Regional Ontologies

Once the relation of existential dependence between Husserl's dynamic
material ontology and his formal ontology has been demonstrated, on the basis
of the latter a *static material ontology* can be developed which lies at a second
level and comprises the various *regional ontologies*.

Husserl stated that the *ontological-formal* categories are eidetic singularities.[63] By this he meant that to each group of 'facts' there corresponds a
'region' of primitive constitutive concepts (essences), and to each region there
corresponds a regional 'form'. The forms of the various regions are typical – in

[58] This analysis is set out in Husserl's *Analysen zur passiven Synthesis* (1920-6) and in his
manuscripts catalogued as *D-Manuskripte*, MS D 13 I (1912), 3; Husserl 1913, II, § 37. On
this see Claesges 1964; Witschel 1964; Diemer 1956.

[59] This topic has been given ample treatment by Koffka 1935, 7 and by Gibson 1979, Ch.
8.

[60] Husserl 1900-1, Third Investigation.

[61] Wertheimer 1923, 318n; Schiller 1933, 179-214. On this see Bozzi 1969, 135-70, 154.

[62] Gibson 1979, Ch. 2, § 30 and § 31.

[63] Husserl 1913, § 13.

the sense that the concept or form of one region cannot be transformed, by variation, into the concept of another. The regions have their own individual sciences which furnish reliable formal descriptions of them but which are *not* formal descriptions of the 'something in general'. In fact, every science that is not formal ontology has its own specific objectual field.[64]

6.1 The regional ontologies are characterized by axioms which yield synthetic a priori judgements. According to Husserl, "the fundamental synthetic concepts, or categories, are the fundamental regional (primitive) concepts essentially tied to that particular region, to its principles or synthetic laws; and there are as many different groups of categories as there are regions to differentiate".[65] However, "the formal ontology does not lie on the same level as the material regions; indeed, properly speaking it is not a region but an empty form of region in general".[66]

At its static level the material ontology is subordinated by the formal ontology, in the sense that the formal ontology comprises all the regional ontologies and prescribes their common formal constitution. It should be borne in mind that each category refers to ultimate substrata – to first-degree or lower-degree objects which are no longer categorial syntactic formations, nor contain any of these ontological forms, but are only correlates to the cognitive functions. These correlates, however, are not merely subjective because, as we have seen, they are connected categorially to the material structure of the world through bodies.

7. Emerging Structures

Husserl's phenomenology derives from an immanentist realism of Brentanian stamp. The fundamental category of this ontology is intentionality or the *inherence relation*, according to which we know objects in inner perception only according to their form and with evidence: in this consists the mental (or intentional) existence of objects.

The function which categorially modifies the structure of material things in inner perception is modification, which constitutes an internal determinant of the act.

---

[64] Husserl 1929, § 54b.
[65] Husserl 1913, 31-2.
[66] Husserl 1913, I, § 10.

Modification is an essential component of intentional inherence. There can be modification of the act of intentional presentation, of the object and of the content. More specifically, every modification of the act entails a modification of the content and the object. There are at least two features of modification that should be borne in mind and kept distinct: one concerns the presented, and therefore categorially modified, object; the other concerns the modifying function internal to the act itself.[67]

7.1 As regards the first of these features, these presented objects exist for us *in so far* as they are known and therefore categorially modified by the structure of intentional inherence in which they are presented.[68] Modification is categorial because it obeys objective laws: for example, a colour can only appear in relation to something substantial which possesses it, namely extension, while speed can only appear in relation to movement, and so on.

The perception of objects is constitutively connected with the perception of principles (*eide*). Sense data (*Erlebnisse*) and essence are always inseparable and are only distinguishable by abstraction.[69] Every aspect of the object presented in inner perception announces and leads to a subsequent aspect, which is incorporated into the structure of the intentional relation.[70] Each aspect of the object can, in turn, be given in various ways.[71] However, the extension of an object as it is given in the presentation, that is, in association with a shape and colour, is something that is *intuited*; it is not a portion of abstract space. Husserl thus asserts that the essential form of any real quality is its form in a certain position or situation, and that this essential form coincides, as a whole, with the material thing.[72]

7.2 As regards the second of the above two features of modification, things are modified not only inasmuch as they are 'presented' but inasmuch as they are 'temporally presented'.

Concerning the nature of the act of presentation (in short, concerning the nature of the psychic present), within immanentist realism Husserl's theory of double intentionality engendered the Graz school's theory and also numerous

---

[67] On this argument, which is of Brentanian origin, see Albertazzi 1994-5.

[68] The characteristics of the 'formal' and 'objective' nature of presentation are analysed by Brentano in Brentano 1967, 80, no. 6; 120, no. 23.

[69] Husserl 1913, I, § 1.

[70] Husserl 1966a, 5.

[71] Husserl MS D 13 I (1921), 2.

[72] Husserl 1913, II, § 12-17; Piana 1988, Ch. 3, 161-2.

laboratory experiments which sought to measure the intervals and duration of an act of perception.[73]

All these attempts – which theoretically and experimentally belong to the mainstream of the Brentanian tradition – were undertaken at the beginning of this century and confirmed by subsequent analyses.[74]

7.3 One theoretical solution to the problem was Husserl's hypothesis of a stratified structure of the act which comprises a double intentionality. When we see a house, for example, there correspond to the various sides or contours of the house appearing in succession within the overall duration of the act of perception, one intentionality directed towards retention of the various aspects of the content considered consecutively, and a second intentionality directed towards the unity of these various aspects taken all together.

Every initial and subsequent *aspect* of the object is *modified* by the intentional structure of consciousness, which retains the object within the individual moments-now of the duration of perception.

Temporal modification consists in characterizing the individual aspects of the object as (to varying extents) past, although their essential nucleus is simultaneously preserved, so that, in the presentation, we recognize as *invariant* the object presented by its various aspects. The unity of consciousness, in short, guarantees the syntactic consistency of semantic contents.[75]

7.4 The theses of immanentist realism were borne out by experimental research conducted in the laboratory.[76] Its basis, in fact, was the presentation, or the phenomenon that occurs within the minimum temporal extension during which psychic activity takes place. It was therefore essential to exemplify its structure and to classify the psychic moments and contents of mental acts.

The ambiguities of perception require careful analysis. For example, one of the most striking features of visual perception is that 'we do not see what is there' – a phenomenon which occurs in cases of camouflage. Or, conversely, 'we see what is not there';[77] we see what in principle it should be impossible to see;[78] we see two different things instead of one[79] and so forth.[80] Thus, within

[73] Meinong 1899; Witasek 1904, Ameseder 1904.

[74] Fraisse 1952, 39-46 and 1964; Vicario 1973.

[75] Albertazzi 1989, 7-19, 14 and Albertazzi 1991, 89-111, 101.

[76] Brentano and Marty were unable to conduct experiments of this kind, but Stumpf at Berlin, Meinong at Graz and Marty at Prague successfully managed to do so.

[77] This is the case of Kanisza's anomalous surfaces. See Kanisza 1980.

[78] As in Escher figures.

[79] For ambiguous figures see Rubin 1921 and 1921.

a given situation there are phenomena of a-modal perception or of formal plurivocity to which correspond different perceptive contents. The same applies to auditory perception.

Laboratory experiments have also shown that the *psychic present* which corresponds to the act of presentation is an extended unit, a stretch of time, not a point-like present (a moment-now). Moreover, its various phases of constitution are governed by laws which *group* and *unify* the apprehended contents of the various consecutive aspects of the object considered.[81] Experiments have also confirmed Meinong's thesis that the act of perception is a unitary whole, although the elements of its content, which are apprehended simultaneously, may be distinct and distributed.[82] The simultaneous apprehension of consecutively presented individual elements reveals a duration: that is, it shows that the single act of perception is divided into successive *phases* and apprehended through a *non-distributed content*.[83] If we take a melody, for example, its elements (i.e. the notes of which it is composed and which follow each other consecutively) are apprehended *simultaneously*, although they are *not apprehended as being simultaneous*.

Laboratory experiments showed that if the temporal structure of the act is altered by adding pauses and *intervals* to it, various assessments are made of its content. In particular, it was found that with shorter intervals (630 milliseconds), the subject of the experiment evaluated the succession of sensations rather than their duration as a whole. With longer intervals (1 second) his or her perception concentrated on the sensations in themselves rather than on whatever delimited the temporal stretch. With average intervals (700 milliseconds), which constitute the limits of the extension of the actual present, the subject intuited these intervals as time and not as succession and, above all, apprehended them in a single act of gestalt perception.[84]

7.5 Analysis of the *perception of form* and its *temporal structure* therefore sheds important light on the relationship between act, object and content in immanentist realism. As we have seen, if the temporal intervals of perception are changed – that is, if the time of the act is altered – then the perceived content also changes. This differing content or conceptual correlate is due to

---

[80] Vicario 1991, 9.

[81] Benussi 1913, 421; Bonaventura 1916; 1924; 1929; 1928a; 1928b; 1931; 1990; Calabresi 1930, 88. Cf. Albertazzi 1993 and 1994.

[82] Meinong 1899, 182-1272.

[83] Meinong 1899, 88; Stern 1897, 325-49; Fraisse 1964, 73 ff.

[84] Benussi 1913, 387.

the different *prominence* or salience acquired by its parts[85] because of the modification of the qualitative structure of the act and of its inner determinant: that is, because of the act's *temporal modes of recognition* of the object of presentation.

For example, given two sounds delimiting an interval, if the intensity of the first sound is greater than that of the second, the first acquires greater prominence and has the effect of 'shortening' the interval. Conversely, if the second sound is more intense, it induces the subject to perceive the duration of the interval as longer.[86] This means that if the *features of the act*[87] (i.e. i particular the temporal features of the structure of the act) are altered, then its conceptual correlates are also altered (that is, the ways in which the object is presented to consciousness). This explains both the perception of optical illusions and the phenomenon of formal plurivocity in the various cases of a-modal presence.[88]

The time of events is a time which does not exactly mirror the chronological sequence of stimuli from the outside world. This is clearly demonstrated, for example, by phenomena of temporal displacement. Given a brief sequence comprising *A notes* (for 100 milliseconds) – *white noise* (for 35 milliseconds) – *G notes* (for 100 milliseconds), what we actually hear is the sequence *A-G – very short pause – noise*. This means that a perceptive rearrangment has taken place which has obeyed the laws of qualitative phenomenal prominence.[89] The belief that the durations of physical occurences are bits of physical time, or that the phenomenal durations of events are bits of phenomenal time, are typical examples of stimulus errors.[90]

7.6 The temporal structure of the act of presentation, however, does not entail an idealism of forms because of the holistic character of the *emerging forms* in Husserl's dynamic material ontology. The Berlin school claimed that individual perceptions do not exist, only perceptions of *form*.[91] For Wertheimer, the phenomenon *phi,* or the perception of movement, was a psychic

---

[85] This is Benussi's definition of salience (*Auffälligkeit*). Cf. Albertazzi 1995.

[86] Benussi 1913, 300 ff.; Calabresi 1930.

[87] Husserl 1966.

[88] Several aspects of Brentano's descriptive psychology had repercussions on the psychological discussion of his time, and not just among his followers. As we have seen, Brentano raised a number of important questions – for instance, the perception of intervals and the magnitude and unitary nature of the present – even though he did so as part of metaphysical inquiry. See Brentano 1976.

[89] Vicario 1973, 38 ff., 41.

[90] The phenomena reported by Lichtenstein and Brown, for example, are part of the time of the duration of events. See Lichtenstein 1963.

[91] For criticism of this thesis see Gibson 1979.

correlate of the function of transverse nervous currents among areas affected by stimuli. These 'cross-functions' (*Querfunktionen*), as Wertheimer called them, are functions of the central nervous system – natural connections which generate perceptions of figural qualities.[92] The perceptive nuclei constitute the initial core of perception from which individual sense data, considered as separate elements in the totality of perception, can only subsequently be abstracted. In short, a psychophysical theory of sensations only applies to a second stratum, once elements have been abstracted from a perceptive continuum.

8. The Morphodynamics of External and Internal Determinants

In recent years, these problems of the material ontology regarding the underlying structures of reality and their transformations have been studied by Thom and Petitot,[93] and they have also been analysed by so-called '*naive physics*'.[94] Petitot draws an interesting parallel between the various levels of the formation of Husserl's noema and Marr's scientific theory of vision.[95] Common to both Husserl and Marr was their conception of the object as invariant and as the *formal principle of coherence among its apparent 'contours'*.[96]

According to this analysis there are three levels of formation of the object. The first corresponds to its boundary (Husserl's *Abschattung*) and is the level at which objects appear – always, however, according to a specific *aspect* or side which continuously varies. The second level corresponds to the object's *borders*, which are distinguished on the basis of the Gestalt law of figure and background. The third level corresponds to the real *object* itself, recognized as a whole. Thus the objects of our experience are phenomenally distinct from those that surround them if there exists a *qualitative discontinuity*, which oc-

---

[92] Wertheimer 1923, 301-51. Brentano 1976, "Was die Philosophen über die Zeit gelehrt haben", written prior to 1902, T4, 53, 66. Müller claimed that physiological processes condition our temporal localizations, thus anticipating the theory of 'personal difference'. On this latter topic see Bessel 1820, Faye 1864. See also Bozzi 1989. For questions relating to Brentanianism see Albertazzi 1992.

[93] Thom 1972; 1980 and 1988; Petitot 1985; 1989; Smith and Petitot 1990. See also the entry 'Naive Physics' by Smith in Smith and Burkhardt 1992.

[94] Hayes 1985; Bozzi 1989 and 1990. Similar ideas were formulated by Whitehead and Woodger.

[95] On Marr see Kitcher 1988.

[96] Petitot 1989, 717.

curs when a moment of the quality that fills its extension undergoes some sort of variation.[97]

The qualitative discontinuities in a spatial extension of the first stratum of experience appears within a *limit* of the qualitative continuum as the *contour* of the object.[98] This is the 'perceptive noema', or the form of the object understood in a morphological and *not yet* ontological-formal sense.

This first stratum comprises *direct perception* of form and *inner and indirect presentation* of reality.[99] The mind is therefore able to understand reality because of a morphism of some sort between the cognitive structures and the fundamental level of reality itself, which possesses some kind of intrinsic intelligibility independently of the mind.

This basic level, however, does not possess a 'semantic' – only a semiotic, an iconic theory of signs. In fact, form is not extracted from meaning, since this belongs to a subsequent level, that of the semantic of the ontological-formal object. Conversely, there does exist a direct, automatic perception of shape, as Gibson has shown in the case of the objects of vision.[100] Things possess *direct information* which is made explicit in the various levels of the presentation, and which is evidence in favour of realism.[101]

Each level, therefore, has diverse objective correlates of reality which correspond to different *kinds* of information.[102] In the visual field, for example, the light signal corresponds to the level of shading, direct information corresponds to the level of the border or limit, and the geometrical sphere of the mechanics of the movement of bodies corresponds to the level of the object.

9. Conclusions

The intentional act (*the mode of presentation of the object*) and presented objects (*the something in general presented in a certain way*) form the categorial structure of objects *and* of meaning. However, from the moment of sensory

---

[97] 'Moment' should be understood in the sense given to it by Husserl 1901, Third Investigation, § 8.

[98] This coincides with Brentano's metaphysical position. See Brentano 1979. On the topic of the contour see Petitot 1984, 101-40.

[99] This definition also corresponds to the theses of the later Brentano. On this see Albertazzi 1992.

[100] Gibson 1972. For criticism of Gibson see Fodor and Pylyshn 1981.

[101] Bozzi 1990.

[102] Petitot 1989, 717.

impression (or of intentional inherence) onwards there is no differentiation between subject and object.

The 'material' aspect of the ontology shapes the initial semiological elements which make it possible for objects to constitute themselves; objects which, at a second level, present themselves to consciousness as formally determined.[103] The entity described by Husserl's formal ontology is therefore the ontological correlate of the objectified phenomenal datum of his material ontology.

The material world is not a particular 'piece' but the basic stratum of the natural world to which the whole of being stands in some sort of relation.

9.1 In the sensible field there is a basic opposition between sensible qualities which present themselves locally fused together, and sensible qualities which locally present themselves separately in a certain configuration, a certain *limit*.[104] Qualities manifest themselves locally and are presented as continuous variations of magnitudes like temperature, wave frequency, and so on.[105]

In a *uniform* perceptive field, fusion consists of the continuous variation of the degree of the quality: for example, the yellow colour of a decreasing surface. If we draw a black line or point on the yellow field, this produces an elementary form of field breakdown; a division such that each part of the field acquires its own homogeneity. And it does so in a twofold way: some sort of unitariness is reconstructed in both parts, while the distinctions between the parts is accentuated.[106]

Furthermore, the spatial extension is occupied by a material substratum which is organized by *morphological accidents* – its *limit* and its *form*. That is to say, the spatial extension is occupied by the set of qualitative discontinuities. A form is an example of *qualitative discontinuity on a substratum space*,[107] so that, both phenomenologically and ontologically, forms act as a sort of *interface* between the perceiving subject and the outside world.

It is precisely this concept of form that comprises those features of Husserl's material ontology which provide his formal ontology with its foundation. The concept concerns, in fact, the *material objects of a qualitative ontology*: more than empty categorial objectualities, forms are signs, physical morphological

---

[103] Goodman 1977.

[104] Husserl 1966.

[105] Husserl's Third Investigation, which analyses ontological-formal concepts and the concept of part-whole, already mentions the concepts of *quantitative discontinuity* and *fusion*. See Husserl 1900-1, Third Investigation, § 9.

[106] Kanizsa 1980; Petitot 1989, 713.

[107] Petitot 1989, 713.

presences, which can be translated into symbols. The relationship between (external) matter and the (internal) features of the act is not a symbolic relationship but one of *natural signs*.

As has been said, immanentist realism envisaged an *inner presentation* of physical reality in 'forms' even before the breakdown of vision into objects.[108] This inner content-based presentation has, however, ontological and not just mentalistic value.[109] Husserl's dynamic ontology, also in its morphogenetic version, permits the cognitive level to be considered as the emergent level.

9.2 Three strata can be distinguished in the complex phenomenon of the formation of objects: passivity, receptivity and spontaneity. The categories of the first stratum are homogeneity, similarity, contiguity, contrast and configuration. These obey the laws of Gestalt. The outcome of this initial stage of the determination of the object is a 'something' which is still indeterminate. Even though Husserl only made passing reference[110] to what, in modern terms, can be called the problem of an *ecological objectivity of forms*,[111] he nevertheless gave an accurate formulation of it. The real problem of his ontology, however, is that overall it fails to explain *singular and concrete forms*. In Husserl's phenomenology, in fact, one can talk about objects only subsequently to the eidetic abstraction that leads from the indeterminate object of the first stratum to the second stratum.

The categories of this second stratum (which corresponds to the level of the formal ontology) are substratum-determination, subject-predicate, substantial part-unsubstantial part. These are categories which concern the internal and external relations of the object and which generate a plurality of determinate objects. This also explains why phenomenology has been developed along predominantly semantic lines: in a phenomenology of essences one can properly speak of objects – that is, know them – only at the ontological-formal level.

The categories of the third level are identity and unity; and they produce meanings, contexts, judgmental propositions and sets. All three of these strata depend genetically on each other, and each of them has an material aspect and a formal aspect. Each stratum leads to another by actualizing in some way the virtual content of its predecessor. The problem of Husserl's phenomenology is, if anything, that it is unable to construct a real and proper ontology of the world: whereas the formal has its noematic and a-temporal status, matter in the last analysis is identified as being functional to the datum of consciousness.

---

108 Brentano 1979; Marr 1982, 269.
109 Properly speaking, this is the level of the perceptive noema. See Gurwitch 1982, Ch. 2.
110 Husserl 1966 and 1966a.
111 Gibson 1979.

9.3 Overall, therefore, Husserl's formal ontology is based on a number of presuppositions that are usually neglected. In particular, his analysis is based on a set of concepts – inherence, place, shape, limit, configuration and modification – which are categories that belong to *material ontology* and which in any case are components of a *categorial* doctrine of consciousness and of descriptive predication.[112]

The form of the objects of formal ontology as given by the aggregate – that is, by the conceptual correlate of each unifying act – is not just an epistemological, relational form produced by the operations of the mind. It is something that emerges from the base strata of material ontology: according to the principle of the non-independence of experience, a particular form is always relative to a particular object.[113]

Of course, differing emphases may be placed on the various components of this general structure. If *epistemological use* is made of forms, the isomorphism between reality and theory resolves itself into a kind of moderate conventionalism.[114] Matters are very different, however, if one makes *metaphysical use* of forms, as did Husserl when he had his material ontology serve as a foundation his formal ontology and gave ontological import to the emergence of form. If it is true that *esse est percipi*, it is so in the sense that the verifiable properties of things are real, although they are in presentation modified.

In sum: on the basis of the ontological category of *inherence* within the structure of the cognitive act, it is possible to distinguish among *objective* conditions, *peripheral* conditions, *subjective* (or non-sensory) conditions and *relational* conditions. Objective conditions are, for example, the particular vibrations of a mechanical device that produces sounds, or the particular vibrations of the cosmic ether than produces light. These are necessary but not sufficient conditions for various perceptive states to occur. Also required are specific peripheral conditions of our organism and subjective conditions of the central nervous system. Relational conditions, finally, are those particular relationships which unite the other kinds of condition: in short, they are those conditions which act upon our sense organs, thereby producing the perceptive fact and giving form to objects.[115]

---

[112] Simons 1986.
[113] Mally 1914. On this see Poli 1990.
[114] Twardowski 1984.
[115] Musatti 1964, 213-65.

In other words, dependence relations stand *ontologically prior* to the part-whole relationship.[116] Husserl's formal ontology is based on a material ontology which distinguishes among different *modes of being* (things, intentional objects, ideal objects, and so on) by means of different moments of existence. Thus the possibility of linking the various genera of objects to one single type of *object*, the most general possible, is certainly still possible, but only at a *second* level: that of the *formal ontology*.[117]

References

Albertazzi, L. 1989a: *Strati*, Reverdito, Trento.

Albertazzi, L. 1989b: "The Noema and the Consciousness of Time", *Supplements of Topoi* 4, 7-19.

Albertazzi, L. 1990-1: "Brentano, Meinong and Husserl on Internal Time", *Brentano Studien* III, 89-111.

Albertazzi, L. 1991: "Il presente psichico tra analisi concettuale e laboratorio: Franz Brentano e Renata Calabresi", *Rivista di psicologia* n.s. 11, 35-76; reprinted in Albertazzi and Poli 1993, 131-173.

Albertazzi, L. 1993a: "Time in Brentanist Tradition: Enzo Bonaventura", Proceedings of the conference *The Legacy of Brentano*, Cracow, November 1993, forthcoming.

Albertazzi, L. 1993b: "Psicologia descrittiva e psicologia sperimentale: Brentano e Bonaventura sul tempo psichico", *Axiomathes* 4, 389-413.

Albertazzi, L. 1994: "Strutture temporali e ontologia", Proceedings of the conference *Francesco de Sarlo e il laboratorio di psicologia di Firenze*, Pisa, April 1994, forthcoming.

Albertazzi, L. 1994-5: "Die Theorie der indirekten Modifikation", forthcoming in *Brentano Studien V*, 1994-5.

Albertazzi, L. and Poli, R, (eds.) 1993: *Brentano in Italia*, Milano, Guerini.

Ameseder, R. 1904: "Über Vorstellungsproduktion", in Meinong 1904.

Bain, A. 1855: *The Sense and the Intellect*, London.

Benussi, V. 1905: "Gli atteggiamenti psichici elementari e i loro oggetti", *Atti* del convegno internazionale di Psicologia, Forzani, Roma, 440-5.

Benussi, V. 1913: *Psychologie der Zeitauffassung*, Winter, Heidelberg.

Bonaventura, E. 1916: *Le qualità del mondo fisico*, Galletti e Cocci, Firenze.

Bonaventura, E. 1924: "Doppio tachistoscopio a caduta per lo studio dell'attenzione, del tempo di apprendimento e della percezione del tempo", *Rivista di psicologia* 20, 76-80.

---

[116] Ingarden 1964.

[117] From this point of view, there is considerably less incompatibility between Ingarden's and Husserl's ontologies. Both of them, in fact, described a material ontology which served as the basis for a formal ontology: the 'existential' ontology in Ingarden's case, the 'dynamic material' ontology in Husserl's.

Bonaventura, E. 1922: "Signification et valeur de la psychophysique", *Journal de Psychologie* 19 , 481-491.

Bonaventura, E. 1929: *Il problema psicologico del tempo*, Ist. Ed. Scientifico, Milano.

Bonaventura, E. 1928a: "I problemi attuali della psicologia del tempo", *Archivio italiano di psicologia* 6, 78-102.

Bonaventura, E. 1928b: "Note di tecnica sperimentale: il metodo tachistoscopico", *Archivio italiano di psicologia* 6, 180-204.

Bonaventura, E. 1931: *Sul problema psicologico dello spazio*, Le Monnier, Firenze (repr. 1961).

Bonaventura, E. 1990: "La metafisica dello spazio e del tempo", in Gori-Savellini 1990, 161-190, 188-189.

Bozzi, P. 1968-9: "Direzionalità e organizzazione interna della figura", *Memorie dell'Accademia Patavina*, Classe di Scienze Morali, Lettere e Arti 81, 135-170.

Bozzi, P. 1969: *Unità, identità, causalità. Una introduzione allo studio della percezione*, Cappelli, Bologna.

Bozzi, P. 1989: *Fenomenologia sperimentale*, Il Mulino, Bologna.

Bozzi, P. 1990: *Fisica Ingenua*, Garzanti, Milano.

Brandl, J. 1987: "Vorwort zu F. Brentanos 'Von der Natur der Vorstellung'", *Conceptus* 53/54, 19-25.

Brentano, F. 1874: *Psychologie vom empirischen Standpunkte (Psychologie I)*, Duncker and Humblot, Leipzig; also ed. by O. Kraus, Meiner, Leipzig 1929; repr. Hamburg 1973.

Brentano, F. 1907: *Untersuchungen zur Synnespsychologie*, Duncker and Humblot; also ed. by R.M. Chisholm and W. Baumgartner, Meiner, Hamburg 1979.

Brentano, F. 1911: *Von der Klassifikation der psychischen Phänomene (Psychologie II)* (O. Kraus, ed.), Duncker and Humblot, Leipzig; repr. Meiner, Hamburg 1971.

Brentano, F. 1976: *Philosophische Untersuchungen zu Raum, Zeit und Kontinuum*, ed. by S. Körner and R. M. Chisholm, Meiner, Hamburg.

Brentano, F. 1968a: *Vom sinnlichen und noetischen Bewusstseins (Psychologie III)*, ed. by F. Mayer-Hillebrand, Meiner, Hamburg.

Brentano, F. 1968b: *Kategorienlehre*, ed. by A. Kastil, Meiner, Hamburg.

Brentano, F. 1956: *Die Lehre vom richtigen Urteil*, ed. by. F. Mayer-Hillebrand, Francke, Bern.

Brentano, F. 1963: *Die Abkehr vom Nichrealen*, ed. by F. Mayer-Hillebrand, Francke, Bern-Munich.

Brentano, F. 1987: "Von der Natur der Vorstellung", *Conceptus* 53/54, 25-33.

Bühler, K. 1934: *Sprachtheorie*, Fischer Verlag, Stuttgart; repr. Ullstein Book 1975.

Burkhardt H. and Smith B. (eds.) 1992: *Handbook of Metaphysics and Ontology*, 2 Vols., Philosophia Verlag, Munich-Wien.

Calabresi, R. 1930: *Il presente psichico*, Bemporad, Firenze.

Chisholm, R.M. 1981: "Brentano's Analysis of the Consciousness of Time", *Midwest Studies in Philosophy* 6, 3-16.

Chisholm, R.M. 1982: "Brentano's Theory of Substance and Accident", *Brentano and Meinog Studies*, Rodopi, Amsterdam , 3-16.

Chisholm, R.M. and Haller, R. (eds.) 1978: *Die Philosophie Franz Brentanos*, Rodopi, Amsterdam.

Claesges, U. 1964: *Edmund Husserls Theorie der Raumkonstitution* (Phaenomenologica 19), Nijhoff, The Hague.

Claesges, U. 1973: Introduction to Husserl 1973.

Cocchiarella, N. 1972: "Properties as Individuals in Formal Ontology", *Nous* 6, 165-87.

Cocchiarella, N. 1974: "Formal Ontology and the Foundations of Mathematics", in Nackhnikian 1974, 29-46.

Cocchiarella, N. 1986: *Logical Investigations of Predication Theory and the Problem of Universals*, Bibliopolis, Napoli.

Cocchiarella, N. 1991: "Ontology II: Formal Ontology", in Buckhardt and Smith 1992, 640-7.

Coniglione F., Poli, R. and Woleński, J. (eds.) 1993: *Polish Scientific Philosophy. The Lvov-Warsaw School*, Rodopi, Amsterdam.

Diemer, A. 1956: *Edmund Husserl. Versuch einer systematischen Darstellung seiner Phänomenologie* (Monographien zur philosophischen Forschung, Bd. 15), Anton Hain, Meisenheim am Glan.

Fodor, J.A. and Pylyshin, Z.W. 1981: "How direct is Visual Perception? Some Reflections on Gibson's 'Ecological Approach'", *Cognition* 9, 139-196.

Fraisse, P. 1952: "La perception de la durée comme organisation du successif", *Année psichologique* 52, 39-46.

Fraisse, P. 1964: *The psychology of time*, Eyre and Spottiswoode, London.

Gibson, J.J. 1979: *The Ecological Approach to Visual Perception*, Houghton Mifflin, Boston.

Goodman, N. 1977: *The Structure of Appearance*, Reidel, Dordrecht-Boston.

Gori-Savellini S. (ed.) 1990: *Enzo Bonaventura*, Firenze, Giunti.

Gurwitch, A. 1964: *The Field of Consciousness*, Duquesne University Press, Pittsburgh.

Hartmann, N. 1948: *Zur Grundlegung der Ontologie*, Westkulturverlag, Meisenheim am Glan.

Hartmann, N. 1949a: *Möglichkeit und Wirklichkeit*, Westkulturverlag, Meisenheim am Glan.

Hartmann, N. 1949b: *Der Aufbau der realen Welt. Grundrisse der allgemeinen Kategorienlehre*, Westkulturverlag, Meisenheim am Glan.

Hayes, P.J. 1985: "The Second Naive Physics Manifesto", in Hobbs and Moore 1985, 1-36.

Hedwig, K. 1978: "Der scholastische Kontext des Intentionales bei Brentano", in Chisholm and Haller 1978, 67-83.

Hobbs J.R. and Moore, R.C. (eds.) 1985: *Formal Theories of the Commonsense World*, Ablex, Norwood, NY.

Husserl, E. 1891a: *Philosophie der Arithmetik. Psychologische und Logische Untersuchungen*, Vol 1, Pfeiffer, Leipzig; edited by L. Eley, Husserliana, HUA XII, 1970.

Husserl, E. 1891b: "Der Folgerungskalkul und die Inhaltslogik", *Vierteljahrsschrift für wissenschaftliche Philosophie* 15, 168-189; repr. in Husserl 1979, 44-66.

Husserl, E. 1894: "Psychologische Studien zur elementaren Logik", *Philosophische Monatshefte* 30.

Husserl, E. 1900-1: *Logische Untersuchungen*, Niemeyer, Halle, 2 ed. 1913; repr. I Vol. edited by E. Holenstein, HUA XVII, 1975; repr. I & II Vol. edited by U. Panzer, HUA XIX 1, 2, 1984.

Husserl, E. 1910-11: "Philosophie als strenge Wissenschaft", *Logos* 1, 289-341; repr. (W. Szilasi ed.), Klostermann, Frankfurt a. Main 1965.

Husserl, E. 1913: *Ideen zu einer reinen Phänomenologie und phänomenologische Philosophie*, edited by W. Biemel (I), M. Biemel (II) and M. Biemel (III), HUA III, 1950, HUA IV, 1952, HUA V, 1952.

230   LILIANA ALBERTAZZI

Husserl, E. 1930: "Nachwort zu meinen Ideen zu einer reinen Phänomenologie", *Jahrbuch für Philosophie und phänomenologische Forschung* 11, 549-570.

Husserl, E. 1939: *Erfahrung und Urteil. Untersuchungen zur Genealogie der Logik*, edited by L. Landgrebe, Academia Verlag, Prague; Claassen and Goverts, Hamburg 1948.

Husserl, E. 1966a: *Zur Phänomenologie des inneren Zeitbewußtseins*, edited by R. Boehm, HUA X; also edited by R. Bernet, Meiner, Hamburg 1985.

Husserl, E. 1966b: *Analysen zur passiven Synthesis*, edited by M. Fleischer, HUA XI.

Husserl, E. 1973: *Ding und Raum*. Vorlesungen 1907, edited by U. Claesges, HUA XIV.

Husserl, E. 1974: *Formale und transzendentale Logik. Versuch einer Kritik der logischen Vernunft*, edited by P. Janssen, HUA XVII.

Husserl, E. 1979: *Aufsatze and Rezensionen (1890-1910)*, ed. B. Rang (HUA XXII).

Husserl, E. 1980: *Phantasie, Bildbewußtsein, Erinnerung*, edited by E. Marbach, HUA XXIII.

Husserl, E. 1983: *Studien zur Arithmetik und Geometrie*, edited by I. Strohmeyer, HUA XXI.

Husserl, E. 1984: *Einleitung in die Logik und Erkenntnistheorie. Vorlesungen 1906/7*, edited by U. Melle, HUA XXIV.

Johansson, I. 1989: *Ontological Investigations. An Inquiry into the Categories of Nature, Man and Society*, Routledge, London.

Kanisza, G. 1980: *Grammatica del vedere*, Il Mulino, Bologna.

Kitcher, P. 1988: "Marr's Computational Theory of Vision", *Philosophy of Science* 55, 1-24.

Koffka, K. 1935: *Principles of Gestalt Psychology*, Harcourt, Brace, New York.

Kraus, O. 1930: "Zur Phänomenognosie des Zeitbewußtseins", *Archiv für die gesamte Psychologie* 75, 1-22.

Ingarden, R. 1964-65: *Der Streit um die Existenz der Welt*: I: Existentialontologie (1964); II: Formalontologie 1 (Form und Wesen) (1965); II/II Formalontologie 2: Welt und Bewußtsein (1965), Niemeyer, Tübingen.

Ingarden, R. 1966: "Remarks pertaining to some of Kasimir Twardowski's ontological Claims in his Book *Zur Lehre vom Inhalt und Gegenstand der Vorstellungen*", *Ruch Filozoficzny* 25, 21-35.

Libardi, M. 1990: "Teorie delle parti e dell'intero. Mereologie estensionali", *Quaderni del Centro studi per la filosofia mitteleuropea* 4-6, 7-302.

Lichtenstein, M. 1961: "Phenomenal Simultaneity with Irregular Timing of Components of Visual Stimulus", *Perception Motor Skills* 12, 47-70.

Mally, E. 1914: "Über die Unabhängigkeit der Gegenstande vom Denken", *Zeitschrift für Philosophie und philosophische Kritik*, 37-52; Engl. transl. by D. Jacquette in *Man and World* 22, 1989, 215-231.

Marr, D. 1982: *Vision*, Freeman, San Francisco.

Meinong, A. 1899: "Über Gegenstände höherer Ordnung und deren Verhältniss zur inneren Wahrnehmung", *Zeitschrift für Psychologie und Physiologie der Sinnesorgane* 21, 182-272; repr. in Meinong 1929, Vol. II, n.iv, 377-469.

Meinong, A. 1904: *Untersuchungen zur Gegenstandstheorie und Psychologie*, Barth, Leipzig.

Meinong, A. 1929: *Gesammelte Abhandlungen*, Barth, Leipzig.

Melandri, E. 1987: "The 'Analogia Entis' according to Franz Brentano", *Topoi* 6, 51-59.

Mulligan, K. 1885: "'Wie die Sachen sich zueinander verhalten'. Inside and outside the *Tractatus*", *Theoria* 5, 145-174.

Mulligan, K. (ed.) 1987a: *Speech Act and Sachverhalt. Reinach and the Foundations of Realist Phenomenology*, Nijhoff, Dordrecht .

Mulligan, K. 1987b: "Promising and Other Social Acts", in Mulligan 1987a, 29-87.

Musatti, C. 1964: *Condizioni dell'esperienza*, Editrice Universitaria, Firenze.

Nakhnikian, G. (ed.) 1974: *Bertrand Russell's Philosophy*, Duckworth, London.

Perzanowski, J.: "Ontologies and Ontologics", in Zarnecka-Biały 1990, 23-42.

Petitot, J. 1984: "La lacune du contour", *Analyse* 1, 101-140.

Petitot, J. 1985: *Morphogènese du sens*, PUF, Paris.

Petitot, J. 1986: "Le morphological turn de la phenomenologie", Document du C.A.M.S, Paris, E.H.E.S.S.

Petitot, J. 1989: "Forme", *Encyclopedia Universalis* XI, Paris, 712-728.

Piana, G. 1977: *La tematica husserliana dell'intero e delle parti, Introduzione alla Terza e alla Quarta ricerca logica*, Il Saggiatore, Milano.

Piana, G. 1979: *Elementi di una dottrina dell'esperienza*, Il Saggiatore, Milano.

Piana, G. 1988: *La notte dei lampi*, Guerini, Milano.

Poli, R. 1989: "Ricerche ontologiche I", *Quaderni del centro studi per la filosofia mitteleuropea*, 2, 5-55.

Poli, R. 1990: "Ernst Mally's Theories of Properties", *Grazer Philosophische Studien* 38, 115-138.

Poli, R. 1992 : *Ontologia Formale*, Marietti, Genova.

Poli, R. 1993 :"Husserl's Conception of Formal Ontology", *History and Philosophy of Logic* 14, 1-14.

Poli, R. 1993b: "Ontologia e logica in Franz Brentano: giudizi tetici e sintetici", *Epistemologia* 16, 39-76.

Rubin, E. 1921: *Visuell wahrgenommene Figuren. Studien in psychologischer Analyse*, Gldenalske, Copenhagen.

Rubin, E. 1927: "Visuelle wahrgenommene wirkliche Bewegungen", *Zeitschrift für Psychologie* 103, 384-392.

Sållstrom, P. (ed.) 1984: *An Inventory of Present Thinking about Parts and Wholes*, Forskningsradsnamden, Stockholm.

Schiller, P. von 1933: "Stroboscopische Alternativversuche", *Psychologische Forschung* 17, 179-214.

Smith, B. 1978: "An Essay on Formal Ontology", *Grazer Philosophischen Studien* 6, 39-62.

Smith, B. 1984a:, "Logical and Philosophical Remarks on Parts and Wholes", in Sällström 1984, vol. I, 29-42.

Smith, B. 1984b: "Reflections on Dependence", in Sällström 1984, vol. I, 29-42.

Smith, B. 1987: "The Substance of Brentano's Ontology", *Topoi* 6, 39-51.

Smith, B. 1989: "The Primacy of Space. An Investigation in Brentanian Ontology", *Topoi* 8, 75-88.

Smith, B. (ed.) 1982: *Parts and Moments. Studies in Logical and Formal Ontology*, Philosophia Verlag, Munich.

Smith, B. and Mulligan, K. 1983: "Framework for Formal Ontology", *Topoi* 3, 73-85.

Smith, B. and Petitot, J. 1990: "New Foundations for Qualitative Physics", in Tiles, McKee and Dean 1990.

Schuhmann, K. 1993: "Husserl and Twardowski", in Coniglione, Poli and Woleński 1993, 41-59.

Simons, P. 1986: "Categories and Ways of Being", *Reports in Philosophy*, Jagellonian University of Cracow 10, 90-104.

Simons, P. 1987: *Parts. A Study in Ontology*, Clarendon Press, Oxford.

Stern, W. 1897: "Über psychische Präsenzzeit", *Zeitschrift für Psychologie und Physiologie der Sinnesorgane* 13, 325-349.

Stumpf, C. 1873: *Über den psychologischen Ursprung der Raumvorstellung*, Hirzel, Leipzig.

Stumpf, C. 1883-90: *Tonpsychologie*, 2 vols., Hirzel, Leipzig.

Stumpf, C. 1907: "Erscheinungen und psychische Funktionen", *Abhandlungen der Kgl. Preussischen Akademie der Wissenschaften*, Berlin.

Tiles, J.E., McKee, G.T. and Dean C.G. (eds.) 1990: *Evolving Knowledge in Natural Sciences and Artificial Intelligence*, Pitman Publishing, London.

Thom, R. 1972: *Stabilité structurelle et morphogénèse. Essai d'une théorie générale des modèles*, Inter Editions, Paris.

Thom, R. 1980: *Modèles mathématiques de la Morphogenèse*, 2 ed., Ch. Bourgois, Paris.

Thom, R. 1988: *Esquisse d'une Sémiophysique*, Inter-Edition, Paris.

Twardowski, K. 1894: *Zur Lehre vom Inhalt und Gegenstand der Vorstellungen*, Höfler, Wien; repr. ed by R. Haller, Philosophia Verlag, Munich 1982.

Vicario, G. 1973: *Tempo psicologico ed eventi*, Giunti e Barbera, Firenze.

Vicario, G. 1991: "L'ipotesi della costanza in psicologia", *Rivista di psicologia* 1-2, 9-19.

Wertheimer, M. 1923: "Untersuchungen zur Lehre von der Gestalt", *Psychologische Forschung* 4 , 301-351.

Witschel, G. 1964: "Zwei Beiträge Husserls zum Problem der sekundären Qualitäten", *Zeitschrift für Philosophische Forschung* 18, 30-49.

Zarnecka-Biały, E. (ed.) 1990: *Logic Counts*, Kluwer, Dordrecht/Boston/London.

JEAN PETITOT AND BARRY SMITH

PHYSICS AND THE PHENOMENAL WORLD[1]

1. Introduction

One of the main problems of the philosophy of science is that of arriving at a plausible conception of the relations between (1) the phenomenal or commonsensical world that is apprehended in perception and described by natural language and (2) the world of standard physical theories, or of such fundamental theories of the microstructure of matter and radiation as: Newtonian mechanics, the Maxwell theory of electromagnetism, special and general relativity, and quantum mechanics. The rise of mathematical physics has long been seen by many as dictating a dismissal of the phenomenal world – the world macroscopically organized in objectual forms, shapes, secondary qualities and states of affairs – from the realm of properly ontological concerns and as dictating a concomitant 'psychologization' of phenomenal structures. There is, then, a reductionist assumption common amongst philosophers to the effect that it is only microphysical reality that has a structure of its own (that the world as it is in itself is a matter of 'minute, widely-separated colourless particles'[2]). In fact, however, the discovery of atoms or quarks in no way served to eliminate molecules, macromolecules, or indeed macroscopic objects together with their macroscopic properties from the realm of physics – all are physical systems of a perfectly well-defined sort.[3] Moreover, recent developments in the cognitive sciences and elsewhere have given rise to a new theoretical relevance of this phenomenal or qualitative level of objective

---

[1] Our thanks go to Eero Byckling (Helsinki) for valuable suggestions.
[2] Jackson 1977, 121.
[3] For the case of colour see e.g. Nassau 1983.

R. Poli and P. Simons, Formal Ontology, 233–253.
© 1996 Kluwer Academic Publishers. Printed in the Netherlands.

reality. We can point, for example, to the idea of a 'naive physics' such as is propagated by Patrick Hayes (1985), to the qualitative physics of Kleer and Brown (1984), as also to the earlier work on perceptual salience of J.J. Gibson (1979).[4] Most scientific work on the phenomenal or qualitative world is however for obvious reasons psychological in orientation.[5] Our thesis here, in contrast, is that it is possible to develop a coherent theoretical understanding of this world as a matter of *objective structures* in a sense to be more precisely determined below.

Already by looking back to the work of pre-Galilean philosophers we can gain some idea of how a theory of the common-sense world ought to go. It must, it seems, amount to one or other form of Aristotelian ontology in the sense of an ontology recognizing enduring animate and inanimate substances manifesting an opposition between form and matter, possessing sensible and non-sensible qualities and undergoing changes of various natural and non-natural sorts. The ontology must in addition recognize species and genera (or 'natural kinds') which these entities, both substances and their accidents, instantiate, and it must recognize that the instances of these species are divided in each case into circles of more and less standard or typical instances.[6]

For Galileo and his successors, in contrast, substances and sensible ('secondary') qualities came to be eliminated from the realm of that which enjoys autonomous existence, along with the whole concomitant apparatus of natural kinds, prototypical instances, and so on – and it is from this perspective one of the most striking features of recent work in naive physics that a fundamentally Aristotelian apparatus is in different forms in process of being once more resurrected.[7]

Clearly, however, the phenomenal or commonsensical ontology – we shall for the moment treat these terms as synonymous – can be Aristotelian only in a broad sense. Thus the space of this ontology is three-dimensional and global in type, as contrasted with the purely local space of Aristotle. Substances occupy volumes of this space and move continuously through it; they have closed

---

[4] See Smith (forthcoming); for a more detailed treatment of the history of naive physics in general see Smith 1995 and Smith and Casati 1993.

[5] See e.g. Bozzi 1958, 1959, 1989, Forguson 1989.

[6] As the Gestaltists have shown, the prototypical instances in each species are more readily discriminable (salient, *prägnant*) than are the non-prototypical instances, and they are more readily able to give rise to correspondingly skilled responses on the parts of perceiving and acting subjects.

[7] Consider, for example, the extent to which Hayes' list of relatively isolated conceptual 'clusters' or sub-theories of naive physics (1985, p. 18ff.) corresponds to the original master-list supplied by Aristotle in the *Categories*.

spatial boundaries which delimit and separate them from other substances, and so on.

How, now, are we to determine the relation between commonsensical ontology and physics of the standard sort? Modern epistemology has concentrated overwhelmingly on reductionistic answers to this question. Thus at the one extreme is the physicalist trend, characteristic in particular of the thinking of some members of the Vienna circle, which strives to eliminate all that would be specific to the phenomenal realm. At the other extreme one has a variety of attempts, beginning with Mach, the early Carnap, and the later Husserl, to reconstruct physics itself on a sensory or phenomenological basis. Here, in contrast, our aim shall be to throw new light on the relation between physics and phenomenal reality in a way which takes each side of this relation seriously on its own terms. The approach that results will be compatible with physics, though not with any physicalist reductionism of the more familiar sort. It is also more cautious than is customary in its account of the reality that is supposedly captured in physical theories.

2. Manifestations of Matter I: Spatial Movement

Modern physics is, crudely defined, a science of matter. It deals with a rather limited number of ways in which matter manifests itself in phenomenal reality (above all, of course, in the controlled context of laboratory experiments). Moreover, it deals with these manifestations not as denizens of the phenomenal world but as it were in purified form, as quantities or magnitudes: qualitative data are treated via mathematical algorithms and concepts. It seeks to use mathematical devices to *explain* the given manifestations by showing how they are consequences of formal laws or principles. Phenomenal reality comes thereby to be filtered entirely through structures of a formal and quantitative sort. The resultant physical models capture only a limited set of the features of phenomenal reality, and many qualitative and morphological structures of phenomenal manifestation are lost to view as such. This is not, as might be supposed, a trivial matter, a consequence of the selective attention that is characteristic of all sciences. Rather, as we shall see, the very entities with which physics deals are in very precise ways shaped and constrained by the filtering structures with which the physicist is compelled to operate.

Classical mechanics, to take the clearest example, seeks to explain in a mathematical way, and in a single, unified framework of principles, all the diverse expressions of that manifest property of matter which is *spatial movement*,

from the movements of pendulums and the orbits of planets to turbulence in
fluid dynamics and the thermodynamic phenomena (such as heat diffusion)
which are captured by statistical mechanics. Such movements are represented
within the theories of mechanics either as vectors (in the case of velocities,
gradients, accelerations, etc.), or as tensors (of angular momentum, of defor-
mation in continuous media, etc.), or as differential forms (flux, divergence,
curl, etc.). Vectors, tensors and differential forms are all mathematical entities
which possess *intrinsic* geometrical meanings in the sense that they are independent of the coordinate frames we use to describe them. Here the admissible
changes of coordinate frame depend in each case on the level of structure
which is relevant. Theses changes form a *group of symmetries* which is characteristic of this level. For instance, for vectors the group is the linear group (or
the orthogonal group when metrical properties are relevant). For inertial frames
in Galilean kinematics it is the Galilean group. For differential forms it is the
group of diffeomorphisms, etc.

One consequence of this, is that the descriptions of movement yielded by
classical mechanics must be independent of whatever we happen to choose co-
ordinate frame among those co-ordinate frames allowed by the characteristic
group. This is an *a priori* (which is to say pre-physical) requirement on the
descriptions of the theory. Thus in Galilean kinematics the differential entities
of which the theory treats must enjoy the specific mathematical property that
they vary covariantly with respect to the Galilean relativity group. Or again:
because no point in time is distinguishable physically from any other, it is
impossible physically to determine an absolute origin of time: with this fact is
associated the relativity sub-group of time-translations. Similarly, it is impossible physically to determine an absolute origin for the co-ordinates of space, or
an absolute direction in space, and with these geometrical facts are associated
respectively the relativity sub-groups of spatial translations and spatial
rotations. It is impossible physically to select an absolute inertial frame; with
this kinematical fact is associated the group of Lorentz transformations, and so
on.

The Galilean group is a group of *symmetries* of space and time: it determines what is called a 'homogeneous' structure within which every point in
space or time is indistinguishable from every other. In general, symmetries
separate the quantities which are invariant under the transformations specific to
the relevant physical system. (If, for example, we take a particle as our physical
system, then its mass is a quantity of this sort.) On the other hand are quantities
which are not invariant but are rather dependent upon the choice of coordinate
system: thus for example we choose arbitrarily a zero for time, a zero for space,
a geometrical co-ordinate frame, and an inertial frame. A mechanical system,

now, is completely described by a certain function, called its Lagrangian, which expresses the 'action' of the system.[8] One of the greatest theorems of classical mechanics, namely *Noether's theorem* (which can be generalized to physical theories of many other sorts), says that if the Lagrangian is invariant through a given group of coordinate transformations, then there are certain physical quantities correlated therewith, which are *conserved* through every movement of the system.[9] Such conserved quantities are called the first integrals of the system. Their role is fundamental in solving the Euler-Lagrange (or Hamilton) equations which are satisfied by the system and whose solutions are temporal trajectories of the system.

Noether's theorem tells us (more precisely) that to every one-parameter group of symmetries of the Lagrangian there is correlated a law of conservation of a physical quantity. A one-parameter group of symmetries is a group of symmetries of dimension one, for example the group of spatial translations in some given direction. If the Lagrangian is symmetric relative to this group, then the component of kinetic momentum in this direction is conserved. Time translations are correlated in this way with the law of conservation of energy. Spatial rotations are correlated with the law of conservation of angular momentum. From correlations of this type, when appropriately applied, we can derive deep physical predictions – to the extent that many physicists will in fact claim that the whole physical content of classical mechanics is exhausted by such laws of conservation. Einstein's celebrated law of the equivalence of mass and energy is itself a direct consequence of Noether's theorem applied to the Poincaré group, which is the relativity group of four-dimensional Minkowskian space-time, and Noether's theorem has played an ever more important role in modern physics, not only in mechanics but also in quantum field theory.[10]

In order to express physical laws mathematically one needs frames of reference. But these frames themselves are pre-physical conditions of description; insofar as they are a matter of conventional fixing on our part, they reflect no objective peculiarities on the side of reality. Thus although for the purposes of objective description one must for example use co-ordinate frames, such frames are in general eliminable in the sense that they lead in most cases to descriptions that are covariant under admissible changes of co-ordinates. It is an implication of our remarks above, however, that this fact has strictly physical consequences, i.e. consequences relating to what the objects *are* (determined by the conservation laws) with which the theory deals. It is in this context that

---

[8] One can also consider the Hamiltonian of the system, which is an expression of the energy the system contains.
[9] See Abraham and Marsden 1978 and Arnold 1989.
[10] See on this Petitot 1992.

we are to understand what Clifford has in mind when he says that 'physics is geometry' and Einstein when he says that 'objectivity is covariance'. For the phenomena of physics, both in classical and modern physics, can to a large extent be described using geometrical concepts. In the resulting models, it is found that the phisically important quantities are precisely those which are invariant under transformations of the sort referred to above; such quantities are intrinsic to the physical system. When a theory is generalized, as when classical mechanics is replaced by relativity theory, the relevant group of transformations become larger. The resulting description is then more exhaustive, and quantities which were previously unrelated are found to be related by law.

Physics is in this sense required to absorb within itself ever more geometrical structures. For instance in classical Newtonian mechanics, force possesses a real (non-relative) physical content (because acceleration is invariant under Galilean transformations). In general relativity, on the contrary, force becomes a relative (non-physical) quantity, as does velocity. This is so because the relevant relativity group is now the huge group of diffeomorphisms of space-time. The covariance principle is therefore more constraining, since invariance has to be guaranteed through a much larger family of transformations.[11]

3. Physics vs. Ontology

With relativity groups and Noether's theorem we see a shift in modern physics away from ontological concerns of the more traditional sort. For Leibniz, matter in the physical sense still had substances and a *materia prima* underlying it, and mechanics was only the mathematical description of one aspect of the ways in which such substances appear. In post-Newtonian (classical) mechanics, however, this Aristotelian world of substances disappears. Thus for Kant, in his *Metaphysische Anfangsgründe der Naturwissenschaft*, the category of substance is seen as expressing no more than the condition of the possibility of permanence of physical quantities. The concept of

---

[11] In contemporary gauge theories it is the physical content of *interactions* which is reduced to covariance principles. Here the quantum numbers (see 4. below) are treated as spatio-temporally varying quantities. For this, the geometrical descriptions of physical systems must use not only the usual space-time geometry but more complex structures which are called *fibre-bundles* over space-time. The relativity group (which is called the gauge group) is now still bigger, and the covariance principle therefore still more constraining. See for instance Quigg 1983 and Petitot 1992.

substance comes therefore to enjoy a largely *normative* role, as a way of lending system and mathematically expressible organization to the phenomena via conservation laws.

A second aspect of the post-Galilean shift away from the Aristotelian ontology is reflected in the move from qualitative to quantitative aspects of reality. An 'observable', in modern physics, must be *measurable*. But for something to be measurable, there has to be the possibility of conservation in certain ideal conditions. Simplifying somewhat, we can say that it is as if the necessary stability is imposed on the phenomena, and in such a way that the sort of stability we impose will determine the sort of theory we end up with.

We can now see why physics of the post-Galilean sort is not capable of serving as an ontology in the classical sense. Post-Galilean physics involves, for better or worse, an ineliminable *Kantian* dimension. Indeed some mathematicians and physicists, and above all Poincaré, have claimed that relativity and invariance groups are the modern form of the Kantian synthetic *a priori*. Modern physics yields a quantified and conceptual-formal reconstruction of reality, a unified system of mathematical regularities in the manifestations of matter, a reconstruction that is in no small part dependent upon constraints which must be satisfied if the relevant quantities are to be graspable at all. Yet still, this Kantian dimension is not of a psychological and cognitive nature: it is linked with the existence of *symmetries* in geometry and physics. As Leibniz already understood, symmetries say something fundamental about the nature of physical phenomena: indiscernibility is not merely an inadequacy on our part, it is a property of the physical system.

4. Manifestations of Matter II: The Wave Function

Matter manifests itself phenomenally not only via mechanical movement but also, for example, via the sort of behaviour captured by a wave function. Quantum physics can be seen as the physics which relates precisely to this mode of manifestation of matter, just as classical mechanics relates to movement. In addition to 'external' space-time, quantum mechanics deals with what are called 'internal' quantum numbers. These are new physical quantities which characterize the states of elementary particles (electric charge, isospin, charm, colour, etc.). And here again there are certain constraints which prove to be of significance in determining the nature of the objects of the theory which results. For example it turns out empirically that in the nexus of strong nuclear interactions the proton and the neutron are indiscernible. The symmetry between the two is called the isospin symmetry. Applying Noether's theorem we are able to derive from this symmetry a conservation law which is the law of conservation of isospin in nuclear reactions.

Another, perhaps even more impressive, derivation of this sort turns on the fact that it is impossible by physical means to individuate an elementary particle in a group of elementary particles of the same type within a single quantum system (for example one electron in an atom with many electrons). This fact, again, seems at first not to have much physical content. The Lagrangian (or the Hamiltonian) here becomes an operator which operates on the wave function describing the quantum state of the system. This Lagrangian is invariant in respect to the symmetry that is represented by the group of permutations of the particles within the system. In some cases permuting the particles leads to no change in the function: the function is symmetric. In other cases such permutation leads to a change of sign: the function is antisymmetric. This opposition is now reflected in those physical properties of matter which are known in quantum mechanics as the correlation between spin and statistic.

Those systems which are antisymmetric are constituted by particles – called 'fermions' – which have a half-integral spin (1/2, 3/2, 5/2, etc.). Such particles, which are particles of matter, are subject to Pauli's exclusion principle, which states that two fermions in the same position in space-time cannot have the same quantum numbers. It is this principle which explains, for example, why all the electrons of an atom must have different systems of quantum numbers (electrons are fermions); and this explains in turn why one needs different orbits of electrons, why matter does not collapse, and therefore also why matter can bunch macroscopically in a smooth and stable manner and so manifest chemical properties.

Those systems, on the other hand, which are symmetric, are constituted by particles of integral spin (0, 1, 2, etc.). These particles, called bosons, are particles vehiculating interactions between particles of matter. The photon, for example, is the particle vehiculating electromagnetic interaction between electrons, protons, etc. For the bosons, Pauli's exclusion principle is not valid. Thus we can have superposition of bosons in the same position in space-time, which explains such fundamental physical phenomena as lasers, superconductivity and superfluidity. Here also, therefore, we have deep, indeed quintessential properties of matter, which are in a certain sense the physical translation of certain constraints pertaining to symmetry and indiscernibility.

5. Manifestations of Matter III: Qualitative Discontinuities

On the one hand, then, we have objective physical determinations of different modes of manifestation of matter (movement, rays, etc.), and on the other hand we have phenomenal (qualitative, morphological) manifestations in the sense familiar to us all pre-theoretically. Our thesis here is that phenomenal manifestation is also a mode of manifestation of matter and that there can indeed exist a sort of phenomenal physics. This phenomenal physics is of course different from standard fundamental physics: it is qualitative, macroscopic and emergent. Yet it is, nonetheless, objective.

There are well-understood ways in which physical theories can be enriched in order to capture the features specific to phenomenal reality. For physics, though in great part restricted to the quantitative, does indeed deal with just the manifestations of matter – color, sound, temperature – from out of which the qualitative, phenomenal world is built up. Physics is not, however, interested from the theoretical point of view in those very special sorts of ways in which manifestations of matter are composed or knitted together which are relevant to the world of qualitative experience. Our task here, therefore, will be that of devising a science of salience in this sense, i.e. a science of the properly qualitative modes of manifestation of matter, with the goal of bridging the gap between quantity and quality, or between the physical and the phenomenal modes of manifestation of matter in such a way as to make the latter, too, able to serve as the object of a genuine theory.

We shall attempt to explain the qualitative structure of a phenomenon as *emergent* in relation to the physical behaviour of the underlying material substrate. For a property on a structure to be emergent we need three things:

1. There must be two levels of reality, a microlevel and a macrolevel, and the emergent property needs to be a property of objects on the macrolevel.

2. Objects on the macrolevel must be made up of objects on the microlevel as their parts, so that we must be able to explain causally the emergent structure exclusively by appeal to phenomena on the microlevel (causal reductionism).

3. But on the other hand we must be able to show that there are holistic and structural or organizational features (morphological properties, properties of self-maintenance, etc.) which are distinct from those structures or organizational features which are proper to the microlevel and captured by the corresponding microlevel sciences.

Here the obvious suggestion is that the qualities manifested locally in phenomenal reality be represented as degrees of appropriate intensive magnitudes: colours via frequencies and reflectances, qualities of hot and cold via temperatures, etc. Such representations will most importantly preserve the spatial or temporal *variations* in the represented qualities, and it seems reasonable to suppose that it is in such variations that the relevant qualitative information will be concentrated. But only some types of physical phenomena will be able to sustain variations of the appropriate sort. Simple mechanical systems (pendulums, for example) fall out of court in this regard. Intuitively speaking we can say that 'qualitative' structures exist where certain fine-grained microstructures are sufficiently smooth to admit a coarse-grained morphological organization via discontinuities (boundaries) on the macroscopic level.

Which microstructures and which associated sorts of discontinuities come into question here depends in part upon accidental features of the human perceptual system. The key theoretical idea, however, which is due to René Thom,[12] turns on the opposition between 'smooth' and 'boundary' regions in the relevant spheres of variation in intensive magnitudes. Thom's idea is that the science we require should take as its main primitive *qualitative discontinuity*, which is to say discontinuous variations in qualities (appropriately smooth quantitative variations) as represented in the given fashion. The theory which results would then be a science of those manifestations of matter which are associated with macroscopic discontinuities of variation in intensive magnitudes in something like the way in which classical mechanics is a science of those manifestations of matter we call spatial movement.

The steps involved in building up a science of phenomenal reality along these lines can here be sketched only in broad terms:

i. We must convince ourselves that the given primitive does yield the central elements of a science of the relevant sort.

ii. We must give a mathematical expression of the idea of qualitative discontinuity.

iii. We must give an account of how we can use this idea to facilitate the move from standard physics to the science of phenomenal reality.[13]

We shall deal with each of these in turn.

---

[12] See Thom 1972, 1980, 1990 and also Petitot 1985, 1992a. In his 1978 Thom distinguished two complementary aspects of an objective phenomenon: as an object of physical experience, a phenomenon 'admits as underlying symmetry group one of the groups of automorphisms of space-time'. As a manifested structure, however, a phenomenon is the result of a certain mathematically determinate type of irreversible process and is 'characterized by observable discontinuities'.

[13] Compare the problem of moving from (laws of) physics to (laws of) psychology, as discussed e.g. in Crane 1991.

Ad i: How do things appear in phenomenal reality? We begin by drawing attention to three characteristic features of the ways things, events, etc. appear in sensation and perception, features that were first clearly isolated by Husserl:

1. The things which appear to us phenomenally (which are observable), appear always from one side, present one face or aspect, and are correspondingly foreshortened or 'adumbrated'.

2. Whatever appears, appears in such a way as to manifest a foreground-background structure.

3. Whatever appears, appears in the context of a spatio-temporally extended whole.[14]

Take, for example, a black dog with brown spots as this appears in visual perception. Here the perceiving subject is responsible, as it were, for fixing the frame (the perspective, the point of origin) within which the contours of the dog at any given time appear. Each such frame is that portion of space that is visually accessible to the relevant subject at the relevant time. (The *granularity* of contours capable of being detected in any given case will of course depend on the subject's powers of discrimination. This aspect however we shall here leave out of account.) First among the perceived discontinuities, now, is the outer contour (exterior boundary) of the dog as this appears within the relevant frame (a matter of projective geometry, with the relevant observer as projection point).[15] The apparent contours of the dog as a whole are a certain sort of discontinuity within the plane (frame) determined by the perceiving subject: not a discontinuity between two different qualities, but a discontinuity between a quality of the appearing thing and the qualities of the background running on behind it. Finally we have the boundaries within the (apparent plane of) the dog itself; and again, each of the apparent colours (spots) on the surface of the dog has a certain spatial extension.

It is in the context of his treatment of this feature that Husserl, in a crucial passage of the 3rd Logical Investigation (§ 8), explains the concept of qualitative discontinuity. Setting out from the ideas of his teacher, the psychologist Carl Stumpf, Husserl points to an opposition between what he calls 'fusion' (*Verschmelzung*) and 'separation' of sensible qualities. Two neighbouring

---

[14] There is, in other words, a relation of foundation in the Husserlian sense between sensible qualities and spatio-temporal extension (no colour can, as a matter of necessity, exist without spatial extension, no sound without duration, etc.). See Husserl's 3rd Logical Investigation, as also the papers collected in Smith 1982, Fine 1993, and ch. 3 of Petitot 1992a.

[15] The fact that, for each given object, we can only perceive one such contour at a time is a typical example of foreshortening or adumbration, as also is the fact that this apparent contour approximates rather to a two-dimensional than to a fully three-dimensional structure (the structure of an envelope). This point has been emphasized by Marr 1982. See also Petitot 1990 for the geometrical theory of apparent contours.

qualities are fused, phenomenally, if there is no observable separation between them (as for example in a smooth transition from a darker to a lighter shade of one colour or indeed from one colour to another). Separation, in contrast, is identified precisely with discontinuous variation. A sensible phenomenon is *set into relief* in relation to other phenomena, now, only where a discontinuity of this sort has been created by the qualitative moments which fill its extension:

> If a content is intuitively separated in relation to co-existing contents and does not flow over into these 'indistinguishably', then it can make itself count on its own and be noticed (stand forth for itself). The intuitively unseparated content, on the other hand, forms a whole with other co-existing contents, and because it is not marked off in the given manner it is not merely bound up with these contents but 'fused' therewith.[16]

It is separation, in other words, which accounts not only for the salience but indeed for the very existence of an item in phenomenal reality.[17] Thus we have strong grounds for supposing that qualitative discontinuities can indeed serve as one central organizing principle of the phenomenal world.

Ad ii: In giving an appropriate mathematical expression to the notion of qualitative discontinuity we follow the topological approach outlined by Thom 1978 and developed further in Petitot 1992a. Suppose that W is the spatio-temporal extension of a given phenomenon (the dog, as this appears to a given subject at a given time). As a portion of space-time, W is of course a topological space with the usual topology. Suppose further that the different qualities which fill W are expressed by degrees of n distinct intensive magnitudes q_1, q_2, ..., q_n. The q_i are functions $q_i(w)$ of points $w \in W$. They are the sensible qualities (colour, texture, temperature, reflectance, etc.), but considered as immanent to the objects themselves.[18]

A point w is called *regular* if all $q_i(w)$ are continuous in a neighbourhood of w. Let R be the set of regular points of W. R contains a neighbourhood of every one of its points and hence it is an open set of W. Let K be the complementary set of R relative to W. K is the closed set of non-regular points w, which are

---

[16] See Husserl 1975/84 (vol. II, A239, B244). The ideas in this work reveal a topological sophistication which is unfortunately lost in the English translation; for this and other reasons Husserl's ideas in this connection have been until recently ignored by his successors.

[17] Cf. Meinong's discussion of the 'prerogative of difference' in § 22 of his 1906.

[18] Of course certain simplifications are involved here. Thus colour might be accounted for in terms of three distinct qualities: hue, saturation and brightness. Similarly there is no single property of reflectance; the latter is rather a macroscopic approximation of a more fine-grained system on the quantum level of a range of properties having to do with the emission-absorption spectra of the atoms constituting the substrate.

called the *singular* points of W. Hence w is a singular point if there is at least one quality q_i which is discontinuous at w. We shall call K the *morphology* of the phenomenon that fills W. K is then the system of qualitative discontinuities – the pattern of boundaries – which sets this phenomenon into relief and makes it salient as a phenomenon. (Consider, for example, the morphological organization of a leaf, or of a dog, or of a wedding-photograph.)

This topological definition of the concept of morphology is as it stands purely phenomenological. It is completely neutral as to what might be the cause or the principle of production of the phenomenon or what might be the realities underlying it. In order to accord physical content to the definition, we must now find some way to conceive a morphology (W, K) as a manifestation of physical properties internal to whatever underlies or causes the phenomenon in question.

Our thesis, now, is that the perceptually salient macrolevel objects are constituted by certain sorts of boundary-patterns to which the physical substrate gives rise. Note that such patterns, together with the phenomenal items which they circumscribe, exist independently of human perceiving subjects. They are objective; but they are of no intrinsic physical interest because they play no role in properly physical *explanations* at the microlevel. Moreover, they would be of no interest at all were it not for the existence of subjects whose perceptual organs are tuned in correspondence to them.

Ad iii: We can understand such boundary-patterns more precisely as follows. In many standard physical descriptions, the instantaneous states of a system with *n* degrees of freedom are represented by points x of what is called a 'phase space' M, which is a differentiable manifold of dimension *n*. For example for a system of N particles in 3-dimensional space, the phase space is the 6N-dimensional space of the positions and velocities of the particles. For a chemical system of N chemical substances in interaction, the phase space is the N-dimensional space of concentrations of the substances. For a magnetic system of N atoms a_i with spins σ_i (or, in an analogous manner, for a neuronal network of N neurons a_i with states of activation σ_i) the phase space is the N-dimensional space of the families $\sigma = (\sigma_i)_{i=1,...,N}$, etc.[19]

The dynamic of the system, now, is described by means of a system of ordinary differential equations, or in other words a *dynamical system* on M.[20] Suppose that X is such a dynamical system on the phase space M. From each in-

---

[19] For an elaboration of morphological ideas in the treatment of connectionism see Petitot 1991.
[20] See again Abraham and Marsden 1978; Arnold 1989.

stantaneous state x the system follows a certain trajectory in M. The instantaneous states taken individually are transient: they are too fleeting to be observable. The effectively observable states of a system correspond rather to the
asymptotic and stable behaviours of trajectories where the energy is minimized.
Such effectively observable states and behaviours, those states and ways of
behaving into which the system falls under normal conditions, are called the
attractors of the system. The simplest case of an attractor is a stable equili-
brium point: think for example of the rest-position of a dissipative pendulum.
Starting from a position away from this point, the pendulum oscillates but little
by little approaches the stable position. Its trajectory is asymptotically attracted
by this fixed point. Or consider an oscillating electric circuit: from any initial
state the system after some time reaches the stable oscillatory state and so its
trajectory is attracted by this state.

Return, now, to our phenomenon having substrate S, spatio-temporal extension W, and morphology K. Here the phase space M is the space of local
physical states of the substrate S. Suppose that the physical behaviour of the
substrate at each point w is physically describable by some dynamical system
X_w on M. Then we can move from the local to a global point of view, and assert that the mapping

$$\sigma: w \longrightarrow X_w,$$

from the extension W to the functional space of the possible dynamical systems
on M expresses the internal properties of the substrate of the phenomenon
taken as a whole. M is referred to as the *internal space* of the system, W as the
external space. X_w is the *internal dynamic* of the system at w, and the attractors
of X_w are the *internal states* of the system at w. We now have enough
machinery to explain physically how it is possible that in the external space W
a morphology K can emerge.

Choose $w \in W$. Let X_w be the internal dynamic at w. In the general (normal)
case, the internal state of the substrate S at w is physically described by an
attractor A_w of X_w. The phenomenal qualities $q_i(w)$ are intensive quantities
associated with A_w. To explain the qualitative discontinuities of the $q_i(w)$, we
now let $w_0 \in K$ be some singular point of W. We consider a path P crossing K
at w_0. The idea is that in moving through points $w \in P$ the attractor A_w
becomes unstable when we cross w_0. That is to say, it is replaced suddenly by
another attractor B_w. In the theory of dynamical systems such a phenomenon is
called a *bifurcation* of attractors. When a system is subject to such a bifurcation, it is subject also to a sudden transition of its internal state and so manifests
a qualitative discontinuity. Similarly we can explain the exterior boundaries of

things by saying that when we cross such a boundary, the internal state A_w disappears entirely. Such boundaries, too, are phenomenally salient.

In macroscopical physics, there are many examples of such phenomena of transition of the internal states of a system. They are known as *critical phenomena*.[21] A typical example is that of phase transitions in thermodynamics, where a system undergoes a sudden change of phase (for example from solid to liquid or from liquid to gas, from a magnetic to a non-magnetic phase, from normal conductivity to superconductivity, and so on). Such changes occur when a parameter such as temperature crosses a critical value. The external space W is the space of (observable) control parameters such as temperature or pressure. The internal space M is the space of molecular states of the system, the internal dynamic X_w is the molecular dynamic and the attractors are the molecular states underlying the phases. Phenomenologically, the internal space M and the internal dynamic X_w are unobservable (their description is the task of standard physics proper). What we experience as salient (and what we possess words to describe) are the qualitative discontinuities which are the phase transitions, together with the smooth regions (for example phonemes) these discontinuities serve to mark out within the relevant phenomenal space.

There are many other critical phenomena: for example shock waves in acoustics, transition to turbulence in hydrodynamics, buckling in elasticity theory, etc. All such phenomena are salient in our perceptual experience. They are the physical support of the qualitative morphological organization of the phenomenal world.

6. A Theory of the Common-Sense World

In this manner we can begin to heal the rift pointed out in our first section between physics and the phenomenal world. We have now at our disposal a theory which is founded in the physics of the substrates and which describes how morphologies or macrolevel boundary-patterns can emerge therefrom. This treatment of morphologies in the phenomenal world employs not the microscopic physics of fermions, bosons, etc., but the resources of a macroscopic physics only. In fact we do not take account of the relation between X_w and the fine-grained physics at w.[22] This relation is not our concern: it is dealt with by

---

[21] See for example the material in Domb and Green 1972-1985 as well as Petitot 1992a (ch. 5).

[22] Consider, for example, the case of a chemical reaction. Here we take for X_w the kinetic chemical equations of the chemical constituents and not the quantum physics of the substrate.

standard physical theories. We simply assume that we can describe macroscopically the relevant internal physical properties via a dynamical system, and this can indeed be shown already to be possible in very many cases.

Of course it might be argued that our 'morphological' science of the qualitative world is at the same distance from an ontology in the strict sense as are classical mechanics, quantum mechanics, etc. We are after all dealing here, too, not with objects (qualities, etc.) in the world, but with products of mathematical reconstruction.[23] The reconstruction here presented allows however a direct mimicking of those central features of the Aristotelian commonsensical ontology that were so fatefully abandoned by Galileo and his successors. Thus not only can it claim to offer a sort of qualitative physics; it can also furnish a theory of substance, of change or process, and of typicality, species and categorization, as also of other pervasive features of the commonsense world. It is this which justifies our use of the terminology of a phenomenal or qualitative 'ontology'.

As concerns the theory of substance and change, here the central problem is that of understanding the relation between the perceived object itself (in our example, the spotted dog) and the family of its apparent contours. There are two abstractly distinguishable systems of continuous development in the latter, one bound up with movements of the object, the other with movements of the perceiving subject. The theory of substance is in the first place a theory of the mathematical properties of the first of these two sorts of continuous development. The geometrical problem to be solved is this: how can the object be unambiguously retrieved from the system of qualitative discontinuities which are given by its apparent contours.[24]

As concerns the problem of categorization and typicality, here we must distinguish two cases. If the entities to be categorized depend on a finite number of characteristic cues (as is the case in relation to colours and phonemes), then a (W,K) model, where W is the space of the cues, *is* a model of categorization. A category C defined by K is a connected component of $W-K$. In each category there is defined statistically a certain centre, the *prototype* T_C of the category. As Petitot 1989a shows, the strategy here outlined can be applied to the elaboration of very detailed models of categorial perception in phonetics (of the ways in which phonetic perception categorizes the continuous audio-acoustic flux by chopping it up into phonemes).

---

[23] For a sketch of some alternatives to this Kantian view of the qualitative morphological ontology – a view criticized in Morton 1990 – see Smith 1995.
[24] See Petitot 1990.

Take, however, the more complicated case of visual forms. Let us suppose that the latter constitute a space F. We can then distinguish within F the structurally stable forms as those whose qualitative type is invariant relatively to small deformations. These constitute an open set R of F. Let K_F be the complementary set of R relative to F. K_F then effects a division of F into stable forms, i.e. categories or species, which are delimited from each other by boundaries made up of unstable forms.

7. Qualitative Ontology and the Science of Cognition

Could something like the phenomenal or commonsensical ontology outlined above constitute a scientific theory in the full sense? Here the most important criticism would be that the theory in question is not predictive in the usual (causal) sense. It can be pointed out, however, that the approach does lead to prediction, though only in the sense that it leads to the possibility of our explicating mathematical constraints for the empirical morphologies. This is prediction of the same sort as, for example, predictions to the effect that if you have a crystal, or the envelope of a virus, or a snowflake, or a honeycomb, or an ornamentation of the Alhambra of Granada, then the symmetry of the structure is necessarily one of the abstract symmetries which are allowed by pure geometry. There exist theorems which make the same type of structural predictions for the possible morphologies K. Even if they are a variety of structural prediction or structural explanation, and not of causal prediction or explanation, these predictions can be interpreted as abstract mathematical constraints upon the universe of morphological phenomena.[25]

Our thesis, therefore, is that a truly scientific theory of the phenomenal world can be rooted in the qualitative macro-physics of the material substrates. But in order to have a plausible theory of the phenomenal world we need in addition a psychological-cognitive theory of *perception* and an account of the link between this theory and the theory of the substrates. How is the subject involved in the perceptual explication and cognitive interpretation of the qualitative structures of the phenomenal world? As far as qualities such as colour are concerned, we already possess considerable work on these problems, and we

[25] Perhaps the best known theorem of this sort is the Whitney-Thom-Arnold theorem classifying elementary catastrophes. But there are also other theorems concerning universal properties of critical phenomena and bifurcation scenarios, for example in relation to the routes towards chaos or turbulence via an infinite number of successive bifurcations, as in Feigenbaum's scenario. See Petitot 1992a.

know something about the chain of steps which lead from physics to the mind. We have first of all, at the microlevel, the absorption-emission spectra of the atoms making up the substrate. At the macrolevel we have the reflectance of the object, which gives rise in its turn to transmission of light of certain wavelengths. At the level of the retina, the light excites the photoreceptors and the information (pattern of wavelengths) it bears is processed by these transducers – which is to say it is transformed by the photoreceptors from photochemical into neuronal information (frequencies of neuron-firings codifying the wavelengths). This gets processed further on its way to the visual cortex, where there at last occurs the registering of the sensible quality of colour.

From our morphological point of view, now, the fundamental link between object and mind is seen as being furnished precisely by the concept of qualitative discontinuity. For this concept can be applied equally to qualities as manifested physically and as apprehended in patterns of sensation in the mind (and it is precisely for this reason that they are phenomenally salient). Wave optics explains (in a non-trivial manner) how the very special type of information provided by qualitative discontinuities can be encoded in the light (that is to say how singularities can be propagated by the light).[26] Theories of visual perception for example of the sort that is propounded by David Marr seek to clarify the perceptive endowment which allows the human cognitive system to detect and to process this information. There is strong evidence for the hypothesis that the retina makes a wavelet analysis of the signal (that is to say, a local and multi-scale Fourier analysis) and picks up the qualitative discontinuities therefrom (Marr's theory of the so-called 2-D primal sketch). Some of these 2-dimensional qualitative discontinuities are then interpreted as apparent contours of 3-dimensional objects.[27]

The interest of the work of Marr and his successors[28] is that it reconciles two apparently antagonistic approaches: the information-processing approach and an ecological point of view in the style of Gibson. In the classical cognitivist paradigm (as exemplified by Fodor, Pylyshyn, *et al.*), information processing is essentially reduced to the operations of calculation on symbolic mental representations.[29] These operations are essentially syntactic: the cognitivists focus exclusively on algorithms and neuronal implementations thereof, and thus, familiarly, they leave no room for the attempt to do justice to the link between the cognitive system and the qualitative features of the world outside.

---

[26] See ch. 5 of Petitot 1992a.

[27] Cf. Marr's theory of the so-called 2-and-a-half-D sketch, and also Petitot 1990 and ch. 3 of Petitot 1992a.

[28] See e.g. Poggio 1984, Koenderink and Doorn 1986.

[29] See Fodor 1980 and Fodor and Pylyshyn 1981.

If, however, one wants to introduce objective structures of the environment into the account of perception and cognition (as the ecologists do), then one is committed to making such structures compatible with the information-processing devices utilized by human perceivers. This is what Marr comes close to doing, and this is why his work is a step along the road to the overcoming of methodological solipsism. Marr shows how what Gibson considered as the 'extraction' (pick-up) of invariants from the environment might be understood in information-theoretic terms as a form of computation.

A truly adequate theory, however, must not only focus on algorithms and neuronal implementations. It must in addition, as Marr himself saw, find a means of comprehending these algorithms in relation to the objective (external) type of information which they process. The algorithms must in this way be determined by objective properties of the environment. The mathematical theory of qualitative discontinuities, now, seems to offer a useful starting point for understanding the sort of determination that is here at issue: for before imagining formal algorithms for the processing of apparent contours, etc., one must know what mathematical type of information such structures consist of. And as we have argued, this information is essentially constituted by singularities: they are drawn from the family of perceptually salient boundary-patterns.

References

Abraham, R. and Marsden, J.E. 1978: *Foundations of Mechanics*, Reading, Mass, Benjamin/Cummings.

Arnold, V. I. 1989: *Mathematical Methods of Classical Mechanics*, New York, Springer.

Arnold, V.I., Gusein-Zade, S.M. and Varchenko, A.N. 1985: *Singularities of Differentiable Maps*, Boston, Birkhäuser.

Boi, L. *et. al.* (eds.) 1993: *1830-1930. A Century of Geometry*, Lecture Notes in Physics, Berlin, Springer.

Bozzi, P. 1958: "Analisi fenomenologica del moto pendolare armonico", *Rivista di Psicologia* 52, 281-302.

Bozzi, P. 1959: "Le condizioni del movimento 'naturale' lungo i piani inclinati", *Rivista di Psicologia* 53, 337-352.

Bozzi, P. 1989: "Sulla preistoria della fisica ingenua", *Sistemi intelligenti* 1, 61-74.

Crane, T. 1991: "All God has to do", *Analysis* 51, 235-244.

Domb, C. and Green, M.S. (eds.) 1972-1985: *Phase Transitions and Critical Phenomena*, New York, Academic Press.

Fine, K. 1994: "The Theory of Part and Whole", in Smith and Smith 1994.

Fodor, J. 1980: "Methodological Solipsism Considered as a Research Strategy in Cognitive Psychology", *Behavioral and Brain Sciences* 3, 63-73.

Fodor, J. and Pylyshyn, Z. 1981: "How Direct is Visual Perception? Some Reflections on Gibson's 'Ecological Approach'", *Cognition* 9, 139-196.

Forguson, L. 1989: *Common Sense*, London and New York, Routledge.

Gibson, J.J. 1979: *The Ecological Approach to Visual Perception*, Boston, Houghton-Mifflin.

Hayes, P.J. 1985: "The Second Naive Physics Manifesto", in Hobbs and Moore 1985, 1-36.

Hobbs, J.R. and Moore, R.C. (eds.) 1985: *Formal Theories of the Commonsense World*, Ablex.

Husserl, E. 1975/84: *Logische Untersuchungen* (Husserliana, vols. XVIII and XIX), Dordrecht, Nijhoff.

Jackson, F. 1977: *Perception*, Cambridge, Cambridge University Press.

Kleer J.D. and Brown, J.S. 1984: "A Qualitative Physics Based on Confluences", *Artificial Intelligence* 24, 7-84.

Koenderink, J.J. and Doorn, A.J. van 1986: "Dynamic Shape", *Biological Cybernetics* 53, 383-396.

Marr, D. 1982: *Vision*, San Francisco, Freeman.

Meinong, A. von 1906: *Über die Erfahrungsgrundlagen unseres Wissens*, Berlin, J. Springer (repr. in Meinong, *Gesamtausgabe*, vol. V, Graz, Akademische Druck- und Verlagsanstalt, 1978).

Morton, A. 1990: "Can't Kant: Smith on Folk Physics", in Tiles, McKee and Dean 1990, 251-261.

Nassau, K. 1983: *The Physics and Chemistry of Color*, New York, John Wiley and Sons.

Petitot, J. 1985: *Morphogenèse du Sens*, vol. 1, Paris, Presses Universitaires de France.

Petitot, J. 1989: "Morphodynamics and the Categorial Perception of Phonological Units", *Theoretical Linguistics* 15, 25-71.

Petitot, J. 1989a: "Hypothèse localiste, Modèles morphodynamiques et Théories cognitives", *Semiotica* 77, 65-119.

Petitot, J. 1990: "Le Physique, le Morphologique, le Symbolique. Remarques sur la Vision", *Revue de Synthèse* 4, 139-183.

Petitot, J. 1991: "Why Connectionism is Such a Good Thing. A Criticism of Fodor and Pylyshyn's Criticism of Smolensky", *Philosophica* 47, 49-79.

Petitot, J. 1992: "Actuality of Transcendental Aesthetics for Modern Physics", in Boi 1993, 273-304.

Petitot, J. 1992a: *Physique du Sens*, Paris, Editions du CNRS.

Petitot, J. and Smith, B. 1990: "New Foundations for Qualitative Physics", in Tiles, McKee and Dean 1990, 231-249.

Poggio, T. 1984: "Vision by Man and Machine", *Scientific American* 250, 68-78.

Putnam, H. 1987: *The Many Faces of Realism*, LaSalle, Open Court.

Quigg, C. 1983: *Gauge Theories of the Strong, Weak and Electromagnetic Interactions*, Menlo Park, Benjamin/Cummings.

Smith, B. (ed.) 1982: *Parts and Moments. Studies in Logic and Formal Ontology*, Munich, Philosophia.

Smith, B. 1995: "The Structures of the Commonsense World", *Logos* 2.

Smith, B. (forthcoming): "Common Sense".

Smith, B. and Casati, R. 1993: "Naive Physics: An Essay in Ontology", *Philosophical Psychology,* forthcoming.

Smith, B. and Smith, D.W. (eds.) 1994: *The Cambridge Companion to Husserl*, Cambridge, Cambridge University Press, forthcoming.

Thom, R. 1972: *Stabilité structurelle et Morphogenèse*, New York, Benjamin; Paris, Ediscience.

Thom, R. 1978: "Formalisme et Scientificité", *Les Etudes philosophiques* 2, 171-78.

Thom, R. 1980: *Modèles mathématiques de la Morphogenèse*, Paris, Christian Bourgeois.

Thom, R. 1988: *Esquisse d'une Sémiophysique. Physique aristotélicienne et Théorie des Catastrophes*, Paris, Intereditions.

Thom, R. 1990: *Apologie du Logos*, Paris, Hachette.

Tiles, J.E., McKee, G.T. and Dean, C.G. (eds.) 1990: *Evolving Knowledge in Natural Science and Artificial Intelligence*, London, Pitman Publishing.

PETER M. SIMONS AND CHARLES W. DEMENT

ASPECTS OF THE MEREOLOGY OF ARTIFACTS

L'intelligence est la faculté de fabriquer des instruments
inorganisés, c'est-à-dire, artificiels.
Henri Bergson, *L'Evolution créatrice*, ch. 2, p. 151.

1. The Need for an Ontology of Artifacts

More ingenuity and creative energy is invested in the design, production and application of artifacts than in any field of human endeavour. We are surrounded by millions of artifacts, we have commerce with them every day, many of us more than with other human beings. The level of civilisation is literally measured by the kind of artifacts of which a culture is capable, from the first palæolithic hand axe to the space shuttle and the supercomputer. It is all the more surprising then that there has been little interest in the general ontological status of artifacts. Perhaps it is assumed that there is little to say beyond the bare dictionary definition, or perhaps that the very variety and heterogeneity of artifacts inhibits such a general study. They lack as a class that simplicity and amenity to formal treatment that attracts the formally inclined, and largely fail to give rise to the kinds of tingling intellectual puzzles that customarily attract philosophers.

Nevertheless, so important a class of entities should not remain outside the general ontological purview. As elsewhere, a sound ontology is the best basis from which to launch further philosophical discussions, such as the ethical ones surrounding the social and ecological impacts of technology, the implications of bioengineering, and others. There are other reasons to urge the development of a general ontology of artifacts. For example, the development of a

255

R. Poli and P. Simons, Formal Ontology, 255–276.

comprehensive and systematic ontology of the everyday or common sense world entails the prior, or at least a parallel development of a general ontology of artifacts. Problems involving the representation of artifacts in computing systems also comprise a key intersection between philosophy and software engineering in general and artificial intelligence research in particular. For instance, there are several efforts underway to establish standards for representing the mereological, geometrical, and economic properties of artifacts in database systems, so that information about them can be more readily exchanged between cooperating organizations.[1] All of these efforts would benefit from the formality, completeness, and consistency that would result from the development of sound ontological foundations. There are also projects to develop software systems that combine very large common sense knowledge bases with sophisticated content manipulation and acquisition capabilities.[2] Such systems cannot function effectively without an explicit representation of the general ontology of the objects they represent that is sufficiently deep to enable the system to manipulate data in ways that correspond to how human beings perform analogous tasks. Since the majority of objects such systems will be representing are artifacts, a general ontology of these entities is essential.

This essay is intended as a step in the direction of such a general ontology of artifacts. We begin by examining the lexical definition of the term, consider some borderline cases, but concentrate primarily on various aspects of artifact mereology, which encompasses several interesting issues. We do not present or even sketch an ontology of artifacts in complete generality, since this is a large and relatively unexplored topic, and is well beyond the scope of a single paper.[3]

---

[1] Among these are the CALS (Continuous Acquisition and Life-cycle Support)-related efforts in the U.S. and the STEP (Standard for the Exchange of Product model data), Parts Library, and MANDATE (Manufacturing Management Data) standards sponsored by ISO (International Organization for Standardization) TCI84/SC4.

[2] Two of these are the PACIS (Platform for the Automated Construction of Intelligent Systems) project at Ontek Corporation, in which we both participate, and the CYC (enCYClopedia) project at MCC (Austin, Texas) led by Doug Lenat.

[3] The philosophical literature on artifacts is woefully inadequate and has tended to focus on tired concerns with Thesean ship part-replacement and identity through time, rather than on more salient problems such as the phenomenological ontology of intersubjective plans, the foundations of metrology, and artifact mereology, among others. Some notable exceptions are Ingarden 1973 and 1989, and Dipert 1993. See also Hilpinen 1993a and 1993b.

2. The Lexical Definition and its Limits

The *Oxford English Dictionary* defines an artifact as "Anything made by human art and workmanship; an artificial product". Looking around this definition, we find for the cognates *artificial*: "Made or resulting from art or artifice, or brought about by constructive skill, and not spontaneously; not natural". And again, *artifice:* "Skill in doing anything as a result of knowledge and practice". There is enough here to be going on with.

Firstly, note that artifacts are products of action. A naturally occurring thing like an acorn or a tidal bar or a thunderstorm is not an artifact. Secondly, not just any kind of action produces an artifact. A person idly scratching herself may produce a red weal on her skin, but the weal is not an artifact (whereas a tatoo is one). Many people may walk along a certain route and so wear a path, but the path is an incidental product of their action rather than an artifact (whereas a paved road is one). The action has to be directed towards producing the product in question, or at least something like it (actions may miscarry, the attempt may be unsuccessful). Further, the definition notes the requirement of a certain level of skill. This is a more delicate matter. A person who writhes around on sandy ground to create a more comfortable place to rest intends to produce the resulting hollow, but the hollow, though a product of action aimed at producing it, is hardly a product of great skill. At best it is a borderline case of an artifact (one can imagine hollow-writhing developing into an art in which certain shapes of hollow are striven after, but the example is rather far-fetched). Nor is every kind of skilled action productive of an artifact. A baseball batter hitting a home run off a 100 m.p.h. fast ball is exercising a skill denied to all but a few, as is Nureyev dancing or Ashkenazy playing, but these actions leaves no artifacts behind them (such is the ephemerality of sport, dance, and music, one might say) although they justifiably excite admiration and may be *recorded in* artifacts such as pictures, films, and sound recordings. Note also that level of skill is on a sliding scale. A child's first gauche daubs may not be Matisse, but they are the first rung on the ladder, and even Matisse had to start somewhere. They are skilled for the child. And skill is not completely relative. Most creatures do not have the ability (or interest) to manipulate brush and paint so as to produce even a single daub, let alone the Lascaux cave paintings. (Some do however: there is an elephant in San Diego Zoo who paints, and her paintings sell well.)

We should distinguish therefore a *product* of an action from a *result* of an action. Any action has results, at the very least, the result that the action has been performed. But a product is something which perdures, if only for a short while. A smoke ring, though it last but a second, is an artifact, as are the short-lived particles produced by particle colliders.

There is a bad factual mistake in the Oxford definition. It is unwarrantedly anthropocentric to confine artifacts to those things made by *human* art and workmanship. The products of nature's star engineers, such as the dam and lodge of a beaver, or the nest of a weaver bird, are well above the level of skill attainable by many human beings (especially young ones), and the making of nests, burrows and other forms of shelter extends through most zoological phyla; though not all of it can count as intentional (because the relevant animals could not have intentions), much of it can. In the case of the nests of social insects like wasps and termites, we may hesitate to call them artifacts not because they do not evince skill but because they are communal products rather than the working out of a plan in the mind of a single individual. But they may be considered another kind of borderline case.

For many centuries it was believed that humans alone make a particular kind of artifact, namely tools. Now we know better. Chimpanzees living in the wild strip leaves off twigs and use them to catch termites: a naturally occurring object is intentionally modified for use to a purpose. The stripped twig is a primitive tool. Its production and use are learned by imitation: they are culturally transmitted. Producing and using the first human tools required little more skill, though the tools were more versatile.

Nevertheless, there is no need to be unduly modest. No creature of our ken remotely approaches historic and prehistoric human levels of skill in artifact making. We can be grateful that the oft-noted combination of large brain, stereoscopic vision, upright posture freeing the forelimbs for manipulation (look at how squirrels eat), opposable thumb, and relative lack of natural armour and weaponry made our ancestors the first systematic artificers.

When and how it becomes important that we can acquire and enhance skills by linguistic instruction is not clear. Even today, most skills are learned by imitating the master rather than reading the manuals: language is surely more important for planning and coordinating complex projects than for providing the necessary manipulative wherewithal. After all, the Tower of Babel failed to meet its completion date not through lack of building skills but because of linguistic hitches, a fact which may strike a chord in those familiar with modern multilingual building sites.

Artifacts are produced by procedures which range from the simplest modification and adaptation of pre-existing natural objects like the stripping of twigs from a branch to make a walking stick to intricate processes which are themselves the children of human ingenuity, such as the etching of circuits on a microchip. Artifacts range from the microscopically small to objects visible from space. Some artifacts take only a second to make, some, like cathedrals, take hundreds of years. Some require little skill, others, like a Stradivarius, require years of apprenticeship. Some can be made by one person, while others, the most complex artifacts like means of transport, communications and weapons systems require whole industries and rest on the work of millions. Some cost nothing, others bankrupt nations. In this dazzling variety it is indeed difficult to find meaningful common denominators beyond the broad lexical definition, and we shall not attempt to do so. There is strong indication that a proper account of artifacts cannot be separated from a general ontology of making, with all that this entails. A taxonomy of artifacts is desirable, but properly carried out it would be a vast undertaking. ·

Rather than attempt the impossible, then, we shall concentrate attention on tractable mereological questions, especially as they pertain to complex artifacts. We do not promise in advance to restrict our attention to formal questions. Rather than strive contentiously to confine our remarks to the formal ontology of part and whole, we shall note simply that the importance of part/whole questions for philosophy is not simply one of form, and allow our considerations to stray into material ontology as necessary.

3. Mereology and Artifacts

It is widely accepted among ontologists that the relationship of part to whole is, apart from the logical relations identity and difference and the relations definable in their terms, as general a relation as can be found applying among objects. Husserl regularly reckoned it among the formal concepts, meaning that it applies to objects of all genera and is not specific to any region or ontological domain. It may be questioned how readily the relation applies to abstract entities, but we shall not be concerned with such things in this paper and so the question is not crucial here. Most of the things we shall be considering are concrete, spatiotemporal objects of one or another sort. For these questions of part and whole are always germane. Indeed, if you ask the person in the street what they associate with the term 'parts', then apart from parts of the body, they will probably think of 'spare parts', things like oil filters, spark plugs, gaskets, fan belts, windscreen wiper blades, or (more expensively) clutches, transmission half-shafts, crankshafts and gearboxes. When one of us published a book with the title *Parts*,[4] it was with the knowledge that this word was most prominently displayed outside emporia where such things are offered for sale.

We shall examine two problems pertaining to the mereology of artifacts. The first is the multivocity of the term 'part' as it is employed in everyday life and its deviation, both in intension and extension, from that term as used by most philosophers concerned with formal mereology. While it is difficult to envision an integration of these different senses into a unifying framework, achieving such a subsumption is necessary for any future mereology of artifacts. The second problem is reconciling differences among alternative mereologies for the same artifact, as represented in distinct types of engineering documents used in complex manufacturing environments. These alternative structures are not arbitrary kinds of mereological sums found in extensional systems. Rather, they arise instead from a combination of the need for intersubjective plans keyed to different stages in the product lifecycle and from the problem of the multiple senses of 'part'. Thus this second problem represents a direct intersection between manufacturing and philosophy.

4. Formal versus Common Sense Concepts of Part

In most systems of formal mereology there is an axiom to the effect that an arbitrary collection or plurality of objects forms a whole, whose parts overlap just those entities which overlap at least one member of the collection, and nothing else besides. The objects in the collection need not be spatiotemporally continuous or joined up, indeed typically they will not. So the object which consists entirely of the knife with which Brutus stabbed Caesar and the football with which Pelé scored his first goal for Brazil, albeit that its disjoint parts are separated by thousands of years and thousands of miles relative to the earth's surface, is a perfectly good object. In those ontologies which include a plurality of basic categories of individual, such as continuants on the one hand like bodies and organisms, and occurrents, like events, processes and states on the other, or perhaps include tropes or states of affairs among their particulars, the adoption of this *General Sum Principle* (GSP) means that there are transcategorial wholes, for example a whole made up entirely of a continuant, say the Eiffel Tower, and an event, say the first cracked note ever sung by Pavarotti in *La Scala*. Now, as one of us has emphasized elsewhere,[5] this prodigality

---

[4] Simons 1987.
[5] Simons 1987, 110.

among objects is not of itself ontologically disastrous, since it is hard to see how it can lead to any contradiction unless either standard mereology is inconsistent (which it provably is not) or even a more restricted mereology leads to contradiction when applied to the objects of the world. The latter cannot completely be ruled out, especially in view of problems such as vagueness, but our (here unsupported) assertion is that this is a problem facing ontology in general and not just the application of mereology. But the sense of acute unease about such scattered and arbitrarily composed objects remains.

Another respect in which the usual mereology is prodigal is that of assuming the existence of arbitrary parts of even ordinary objects. This does not follow directly from the application of the formalism, it is true, but it is a standard account which is at it were part of the mereologist's patter. Take an object, like this house here. Not just its parts standardly so called, like its walls, roof, foundation, doors, windows etc. are parts, but also many others. For example, take any imaginary surface (plane or otherwise) that cuts the house in at least one point: then the parts of the house to either side of this surface form a partition into two objects (we are ignoring the surface itself). The horizontal planes dividing ever thicker bits of the top of the house from ever thinner bits of the bottom yields just one particularly straightforward family of such partitions. Another way to arrive at such parts is to consider the house as the sum of its smallest or simplest parts (if there are such, we shall assume for the moment there are). Let H be the house and AP(H) this collection of smallest (atomic) parts. Then any partition of AP(H) into subcollections (whether disjoint or not) yields parts of H: if C is any such subcollection of AP(H), then SUM(C) is, by GSP, an individual and it is a part of H. Indeed, if H is made up completely of atomic parts, then the collection of *all* parts of H is the collection of all sums SUM(C), for all subcollections C of AP(H). The collection AP(H) itself yields H as its sum. While the matter is more complex if H is not made of mereological atoms, or only partly so, the basic idea that the parts of H are arbitrary and highly numerous (if there are atomless parts of H then H must have non-denumerably many parts) carries over.

The existence of arbitrary sums and the existence of arbitrarily demarcated parts are repugnant to the common or garden way of thinking about parts and wholes. As David Sanford has argued in a recent paper,[6] if we take a simple artifact like a garden sprinkler, then we can easily and finitely list its parts. Further, parthood in this sense is not always transitive, and parts are often taken not to overlap.

<hr />

[6] Sanford 1993, 220.

A further problem with classical extensional mereology is that GSP makes much less sense for an ontology espousing various basic categories of concrete objects than for a monistic ontology. Someone who countenances continuants alongside occurrents will be unhappy at summing them, whereas the upholders of a four-dimensional ontology in which continuants are understood as having temporal parts is in effect collapsing the continuant/occurrent distinction and in this monistic climate arbitrary sums are much less repugnant. The distinction between continuants and occurrents is mereologically defined in any case: continuants are those things which exist for more than a moment but do not have temporal parts, whereas occurrents are those things which either exist for only a moment or exist for longer by virtue of having temporal parts or being spread out in time.[7] Because it makes sense for continuants to talk about the parts they have at a certain time, but not for occurrents, the mereologies of continuants and occurrents have to be treated separately. In this essay, since we are considering artifacts, which are the continuant *products* of certain kinds of action, we can confine our discussion to continuant mereology alone, though there will, in an adequate ontology of artifacts, have to be links between the two kinds of mereology, not least in considering how different (spatial and temporal) parts of production processes produce different parts of the product. But we leave this complication aside here.

Hence if we wish to make headway in establishing what makes some parts (of continuants) common or garden naive parts whereas others are sophisticated mereological parts, we need to arm ourselves with more than one part/whole relation. The most expedient procedure from an explicatory point of view is to start with a broad and maximally theoretically neutral concept of part,[8] and consider what restrictions must be placed on it to obtain various more homely concepts. We shall accordingly stipulate that the term 'part' is to be understood broadly, whereas for narrower concepts we shall use other terms as appropriate, reserving the word 'component' to cover all such terms. This word, which is etymologically inappropriate if we consider natural objects, is almost wholly unobjectionable when we confine attention, as here, to artifacts.

The relation of part to whole shall be tensed: we express this by the convenient 'at *t*' locution. Defining as follows:

PROPER PART: *a* is a proper part of *b* at *t* iff (Df.) *a* is part of *b* at *t* and *b* is not part of *a* at *t*.

---

[7] Simons 1987, 129-132.

[8] By contrast with the ordinary language approach espoused by Sanford 1993, 221.

OVERLAP: *a* overlaps *b* at *t* iff (Df.) some *c* is part of *a* at *t* and part of *b* at *t*.

The principles we take to hold for the broad relation of (proper or improper) part to whole among continuants are then:[9]

REFLEXIVITY: If *a* exists at *t* then *a* is part of itself at *t*
EXISTENCE: If *a* is part of *b* at *t* then *a* and *b* exist at *t*
TRANSITIVITY: If *a* is part of *b* at *t* and *b* is part of *c* at *t* then *a* is part of *c* at *t*
SUPPLEMENTARITY: If *a* is part of *b* at *t* and *b* is not part of *a* at *t* then some *c* is a proper part of *b* at *t* and does not overlap *a* at *t*

This, we suggest, is as far as a formal theory of part and whole for continuants is obliged to go. It does not entail any sum principle, nor does it pronounce on arbitrarily engendered parts, nor does it assume that objects with the same parts are identical, nor does it tell us anything about the parts of a continuant at different times.

What, then, makes a part a component, a part in the common or garden sense? Our answer is that there is no single answer, but a variety of answers. The consequences of this will become apparent below in Section 5. Without even claiming completeness as to what different kinds of component there are, we list some which are important for what follows later.

Firstly, something can be a component because it is manipulated as a unit during the assembly or manufacture of the artifact. There are two kinds of what we shall call *assembly components*. The first are parts which are not themselves assembled but which come to the assembly process ready to be put together with others. We call these *simple assembly components* or *assembly atoms*. The 41 parts of Sanford's garden sprinkler are assembly atoms. Next, there are *assemblies*, which are assembly components made up out of two or more assembly atoms. The carburettor of a car is an assembly, for example: it has a float bowl, float, jet, butterfly valve, springs, washers and so on. The float itself is a *subassembly*, that is, an assembly which is an assembly component of an assembly, here consisting of the float body, pins, hinges etc. The carburettor is itself a subassembly, being an assembly component of the engine. When assemblies are mated, new wholes are created bridging the join between the assembly which are not themselves assembly components. When the carburettor is attached to the engine a new contiguous whole is created

---

[9] Simons 1987, 179.

consisting of the carburettor body and the inlet manifold, but since this is not manipulated as a whole during assembly it is not an assembly component.

Of course even an assembly atom has parts in at least the broader sense, and will be the end-product of its own production process. A humble hexagonal-headed bolt, for example, has a head and a shaft, neither of which may be an assembly component since such bolts may be produced not by assembly but for example by turning a piece of hexagonal rod along most of its length to produce the shaft, then cutting a thread onto this shaft, or by die casting the head and shaft before cutting the thread, or by forging the head from round rod stock. Head and shaft could be assembly atoms if they were welded together: the weld would be the joining material rather than a third component.

This highlights another mereological aspect of manufacture: many artifacts and components thereof are produced not by assembly but by the removal or forming of parts: the processes of turning, milling, drilling, planing, sanding, polishing and etching, to mention a few, all entail the removal of parts from a larger pre-existing object. The chimpanzee's termite-catching twig and the early human chipped flint hand-axe are simple products of such removal. Other processes such as bending, forging, moulding, casting, plating and weaving, are examples of forming and serve to remind us how diverse the procedures are which are used in manufacturing artifacts, and how one should not become too obsessed with the procedures of fastening, bonding, or welding, important though these are.

A second kind of component is one which fulfils a single purpose, office or function in the working of the artifact. We call these *functional components*. Another and sometimes better term for them in the case of complex artifacts is *subsystems*. For example, the braking system on the car is a functional component, the transmission is another. Sometimes functional components are assembly components, for example the carburettor. Other are not, for example the braking system, consisting of brake pedal, brake pipes, servo system, hydraulic fluid reservoir, cylinders, plungers, valves, brake pads and disks etc. is so relatively filigree and so spread around the vehicle that it would be physically impossible to mount it into the car as an assembly component: it comes into being as the car is assembled, and only then can it work.

A difficulty with the concept of a functional component of subsystem is the vagueness and open texture of the concept of a single office or function. Even very minor components may have a function, for instance a screw has the function of holding two objects together. There will also often be parts of artifacts which have no function in the sense of being useful towards the practical end for which the artifact exists, but are simply decorative, like the chrome trimming on 1950s cars. Of course components can be both functional and decorative too. But for the most part the concept of a functional component is sufficiently clear for it to be well understood in concrete cases.

A third kind of component is a *maintenance component*. This is something which is manipulated as a unit during disassembly and reassembly during repair and overhaul of an artifact. Often maintenance components will be assembly components and vice versa: again the carburettor is an example, but they need not be. For example, the resistors on a circuit board in a television receiver are assembly components, because at some point they were soldered into the board's circuitry as units, but no one would repair a single resistor on a defective TV set; more likely the whole preassembled board would be replaced. There was a time when it was possible to replace a headlamp reflector in a car headlight, but now the whole sealed unit is replaced (at much greater expense to motorists, as they find out to their cost, literally). But the reflector was certainly an assembly component.

These are perhaps the kinds of component that would probably occur to most of us. But there are at least two others, somewhat less obvious. One is the *disassembly component*. It may seem fatuous to even mention this, as surely disassembly is simply the reverse of assembly? Not necessarily. Apart from the fact that artifacts are often disposed of by less mereologically discriminating means, such as burning, crushing, cutting apart, shredding and the like, in most cases the way in which an artifact is taken apart is quite different from the way it is put together. One reason is that bonding methods ensure that assembly components cannot be taken apart non-destructively; another is that the functioning of the artifact or simply its longevity may cause changes in its parts which render disassembly as the reverse of assembly impossible, for instance chemical changes like rusting or the accumulation of other encrusted deposits. Also in some cases it would be highly dangerous to attempt disassembly, for instance in the handling of toxic or radioactive materials.

Another kind of component which it is easy to overlook, because it is closely connected with the manufacturing process and so tends to run together with assembly components, are *design components*. These are wholes which are conceived and planned as assembly components but do not in fact fulfill this role, usually for practical reasons. We shall give examples below.

A further concept of part – it is less appropriate to speak of components here – is the rather vague one of a prominent or *salient* part, which applies to any material object, not just an artifact. Some parts literally stick out geometrically from the whole, or are distinguished from the rest by their colour or texture. In most automobiles the engine compartment sticks out at the front of the vehicle; while it has several functions, such a part would stick out and be prominent even if it were there only for show. Salient parts may arise incidentally rather than as assembly or functional components, and their salience consists in their being obviously discernible in perception. There is another conception of salience used in manufacturing, meaning simply the relative *importance* of the part to the functioning and safety of the artifact. The wheels of a car are salient in this respect, the hubcaps on the wheels are not.

It may seem that some of these distinctions are rather trifling. Philosophically they are all obtained by different, empirical restrictions on the broad part concept, according to the role played by the part in question in various processes during the life-cycle of an artifact, from its conception and detailed planning, through manufacture, use, maintenance, to retirement and disposal. The trouble is, however, that designers, manufacturers, users, maintenance people and scrap merchants all use not the philosophical concept of part, delicately modulated to their roles, but common or garden concepts, usually with no clear conception that there is more than one. As we shall see in the next section however, this entails giving up the idea that there is such a thing as *the* mereological analysis of a complex artifact.

5. Complex Artifacts and Multiple Bills of Materials

Vast amounts of technical data are produced and used by people engaged in designing, producing, using, and maintaining complex artifacts, such as computing machines, aircraft, and buildings. For example, the design, manufacturing, and logistical support documentation required for an F-18 is so voluminous that when Northrop rents a railroad car to ship one of these aircraft to McDonnell-Douglas for final assembly, they have to rent *another* railroad car just to ship the documents that go with it.[10]

There are also hundreds of distinct kinds of technical documentation associated with complex artifacts: requirements analysis and allocation documents, engineering drawings, material, process, and test standards and specifications, manufacturing process and inspection plans, end user and maintenance guides, to name but a few. One of these – the Bill of Materials (BOM) – plays a central role throughout the life-cycle of any complex artifact and is, more importantly to us here, a source of several interesting philosophical problems.

A BOM is an abstract representation of the mereological structure of an artifact. Its formal structure is typically an acyclic graph forming a hierarchical

---

[10] One doesn't have to buy a forty million dollar airplane to have a 'railroad car' experience – simply purchase a personal computer and a word processing program.

tree, intended to mirror the mereological structure of the artifact.[11] The root of the BOM represents the whole artifact (individual or type). The next level down represents all the major subcomponents or assemblies, for instance in the case of an airplane the wings, fuselage, tail, and engines. Each of these is further decomposed into a list of its immediate subassemblies, and so on down through the levels until we reach the leaves of the tree, the parts that are not further subdivided. There are some deviations from this; for instance paint, glue, frequently repeated simple parts like rivets and washers are not listed individually but by weight or volume as 'materials'. But these details aside, in principle a BOM is a representation of the artifact's structure of parts, in the common or garden sense of the term 'part', and a BOM is essential for constructing and maintaining any complex artifact. Imagine trying to build the World Trade Center without a floor plan and materials list, or repairing a jet engine without the relevant assembly drawings.[12]

There is a problem involving BOMs, which is known in manufacturing circles as the *multiple* BOM *reconciliation problem*. The difficulty is this: any reasonably complex artifact has not one, but *several* BOMs, each representing a *distinct mereological configuration* of that artifact, and these BOMs differ from each other, both in structure and in the number and kinds of parts that comprise them. Some of these alternative configurations represent the mereological structure of the artifact during different periods in its life-cycle, while others are differentiated by characteristics other than temporal or existential modalities. In any case, all producers of complex products are faced with the need to accommodate continuous changes in the configurations of the artifacts they build, and, because there is no such thing as 'the' mereological configuration of a given artifact, managing change is perhaps the most complex and costly process in a manufacturing enterprise. Identifying and propagating the consequences of even a single modification to *one* feature of *one* component in *one* BOM, to its counterparts in other BOMs for the same artifact – if in fact any such counterparts exist at all – often requires the coordinated expertise of a team of people that span several distinct speciality disciplines, such as materials and process, mechanical, electrical, and software engineering.

The existence of multiple and distinct mereological configurations of the same artifact is not symptomatic of some fundamental empirical or logical flaw

[11] Prior to the advent of electronic computers, BOMs were implemented either as parts lists on engineering drawings, or as assembly drawings with affiliated subassembly drawings and their parts lists, or some combination of both. Most manufacturing enterprises today implement BOMs as hierarchically related records in electronic databases.

[12] For that matter, one doesn't have to be an architect or A&P mechanic to appreciate this point; simply buy a bicycle that 'requires some assembly' for a child the day before Christmas.

in manufacturing theory or practice. Instead, multiple BOMs reflect actual ontological structure exemplified by complex artifacts, especially as they relate to the processes that involve their conception, realization, use, and support. And, there are at least two issues of philosophical import associated with this phenomenon; that is, the multiple BOM reconciliation problem represents a direct interface, or point of contact, between manufacturing and philosophy. We will discuss the philosophical issues after we have described the plural configuration phenomenon in more detail.

Three commonly represented and distinct mereological configurations of a given artifact are its *nominal, constructive,* and *sustainment* configurations. These are called respectively the *engineering, manufacturing,* and *logistical support BOMs* (E-BOM, M-BOM, and L-BOM) in industry. All three kinds of BOM (along with others we will present later) are customarily produced by the manufacturer of a particular complex artifact, and any one of these three is distinct, both in structure and in content, from the other two.

The E-BOM for a given artifact represents the mereological component of its abstract physical architecture. The physical architecture of an artifact is a product of a systems engineering process called *synthesis.* Synthesis translates a functional architecture, developed by performing requirements analysis, decomposition, and allocation, into 'system product and process solutions' – a physical architecture – that will satisfy or realize the functional architecture. The mereological structures represented by E-BOMs reflect this 'top-down' emphasis on implementing functional requirements. Hence the assemblies, subassemblies, parts, and materials constituting an E-BOM appear on it only because they implement one or more requirements defined in the functional architecture. For example, the F-18 E-BOM specifies two parts – left and right wing spars – whose geometric configurations and material constitutions reflect a synthesis of several interacting requirements, such as static and aerodynamic load, weight, and service life.

The M-BOM for a given artifact represents the mereological structure delineated by an implementation plan or manufacturing system scheme for constructing it. The implementation plan for constructing an artifact is a product of a process customarily called *manufacturing engineering.* Unlike detailed design (considered to be part of synthesis), the process of manufacturing engineering is focused on developing designs and specifications for the manufacturing systems and processes required to actually build the artifact. The mereological structure of an artifact represented by its M-BOM reflects this 'bottom-up' orientation, and, as a result, frequently diverges from the mereological structure represented by the E-BOM for that same artifact. For example, as we mentioned above, there are left and right wing spars represented as *atomic parts* ('monodetails') on the F-18 E-BOM. However, these spars are actually constructed by first machining and then welding several parts together; accordingly they are represented as *subassemblies* on the F-18 M-BOM.[13] This *articulation* (breaking one part into two or more components) is one common cause of divergence between E-BOMs and M-BOMs.

Another cause of divergence between E-BOMs and M-BOMs is *factoring,* which is the practice of producing two or more parts (of the same or different kinds) from a single progenitor. While articulation establishes a correspondence between one part and many, factoring delineates a correspondence between many parts and one. There are several kinds or 'modes' of factoring. Some of the most common ones are:

INCLUSION: A very common factoring technique is to design one part type – the generic template – which, in conjunction with one or more differentiating features, is used as a basis for an entire family of specific part types. Instances of a specific part type are then produced by realizing the appropriate differentiating features on instances of the generic part type.[14] Factoring to exploit inclusion will usually result in structural divergences between an E-BOM and an M-BOM for an artifact, since the mereological positions of the specific parts made from the generic template, as represented in the M-BOM, will be distinct from the location of the generic template itself in the E-BOM.

ABSTRACTION: Some parts of complex artifacts inevitably have one or more complex and difficult to produce features, such as 5-axis surfaces, long holes with small diameters and tight perpendicularity tolerances, and helical gear teeth, to name a few. Manufacturing engineers commonly factor these into what are sometimes called *phantom* parts. The idea is to produce the feature once, obtaining that feature on several parts by subsequently splitting or dividing the phantom into two or

[13] There are two major reasons why the wing spars are welded rather than machined from single pieces. First, it is almost impossible to obtain the required size of aluminum bar that is free of internal voids and other imperfections that might cause the parts to fail under high load conditions. Second, a spar could not be assembled as a single piece; there isn't enough maneuvering room to do anything other than weld several parts together once they are 'in rig'.

[14] One example of a generic template is a standard flanged 'elbow', with standard geometric, dimensional, and materials characteristics, excepting the flange hole patterns (e.g, 4, 6, and 8 holes) that differentiate specific types.

more actual parts. The geometric forms of these kinds of factored parts are determined almost entirely by the geometry of the feature to be produced, and their spatial extents are determined by the types and number of actual parts the phantom is to be divided into.[15] This mode of factoring will result in a structural divergence between the E-BOM and the M-BOM for an artifact, since the phantom does not even exist on the E-BOM.

COMPLEMENTARITY: Occasionally there are parts comprising artifacts that have complementary features, such as cylindrical sections or parallel surfaces. Such parts are usually encountered in artifacts with bilateral or rotational symmetry, such as bridges and propulsion systems. Depending on feature complexity and topology, manufacturing engineers will factor the complementary features into a new *synthetic feature* on a phantom part. Producing this synthetic feature, then dividing the phantom into actual parts, enables the individual complement features to be produced in one operation.[16] Factoring for complementarity results in the same structural divergence patterns between E-BOMs and M-BOMs that factoring for feature abstraction produces. That is, parts will exist on the M-BOM (the phantoms) that do not exist on the E-BOM. While this mode of factoring appears at first glance to be the same as factoring for abstraction, it is in fact very different. Factoring by abstraction produces a new part but not a new

---

[15] One illustrative example would be a phantom for several helical gears. Consider that an E-BOM for a transmission specifies six helical gears as components, and that all six gears are identical (same outside diameter, pitch, lead, thread form, etc.) excepting their lengths: *two* being 75mm long and four 60mm long. The obvious thing to do as a manufacturing engineer is to specify a single phantom, 395mm long (plus some overage), on the M-BOM. The six parts would then be produced by first cutting the helical teeth on the phantom gear blank, and then parting the blank into six pieces of *two* distinct lengths). This is a simple example involving a monadic homogeneous phantom. We have also seen collective phantoms (i.e., those involving *multiple* feature abstraction), heterogeneous phantoms (i.e., those dividing into more than one type of part), and collective heterogeneous phantoms, which are unions of both the prior cases.

[16] A simple example would be four pillow blocks for shaft bearings in a transmission. Since each block has a quarter-radius as a surface, the most efficient production technique would factor these surfaces into a single synthetic feature – namely a hole of the proper diameter – of a single phantom part. The quarter radii of the four blocks would then be realized by boring the hole.

feature, while factoring for complementarity produces a new
feature, and frequently a new part as well.

COLLOCATION: Given certain configurations of the relations between the
spatial envelope of a part, its geometry, its material constitution, and the processing techniques used to make it, it is frequently possible to simultaneously make n complete instances of the part, n partial instances, or at least n 'blanks' from
a single piece or amount of raw material. Depending on the
particular four-fold configuration at hand, manufacturing
engineers will (i) design a *collective synthetic* part, or (ii)
specify a particular raw material configuration with a *make
multiple* quantity.[17] In either specific case, factoring by collocation yields both structural and quantitative divergences
between E-BOMs and M-BOMs. The structural divergences are
similar to those caused by factoring for abstraction or
complementarity.

The last member of the three mereological configurations we mentioned in the
beginning of this discussion is the sustainment configuration, represented by
the structure known in industry as the logistical BOM (L-BOM). The mereological structure represented by an L-BOM for a given artifact is determined by a
combination of physical constraints and the procedures required to maintain the
artifact in a state of readiness. Accordingly, the majority of components
comprising an L-BOM are parts, subassemblies, and subsystems that are non-
destructively accessible under disassembly, maintenance, and reassembly
operations, or are essential consumables that must be periodically replenished.
More precisely, many (although not all) components on a L-BOM for a given
artifact constitute a *fusion* of two or more components on the E-BOM (and, in
consequence, on the M-BOM) for that artifact. For example, while the transistors
on a processor chip would be on both the E-BOM and M-BOM for a circuit board
using that chip, they would *not* be on the L-BOM for the board, since obviously
one cannot remove or replace or repair a single transistor in a VLSI chip. In fact,
the chip itself probably would not be on the L-BOM – the whole board would a
single component. Similarly, the control surface on the F-18 speed brake (a

[17] A common example of achieving collocation with a complex collective phantom is a
part produced by injection or compression molding a 'tinker-toy' synthetic part, containing
several complete actual parts connected to each other by small diameter 'wires' or tabs of the
same material. The parts comprising Revell models are prosaic examples of collective
synthetic parts. The most common example of a make multiple material configuration is a
sheet, rod, or tube (of any material) that is cut into two or more blanks.

graphite-epoxy composite panel) is on the E-BOM and M-BOM for the aircraft, but that same panel is not on the L-BOM, as it cannot be removed from the frame surrounding it without destroying it. (It can be repaired, however.)

One might be tempted to think that the structures and relations we have thus far presented are just special cases of those involved in a more fundamental and philosophically familiar distinction: namely, the distinction between the abstract and the concrete. Thus one might believe that all we have demonstrated so far is the relatively unsurprising fact that an ontology of artifacts, like an ontology of any other category, necessarily brings in a discussion of the deeper distinction between the abstract and the concrete, which is already a well-known and central issue in ontology, and certainly not unique to artifacts alone. However, this is simply not the case. The three classes of BOMs we have discussed so far are *all abstract,* in that they each represent the mereological structure of a *class* of artifact (the class 'F-18', for example) rather than any particular concrete instance of that class (for example, 'F-18 #42'). Therefore, whatever the ontological bases of the distinctions between these three types of BOMs are, they are not simply empirical realizations of the ontological distinction between the abstract and concrete, or the universal and the particular.

To reinforce this point, we can demonstrate that the multiple BOM phenomenon also exists at the 'instance level'. That is, there are BOMs, in addition to those already discussed, that represent multiple and distinct mereological configurations of the same *concrete* artifact. The two most common of these are the *actual* and the *effective* configurations, represented by what are called the 'as-built' and the 'as-used' BOMs in industry.

The 'as-built' BOM for a given artifact represents its actual concrete mereological structure. For many kinds of complex artifacts, especially aircraft, spacecraft, nuclear reactors, and many medical products, these BOMs include explicit identifiers for the artifact itself and all its significant elements, such as the serial number of every single component part and the lot or batch number of every piece of material in the artifact. An 'as-built' BOM can be thought of as an 'instance' of an M-BOM; and, as one would expect, there can be, and usually are, significant differences between its anticipated constructive configuration and its actual configuration, even for a single particular artifact.

The 'as-used' BOM for a given artifact represents its operational mereology. Because any complex artifact can usually be configured in a variety of ways, depending on the specific use intended, there are normally several BOMs of this kind for a single artifact. For example, a particular F-18 can be configured to fly interceptor missions, in which case air-to-air missiles will be components on an 'as-used' BOM. However, that same plane can also be used to perform electronic countermeasure and coordination missions, in which case communication and ECM pods will be components on another distinct effective configuration.

While both 'as-built' and 'as-used' BOMs represent concrete, rather than abstract mereological structure, 'as-used' BOMs will almost always contain elements that 'as-built' BOMs do not. For example, the fuel rods for a nuclear reactor are not components on its actual configuration; they only appear on its effective configuration. Similarly, jet fuel, pilots, and some software modules downloaded only for particular kinds of missions are not components on the actual configuration of an F-18; however they are components on its effective configurations. Thus both the 'as-built' and the 'as-used' BOMs for an artifact represent concrete mereological structure; yet both are distinct in structure and in content.

So far we have presented five distinct types of mereological configurations, each represented by distinct types of BOMs. Three of these (the E-BOM, M-BOM, and L-BOM), are all abstract but distinct: two (the 'as-built' and 'as-used' BOMs) are both concrete but also distinct. The differences between the first three as a group and the second two as a group *are* specific cases of the familiar distinction between the universal and the particular. However, it should be clear that the distinctions among the members of these two groups are not explicable in those terms. A single artifact, either abstract or concrete, does, in fact, simultaneously exemplify more than one mereological structure. There really is no such thing as 'the' mereology of an artifact.

The obvious logician's thought, that what is needed to solve the reconciliation problem is some kind of logical product of the various BOMs – a 'master' BOM in which all the others are joined into a single object – ignores the utility of having different concepts of part, and disregards the fact that there really are distinct mereological structures for the same artifact represented by different types of BOMs. Further, such an approach presupposes that these distinct mereological configurations are *specific* cases of some more general mereological structure, and that all of the relations *between elements* in the different kinds of BOMs we have presented here (articulation, factoring, and fusion) are also special cases of this same general structure, which is flat out not true. While it is true that articulation and fusion are specific kinds of the part-whole relation between elements in different BOMs, and that factoring is a specific kind of dependence relation between elements in different BOMs, it is *not* true that any of these are *identical to* or reducible to the generic composition and materiality relations that hold between the elements comprising a single BOM.

Any viable solution to the multiple BOM reconciliation problem must formally explicate – not ignore or eliminate – the plural nature of artifact mereology. A formal explication of this phenomenon will, in turn, rest on a formal ontology of two categories: FEATURE and INVOLVEMENT (the relation between occurrents and continuants).

Earlier we stated that factoring many parts into one is a fundamental cause of differences between the E-BOM and the M-BOM for a given artifact, and that there are at least four distinct kinds or modes of this relation; namely inclusion, abstraction, complementarity, and collocation. Accordingly, the ability to solve the multiple BOM reconciliation problem hinges, in part, on an ability to formally define and explicitly represent these relations between BOMs. While factoring (of any kind) is itself a specific kind of dependence relation,[18] the entities that stand in those relations are features and parts, rather than materials and parts, which are the entities that stand in materiality relations represented in a single BOM. The ability to formally characterize and veridically represent factoring relations between elements across distinct BOMs presupposes an ontology of the features that can stand in those relations, and no such ontology has yet been developed.[19]

The structures and the types of components comprising the five mereological configurations of complex artifacts we have discussed in this paper are determined, almost entirely, by the occurrents that involve them. The nominal configuration of an artifact is determined by its 'functional architecture' (the process or processes it is intended to implement); its constructive configuration is determined by the processes required to produce it; its sustainment configuration is determined by the processes required to maintain it; its actual configuration is determined by the events that realized it; and, its effective configuration is determined by operations involving its use. Some of these configurations are also temporally related, simply because their corresponding occurrents are; some are not or at least are not necessarily related in that way. Further, the five examples we have presented are far from exhaustive. There are many other distinct kinds of BOMs used in the manufacturing industry, besides those mentioned here. Just exactly how many distinct kinds of mereological

---

[18] In all of the specific modes of factoring we discussed earlier, the part resulting from the factoring is a *fundament* of the specific parts made from it (a sortal 'material'). Notice that the basis for factoring any of parts in our examples were *features of* those parts (e.g, the bolt circle pattern, the helical gear form, and the quarter radius), and not the parts themselves. Features are also fundaments – not parts, not properties – of their respective parts, and thereby also stand in a specific kind of dependence relation to them, albeit they, like factors, are sortal entities rather than masses.

[19] An excellent demonstration of just what an ontology of features should encompass, both in content and in methodology, can be found in Casati and Varzi 1994. The work presented in this book is outstanding. It is precisely the kind of philosophical analysis needed to formulate solutions to the problems we have been discussing here.

configurations of artifact are there? How does each kind differ from the others? What are the relations between them? That is, what are the properties and kinds of the relations that can obtain between a particular element in one kind of configuration and its counterparts in any of the others? What is the ontological status of these configurations? Given that these mereological configurations are conditioned by occurrents, formal answers to these and other related questions requires a comprehensive, formal, and non-reductive ontology of occurrents (especially intentional occurrents), as well as an ontology of the involvement relation between occurrents and continuants in general, and between intentional processes and artifacts in specific.

6. Conclusions

We have demonstrated that solving the problems left open in the last two sections requires a plunge deep into general ontology. The issues of time, modality, generation, change, qualities, quantities, composition, essence and accident, dependence, abstract and concrete, generic and specific all need to be addressed to arrive at a satisfactory solution. Clearly, this is not going to happen overnight. In our view the mereology, and more generally, the metaphysics of artifacts and their manufacture, especially when realistic examples are brought into the discussion, encompass a far wider range of philosophical issues than the hackneyed question of artifact identity versus organic or personal identity: we have touched on only a few. There is much more waiting.

References

Casati, R. and Varzi, A.C. 1994: *Holes and Other Superficialities,* M.I.T. Press, Cambridge, MA.
Dipert, R.R. 1993: *Artifacts, Art Works, and Agency,* Temple University Press, Philadelphia, PA. (This book, though we do not agree with all its theses, is an immeasurable improvement over what has existed before, excepting the two works of Ingarden cited above. We were heartened by Dipert's recognition of the importance of intention to artifact production, of tools and instruments, the issue of group agency, and the need for a metaphysics of artifacts in general. While most philosophers will probably read this book for what it says about works of art, we think the really important advances are in its earlier chapters on artifacts in general. Since reading Dipert's book, we have modified our earlier outline for our paper, eliminating a summary of issues pertaining to

artifacts in general in favor of a reference to this book, as Dipert covers this subject in greater detail than we would have been able to here.)

Hilpinen, R. 1993a: "Authors and Artifacts", *Proceedings of the Aristotelian Society,* Volume 93, 155-178.

Hilpinen, R. 1993b: "On Artifacts and Works of Art", *Theoria.*

Ingarden, R. 1973: *The Literary Work of Art: With an Appendix on the Functions of Language in the Theater.* Translated by George G. Grabowicz. Northwestern University Press, Evanston, IL. (Originally published in German as *Das literarische Kunstwerk: Eine Untersuchung aus dem Grenzgebiet der Ontologie, Logik, und Literaristeratur-wissenschaft,* Max Niemeyer Verlag, Halle an der Saale, 1931.)

Ingarden, R. 1989: *Ontology of the Work of Art,* Translated by Raymond Meyer with John T. Goldthwait. Ohio University Press, Athens, OH. (Originally published in German as *Untersuchungen zur Ontologie der Kunst,* Max Niemeyer Verlag, Tubingen, 1933.)

Sanford, D.H. 1993: "The Problem of the Many, Many Composition Questions, and Naive Mereology", *Nous,* Volume 27, 219-228.

Simons, P.M. 1987: *Parts,* Clarendon Press, Oxford.

INGVAR JOHANSSON

PHYSICAL ADDITION

Modern physics is unthinkable without mathematics. Its conceptual apparatus is permeated by numbers. In ancient and medieval times it was a problem whether mathematics could be useful in fundamental physics. Today we face the opposite problem. Are there any interesting non-mathematical concepts in physics?

In the center of mathematics we find the natural numbers and the operation of adding these numbers. Usually, when philosophers of science have been discussing addition in physics, they have looked upon pure mathematical addition as something well-known and then explained physical addition as an *application* of mathematical addition. Thus, the direction has been from operations between numbers to operations between things. Physical addition has, in such approaches, no identity of its own. The distinction between additive and nonadditive quantities gets its whole identity from mathematics. I shall try to show that this traditional view is false. There are properties which are naturally called additive (and subtractive) independently of whether these properties are quantifiable or not. When the properties in question lend themselves to quantification we get what is sometimes called extensive, sometimes additive quantities (or magnitudes).

1. 'Top-Down' and 'Bottom-Up'

Once upon a time in analytic philosophy, nominalist and operationist accounts of quantities reigned supreme. According to nominalism, even ordinary properties are structures which we impose, by means of our language, on particulars. Nominalism with regard to quantities, then, becomes a mere corollary.

R. Poli and P. Simons, Formal Ontology, 277–288.

However, it is possible to be a realist with regard to properties but a nominalist with regard to quantities. A realist view of quantities says that quantities are ordinary properties that admit of degrees and that quantities, therefore, can inhere in particulars; nominalism about quantities says that even if properties can inhere in particulars, quantities have to be conceptual constructs.

In a similar way it is possible to distinguish between an all-embracing operationism and operationism with regard to quantities. General operationism claims that *all* properties are logically secondary to operations; 'quantity operationism' claims only that, even if some properties can precede measuring operations, quantities cannot. There is a close relationship between nominalism and operationism in general as well as between quantity nominalism and quantity operationism.

Let us now, as an introduction to the distinction between additive and nonadditive quantities, take a quick look at Carl Hempel's analytic philosophical classic *Fundamentals of Concept Formation in Empirical Science*. According to Hempel, quantities are functions. A function which assigns to every element, x, in a domain exactly one real number, $s(x)$, constitutes a quantity.[1] Quantities, though, as Hempel makes clear, can be of different kinds:

The distinction of additive and nonadditive quantities refers to the existence or nonexistence, for a given quantitative concept, of an *operational interpretation for the numerical addition* of the s-values of two different objects. In this sense, length is called an additive quantity *because* the sum of two numerical length-values can be *represented* as the length of the interval obtained by joining two intervals of the given lengths end to end in a straight line; temperature is said to be nonadditive because there is no operation on two bodies of given temperatures which will produce an object whose temperature equals the sum of the latter. To state this idea more precisely, we first define a relative concept of additivity:

(14.1) A quantity s is additive relatively to a combining operation o if $s(x \text{ o } y) = s(x) + s(y)$ whenever x, y, and xoy belong to the domain within which s is defined.[2]

It is not quite clear whether Hempel has a realist view of the property of length or not, but even if he has (though I think he leans heavily towards a general nominalism), there is for him, obviously, nothing in the property length itself which makes it additive. It is by accident, so to speak, that addition can be represented by an operation of concatenation.

Another classic in the field was Brian Ellis' *Basic Concepts of Measurement*.[3] Ellis criticized not only operationism about quantities but also a realist

---

[1] Hempel 1952, 63.

[2] Hempel 1952, 75, emphases added.

[3] Ellis 1966.

account of quantities. He regarded quantities as objective linear orders not dependent upon quantitative universals. He himself, however, has subsequently
changed his mind. Now he thinks that quantities can have magnitudes independently of our measuring operations.[4] There are though, still, philosophers
(John Forge[5] in particular) who explicitly defend positions closely related to
those of (early) Ellis.

The similarity between Hempel, (early) Ellis, and Forge is, firstly, that they
defend a nominalism about quantities, and, secondly, that their position with
regard to non-quantitative properties is ontologically unclear.

Mario Bunge has always explicitly been a realist with regard to properties,
but, like Hempel, he regards quantities or magnitudes as functions. Bunge says
that "Functions are the structure of quantitative concepts or *magnitudes*, also
called quantities"[6] and that:

In general, any magnitude M involving an object variable and a numerical variable – such as
length and population density – can be analyzed as a function M from a physical set P × S to a
numerical set $R_0 \subseteq R$.[7] (P is a set of physical objects and S a set of scales.)

Certainly, Bunge distinguishes between mathematical addition and physical
addition as an operation of concatenation, but, nonetheless, his distinction
between additive and nonadditive magnitudes is founded not in the properties
themselves but in a contingent similarity between concatenation and mathematical addition. He says that:

If two or more objects are considered for measurement, more than one object variable may
enter the magnitude. For example, if two rods, x and y, are juxtaposed end to end, a third object
z is produced which may be said to be the *physical sum* (or joining) of x and y. We have
denoted physical addition by '+' to distinguish it from the corresponding arithmetical operation: the former regards bodies, the latter numbers. If we now ask what the length $L(x + y)$ of
the composite rod z Æ x + y is, the answer will be: the numerical value of the total length
equals the sum of the partial lengths, i.e. $L(x + y) = L(x) + L(y)$ regardless of the length scale
and unit.

The foregoing is a synthetic (nonlogical) formula: universes are conceivable in which
lengths do not add in this simple way – i.e. in which length is not an additive measure.[8]

I think Bunge in his nominalist view of quantitaties moves too fast between
properties realistically conceived, numbers, and quantities or magnitudes.

[4] See Ellis 1987, 319-25.
[5] In particular, see Forge 1987a.
[6] Bunge 1967, vol. I, 61.
[7] Bunge 1967, vol. I, 70.
[8] Bunge 1967, vol. II, 199.

Something more has to be said about relations like 'being larger than', 'being more massive', 'being more dense', etc. Some Australian philosophers, however, have (from my point of view) tried to remedy this defect and made relations important in the analysis of quantities. David M. Armstrong, in a comment on these attempts, distinguishes between two realist approaches, a *top-down* strategy and a *bottom-up* strategy.[9] The top-down strategy is put forward in a paper by John Bigelow and Robert Pargetter.[10] They claim that quantities are in essence relations (conceived as realist universals). Chris Swoyer[11], and Armstrong himself, on the other hand, claims that quantities are properties. In the top-down approach relations are logically prior to quantitative properties; in the bottom-up approach properties are logically prior to relations.

Armstrong's metaphors 'top-down' and 'bottom-up' are telling. It seems natural to regard relations as in some way hovering above properties. The same is true for concepts and functions, which means that not only Bigelow and Pargetter's analysis, but also Hempel's, Ellis', Forge's, and Bunge's analyses of quantities may be called top-down procedures. All these attempts have something in common which makes them differ from bottom-up procedures. I think Armstrong has hit upon the really interesting divide in the philosophy of quantities.

I am myself confident that the bottom-up procedure is the ontologically correct one, and I shall now try to show that not only quantities, but also the distinction between additive and nonadditive quantities, can be explained in a bottom-up fashion. Not only some properties and quantities, but also the distinction between additive and nonadditive quantities does in some cases precede actual measurement. Some properties are in virtue of their 'nature' additive and some are not. Neither Armstrong nor Bigelow and Pargetter have really focussed attention on this issue.

2. Properties and Their Relation to Space

My fundamental thesis is that different properties can be *differently related to space* and that their relation to space explains why some of them are naturally additive and others nonadditive. Kant pointed out that the difference between a right hand and a left hand cannot be explained by any intrinsic differ-

---

[9] Armstrong 1988.
[10] Bigelow and Pargetter 1988.
[11] Swoyer 1987.

ence between the hands, but only by their different relationships to space. It is logically possible that there exists a right hand and a left hand which are exactly identical in all their ordinary properties. Nonetheless they are different, and that is because of their relation to space. The point I am going to make about additive and nonadditive properties has affinities with Kant's remark.

Graham Nerlich has generalized Kant's insight, and Nerlich regards the properties of being a left hand and a right hand as particular cases of the general concept of *enantiomorphic properties*.[12] In order to give a definition of this concept we need the concepts of 'rigid motion' and 'reflective mapping'. A rigid motion is a movement in which the moving thing neither bends nor stretches; a reflective mapping is a function which takes one from the space of a thing to a space where a mirror image of the thing exists. In a three-dimensional space this may mean simply that, in the function describing the thing, the sign of the x-values are changed, i.e. the y-z plane acts as a mirror. Having introduced these concepts Nerlich says:

Now we can express the idea of enantiomorphism in a new way which has nothing to do with possible worlds or with the relation of one hand to another (actual or possible) hand or body. It does, however, *quantify over all mappings* of certain sorts. We can assert the following: Each reflective mapping of a hand differs in its outcome from every rigid motion of it.[13]

The concept of enantiomorphism requires that space is a real unity independently of the contained objects. In such a three-dimensional space there is no rigid motion which can move a hand into a reflective mapping of it. In a two-dimensional space there is no rigid motion which can move an L into an J, although there is such a motion in a three-dimensional space. Being an 'L' is an enantiomorphic property in a two-dimensional space but a homomorphic property in a three-dimensional space. Whether a property is enantiomorphic or not depends on the space containing it. If space were four-dimensional, being a left hand would *not* be an enantiomorphic property.

3. Pre-Mathematical Addition

Instead of 'rigid motions' and 'reflective mappings' of things we shall look at 'shortenings' of 'causally rigid' things. In thought we shall investigate what necessarily happens and what necessarily cannot happen with different proper-

[12] See Nerlich 1976, chapter 2.
[13] Nerlich 1976, 35.

ties when a thing in which they inhere is shortened. We shall be doing
Gedankenexperimente.[14]

Let us assume that we have a body (let's say a rod) with a specific colour
hue, a specific volume, a specific mass, a specific shape and a specific density
placed along a straight line. Furthermore, assume that no properties of the body
will change due to causal processes triggered by a shortening of the body. The
body is, we shall say, 'causally rigid'.

If, now, we make a cut orthogonal to the line along which our causally rigid
rod is placed, and take away a bit from the rod, then, what happens with the
inhering properties? Let us first compare volume and phenomenological colour
hue. In our thought experiments we shall regard colours not as electromagnetic
radiation but, with common sense, as properties inhering in things, i.e. we shall
regard colours as primary qualities like volumes and shapes. The shortened rod
will, given our presuppositions, instantiate the same specific colour hue as the
original rod, but it will necessarily instantiate another and smaller volume. If
we repeat this operation of shortening, then the remaining rod still instantiates
the same colour hue but an even smaller volume. Obviously, such an operation
can be repeated an arbitrary number of times.

This simple thought experiment shows that determinate[15] colour hues
(regarded as primary qualities) and determinate volumes are differently related
to space. A colour-determinate can be instantiated in a thing without other colour-determinates being instantiated in the possible spatial parts of the thing, but
a volume-determinate cannot possibly be instantiated if other volume-determinates are not instantiated in the possible spatial parts of the thing. There is
a part-whole relation between volume-determinates which is lacking in the case
of colour-determinates. A volume-determinate *spatially includes* other volume-
determinates (those which are of less volume) as parts, while a colour
determinate *spatially excludes* other colour-determinates.

It may be argued that the difference just pointed out is, for two reasons, of
no ontological importance. First, volume is a special property with a very close
relation to spatial extension; second, colour hue is in fact not a primary but a
secondary quality. However, there are other properties which embody the distinction I am trying to unfold. Let us now see how the masses and densities of
causally rigid rods behave when the rods are shortened.

---

[14] This part of the paper repeats views earlier put forward in chapter 4 of my Johannson
1989.

[15] 'Determinate' is here and in what follows used in the sense it has in the philosophical
distinction between determinates and determinables. A specific colur hue is a determinate of
the determinable colour hue.

Assume that we have two compact and homogeneous rods with different masses. Compactness means that the rods contain no void, and homogeneity means that all parts of the rods of the same volume are equal in all respects. If we imagine successively smaller parts of these two rods (the corresponding parts however being equally large), then the mass necessarily diminishes successively in both cases. But for arbitrarily small parts there nevertheless remains the difference that the mass of the one rod is greater than that of the other. This difference is due to the fact that the rods have different densities.

There are two kinds of densities of a thing, real density and nominal density. On the one hand there is the real density of each compact and homogeneous part, on the other there is the mean value density. In homogeneous things the two densities are numerically identical; in heterogeneous things the mean value density always differs from the real density of at least some part. Mean value density has to be conceived nominalistically; it is merely a conceptual construct. This construct, however, gets its content from really existing densities, because if mass is a real property then the densities of homogeneous parts have to be real properties, too. If the densities were not real properties, the real difference between two rods of equal volume but different masses would be inexplicable. A real difference cannot be explained by a conceptual construct.[16] As a tone has to have both pitch and volume, a material body has to have both mass and density. This seems to be a kind of synthetic *a priori* truth.[17]

Let us now take a second look at the shortenings of the rods in our thought experiment. Whereas the masses of the rods necessarily are diminished when the rods are shortened, the density of the homogeneous rods necessarily remains the same. In this thought experiment mass behaves like volume in our first experiment and density behaves like colour hue. Mass and density are differently related to space. A mass-determinate *spatially includes* other mass-determinates (those which are of less mass) as parts, while a density-determinate is only itself and *spatially excludes* other density-determinates.

Both mass and density can be linearly ordered in a relation of greater-less and quantified. But while an instance of a greater mass necessarily has potential spatial parts which have less mass, an instance of a larger density has no spatial parts at all with less density. Each density is, like each (phenomenological) colour hue, an indivisible unit which excludes other similar units, i.e. other densities. It should to be noted, though, that densities and colour hues

[16] Armstrong, though, claims that density is a reducible property; see Armstrong 1988, in particular 313-15.

[17] For a defence of *a priori* knowledge, see my 1989, chapter 16.2, 'A new way of looking at the synthetic *a priori*'.

have to be distinguished from density *patterns* and colour *patterns*. If one removes a part of a pattern one usually gets a different pattern, which means that the patterns behave more like volume and mass. Different parts of a thing may of course have different densities, but each such density behaves in the way explained.

The properties of volume and mass are such that, in and of themselves, when instantiated in space, they *include* other volume-determinates and mass-determinates, respectively. Therefore, I shall call them *spatially inclusive properties*. A specific (phenomenological) colour hue, on the other hand, *excludes* other colur hues in the space where it is instantiated. Colour hue is, I shall say, a *spatially exclusive property*.[18]

The converse operation of shortening is lengthening or *physical addition*, which means that the distinction between inclusive and exclusive properties is of relevance for such addition. Inclusive properties are physically additive whereas exclusive properties are necessarily physically nonadditive. When two things are joined to each other, then the inclusive properties of the original thing necessarily become included in a new instance of the same determinables, whereas an exclusive property cannot possibly be included in a new instance of the determinable to which it belongs. If two things are joined to each other then necessarily both a new volume-determinate and a new mass-determinate become instantiated; the new determinate volume and mass are the sums of the old volumes and masses, respectively. However, no new instance of any real density comes into being. Densities cannot because of their 'nature' be physically added.

Both Hempel and Bunge talk of the joining or adding of things on the one hand and mathematical addition on the other. According to my account there is something in between these two operations: there is also physical addition *of properties*. When things are joined, some properties (the inclusive ones) by their 'nature' combine together additively whereas other properties (the exclusive ones) because of their 'nature' cannot do so. This is a fact which is lost from view in the top-down approaches, and this is the fact which makes a realist distinction between additive and nonadditive quantities possible.

When an inclusive property is quantified we necessarily get an additive or extensive quantity, and when an exclusive property is quantified we necessarily

---

[18] My concept of inclusive property is very similar to Armstrong's concept of *non-relationally structural property*; see Armstrong 1978, 68-71. I noted already in my 1989 (see note 14) that probably the concepts have the same *extension*. There are however differences which are mentioned in the book, the most important being that Armstrong does not have a realist view of determinables and does not give space the central function I give it.

get a nonadditive quantity. Inclusive and exclusive properties differ in their relation to space independently of whether they are quantified or not. Some exclusive properties (e.g. density) are quantifiable whereas other exclusive properties (e.g. phenomenological colour hue) are not. Also, many inclusive properties (e.g. volume and mass) are quantifiable; but not all are such. Shape is an inclusive property which is not quantifiable. Let us see why.

Imagine a causally rigid thing with a certain shape, and imagine a straight partition line through it. If we imagine orthogonal cuts and shortenings of the thing, we see that the remaining thing instantiates constantly new shapes (i.e. shape-determinates). Conversely, if we join two things to each other then the original shape-determinates are added and a new shape becomes instantiated. Shapes behave in relation to space just like volumes and masses; shape is an inclusive property. It differs, however, from volume and mass in the following way. The partition line in our thought experiments of shortening (and lengthening) can be drawn in a variety of ways. In the case of quantifiable properties like volume and mass, *every* determinate which can be found along one partition line can also be found somewhere along every other partition line, but this is not the case with shapes. As can easily be seen by drawing some figures, shortenings along one partition line can yield shapes which cannot possibly be found along a certain other partition line. This fact explains why shape is spatially inclusive and additive but is nonetheless not quantifiable and does not give rise to an additive *quantity*.

The approach to physical additivity taken here, with shortenings and lengthenings along a conventionally determined partition line, allows shape to be considered an additive property. If such a line is given, one shape can be conjoined to another, and these two can be added in a well-defined way. They form *one* new shape, not a shape pattern, as would have been obtained if shape were an exclusive and nonadditive property. Thus there is physical addition even for non-quantifiable properties, but only for inclusive properties.

The important point which emerges from the discussion above is that there is a kind of addition (property addition) which is independent of the existence of numbers and mathematical addition. This kind of physical addition amounts to more than merely forming an aggregate out of different things. Therefore, I want to call it pre-mathematical addition. Of course, one can speak of the converse operation as pre-mathematical subtraction.

4. Pre-Mathematical Vectorial Addition

The pre-mathematical addition discussed above relates to *scalar* addition. Now I want to show that there is also a kind of pre-mathematical *vectorial* addition. Thus even some vectors can be construed bottom up.

Vectors differ from scalars in that they have a direction. The concept of space used when pre-mathematical scalar addition was defined was that of an isotropic space, i.e. a space without intrinsic directions. Time, however, is directed, which affords me the clue to the next thesis:

Pre-mathematical vectorial addition is addition in time of temporally inclusive properties, whereas pre-mathematical scalar addition is addition in space of spatially inclusive properties.

The kind of thought operation by means of which I introduced the distinction between spatially inclusive and exclusive properties can equally well be applied in time. Instead of spatial shortening we then have temporal shortening. In thought we take away parts of a thing's 'lifetime'. It is, in analogy with spatially inclusive and exclusive properties, possible to distinguish between *temporally* inclusive and exclusive properties.

All the properties so far discussed (volume, color hue, mass, density, and shape) are temporally exclusive properties. Assume that we have a thing which does not change any of these properties during a five minute interval. If we take away the last minute, or any part of the interval you like, this does not affect the thing's properties. These properties do not add in time, and that is because of their 'nature'; they are *exclusive* in time. Therefore, also, their physical dimension need not and does not contain any reference to time. This, by the way, seems to be true for most of the properties referred to by modern physics.

What is true for a temporally exclusive property is, however, not true for a *change* of the same property. Changes of temporally exclusive properties constitutes *patterns in time*. Ordinary patterns, i.e. spatial patterns, are inclusive in space and temporal patterns are inclusive in time. If you think away part of the change, what remains is *another* change which was part of the larger change.[19]

Movement, or change of place, is a temporally inclusive property. If one thinks away one part of a movement then, necessarily, another and shorter movement remains. A spatially inclusive property is necessarily extended in space, but movement is necessarily extended in time. There can be no movement (speed or velocity are other properties, see below) or change of place in a point of time. This is true even mathematically. When you integrate a velocity

[19] Cf. Johannson 1989, chapter 6.1.

function in order to get a particular movement between t_1 and t_2, you get the result zero if t_2 equals t_1.

The similarity between spatial and temporal inclusiveness goes even further. Movements can, pre-mathematically, be added in time just like spatially inclusive properties can be added in space. Two movements which are joined in time constitute a new movement which is the sum of the two included movements. Also, speed is to movement (in time) as density is to mass (in space).

Just as a two things may be of equal volume but differ in mass, so two movements can be of equal length but differ in time. In the former case the difference shows the existence of density or intensity of mass; in the latter case the difference shows the existence of speed or intensity of movement. If we look at a homogeneous (i.e. uniform) motion, we realize immediately that speed is temporally exclusive. We can shorten the movement we are considering as many times as we want without, thereby, affecting the speed of the movement. This means that, in contradistinction to movements, speeds cannot possibly be added in time.

Just as mass and density are differently related to space so movement and speed are *differently related to time*.

A rod and a movement may be equally long, but the length of the rod lacks direction whereas the length of the movement has direction. A movement is *from* a place *to* a place. True, an ordinary *measurement* of the length of a rod has a direction, but that is not because the rod has a direction but because the measurement is extended in time. First you look at one end of the metre rod and then you look at the other. The one who makes the measurement goes ("moves") *from* one end *to* the other end. The direction is not in the rod itself as there is direction in the movements themselves.

Movements can be added in time independently of their mathematical representation, and when they are so added they are added with their direction. Time-extended motion is inclusive in time and quantifiable. Therefore, it can be added vectorially both physically and mathematically.

5. Concluding Remarks

I have argued that some quantities are such that their additivity has to be understood realistically or 'bottom up'. That is, some predicates refer to properties which exist *in re* and which, by their 'nature', are such that they are additive. In these cases, we can add only because the properties are possible to add – either spatially or temporally. I have put 'nature' within scare quotes because this nature is not something internal to the properties; it is a relationship between the properties in question and space (or time). Even simple properties can be differently related to space and time.

Now, of course, the fact that some quantities and their additivity has to be understood realistically does not mean that no quantities should be understood nominalistically. With regard to modern physics, with its heavy reliance on spatially and temporally punctual quantities, a really interesting question is whether any of the postulated point-magnitudes should be given a realist interpretation. What about, for instance, density in a zero-dimensional point and velocity in a momentary point of time? Can there be density without mass and velocity without movement? These questions, however, will not be dealt with here. I want to end by putting them forward because I think that, with respect to point-magnitudes, too, many philosophers too easily take a nominalist stand as self-evident.[20]

References

Armstrong, D. 1978: *A Theory of Universals. Universals & Scientific Realism vol. II*, Cambridge University Press, Cambridge.

Armstrong, D. 1988: "Are quantities relations? A reply to Bigelow and Pargetter", *Philosophical Studies* 54, 305-16.

Bigelow, J. and Pargetter, R. 1988: "Quantities", *Philosophical Studies* 54, 287-304.

Bigelow, J. and Pargetter, R. 1989: "Vectors and Change", *The British Journal for the Philosophy of Science* 40, 289-306.

Bunge, M. 1967: *Scientific Research*, Springer-Verlag, Berlin, Heidelberg & New York.

Ellis, B. 1966: *Basic Concepts of Measurement*, Cambridge University Press, London.

Ellis, B. 1987: "Comments on Forge and Swoyer", in Forge 1987.

Forge, J. (ed.) 1987: *Measurement, Realism and Objectivity*, Reidel, Dordrecht.

Forge, J. 1987a: "On Ellis' Theory of Quantities", in Forge 1987.

Hempel, C.G. 1952: *Fundamentals of Concept Formation in Empirical Science*, University of Chicago Press, Chicago & London.

Johannson, I. 1989: *Ontological Investigations*, Routledge, London.

Nerlich, G. 1976: *The Shape of Space*, Cambridge University Press, London.

Swoyer 1987, "The Metaphysics of Measurement", in Forge 1987, 235-90.

---

[20] For attempts at realist interpretations see my 1989, chapters 6.2, 6.3, and 7.2 and Bigelow and Pargetter 1989.

INDEX OF NAMES

— A —

Abelard, P. 10, 23, 42, 43, 51
Abraham, R. 237, 245, 251
Ajdukiewicz, K. 176, 186
Albertazzi, L. 1, 6, 11, 21-23, 200, 201,
    206, 207, 218-222, 227
Albertus Magnus 13
Ameseder, R. 219, 227
Anderson, J. 168
Anscombe, G.E.M. 169, 171
Anselm 157
Aquinas, T. 1-3, 6, 13
Aristotle 3, 7, 10, 17, 21, 24, 26, 28, 39,
    43, 45, 74, 75, 80, 157, 234
Armstrong, D.M. 23, 24, 161, 162, 167,
    170, 171, 280, 283, 284, 288
Arnold, V.I. 237, 245, 251
Ashkenazy, 257
Austin, J.L. 135, 158

— B —

Bacon, J. 171
Bain, A. 212, 227
Bar-Hillel, Y. 107, 129
Barwise, J. 149, 158
Baumgartner, W. 228
Belnap, N. 194
Bencivenga, E. 193, 198
Benussi, V. 220, 221, 227
Bergmann, G. 160, 163

Bernet, R. 230
Bessel, F.W. 222
Biemel, M. 230
Biemel, W. 230
Bigelow, J. 163, 171, 280, 288
Black, M. 60
Bloom, S.L. 178, 186
Bodnár, 62, 77, 128
Boehm, R. 230
Boi, L. 251, 252
Bolzano, B. 71, 129
Bonaventura, E. 220, 227, 228
Bormann, K. 62, 129
Bozzi, P. 216, 222, 223, 228, 234, 251
Branch, G. 131
Brandl, J. 24, 25, 228
Brentano, F. 17, 22, 23, 24, 39-41, 60,
    209, 218, 219, 221-223, 225, 228
Brown, J.S. 222, 234, 252
Brutus 260
Brückner, A. 78, 129
Bühler, K. 213, 228
Bunge, M. 279, 280, 284, 288
Burkhardt, H. 24, 129, 222, 228, 229
Burnet, J. 62, 129
Byckling, E. 233

— C —

Caesar 260
Cairns, H. 130
Calabresi, R. 220, 221, 228
Campbell, K. 171

290

Capitan, W.H. 171
Carnap, R. 34, 235
Casati, R. 234, 252, 274, 275
Chisholm, R.M. 24, 25, 200, 228, 229
Claesges, U. 213, 214, 216, 229, 230
Clifford, W.K. 238
Cocchiarella, N. 1, 12, 17, 18, 24, 29-31, 33, 38-41, 46, 47, 50, 52, 53, 57, 59, 60, 199, 229,
Coniglione, F. 229, 232
Crane, T. 242, 251
Czezowski, T. 9, 24

— D —

Dal Pra, M. 23
Dalen, D. 129
Dappiano, L. 10, 26
Davidson, D. 135-137, 140-142, 148, 158
Dean, C.G. 232, 252, 253
Denise, T. 131
Dias, M.F., 128
Diels, H. 62, 80, 129
Diemer, A. 216, 229
Dipert, R.R. 256, 275, 276
Domb, C. 247, 251
Doorn, A.J. 250, 252
Doyle, C. 57
Dretske, F. 170

— E —

Eccles, J.C. 54, 55, 60
Eckhart, Meister 93
Edghill, E.M. 24
Einstein, A. 238
Eley, L. 229
Elie, H. 2, 3, 24
Ellis, B. 278, 279, 288
Englebretsen, G. 131
Epstein, R.L. 12, 24
Escher, M.C. 220
Euclid 20
Evans, G. 149, 150

— F —

Fausti, G. 2, 24
Faye, 222

Findlay, J.N. 3, 24
Fine, K. 6, 24, 166, 171, 175, 243, 251
Fleischer, M. 230
Fodor, J.A. 223, 229, 250, 251
Føllesdal, D. 24, 26
Forbes, G. 23, 24
Forge, J. 279, 288
Forguson, L. 234, 252
Forrest, P. 163, 167, 171
Fraassen, B. van 194, 198
Fraenkel, A.A 107, 129
Fraisse, P. 219, 220, 229
Freddoso, A.J. 143, 158
Frege, G. 12, 19, 20, 32-36, 55, 56, 60, 131-135, 142, 147-149, 151, 158, 175, 176

— G —

Gabbay, D. 24, 60,
Galileo, G. 234, 248
Geach, P.T. 60, 158
Gibson, J.J. 216, 223, 225, 229, 234, 250-252
Goldthwait, J.T. 276
Gombocz, L. 24, 25
Goodman, N. 30, 60, 224, 229
Gori-Savellini, S. 228, 229
Gorzka, C. 128
Grabowitz, G.G. 276
Green, M.S. 247, 251
Gregor, M.J. 129
Gregory of Rimini 1-3, 9
Grossmann, R. 23, 24, 168, 171
Guenthner, F. 24, 60
Gurwitch, A. 214, 225, 229
Gusein-Zade, S.M. 251

— H —

Haller, R. 1, 24, 25, 229, 232
Hamilton, E. 130
Hartmann, N. 200, 229
Harvey, C.W 22, 24
Hayes, P.J. 222, 229, 234, 252
Heatcote, A. 169, 171
Hedwig, K. 200, 229
Heidegger, M. 62, 71, 80, 129
Hempel, C. 278, 279, 284, 288

Henry, D.P. 10, 24, 25
Hermes, H. 60
Hilpinen, R. 256, 276
Hintikka, J. 22, 24
Hobbs, J.R. 229, 252
Hochberg, H. 23, 25, 164, 171
Holenstein, E. 229
Humboldt, W. 211
Hume, D. 167
Husserl, E. 4, 5, 13, 22, 25, 199-219, 221-
227, 229, 230, 235, 243, 244, 252, 259

— I —

Ingarden, R. 5, 25, 227, 230, 256, 276

— J —

Jackson, F. 233, 252
Jacquette, D. 230
Janssen, P. 230
Johansson, I. 200, 230, 286, 288
Johnson, W.E. 162

— K —

Kahn, C. 81, 129
Kambartel, F. 60
Kanisza, 220, 224, 230
Kant, I. 14, 74, 126, 129, 131-133, 137,
138, 141, 213, 238, 280, 281
Kaplan, D. 11, 25, 149, 150-153, 155,
156, 158
Kastil, A. 228
Körner, S. 228
Kaulbach, F. 60
Kelley, D. 131
Kerry, B. 5, 25
Kirk, G.S. 62, 80, 129
Kisielewicz, A. 70, 129
Kitcher, P. 222, 230
Kleer, J.D. 234, 252
Koenderink, J.J. 250, 252
Körner, S. 228
Koffka, K. 216, 230
Kotarbiński, T. 5, 17,
Kraus, O. 60, 200, 228, 230
Kretzmann, N. 157, 158
Kripke, S. 156, 158, 175

— L —

Laerzio, D. 2, 25
Lambert, K. 12, 25, 198
Landgrebe, L. 230
Lascaux, 257
Leibniz, G.W. 93, 111, 126, 129, 238, 239
Lenat, D. 256
Leonard, H. 189-194, 198
Leśniewski, S. 5, 68, 129
Levi, A. 107, 129
Lewis, C.I. 135-137, 140
Lewis, D.K. 57, 157, 161-162, 164, 169,
171
Libardi, M. 1, 10, 26, 202, 230
Lichtenstein, M. 222, 230
Locke, J. 164
Loemker, L.E. 129
Lorenz, K. 154
Łoś, J. 176, 186
Łukasiewicz, J. 100, 129, 175, 177
Lüthe, R. 128

— M —

Mach, E. 235
Mally, E. 12, 25, 26, 226, 230
Mannheim, K. 62, 80
Marbach, E. 230
Margalit, A. 158
Marr, D. 222, 223, 225, 230, 243, 250-
252
Marsden, J.E. 237, 245, 251
Marsh, R.C. 158
Martin, C.B. 160
Marty, A. 219
Mates, B. 149, 158
Matisse, P. 257
Mayer-Hillebrand, F. 228
McKee, G.T. 232, 252, 253
Meinong, A. 1, 3-6, 12, 25, 41, 58, 59,
219, 220, 230, 231, 244, 252
Meixner, U. 23, 25
Meyer, R.K. 194, 198
Melandri, E. 2, 25, 231
Melle, U. 230
Mendelson, E. 69, 70, 107, 129
Merrill, D.D. 171
Mezei, B. 128

Michaels, A. 186
Mill, J.S. 168
Mohanty, J.N. 24, 26
Moore, R.C. 229, 252
Morton, A. 248, 252
Mulligan, K. 24-26, 199, 231, 232
Munitz, M.K. 129
Musatti, C. 227, 231

— N —

Nagel, E. 148
Nakhnikian, G. 24, 25, 229, 231
Nassau, K. 233, 252
Nerlich, G. 281, 288
Nureyev, 257

— O —

Ockham, W. 143, 158
Olvera-Mijares, R. 128
Omyła, M. 20, 22, 180, 185-187
Owens, J. 75, 129

— P —

Panzer, U. 229
Pargetter, R. 163, 171, 280, 288
Parikh, R. 25, 26
Parmenides 62, 63, 67, 74, 75, 77, 80, 81
Parsons, T. 12, 25,
Paśniczek, J. 23, 25, 129, 130
Patin 77
Pavarotti, L. 260
Peirce, C.A. 19
Pelletier, F.J. 99, 101-103, 129
Perry, J. 149, 150, 158
Perzanowski, J. 1, 19, 20, 25, 67, 129,
    130, 200, 231
Petitot, J. 222-225, 231, 232, 237, 238,
    242-245, 247-250, 252
Piana, G. 200, 213, 219, 231
Pietruszczak, R. 128
Plato 62, 63, 67, 74, 80, 81, 101, 130,
    162,
Plotinus 80
Poggio, T. 250, 252
Poincaré, H. 239

Poli, R. 5, 6, 10, 12, 14, 17, 21, 23, 25,
    26, 75, 128, 130, 199-201, 206, 207,
    226, 227, 229, 231, 232
Popper, K.R. 54, 55, 60
Porębski, C. 128
Post, E. 175
Prior, A. 193, 196
Putnam, H. 168, 171, 252
Pylyshyn, Z.W. 223, 229, 250, 251

— Q —

Quigg, C. 238, 252
Quine, W.V.O. 11, 26, 28, 76, 130, 138,
    168, 194

— R —

Ramsey, F.P. 148
Rang, B. 230
Raven, J.E. 62, 80, 129
Reinhardt, L. 171
Rijk, L.M. 130
Rosen, S. 130
Ross, W.D. 23
Rorty, R. 137, 141, 142, 158
Routley, R. 12, 26,
Rubin, E. 220, 231
Russell, B. 12, 33, 34, 36, 53, 121, 130,
    133, 134, 158, 166, 192, 196

— S —

Santambrogio, M. 6, 26,
Sållstrom, P. 231
Sanford, D.H. 261, 262, 276
Schiller, P. 216, 231
Scholz, H. 100, 130
Schuhmann, K. 232
Schuurman, H. 158
Scott, D. 194, 198
Scotus, I.D. 162
Sebestik, J. 25, 26
Seebohm, T.S. 24, 26
Shoenman, R. 171, 198
Simons, P. 23, 26, 71, 128, 199, 202, 226,
    232, 259, 260, 262, 263, 276
Skyrms, B. 166, 171, 191, 198

Smith, B. 1, 8, 18, 19, 21, 24, 26, 128, 129, 199, 207, 222, 228, 229, 231, 232, 234, 243, 248, 251, 252
Smith, D.W. 251, 252
Sommers, F. 12, 26, 158
Sosa, E. 171
Soulez, A. 25, 26
Stern, W. 220, 232
Stoics 1, 2
Stoothoff, R. 158
Strawson, P.T. 135-137, 139, 140, 141, 148, 158, 162,
Strohmeyer, I. 230
Stump, E. 157, 158
Stumpf, C. 212-214, 219, 232, 243
Suszko, R. 19, 26, 173-178, 186, 187
Swoyer, 280, 288
Szilasi, W. 230

— T —

Tarán, L. 62, 130
Tarski, A. 20, 148,
Tatarkiewicz, W. 62, 130
Thom, R. 222, 232, 242, 244, 253
Thomas: see Aquinas, T.
Tiles, J.E. 232, 252, 253
Tolkien, J.R.R. 138, 157
Tooley, 170
Twardowski, K. 5-8, 12, 13, 26, 75, 76, 226, 232

— U —

Ueberweg, F. 13, 26

— V —

Vaihinger, H. 14, 26
Valla, L. 13
Varchenko, A.N. 251
Varzi, A. 274, 275
Vicario, G. 219-221, 232

— W —

Wertheimer, M. 216, 222, 232
White Beck, L. 129
Whitehead, A.N. 222
Whorf, B.L. 211
Williams, C.J.F. 133, 158, 196, 198
Witschel, G. 216, 232
Wittgenstein, L. 20, 21, 33-35, 166, 173, 176, 185, 187
Woleński, J. 229, 232
Wolff, C. 5, 14
Wolniewicz, B. 176, 181, 187
Woodger, J.H. 222

— Y —

Yourgrau, P. 131, 150, 158
Yourgrau, W. 25, 26

— Z —

Zalta, E. 12, 26
Zanatta, M. 13, 26
Zarnecka-Biały, E. 129, 130, 231
Zemach, E. 131
Zeno 62
Zimmermann, R. 5
Zygmunt, J. 187

Nijhoff International Philosophy Series

17. İ. Dilman (ed.): *Philosophy and Life.* Essays on John Wisdom. 1984
ISBN 90-247-2996-3

18. J. J. Russell: *Analysis and Dialectic.* Studies in the Logic of Foundation Problems. 1984 ISBN 90-247-2990-4

19. G. Currie and A. Musgrave (eds.): *Popper and the Human Sciences.* 1985
ISBN Hb 90-247-2998-X; Pb 90-247-3141-0

20. C. D. Broad: *Ethics.* Lectures given at Cambridge during the Period 1933–34 to 1952–53. Edited by C. Lewy. 1985 ISBN 90-247-3088-0

21. D.A.J. Seargent: *Plurality and Continuity.* An Essay in G.F. Stout's Theory of Universals. 1985 ISBN 90-247-3185-2

22. J.E. Atwell: *Ends and Principles in Kant's Moral Thought.* 1986
ISBN 90-247-3167-4

23. J. Agassi, and I.C. Jarvie (eds.): *Rationality: The Critical View.* 1987
ISBN Hb 90-247-3275-1; Pb 90-247-3455-X

24. J.T.J. Srzednicki and Z. Stachniak: *S. Leśniewski's Lecture Notes in Logic.* 1988 ISBN 90-247-3416-9
For 'The Leśniewski's Collection' *see also Volume 13 and 44.*

25. B.M. Taylor (ed.): *Michael Dummett.* Contributions to Philosophy. 1987
ISBN 90-247-3463-0

26. A. Z. Bar-On: *The Categories and the Principle of Coherence.* Whitehead's Theory of Categories in Historical Perspective. 1987 ISBN 90-247-3478-9

27. B. Dziemidok and P. McCormick (eds.): *On the Aesthetics of Roman Ingarden.* Interpretations and Assessments. 1989 ISBN 0-7923-0071-8

28. J.T.J. Srzednicki (ed.): *Stephan Körner – Philosophical Analysis and Reconstruction.* Contributions to Philosophy. 1987 ISBN 90-247-3543-2

29. F. Brentano: *On the Existence of God.* Lectures given at the Universities of Würzburg and Vienna (1868–1891). Edited and translated from German by Susan F. Krantz. 1987 ISBN 90-247-3538-6

30. Z. Augustynek: *Time. Past, Present, Future.* Essays dedicated to Henryk Mehlberg. 1991 ISBN 0-7923-0270-2

31. T. Pawlowski: *Aesthetic Values.* 1989 ISBN 0-7923-0418-7

32. M. Ruse (ed.): *What the Philosophy of Biology Is.* Essays dedicated to David Hull. 1989 ISBN 90-247-3778-8

33. J. Young: *Willing and Unwilling.* A Study in the Philosophy of Arthur Schopenhauer. 1987 ISBN 90-247-3556-4

Nijhoff International Philosophy Series

34. T. Z. Lavine and V. Tejera (eds.): *History and Anti-History in Philosophy.*
1989   ISBN 0-7923-0455-1

35. R.L. Epstein: *The Semantic Foundations of Logic.* Volume 1: Propositional
Logics. With the assistance and collaboration of W.A. Carnielli, I.M.L.
D'Ottaviano, S. Krajewski and R.D. Maddux. 1990   ISBN 0-7923-0622-8

36. A. Pavković (ed.): *Contemporary Yugoslav Philosophy.* The Analytic Approach. 1988   ISBN 90-247-3776-1

37. A. Winterbourne: *The Ideal and the Real.* An Outline of Kant's Theory of
Space, Time and Mathematical Construction. 1988   ISBN 90-247-3774-5

38. K. Szaniawski (ed.): *The Vienna Circle and the Lvov-Warsaw School.* 1989
                                                               ISBN 90-247-3798-2

39. G. Priest: *In Contradiction.* A Study of the Transconsistent. 1987
                                                               ISBN 90-247-3630-7

40. J. Woleński (ed.): *Kotarbiński: Logic, Semantics and Ontology.* 1990
                                                               ISBN 0-7923-0865-4

41. P. Geach (ed.): *Logic and Ethics.* 1991   ISBN 0-7923-1044-6

42. U. Wybraniec-Skardowska: *Theory of Language Syntax.* Categorial Approach.
1991.   ISBN 0-7923-1142-6

43. J. Bransen: *The Antinomy of Thought.* Maimonian Skepticism and the Relation
between Thoughts and Objects. 1991   ISBN 0-7923-1383-6

44. J.T.J. Srzednicki, S.J. Surma, D. Barnett and V. F. Rickey: *S. Leśniewski's
Collected Works.* 1992   ISBN 0-7923-1512-X
For 'The Leśniewski's Collection' see also Volumes 13 and 24.

45. P. Simons: *Philosophy and Logic in Central Europe from Bolzano to Tarski.*
Selected Essays. 1992   ISBN 0-7923-1621-5

46. J. T. J. Srzednicki and D. Wood (eds.): *Essays on Philosophy in Australia.*
1992   ISBN 0-7923-1695-9

47. B. Dziemidok: *The Comical.* A Philosophical Analysis. 1993
                                                               ISBN 0-7923-2103-0

48. S. Read (ed.): *Sophisms in Medieval Logic and Grammar.* 1993
                                                               ISBN 0-7923-2196-0

49. K.J. Perszyk: *Nonexistent Objects.* Meinong and Contemporary Philosophy.
1993   ISBN 0-7923-2461-7

50. P.J. Hager: *Continuity and Change in the Development of Russell's
Philosophy.* 1994   ISBN 0-7923-2688-1

Nijhoff International Philosophy Series

51. D.F.B. Tucker: *Essay on Liberalism*. Looking Left and Right. 1994
ISBN 0-7923-2705-5
52. L. Albertazzi, M. Libardi and R. Poli (eds.): *The School of Franz Brentano.*
1996
ISBN 0-7923-3766-2
53. R. Poli and P. Simons (eds.): *Formal Ontology.* 1996   ISBN 0-7923-4104-X

Further information about our publications on *Philosophy* are available on request.

Kluwer Academic Publishers – Dordrecht / Boston / London

FORMAL ONTOLOGY

Nijhoff International Philosophy Series

VOLUME 53

The titles published in this series are listed at the end of this volume.

Printed in the United States
77930LV00002B/136